Born in New York City, educated at City College and Columbia University, Seymour Martin Lipset has been a professor of sociology and government at Harvard University since 1965. Prior to that he taught sociology at the University of California at Berkeley where he witnessed the celebrated Berkeley Revolt of 1964–1965, and served as the faculty adviser of the Young People's Socialist League. Lipset has written and edited many books dealing with the social bases of political action including AGRARIAN SOCIALISM, POLITICAL MAN: *The Social Bases of Politics*, REVOLUTION AND COUNTERREVOLUTION and STUDENT POLITICS. He is the co-author of THE POLITICS OF UNREASON: *Right-Wing Extremism in America, 1790–1970* and the co-editor of STUDENTS IN REVOLT and THE BERKELEY STUDENT REVOLT. His books have been translated into fifteen languages.

Gerald M. Schaflander was born in Detroit in 1920 and educated at the University of Michigan. At the age of forty-five he left his position as national sales manager of the Ronson Corporation to study and to teach, attending both the Harvard University department of social relations and the New School for Social Research. Since then Schaflander has conducted action-research on university campuses and in black ghettoes such as Bedford-Stuyvesant. He has also taught at Boston University and Brooklyn College. Gerald Schaflander is co-author of GHETTO CRISIS.

Books by Seymour Martin Lipset

Agrarian Socialism

With Martin Trow and James S. Coleman: *Union Democracy*

With Reinhard Bendix: *Social Mobility in Industrial Society*

Political Man: The Social Bases of Politics

The First New Nation: The United States in Historical and Comparative Perspective

Estudiantes universitarios y política en el Tercer Mundo

Revolution and Counterrevolution

With Earl Raab: *The Politics of Unreason: Right-Wing Extremism in America, 1790–1970*

With Gerald M. Schaflander: *Passion and Politics: Student Activism in America*

Edited by Seymour Martin Lipset

With Sheldon S. Wolin: *The Berkeley Student Revolt*

Student Politics

With Philip G. Altbach: *Students in Revolt*

Books by Gerald M. Schaflander

With Henry Etzkowitz: *Ghetto Crisis*

With Seymour Martin Lipset: *Passion and Politics: Student Activism in America*

Passion and Politics: Student Activism in America

Part One by Seymour Martin Lipset

Part Two by Gerald M. Schaflander

Little, Brown and Company · Boston · Toronto

LIBRARY OF CONGRESS CATALOG CARD NO. 70–149459

FIRST PRINTING

T11/71

"Experiment in Education" by Martin Duberman is reprinted by permission from *Daedalus,* the Journal of the American Academy of Arts and Sciences, Boston, Massachusetts, Volume 97, Number 1 (Winter 1968).

Published simultaneously in Canada
by Little, Brown & Company (Canada) Limited

PRINTED IN THE UNITED STATES OF AMERICA

Acknowledgments

This volume is an outgrowth of a program of studies of problems of the university and of student unrest undertaken at the Center for International Affairs at Harvard University and supported by a grant from the Hazen Foundation. Other books in this program, which will be published in 1972, are *Latin American Students* by Arthur Liebman, Kenneth Walker and Myron Glazer, *Higher Education in a Transitional Society* by Philip G. Altbach, and *Higher Education in India* edited by Amrik Singh and Philip G. Altbach. Earlier books sponsored by the Center's research program dealing with student activism were written under grants for comparative and international research made by the Ford Foundation and the Carnegie Corporation. These include:

Seymour Martin Lipset, ed. *Student Politics*. New York: Basic Books, 1967.

Philip G. Altbach. *Student Politics in Bombay*. Bombay: Asia, 1968.

———, ed. *Turmoil and Transition*. New York: Basic Books, 1968.

Seymour Martin Lipset and Philip G. Altbach, eds. *Students in Revolt.* Boston: Houghton Mifflin, 1969. Paperback ed.: Boston: Beacon, 1970.

Philip G. Altbach, ed. *Student Revolution: A Global Analysis.* Bombay: Lalvani, 1970.

Arthur Liebman. *Politics of Puerto Rican Students.* Austin: University of Texas Press, 1970.

Philip G. Altbach. *Student Politics and Higher Education in the U.S.: A Select Bibliography.* Cambridge: Center for International Affairs, Harvard University, 1968.

_______. *A Select Bibliography on Students, Politics and Higher Education.* Cambridge: Center for International Affairs, Harvard University, 1968.

_______. *Higher Education in Developing Countries: A Select Bibliography.* Cambridge: Center for International Affairs, Harvard University, 1970. Occasional Paper 24.

Various individuals and institutions contributed to making this book possible. William Creed, Fred Rackmil, and Bartley Horwitz were particularly helpful as research assistants. Mrs. Meena Vohra helped supervise the production of different drafts. I am particularly grateful to a number of executives of various American polling organizations for furnishing me with detailed reports of their national surveys of college students. These include Dr. Irving Crespi of the American Institute of Public Opinion Research (the Gallup Poll); Dr. Daniel Yankelovich of Daniel Yankelovich Associates; Louis Harris of Louis Harris Associates; Burns Roper of the Roper Organization; and George Mihaly of Gilbert Youth Research. Access to the findings of studies completed for projects associated with the White House was made possible through the good offices of the staff of the President's Commission on Campus Unrest, particularly Dr. Richard Braungart. Some of the material in Chapters 2 and 3 was initially written as research memoranda for the Commission, and has been substantially revised since. Other parts of the book have drawn upon articles published earlier. All of the previously published material has been substantially rewritten and revised. The articles include:

"Youth and Politics." In Robert K. Merton and Robert Nisbet, eds., *Contemporary Social Problems*. 3rd ed. New York: Harcourt, Brace and Jovanovich, 1971. Pp. 743–791.

"The Possible Effects of Student Activism on International Politics." In Seymour Martin Lipset and Philip G. Altbach, eds., *Students in Revolt*. Boston: Houghton Mifflin, 1969. Pp. 495–524.

"The Activists: A Profile." *The Public Interest* (Fall 1968), pp. 38–50.

"Student Opposition in the United States." *Government and Opposition* 1 (April 1966), pp. 351–374.

I would also like to acknowledge the helpful advice in my efforts to make sense out of the events and research in this area of my colleagues, Chaim Adler of the Hebrew University, Philip Altbach of the University of Wisconsin, Arthur Liebman of the State University of New York at Binghamton, and Nathan Glazer of Harvard University. My principal intellectual debt, however, is to the large number of students who have sought in different ways to describe the way in which they and their peers see the world.

Seymour Martin Lipset

Contents

Introduction

The American university has been a place of turmoil since the Berkeley revolt of 1964–65. A literal flood of books and articles has poured forth seeking to describe, advocate, or analyze different modes of campus behavior. These analyses have ranged from those that place the responsibility for campus discontent on aspects of the social structure to some that see the university itself as the source. Still others argue that specific political events, especially the war in Indo-China and the civil rights struggles, are the principal energizing factors. These theories, of course, are not mutually exclusive. Each of them would appear to contain some validity.

The approaches which stress societal factors include the proposition that changes in child-rearing and educational practices have produced a generation of students who combine belief in equalitarian doctrines with an insistence on instant gratification. The scions of the liberal segment of the upper-middle class were reared by parents who did not discipline them strongly for fear of injuring their personalities, and sent them to "progressive" private or suburban public schools. These parents also accepted the belief, as David Cohen has argued, that youth should not be restrained or coerced, that education should reflect the desires of the students, that education (and work) should be play, that is, should be unalienated behavior reflecting the free choice of the individual. And it follows from this analysis that when these students came of age, they began to insist that the rest of the world conform to the idealistic state of freedom and comparative equality which they had experienced. The year 1965 is twenty years after the end of World War II, and therefore corresponds to the time in which one would expect the children of the parents of the liberalizing thirties to have come of age.

There are, of course, other structural change theories which have been advanced to account for the growth in student discontent. These stress, particularly, technological determinants which supposedly have made life more difficult, e.g., more population, more pollution, and more noise, or have opened the door to new vicarious experiences and instantaneous communication about events in other parts of the country and world through television.

Much of the literature in the field, of course, emphasizes the role of the educational system as a cause of unrest. Ever since protest erupted on the senior campus of the University of California, Berkeley, numerous interpreters of what is bothering the students have suggested that the large bureaucratic educational institutions have turned them off. Specifically, the large university is seen as inherently impersonal, relying on the large lecture course, the graduate teaching assistant, and a very big student–senior faculty ratio, which frustrates students seeking an educational experience with distinguished scholars. Instead of being treated as a total individual, the student in the megauniversity finds himself a number on an IBM card, registered and graded through use of computers. The presumed decline of close faculty-student relationships has also been blamed by many on the emphasis within the universities on research – on the fact that professors secure prestige and higher salaries through their publications, rather than as a result of the quality of their teaching. The emphasis on research has grown since World War II in response to the enormous increase in funds available through government, industry, and foundations. The teaching loads have declined sharply, and presumably, as Clark Kerr argued in 1963 just before the current wave of unrest began, the undergraduates are shortchanged.

The third approach, that which stresses the role of specific politically relevant historical events as a catalyst which initiated the current wave of protest, points to the recurrent role of student violence and protest since the Middle Ages. Basically, it argues that those revolutionary theorists like Bakunin and Blanqui, who stressed the revolutionary role of intellectuals and students as the inspirers, leaders, and often mass troops of the revolution, were correct. Bringing together evidence of the large-scale student involvement in the revolutionary movements in czarist Russia, nineteenth century France, Germany, and Italy, and various colonial and third world countries more recently, it suggests that the social situation of the students makes them, even more than the proletariat, the revolutionary class par excellence. Elements inherent in the marginal status of youth and students, the lesser commitment to authority demanded of sociological adolescents, freedom to sow "wild oats," the socialization of young people into the idealism of the adult group to which they belong, and the relative ease with which those on campus can be reached and mobilized, all make students more likely than any other stratum to respond to events which undermine a social system. From this perspective, the socially available and idealistic students were activated by two sets of issues which undermined the American polity, first the frustrations endemic in the efforts to secure civil rights and economic equality following the Supreme Court's desegregation decision, and subsequently the immorality or weakness exhibited by the United States in fighting a seemingly weak little nation-enemy in Southeast Asia.

The whole development of student and academic protest had an effect far beyond that which American universities had ever experienced — because of the tremendous increase in the sheer numbers of persons connected with academe. In 1930, there were about a million students and eighty thousand faculty, figures which grew to one million, six hundred seventy-five thousand students and one hundred sixty-five thousand professors by the end of World War II. Twenty-five years later in 1970 there were seven million students and over half a million full-time faculty. These absolute figures mean, among other things, that a relatively small percentage constitutes a large enough critical mass to sustain the demonstrations, organizations, and subscriptions to journals necessary to create a viable social movement. Five percent of the student body now equals over three hundred fifty thousand students. One tenth of the faculty nationally means a body of over fifty thousand people. Faculty and student groups are vocal, mobilizable, and noticeable. Hence, the sheer jump in numbers since 1945, combined with a set of events which activate a minority, can be enough to impress the country that the campus is in revolt.

But politics has not been the only arena which brought tension between students and their elders in the 1960s. Many students exhibited their renunciation of the culture of their parents through innovative forms of dress, hairstyles, use of drugs, obscene language, and more widespread willingness to have a variety of sexual experiences. In this sense, the sixties showed some resemblance to the 1920s, when illegal alcohol, premarital sex, and short skirts also shocked elders into discussions of the generation gap – of the differences between those under and over thirty. And many adults who could accept revolutionary politics as the idealism of young people who would grow more conservative as they grew older, a frequently made observation about student radicals in many countries, found themselves horrified by the new morality of a renunciatory segment of the young.

Whatever the nature and underlying causes of the new style of student protest of the 1960s, the authors of this book found themselves strongly reacting to it. Schaflander, employed as an advertising-sales executive when the decade opened, had student-generation children who were directly and indirectly involved in early civil rights and SDS activities. Active in the New York

Reform Democrats, he was quite sympathetic to efforts to bring "participatory democracy" to the ghetto and other areas. He helped raise funds for the so-called Newark Project of SDS, for SANE and for Martin Luther King, in the early sixties, and on the graduation of his children from high school and college decided to return to graduate school and shift into an academic career. He and Lipset first met when Schaflander took a course of Lipset's as a special graduate student at Harvard in 1965–66. Schaflander subsequently was involved in action-research in Bedford-Stuyvesant and other ghettoes, experiences written up in the book *Ghetto Crisis* by Schaflander and Henry Etzkowitz.[1] Schaflander also began teaching, and joined with student groups in demanding structural changes which would increase student power within academe. Some of his experiences in such activities are described in his section of this book.

Lipset was on the staff of the University of California at Berkeley, the year of the celebrated Berkeley revolt, 1964–65. Contrary to published gossip, his departure from Berkeley was not a result of his reaction to that event. He had made arrangements in the spring of 1964 to move to Harvard a year later. Ironically, given the contrary rumors, these arrangements were not finalized for another year because of a request from Berkeley administrators that he delay any resignation to avoid the impression that he was leaving because of the turmoil at Berkeley. Previous to the revolt year, and during it, Lipset had been the faculty adviser of the Young People's Socialist League (YPSL), the youth section of the Socialist Party, a group which was involved in the protest movement which became the Free Speech Movement. During the Berkeley protests, he also served as faculty adviser to the Cited Students' Organization, an association formed of FSM students who had been charged with violating university rules, and which was the only formally recognized campus organization of the FSM. He favored the proposals of the FSM "moderates" (from Students for Goldwater to the YPSL) for liberalization of the university rules which inhibited certain forms of political activity on campus – chiefly fund-raising for political purposes and organizing demonstrations for off-campus protests, particularly civil rights sit-ins — while at the same time urging with them that the goals pursued by the FSM and favored from the start by most faculty could and should be pursued without using illegal tactics that might create confrontations with the police.[2] He argued publicly on many occasions that civil disobedience is only justified in the absence of democratic rights.

As in subsequent large-scale student demonstrations elsewhere, the FSM was divided between extremists who openly advocated radicalizing tactics deliberately designed to create a conflict between police and students, and those who saw such tactics as unnecessary to attain the manifest goals of the movement.[3] Few observers, inside or outside of Berkeley, at the time, noted that the plan to occupy Sproul Hall in December 1964 was opposed by some of the groups involved in the movement from its beginning. The Berkeley Revolt was the prototype event of the student movement. The radical wing sought successfully to exacerbate the tactics even after the initial widely supported demands of the movement had almost entirely been met. Most of the faculty supported agreeing to the demands, and backed total amnesty, and assumed that once the issues were settled on the FSM's terms the demonstrations and confrontations would end. But when it became clear that the radical wing of the movement had wider and continuing objectives justifying further civil disobedience, the faculty divided bitterly into distinct caucuses, divisions which have lasted to the present (1971).

Lipset reacted to the seeming "solution" of the Berkeley crisis in December 1964, when the faculty voted by a large majority to endorse the total position of the FSM *after* the sit-in, with pessimism. In an article which he and Paul Seabury wrote during the Christmas vacation, he expressed considerable uneasiness about the consequences for the university of the introduction of tactics of civil disobedience, in terms which he still believes are deserved:

> Most shaken by this sudden crisis . . . has been the human trust that is the ethical basis of any university — or, for that

> matter, of any community. This delicate though often impersonal confidence between teachers and students, professors and professors, students and students, was severely breached. The wounds left by suspicion and resentment over apparent betrayals of trust will remain for a long time. This is a poignant future problem for the teacher and his students. Once classrooms have been bitterly divided with covert and overt defamation of faculty members as "stooges of the administration" or "tools of the FSM steering committee," the community of scholarship is clearly endangered. . . .
>
> The Berkeley Revolt is not just another California curiosity. This new style of campus political action may affect other campuses, and eventually our national political life. The new student generation is brilliant and aggressively serious. The number of graduate students who spend years at a university increases steadily. The student leftist movements are growing and probably will continue to grow as they demand totally moral solutions to issues of racial discrimination and foreign policy. The indifference to legality shown by serious students can threaten the foundations of democratic order if it becomes a model for student political action. Extremism in the pursuit of liberty was quite recently a favorite slogan of the radical right. Berkeley has shown that anyone can play this game. The danger now exists that students at other universities will have learned how easily a great university can be brought to its knees if but two or three percent of the student body are willing to engage in actions which may force the police on campus. Universities are probably more vulnerable to civil disobedience tactics than any other institution in the country precisely because those in authority, whether administration or faculty, are liberal. They are reluctant to see force invoked against their students regardless of what the students do. Now that this secret is out, it may be difficult to restrain students from having their way on many university issues, much as occurs on Latin-American campuses.[4]

The concern that deliberate use of the Blanquist tactics of confrontation designed to provoke authority to be repressive would spread through the university world has, of course, been warranted. Given the suspicion against authority which exists among the majority of liberal-to-left-disposed students and faculty, the more extreme groups can rely on mass support if their actions result in a clash between police and demonstrators. Steve Weissman, theoretician of the FSM, openly described to a journalist the discussions among FSM leaders as to how they could force the university to call the police. They regarded an incident in which the police came on campus as necessary for the success of the movement, to further the process of radicalization. The conscious character of this tactic has been attested to by various leaders of the national movement since Berkeley.[5] Thus, two years later in 1967, Stokely Carmichael, former head of the Student Nonviolent Coordinating Committee (SNCC) in a discussion with Carl Oglesby, former president of the Students for a Democratic Society (SDS), published as a lead article in the New Left weekly, the *National Guardian,* described revolutionary strategy in the following terms:

> People won't fight; they won't fight unless you push — so you push. You create disturbances, you keep pushing the system. You keep drawing up the contradictions until they have to hit back; once your enemy hits back then your revolution starts. If your enemy does not hit back then you do not have a revolution.[6]

A writer in the British *New Left Review* in 1968 also generalized in much the same terms as Weissman and Carmichael. It is necessary, he argued, for student radicals

> to behave as provocatively as necessary and to effectively sanction the University to the extent that they *need* to use force, probably the police. Complete occupation of offices rather than corridors will achieve this. It is at this stage that the administrations commit their ultimate folly, and it is at this stage that the staff [faculty] and less political students will feel encouraged to enter a situation already politically structured.[7]

Perhaps the height of cynicism with respect to boasting about the ability of radicals to manipulate the progressive sympathies of the majority of academia came from Mark Rudd, the leader of the Columbia SDS sit-in demonstration in the spring of 1968. In a speech in the fall of that year, urging Harvard and other Boston area students to launch their own sit-in demonstrations, Rudd advised them not to worry about issues, since the two major Columbia issues were basically non-issues for him.

> Let me tell you. We manufactured the issues. The Institute for Defense Analysis is nothing at Columbia. Just three professors. And the gym issue is bull. It doesn't mean anything to anybody. I had never been to the gym site before the demonstration began. I didn't even know how to get there.[8]

Citing these statements is not intended to suggest that the issues which have been the ostensible causes of various campus demonstrations from Berkeley to Harvard were not legitimate concerns about which many students felt deeply before the confrontation. What is in controversy about many of these affairs is whether the particular problem justified the use of extralegal methods which sharply divided the campus communities, heightened the antiintellectual right-wing backlash, and ultimately, according to Sam Brown, the founder of the McCarthy peace campaign in 1968 and of the antiwar Moratorium movement in 1969, even had a counterproductive effect on the efforts of the peace movement to influence policy.[9] These issues which have been argued on many campuses of the nation are essentially the same as those which divided the Berkeley faculty and student body through the fateful fall semester of 1964.

Since moving to Harvard in 1965, Lipset has continued his connection with student politics by serving as one of the faculty advisers for the Harvard chapter of the Young People's Socialist League.[10] In addition, he has edited a number of books, and written many articles dealing with student activism as a social and political phenomenon both in foreign countries and in the United States.[11] This interest also predates the rise of mass activism in this country, since he published a long article in the summer of 1964, analyzing the factors affecting student political activism as a force for social change in underdeveloped countries.[12]

Since Lipset has been involved in considerable writing and lecturing on the subject of academic politics, his views, analyses, and activities have been the subject of frequent comment. Some have attributed a policy-related role to his work in this field. It may, therefore, be worth noting that he has never served as adviser or consultant on the subject of student unrest or related topics to any administrative agency, although he has submitted memoranda to both the House Committee on Education and to the President's Commission on Campus Unrest, which presented his views on the university situation. It might also be noted, given reports to the contrary, that he has never been personally involved in research on the activities of students in any given overseas country or area. He has, however, attempted at times to integrate the knowledge gathered in various places in different publications. Given his interest in the role of students, intellectuals, and universities, and in affecting social change, Lipset has encouraged the work of graduate students and junior colleagues both in this country and elsewhere through helping to raise funds for their research in various parts of the world. These efforts have involved studies in North Africa, Yugoslavia, Iran, India, Japan, western Europe, and Latin America, and have resulted in a variety of doctoral dissertations and books which are cited in the Acknowledgments.

The politicization of academic life, a subject discussed at some length in this book, particularly in Chapters 3 and 6, has greatly affected intellectual judgments and reviews of social science research generally, but particularly in this area. Much of the comment on such research is often closely related to whether the reviewer agrees or disagrees with the political assumptions or conclusions of the author. Thus, beyond those who agree with and praise his writings, Lipset has been sharply criticized by leftists for his "conservative" biases, which allegedly inform his analyses of student unrest, and by right-wingers for his "leftist" or pro-activist orientations.[13] A Mexican paper, *El Universal,* described his writings on student politics as "containing revolutionary directives," and concluded that he was a supporter of the "extreme left in the United States."[14] The right-wing Church League of America in a publication on *Subversion by the Volume,* an attack on publishers for putting out left-wing books, cited Lipset as giving support to "students who rioted," and for being active "among the protesters against the war in Vietnam."[15] The same disparity in evaluation of Lipset's general political sociological writings has led some commentators to see him, in the words of the author of an SDS pamphlet, as seeking "to maintain the American celebration," and others as a partisan of social stability, while a variety of political scientists and sociologists have described his work as "reflecting a Marxian frame of reference," or according to two recent works as espousing the same conflict-oriented approach to social analysis followed by C. Wright Mills.[16]

Although the two authors of this book had some serious discussions about student activism in 1965–66 when Schaflander was a student at Harvard, they did not follow these up until 1969, when Schaflander approached Lipset with a request for cooperation in creating a new research center dealing with social and educational change. This effort never matured in any permanent organization, but discussions concerning the nature of the contemporary university and student body led them to the writing of this book. Since they disagreed in their interpretations of what was happening on campus, and what, if anything, ought to be done about it, it was clear that they could not write the common type of jointly authored volume, in which two authors work together to develop a set of common themes. Rather, they thought a book in which each of them wrote up his analysis and suggestions about the current state of academe might make for an interesting work precisely because it presented conflicting points of view and analytic styles.

As will be clear to the reader, Lipset prefers to deal with student activism using a more conventional academic approach, i.e., presenting analytic hypotheses and discussing the evidence for them. Schaflander, who is much more action-research oriented, has written his section in terms of institution conflicts, consequent problems and proposed solutions, particularly for and by the nonradical but change-oriented (liberal-moderate) "marginal ambivalents," who are analyzed and discussed in detail in his section.

The Lipset section, in addition to presenting a variety of material relevant to the current university scene, includes two chapters discussing the history of student activism from the American Revolution down to the 1950s. These analyses are clearly not intended to be definitive in any sense. They are presented here because the paucity of published information about the history of American student protest has seemingly contributed to many erroneous assumptions about the uniqueness of much of what has gone on during the past decade. Little in the way of comparative data is presented here, since this is readily available elsewhere.

Schaflander's section, besides reporting on the behavior of the marginally ambivalent students, and proposing various basic institutional reforms in academe, also contains an analysis of some conflicts and controversies in which he was a major participant at Boston University. Clearly, his statement about his own role, his analyses, and Lipset's discussions both of past and present student activism, cannot be considered as "objective" statements about the nature of the student movement or the university. Neither has *ever* believed that such a thing as "value-free" scholarship occurs in social science, and certainly not in as highly controversial an area as this one. Each of Lipset's earlier books, in fact, contains an introduction or preface in which he seeks to give the reader some sense of his own values as they relate to the subject treated in the book, so that the reader may consider these in evaluating the conclusions of the work. Like Max Weber, whose views on these matters are frequently misinterpreted, the authors believe that there is no such thing as an "ethically neutral" approach. These issues are discussed in some detail by Lipset in Chapter 6.

Since Lipset's discussions of the social sources of student activism, of its history, and of faculty-student conflict address themselves to a general picture of student activism as a whole, these have been presented first in this book. Schaflander's chapters dealing with the way the "marginal ambivalents" react to the breakdown of the family as a primary socialization institution and the issues of their own repetitive behavior patterns with respect to passion (sex), pot (drugs), and politics, come next. The book concludes with Schaflander's suggestions for institutional changes. The reader should not feel concerned about finding differences in the analyses, understanding of the relevant underlying facts, and values of the two authors. They do disagree about a number of matters. But they agree completely in their belief that the method of the dialogue, of reasoned discussion and sharp controversy, is necessary both for the advancement of knowledge and for the body politic. Force may end an argument; it can never win it. No one who believes that truth is on his side can honestly object to scholarly investigation, even of himself, his motives, and his actions. And no argument is won by *ad hominium* or guilt-by-association tactics. To accuse a man of being a communist, a fascist, "crazy," or a tool of the establishment has no bearing on the validity of his statements. It is, of course, quite legitimate to seek to demonstrate that a given course of action or public advocacy will serve the interests of a certain group, or that the methods employed may lead to a result quite contradictory to that advocated by those employing them. But such an argument must be an effort at tracing a logical chain of thought. To state such simple truisms may seem insulting to the reader. Yet it is necessary to make them in this era of heated intellectual controversy, since men on all sides of current issues often forget them.

Cambridge, Mass. — Seymour Martin Lipset
New York, N.Y. — Gerald Schaflander

Part One:

The Dimensions of Student Involvement

by Seymour Martin Lipset

Dedication

To the memory of
Richard Hofstadter, Joseph Levenson,
Robert S. Lynd, and Robert McCloskey

1

Sources of Student Activism

Any effort to interpret the changing political behavior of American students in recent years is subject to the difficulty that it is dealing with a local aspect of a worldwide phenomenon.[1] Although the events which precipitated student activism vary from country to country, and the targets of student attack differ, there are more common themes than differences in the tactics and ideologies of the movements. Unlike the leftist youth and student movements of the 1930s which were linked to adult political parties, the dominant ones of the 1960s constituted a genuine youth rebellion, one which was almost as much levied against the major parties of the Left, and the Soviet Union, as it was against the moderates and conservatives. The lack of involvement in adult politics gave free rein to the propensity of youth to adhere to absolute principles, to engage in expressive rather than instrumental politics. Relatively unconcerned with the long-term consequences of their actions, the New Left student movements appeared ready to attack all existing structures, including the university, and to use tactics which alienated the majority, in order to make manifest their contempt, their total rejection of the intolerable world created by their elders. This rejection of the ethic of "responsibility" has characterized student groups in Japan, France, Germany, the United States and many other countries.

Most recently, however, this situation has changed somewhat. The American New Left turned during 1969 to an endorsement of Marxism-Leninism.[2] The currently dominant wing of the Students for a Democratic Society (SDS), the Worker-Student Alliance, is in fact the student movement of the Maoist Progressive Labor party. The Young Socialist Alliance, affiliated to the Trotskyist Socialist Workers party, has also achieved an important position within the radical movement, particularly through its major role in the formation of the New Mobilization Committee Against the Vietnam War. Even the old Communist party has begun to regain a position within the student left. And the emergence in strength of the various communist parties within the left-wing student movement has ironically made for a more responsible, less violent and adventuristic, movement. Each of these parties, desirous of winning adult noncampus support, has opposed aggressive confrontationist tactics which antagonize those outside of the movement. Only the so-called Weatherman faction of SDS, which remains unattached to an adult party, continues to advocate confrontationist tactics as a major activity of the student radicals.

The beginning of a new decade has resulted in the usual efforts to predict the future of campus-based activism. Since no one anticipated that the sixties would be characterized by widespread protest, there is no good reason to assume that more recent efforts at prognostication will be more accurate. In any case, these tend to be sharply contradictory. Some fear or hope that the era of unrest and confrontation politics will continue; others venture the conviction that the seventies will produce a new stage in the political cycle, one that sees a return to more scholarly pursuits. The record of the 1969–70 school year would support the first assumption; that of 1970–71 would appear to validate the conclusions of the second.

Certainly those bold enough to proclaim the "end of the

student revolution" during the final year of the sixties had their conclusions severely challenged by events.[3] In spite of extensive effort to "cool" or "repress" campus unrest, the early winter months of 1970 witnessed an increase in the protest wave. The Urban Research Corporation, which has been monitoring student demonstrations, reported more "major incidents" between mid-January and March 23, 1970, than had occurred in a corresponding period of 1969. Reports gathered for the President's Commission on Campus Unrest indicated that there were many more "disruptive" demonstrations in 1969–70, *before* the Cambodian incursion, than in the two previous academic years.[4] The Cambodian events and the killings at Kent State and Jackson State resulted in the first national student strike of long duration.[5] The data from opinion polls, discussed later, indicated that close to half the undergraduate campus population was involved.

Many college administrators and political activists were convinced that the fall semester would witness a continuation of massive political involvement of May and June. Instead, the campuses of the United States probably were less politically involved during 1970–71 than at any time since the beginning of the Vietnam war. Most of the journalistic articles written during this year have been devoted to describing and explaining the reasons for the seeming depolitization of the college community. There were few major demonstrations linked to any given campus. A Harris poll of a national sample of students taken in November 1970, reported that only 7 percent identified their politics as "radical," a drop from the 11 percent who did so during the spring protest wave, a pattern reflected in other surveys. This decline in support for radical politics was the first such reported since 1965.

As the American educational system enters the 1970s, it is clear that two characteristics are present which differ largely from the beginning of the 1960s. There is much less respect for the authority of heads of institutions, whether public, private, or educational; and the large, passive majority of students are much more liberal in their social, economic, and political values. Nevertheless, the bulk of politically active students support "liberal" political activities which basically accept the premises of the American political system. Thus the major student activities of recent years involved participation in the nomination campaigns of Robert Kennedy and Eugene McCarthy, in the 1969 antiwar Moratorium, and in the 1970 strikes – all led by youth still committed to electoral efforts. It would appear that the dominant form of student activism in the 1970s will involve efforts to build reformist political tendencies and pressure group movements, that the resort to civil disobedience which characterized much of the sixties will be less in evidence. This prediction, of course, may go completely awry should American participation in the Vietnam war continue at a high level. As in the case of earlier protest and radical movements, the extent to which such groups accommodate to the rules of the game of a democratic political system will depend on how responsive the system seems to be, or as the radicals would put it, how successful it is in co-opting protest. Co-optation and responsiveness are two words often used to describe the same process. The more responsive the system, the more moderate the leftist and trade-union groups have become in the past; a similar reaction may be anticipated from the current "out" groups, the antiwar students and the black militants.

This prediction, of course, applies largely to the mass of politically concerned students whose political interests have been activated by the major issues of the sixties – racism and war – or who have been drawn into the "counterculture" of youth which has sought to deemphasize materialist goals. Many of them, like Sam Brown, the Harvard Divinity School student who organized the movement which resulted in the McCarthy presidential campaign in 1968, and who also founded the antiwar Moratorium movement which precipitated large demonstrations in the fall of 1969, have concluded that the undifferentiated anti-system attacks of extremist student groups that have gone outside of the regular pressure group and campaign tactics of American politics have been counterproductive. Such efforts have

actually reduced rather than increased the efficacy of the antiwar movement in accomplishing its objective of ending the war. In a long analysis to this effect, Brown quotes the statements made by the foreign minister of the Provisional Government of South Vietnam (the Vietcong), Madame Nguyen Thi Binh. She told a visiting delegation of antiwar leaders from the United States that many American student radicals appeared to be "reluctant to touch political power" and help end the war.[6] By their aggressive tactics and personal life-styles, they have antagonized many older Americans who have been ready to support efforts to force the government to change its war policies.

But while the large majority show signs of returning to ends-oriented politics as distinct from involvement in expressive forms of salvation-oriented styles of life, a small, almost infinitesimal minority has adopted terroristic tactics in frustration against failure to gain any effective base of support either on or off campus. The Weatherman faction is perhaps the best known of a variety of such groups which are prepared to engage in terrorism, assassination, bombing, arson, and kidnapping. Since a few hundred determined terrorists can literally tie up a nation, the changes in the mood of the student population will not serve to moderate the ultramilitant groups. If anything, greater moderation by the mainstream activists may only inflame the terrorists. And the danger exists that such terrorism will give rise to counterterrorism, to the use of repressive tactics by the police and other authorities. A struggle to wipe out urban guerrillas who base themselves in campus communities could, of course, upset the trends pressing the American university to reject confrontation tactics.

The Change from the Fifties

To understand the reasons why the relatively passive postwar generation was replaced by one which contains an activist minority of the "enraged," it is important to note the extent to which some of the conditions that dampened ideological controversy among intellectuals during the forties and fifties changed in the sixties. Essentially, the politics of the two earlier decades were dominated first by the Second World War and then by the cold war. Given a high degree of support among liberal intellectuals concerning these events, many who were deeply critical of various domestic institutions and practices found themselves defending the fundamental character of their societies as moral and decent against the totalitarian critics. For a brief period, historically speaking, Western democratic intellectuals found themselves engaging in actions which belied their role as critics. This period was broken by changes within Communist society, as well as increasing awareness of the social conditions existing in the underdeveloped third world. The breakdown of monolithic communism, the rise of liberal opposition tendencies in various Eastern countries, the intensity of the Sino-Soviet split, all served to undermine the conviction that all men of goodwill and all non-Communist nations must unite to fight totalitarian expansion. In a real sense, as far as many intellectuals were concerned, the cold war came to an end.[7]

This change had considerable impact on those members of the older generation who had remained liberal critics, but had kept quiet either because they agreed with the assumptions justifying unity against the Communist threat, or because they feared social or political sanctions from the supporters of anticommunism. Many of them had been active when younger in various radical movements, and though publicly quiescent had continued their criticisms within private circles. As a group, they were concentrated among college-educated professionals and intellectuals, including, particularly, university faculties. Jews had been relatively heavily involved in radical activities in the 1930s and 1940s, a phenomenon which stemmed from continuity with the political values brought over from the ghettoes of Eastern Europe, from experience with domestic anti-Semitism which was particularly strong in the United States until the end of World War II, and from an identification of Nazism with conservatism and militant anticommunism.[8] As ideological anticommunism lost strength, some former radicals and left-liberals returned in some measure to their earlier beliefs. More significant, however, was the emergence among younger intellectuals and students of widespread social criticism, sentiments which were often encouraged by their "liberated" elders. The new generations of liberals who knew not Hitler and Stalin, the 1948 Czech coup or the Hungarian revolution from firsthand experience, found little reason to restrain applying their moral beliefs to politics.

This shift in ideological climate, as well as the rather rapid escalation of protest from words to action, was facilitated by the struggle for Negro rights which emerged in the years following the Supreme Court's school desegregation decision of 1954. This was the perfect issue around which to create a new activist movement, since it engaged the principal aspect of American society, in which the system engaged in actions which were at sharp variance with its manifest creed of equality and democracy. Most Americans, and the university system in toto, recognized that Negro inequality is evil, and in principle approved all actions designed to reduce or eliminate it. Hence race was the easiest issue around which the new political criticism could mobilize. To organize to fight segregation, particularly in the South, was not a radical act. Yet the struggle contributed greatly to radicalizing sections of the young. In this situation, the conservative or traditionalist forces introduced the tactics of civil disobedience, and even of violence; the Southern segregationists refused to accept the law as laid down by the Supreme Court and Congress, and taught the advocates of civil rights, both the black community and the white students, that the regular peaceful methods of democracy would not work. The confrontationist tactics of civil disobedience, which first emerged in the South, were then diffused by the American student movement to other parts of the country and the world, and to other issues both inside and outside of the university.

The aggressive tactics of the civil rights movement were successful, judged by the criteria of actions taken by different agencies of government to outlaw discrimination, and to foster economic and educational improvements. Whatever the profound limitations of these, the fact remains that more has been attempted by government to improve the situation of the black in recent years than in all the preceding years since Reconstruction. Many of these actions, particularly by the Administration, Congress and local agencies, can be credited as responses to political militancy or the fear of ghetto riots. But though these efforts attest to the value of political action, they have not resulted in any major *visible* change in the position of the bulk of the Negroes. (Statistical gains are often invisible to all not directly involved.) They remain preponderantly poor, segregated and uneducated, securing the leavings of the labor market. To each group of civil-rights-concerned youth who have come to political consciousness during this period, the gap between what ought to be and what actually exists appears to have increased rather than decreased. They take for granted the existing structure, including the changes which had been made, and react with outrage against the continued sources of black deprivation. Older liberals, on the other hand, have often reacted with pleasure at the considerable progress that has been made within the past few years. Thus an inevitable age-related split has occurred.

This division between the generations has been particularly acute within the Negro community. To younger blacks, the gains made since the 1950s appear empty, in face of the existing pattern of Negro social and economic inferiority. And on the major campuses of the nation, the growing minority of black students have found themselves in a totally white-dominated world, facing few, if any, black faculty, and a white student body whose liberal and radical wing turned increasingly after 1964 from involvement in civil rights protest to activity directed against the Vietnam war. The concern with black power, with Negro control over their own communities, and particularly civil rights organizations, has won growing support among black college students. Most recently, these students have played a major role in confronting university administrations with demands for more black students and faculty, and for changes in the curriculum.[9] Black students have been among the major forces initiating sit-ins at schools as diverse and separated as Cornell University, San Francisco State College, Columbia University, Boston University, Northwestern University and many predominantly Negro institutions as well.

The issue of the acceptable pace of reform also has been affected by events abroad, particularly in Cuba and Vietnam. The triumph of the Castro movement, an event dominated by young men, produced an example of a revolution seemingly uncontaminated by Stalinism. Cuban events helped to generate the sense that revolution was both possible and desirable as a way to eliminate social evils. Again generational differences divided the liberal-left communities. The older ones had learned from experience that revolutions could lead to totalitarianism, to new intense forms of exploitation and to cynical betrayals of the popular will. To many youth, raising such matters seemed only to justify inaction against the intolerable aspects of the status quo.

The spread of opposition to the Vietnam war has, of course, become the dominant political issue affecting student activism. To the older generation, including initially most liberals, Vietnam was but the most recent episode in a two-decade-long struggle against Communist imperialist expansion. To the new generations of the children of liberals and former radicals, Vietnam became defined in terms which placed American actions at odds with certain basic American beliefs, those of antiimperialism, and of the right of self-determination of politically weak peoples. Given the existence of a polycentric divided Communism, it simply did not make sense to perceive Vietnamese Communism as an extension of Russian or Chinese power. The very failure of the powerful United States to quickly defeat its small poor Vietnamese opposition has been evidence of the oppressive character of the war, of its being a war in which a foreign power seeks to impose its will by force over another people. The very values which led Americans to be suspicious of, and opposed to, the British, French and Dutch empires, which were called into play to justify World War I and II, and the Korean War, have now been turned against the United States.

To comprehend the reasons for the special confrontationist character of the student antiwar movement, it is necessary to recognize the direct link between it and the tactical lessons learned from the civil rights movement. Sam Brown put it well:

> In the early sixties, young people learned that voting and precinct meetings were not the only effective forms of political activity, that extralegal demonstrations worked in the face of a moral horror, and that American leaders often displayed both cowardice and hypocrisy in race relations. The civil rights movement, with all its implications about American politics, was almost a necessary [prior] condition for antiwar activism on the campus.[10]

It was also important to understand that the passion unleashed by the antiwar movement is strongly related to basic aspects of the American value system. To decry wars, to refuse to go, is at least as American as apple pie. Sol Tax, of the University of Chicago, who has attempted to compare the extent of antiwar activity throughout American history, concluded that the Vietnam war is only our fourth least popular military conflict with a foreign enemy since the Revolutionary War, up to the point negotiations to end it began.[11]

The War of 1812 was intensely unpopular among the merchants and other strata; some New England states threatened to secede on the issue.[12] A vigorous peace movement emerged after the war, whose success among students "was evidenced by the formation of peace societies at Amherst, Dartmouth, and Oberlin and less organized student activities at Harvard, Union, Knox and other colleges".[13] Abraham Lincoln and many Whigs denounced the Mexican War. The abolitionists regarded it as an immoral conflict fought to extend the domain of slavery, and innumerable Catholics objected to fighting a Catholic country. Indeed, the Mexican army was able to form units composed of American deserters.[14] By paying $300, men could and did buy themselves out of the Civil War, which, ironically, since Karl Marx enthusiastically supported it, was the only war regarded popularly as "a rich man's war and a poor man's fight." The antidraft riots of 1863 were the bloodiest of our history.[15] Professors and other intellectuals were vilified in the press and pulpit as traitors for their opposition to the Spanish-American War. Oliver Wendell Holmes expressed his disgust at the "self-righteous" antiimperialist and antiwar talk "which has prevailed to some extent at Harvard College and elsewhere."[16]

In August 1917, the New York *Herald* reported that "in New York City ninety out of the first hundred draftees claimed exemption." The War Department listed 337,649 draft evaders in World War I. The antiwar Socialist party secured its largest vote in history in many cities in the 1917 municipal elections.[17] Our entry into World War II was strongly opposed by an extensive mass movement. Had the United States entered World War II in any way other than through having been attacked, it is clear that a large segment of the country would have continued its opposition to the war after Congress declared it. Opinion surveys taken during the Korean War reported significant majority opposition to it among the population and among college students within two years of its beginning.[18]

The same Protestant propensity for moralistic crusades which has been expressed in various efforts to reform the rest of the world by war also underlies the endeavor of numerous Americans to resist each war as immoral. For many Americans, wars must be moral or immoral; one must do God's work in supporting or opposing them. The United States is the only country in which the majority of the citizens have adhered to what the British called the "dissenting" or "nonconformist" denominations, rather than to groups that are or once were state churches. The values of moralistic dissenters, mainly the Baptists and Methodists, have deeply informed our political history, in terms of a propensity for domestic and international crusades against satanic enemies.[19]

The Sources of Student Unrest: Motivating Factors

A general analysis of the changing political climate as it has encouraged student dissatisfaction, of course, does not explain why students *qua* students have played such an important role in stimulating protest. Here it must be noted that students have almost invariably been more responsive to political trends, to changes in mood, to opportunities for social change, than any other group in the population, except possibly intellectuals. As a result students have played a major role in stimulating unrest and fostering change in many countries. The special role of students has been particularly noted in the revolutions of 1848; in the Russian revolutionary movement, which was largely a student one until 1905; in the various Chinese movements during the first half of the twentieth century; in the different fascist movements in Italy, Germany and Spain before the fascists took power; in a host of colonial and underdeveloped states; and in various communist countries since 1956.[20]

Historically then, one would expect a sharp increase in student activism whenever events call accepted political and social values into question, in times particularly where policy failures seem to question the adequacy of social, economic and political arrangements and institutions. Although it may be argued that student activism is the result rather than the cause of social discontent, it is important to recognize that once activated, student groups have played a major role in mobilizing public opinion behind the causes and ideologies fostered by them. Social unrest causes student unrest, but once they start expressing their disquiet, students and intellectuals have been in many ways the vanguard of political change.

Awareness of the important role of students has led to efforts to detail those aspects of the situation of students generally, as well as in specific times and places, which press them to act politically.

The factors to which attention has been called in the growing literature on the subject may be differentiated between those which *motivate* students to action and those which *facilitate* their participation.

Perhaps the most general hypothesis which has been repeatedly advanced to account for youth protest suggests that it is a result of a process set in motion by rapid rates of social change, by events which create a sharp discrepancy between the formative experiences of parental generations and those of a given generation of youth. Both laymen and experts on youth behavior have agreed with Kingsley Davis's proposition that "rapid social change . . . has crowded historical meaning into the family time-span, has thereby given the offspring a different social content from that which the parent acquired, and consequently has added to the already existent intrinsic differences between parent and youth, a set of extrinsic ones which double the chance of alienation."[21] Or as Norman Birnbaum has put it more recently: "Generational dissidence and revolt are not a perpetual social problem, but assume acute forms only under conditions of extreme dissonance between generational experiences."[22]

As the discussion of the sources of repeated periods of American campus unrest presented in Chapters 4 and 5 should make clear, any wave of discontent can be and has been explained by the concurrent social changes which have upset the normal sources of youthful deference to older generations. While this approach may be valid in the sense that Kingsley Davis presented it, as accounting for greater youthful protest in "modern civilization, in contrast to most societies," it does not explain why certain epochs of rapid change lead to student activism, while others have not. An effort to do so derivative from Freudian analysis suggests that student movements occur whenever "the elder generation, through some presumable historical failure, has become de-authorized in the eyes of the young. . . . They arise wherever social and historical circumstances combine to cause a crisis in loss of generational confidence, which impels the young to resentment and uprising. . . . Rapid social change in and of itself does not necessarily involve student unrest."[23] The emphasis on the causal role of "de-authorization," however, suffers from the same methodological problem as the theory of "rapid social change," in that its advocates seek to demonstrate the congruence of specific events with the presumed presence of the causal process, and ignore circumstances in which the resultant event—student unrest – did not take place, though rapid social change or de-authorization did.

But though various historical sociological theories have been advanced to account for greater or lesser periods of youth-based unrest, other hypotheses have been suggested to explain why youth generally, and students in particular, have shown a more intense commitment to and greater involvement in movements favoring radical social change and millenarian hopes, than their elders. Much of the writings on the subject by psychologists have been an insistence that youth still resemble Aristotle's portrait of 2,500 years ago that they do "things excessively and vehemently," that they "have exalted notions, because they have not yet been humbled by life or learnt its necessary limitations."[24] Some contemporary psychologists see a special contemporary disposition toward excessive anxiety and commitment in the strains of adolescence, a period which in modern society with its prolongation of education and career preparation lasts into the twenties for college students. During this stage of personality development, the individual is faced with the need to establish a personal identity and select an adult role. The very openness, freedom to choose alternative paths, characteristic of modern society, faces the modern adolescent with a more ambiguous, ego-threatening period than that which confronted his predecessors, who were much more likely to have an identity and career handed to them. The reaction of adolescents to this state of prolonged uncertainty has been well described by Erik Erikson:

> Clearly the adolescent looks most fervently for men and ideas to have faith in, which also means men and ideas in whose service it would seem worth while to prove oneself trustworthy. . . .

> The adolescent now looks for an opportunity to decide with free assent on one of the available or unavoidable avenues of duty and service, and at the same time is mortally afraid of being forced into activities in which he would feel exposed to ridicule or self-doubt.
>
> . . . The adolescent's willingness to put his trust in those peers and leading, or misleading, elders who will give imaginative, if not illusory, scope to his aspirations is only too obvious.[25]

Gordon Allport in analyzing the changes in personality that accompany "maturing" suggested that youth are inherently less able to handle ambiguity, to accept their weaknesses as well as strengths, tend to overreact to stimuli, and lack a high capacity for tolerance.[26]

The sociological analysis has pointed to the same aspects as inherent in the fact that youth, and students in particular, are marginal men. They are in transition between having been dependent on their families for income, status and various forms of security and protection, and taking up their own roles in jobs and families. Studenthood is inherently a tension-creating period. The rapid growth in the number of students, almost eight million today as compared with one and a half million at the end of the 1930s, means both that the composition of the college population, as a group, has come from increasingly less privileged families, and that the value of a college degree for status placement has declined.

The university has become more meritocratic; it is how well you do, rather than who you are that counts. Hence, young people in a society in which education increasingly determines how well they start in the struggle for place, find themselves facing a highly competitive situation. The pressures to conform to the requirements of the education establishment begin for many middle-class and aspiring working-class youth in elementary school and intensify in high school. Hard work and ability at each level only serve to qualify the individual to enter an even more difficult competition at the next rung in the educational ladder. While some succeed, many must show up as mediocre or must rank low.

A number of radical theorists in different countries have suggested that the growing protest movement among students reflects the fact that the student role in capitalist society has essentially become one of an apprentice low-paid member of the new class of professional employees who are essentially workers denied the opportunity for true self-expression in their work role.[27] Society forces increasing numbers of youth to go to university to acquire the skills necessary for the highly specialized jobs which advanced industrial societies must fill. Hence, the student is increasingly a member of an exploited alienated sector of the powerless strata. His protests represent his increased awareness that he is coerced by the elite. As two Canadian Marxists put it:

> [S]tudying has lost any trace of the self-directed activity that it may once have been and has become a form of labor. . . . The ideological mystification of student alienation . . . is the idea that the student is investing in himself. Yet if he asks himself why he is in school, the student must honestly respond with answers that have little or nothing to do with his personal development and growth. . . .
>
> Student labor is alienated in the same sense that the product is for the future employer rather than for the student himself. Since the product is embodied in the skills of the student himself, he becomes alienated from himself. Thus modern education and technology, when continued in the capitalist mode, frequently gives rise to the individual psychological estrangement often confused with the conception of alienation.[28]

This type of analysis, though coming from different roots than that which stresses the adverse consequences on youth of the emphasis on meritocratic competition in the context of sharply increased numbers of students, joins hands with it in specific empirical deductions. Thus, the Belgian Marxist Ernest Mandel stresses the causal impact of the "university explosion," of the fact that a "new social grouping has emerged from the very vitals of capitalism," the millions of university students in America, western Europe, and Japan who are faced with the "insoluble contradictions" of capitalism; that it is impossible to integrate them into "the kinds of jobs they rightly expected when they started their university education."[29] Whether the expansion of the university system is credited to the inherent logic of increasingly equalitarian societies open to merit, whether socialist or capitalist, or is blamed on the need of a more developed industrial capitalism to press an ever growing proportion of youth to continue their education to facilitate the profit system, proponents of each assumption agree that modern university students are increasingly subject to anxieties derivative from the pressures on them to succeed.

There is a variety of evidence which suggests that these tensions affect the emotional stability of many teenagers and college youth, even the most able among them.[30] Such tensions may find varying outlets, of which a rejection of the competitive social system which forces them into a rat race for grades is one. Although such tensions have always been present in the student role, it should be noted that they have intensified considerably in the last decade and a half. The very expansion of the numbers going to universities throughout the world has made the situation worse, more competitive, than before.

The idealism of youth, to which reference is frequently made, is another stimulating factor which is an outgrowth of social expectations. Societies teach youth to adhere to the basic values of the system in absolute terms – equality, honesty, democracy, socialism, and the like. There is a maxim which exists in various forms in many countries: "He who is not a radical at twenty does not have a heart; he who still is one at forty does not have a head." This statement is usually interpreted as a conservative one, assuming radicalism is an unintelligent response to politics. But the first part of the maxim may be even more important than the second, for it denotes a social expectation that young people should be radicals, that the older generation believes that youthful people should be radicals, that the older generation agrees that youthful radicalism is praiseworthy behavior. It is the young conservative, the young "fogie," not the young radical who is out of step with social expectations.[31] The emphasis on youthful reformism is even greater in the United States than in many other countries, for American culture places a premium on being youthful and on the opinions of youth. It tends in general to glorify youth and to deprecate age.

Many American adults are reluctant, even when they consciously disagree sharply, to call students or youth to task. Rather they may encourage youth and students to take independent new positions, rather than emphasize the worth of experience. This ties in with the part of the American self-image which assumes that the United States is a progressive country, one which accepts reform and change.[32] And the truism that the youth will inherit the future is linked with the sense that the youth are the bearers of the progressive ideas which will dominate the future, that youth will contribute to the enduring struggle to make the American creed of equality more meaningful.

The real world, of course, necessarily deviates considerably from the ideal, and part of the process of maturing is to learn to operate in a world of conflicting values, roles, interests, and demands. Such compromises as this requires are viewed by youth as violations of basic morality. They have not established a sense of affinity with adult institutions; experience has not hardened them to imperfections. Their contact with the moral principles of society is abstract and pure; they are not yet tested by personal experience, by contact with reality. Students hang on to idealistic beliefs longer than others. They tend, as Max Weber suggested, to develop an ethic of "absolute ends" rather than of "responsibility."[33] They tend to be committed to ideals rather than institutions. Hence, those events which point up the gap between ideals and reality stimulate them to action.

Many observers of American behavior have pointed to the codification of equalitarian values in the American creed. Americans are taught to believe "that all men are created equal," that they should be given equal opportunity to gain the good things of life, and that all are worthy of equal respect in interpersonal relations. This stress on equality presumably creates an inherent tension with the reality of inequality of income, respect, and power, particularly when it is linked to as obvious a violation of the creed as racial inequality. Yet David Cohen has suggested that the heightened student discontent of recent years has been further stimulated by the fact that an important segment of society, those involved in education, communication, culture creating and diffusing, and the social welfare occupations – and the schools to which this segment of society sends its children – increasingly since World War II have favored an ethos which "resembles nothing so much as that utopia which Marx and subsequent generations of radical critics envisaged." This may be seen most clearly in the elite private schools which "stress spontaneity, creativeness, and a general freedom from rigid constraints in learning. . . . Schooling, in short, is justifiable only when it is playful. . . . This, then, is a situation in which all the tables have been turned: the only acceptable work is that which is play. . . ." And the values and practice of such schools which are "efforts to create utopian enclaves in the midst of capitalist society," enhance for the children of the affluent intelligentsia of America the gap between what is desirable and the need to conform to the class and work ethos of a competitive capitalist society.[34] A similar point has been made by Charles Hampden-Turner, who, in coming to this country from England, was "struck by the strength of developmental and humanist themes in American educational and child rearing philosophers, and the relative weakness of the same themes in commerce and politics. . . . It has long seemed to me only a matter of time before the developmental themes in American life confronted the repressive themes, and before those students nurtured in the better homes and schools came to regard the opportunities offered by business and government as an insult to their achieved levels of psycho-social development."[35]

The strain between the emphases on equality, play, and lack of repression, which characterize many of the private and suburban public schools of the intelligentsia, and the onerous requirements of bureaucratic industrial society, is brought to a head by the requirement that students compete for success through working hard, while remaining sociological adolescents in the university.[36] Their physical maturation which is not paralleled by increased power is another source of frustration for those reared in such families.

Although physiologically mature, and often above the age legally defined as adult, students are expected to refrain from full involvement in the adult world. The very nature of university education is seen as calling for a withdrawal by the institution from the mainstream of society into an ivory tower, free from the constraints of politics and religion. Although living in a society which stresses that adults should establish their own status based on their individual abilities and achievements, students are expected to maintain a status in limbo, or to remain dependent on their family status. Such a situation can be a source of bitterness, especially in a culture like the American, which places so much stress on individual achievement. Thus the student, in addition to the opportunity to acquire an education, also demands the chance both to experiment with adult roles, and to exhibit his ability to achieve a position on his own.[37]

Dependency is, of course, built into the very essence of the university system. Students are dependent, as to the chances of their future placement, on their standing with the faculty. The faculty has the power of certification through its control over grades. This gives them the right to influence what students read, and how they spend much of their time. The American university, in particular, with its stress on frequent examinations and faculty judgments, emphasizes this dependent relationship even more than does the university in most other countries. Hence, the student who leaves home to attend a university finds that he has actually entered a highly controlled situation, while many aspects of the society urge him to become independent.

The constraints imposed on students living in university dormitories have proved to be particularly onerous. By acting in *loco parentis,* universities in America took on the role of constraining agent over the social life of individuals who increasingly have claimed the right to be autonomous. And in a world in which eighteen-year olds are eligible for the draft, the effort of the university to maintain these controls has been inevitably doomed to failure. With the decline in average age at which Americans reach sexual maturity from a physical point of view, and the accompanying changes in the accepted norms concerning sexual relations, the university has placed itself in the impossible position of seeking to enforce a status of social dependency—which even middle-class parents have found difficult to maintain.

The Youth Culture as Motivating Force

It may be argued, however, that student activism in particular, is among other things, an expression of the need for a distinct youth culture.[38] The student stratum, as such, tends to create a whole array of age-group symbols, which sets it apart from others in society, and from adults in particular. These include unique patterns of personal appearance, peculiar modes of communication, and special styles of life (relatively low standard of living, but major expenditures on music or travel, or use of drugs as compared with adults' consumption of liquor). In their desire to demonstrate their rejection of the adult world, youth rebels have repeatedly engaged in forms of expressive behavior which have been noteworthy for their similarity. Some of those in the American past are presented in Chapters 4 and 5, but it should be noted that descriptions of such activities in France, Russia, and Germany in the nineteenth century and the pre–World War I period read like contemporary accounts of the scene at Telegraph Avenue, Berkeley, or Harvard Square. A report on the behavior of the young Bohemians in the left bank of Paris, on the same spot as the May 1968 riots, clearly has this effect.

> [They] held radical-sounding, erratic political ideas which somehow were never followed by practical action. According to

> Balzac they could be recognized by their off-center cravats, greasy coats, long beards, and dirty fingernails. The Bohemians of the 1830s and 1840s were young, actually and ideologically; they claimed that youth itself was the collective expression of genius. It is exaggerating very little to say that Bohemians hoped to be seen as a band of intellectual raiders and freebooters, who routed convention everywhere and kept all contented souls in a state of dazzled alarm . . . In all accounts of the Bohemia of the Orleanist years, the first impressions have always to do with its ingenious techniques of social outrage. When Thackeray first came on the Paris Bohemia, he was astonished enough to make a careful record of their appearance – their ringlets, straight locks, toupees, English, Greek and Spanish nets, and the variety of their beards and jackets.[39]

Similar modes of behavior occurred in czarist Russia:

> Among the students of the universities and the higher technical schools [there appeared] . . . a new and striking original type – young men and women in slovenly attire, who called in question and ridiculed the generally received convictions and respectable conventions of social life, and who talked of reorganizing society . . . They reversed the traditional order of things even in trivial matters of external appearance, the males allowing the hair to grow long and the female adepts cutting it short, and adding sometimes the additional badge of blue spectacles. Their appearance, manners and conversation were apt to shock ordinary people, but to this they were profoundly indifferent, for they had raised themselves above the level of so-called public opinion, despised Philistine respectability, and rather liked to scandalize people still under the influence of what they considered antiquated prejudices. . . .[40]

The activities of the pre–World War I German youth movement have been invidiously described in similar terms:

> Turbulent gangs of untidy boys and girls roamed the country. . . . In bombastic words they announced the gospel of a golden age. All preceding generations, they emphasized, were simply idiotic; their incapacity has converted the earth into a hell. . . .

> The inflated verbiage of these adolescents was only a poor disguise for their lack of any ideas and of any definite program. They had nothing to say but this: We are young and therefore chosen; we are ingenious because we are young; we are the carriers of the future; we are the deadly foes of the rotten bourgeois and Philistines.[41]

The effort to formulate a specific youth culture which rejected that of the adult world has also repeatedly taken the form of student political groups and ideologies which have little to do with those of the adult political world, often including the revolutionary parties. As the British sociologist Donald MacRae has generalized in his analysis of these cultures:

> Adolescent rebellion is older than the universities of the middle ages. It has constantly presented a pattern of temporary bohemianism and a defined and legitimated licence of behavior. Since 1789, it has also involved experiment with radical politics—left and right, nationalist and internationalist. . . .[42]

And these experiments, as S. N. Eisenstadt has indicated, have often taken the form of "various youth and student movements . . . which . . . aim to reform the society in terms of distinct, specific youth values."[43]

The pure youth and student movements have tended toward an ahistorical rejection of a detailed, worked-out, means-ends related form of radical politics. Rather, as one description of Martin Luther's student followers reports, there is "an inclination to primitivism among students. Some of them carried their opposition to Aristotle and scholasticism to the point of rejecting all scholarship, and advocated the innocent simplicity of the Apostles."[44] In the nineteenth century, the chief Marxist leaders, including Karl Marx and Friedrich Engels, themselves, though recognizing that students had, for example, played a major role in all the French revolutions, condemned as irresponsible the expressive politics and personal styles of revolutionary students.[45] The desire of youth to make the revolution at once, without consideration of realistic possibilities, was seen by them and their successors as "putschism" or "left-wing adventurism," behavior which they related to the "bourgeois" origins and positions and aspirations of the radical students, as well as to their youth and inexperience. Marx and Engels denounced various groups of left-wing youth for their antiintellectual attitudes and behavior, that is, an unwillingness to acknowledge that they could learn from any segment of the adult world. In 1870, Engels wrote to Marx in harsh terms concerning a rumor that large numbers of Russian students were planning to emigrate in great numbers to Western Europe to join the revolutionary movement there. "If there is anything which might ruin the Western European movement, then it would be this import of 40,000 more or less educated, ambitious hungry Russian nihilists."[46] Some indication of what Engels feared may be seen in a description of the Russian student movement of that day.

> With the impulsiveness of youth and the recklessness of inexperience, the students went . . . much further than their elders.
> . . . they wanted an immediate, thoroughgoing transformation of the existing order of things according to the most advanced socialistic principles, and in their youthful, reckless impatience they determined to undertake the work themselves.
> . . . some of the Nihilists maintained that things were not yet ripe for a rising of the masses, that the pacific propaganda must be continued for a considerable time, and that before attempting to overthrow the existing social organization some idea should be formed as to the order of things which should take its place. The majority, however, were too impatient for action to listen to such counsels of prudence, and when they encountered opposition on the part of the government they urged the necessity of retaliating by acts of terrorism. In a brochure issued in 1874 one of the most influential leaders (Tkatchev) explained that it was a mistake to attach great importance to questions of future social organization . . . [T]he reconstruction of society on the *tabula rasa* might be left, it was thought, to the spontaneous action of natural forces.[47]

The German students were largely supporters of different forms of right-wing nationalism from the mid-nineteenth century through their early (1931) majority support in student council elections for the Nazis. The Nazis sought to build on the history of pure antisystem, antiadult youth movements in Germany by alluding to themselves as a youth movement.[48] And the descriptions of the expressive youth culture of the German rightist students closely resemble those of the Russian leftists. Thus the German sociologist, Max Weber, writing about his fellow students in 1885, when he was twenty-one, noted their nationalist and anti-Semitic enthusiasms, and stated that "the most incredible part of the matter is the fantastic ignorance of my age mates about the history of this century. Those from the metropolis are a bit more knowledgeable than the others. But for the rest, there is *tabula rasa*. . . . In their heads domestic politics began less than a decade ago."[49]

Historians of youth movements have noted the similarities in expressive style, in romanticism, in idealism, in commitment to violent actions, which have occurred among groups which have varied considerably in their social and political values. Walter Laqueur, the foremost student of the pre–World War I German movement, has emphasized these common elements:

> The idealism, spirit of sacrifice, devotion to one's people, and revolutionary fervor that marked the *Burschenschaft* [early nineteenth century nationalistic, anti-Semitic, terrorist student groups] have been an inherent part of all youth movements over the last hundred years. It is a mistake to assume the fascist youth movements were an exception to this rule. . . . To be sure, they preached a doctrine of violence, but as Mussolini said, "There is a violence that liberates, and there is a violence that enslaves; there is moral violence and stupid, immoral violence." (Compare Marcuse: "In terms of historical function, there is a difference between revolutionary and reactionary violence, between violence practiced by the oppressed and the oppressors.") . . . .
>
> Youth movements have never been out for personal gain. Whoever describes a youth movement as idealistic only states the obvious. What motivates youth groups is different from what motivates an association for the protection of the interests of small shopkeepers. The fascist experience has shown the immense

potential which inheres in every youth movement can be exploited in the most disastrous way. . . .

Most of the basic beliefs and even the outward fashions of the present world youth movements can be traced back to the period in Europe just before and after the First World War. The German *Neue Schar* of 1919 were the original hippies: long-haired, sandaled, unwashed, they castigated urban civilization, read Hermann Hesse and Indian philosophy, practiced free love, and distributed in their meetings thousands of asters and chrysanthemums. They danced, sang to the music of the guitar, and attended lectures on the "Revolution of the Soul." The modern happening was born in 1910 in Trieste, Parma, Milan, and other Italian cities where the Futurists arranged public meetings to recite their poems, read their manifestos, and exhibit their ultra-modern paintings. No one over thirty, they demanded, should in future be active in politics. . . . The idea of a specific youth culture was first developed in 1913–14 by the German educator Gustav Wyneken. . . .

For the historian of ideas, the back issues of the periodicals of the youth movements, turned yellow with age, make fascinating reading. . . . It is indeed uncanny how despite all the historical differences, the German movement preempted so many of the issues agitating the American movement of today, as well as its literary fashions.[50]

In 1920, Lenin, like Engels before him, expressed serious concern over the expressive behavior of those involved in the radical youth culture.

The little yellow-beaked birds who have just broken from the egg of bourgeois ideas are always frightfully clever. . . . The youth movement . . . is attacked with the disease of modernity in its attitude towards sexual questions. . . . [T]he so-called "new sexual life" of the youth . . . often seems to me to be . . . an extension of bourgeois brothels. . . . Of course, [the sexual need like] thirst must be satisfied. But will the normal man in normal circumstances lie down in the gutter and drink out of a puddle, or out of a glass with a rim greasy from many lips? . . .

Young people, particularly need the joy and force of life.

> Healthy sport, swimming, racing, walking, bodily exercises of every kind, and many-sided intellectual interests. . . . That will give young people more than eternal theories and discussions about sexual problems and the so-called "living to the full." . . .
>
> The revolution . . . cannot tolerate orgiastic conditions. . . . Dissoluteness . . . is bourgeois, is a phenomenon of decay. The proletariat . . . doesn't need intoxication as a narcotic or stimulus. Intoxication as little by sexual exaggeration as by alcohol. . . . I am deeply concerned about the future of our youth.[51]

Most recently, various commentaries on contemporary American student unrest, such as those of John Seeley and Theodore Roszak, which are summarized and accepted in the 1970 *Report of the President's Commission on Campus Unrest,* emphasize in their causal analysis "the formation of a new youth culture that defines itself through a passionate attachment to principle and an opposition to the larger society. At the center of this culture is a romantic celebration of human life, of the unencumbered individual, of the senses, and of nature."[52]

The "counterculture" of youth need not take a political form. Indeed, much of the pre–World War I German youth revolt, as well as lesser similar manifestations in the United States, were not political. The youth culture has often evidenced itself in expressions of cultural renunciation of predominant adult values and behavior with respect to morality, dress, work orientations, achievement norms and the like. Sometimes, it has taken the form of youth-based new varieties of religious expression. Various forms of "deviance" from the point of view of the adult world have served as anchorage points to bring large numbers of young people together in a solidaristic relationship. As Walter Laqueur has noted: "Whether a certain movement became political or unpolitical, whether it opted for the Left or the Right, depended on the historical context: it hardly needs to be explained in detail why youth movements were preponderantly right-wing after the First World War, while more recently most have tended to the left. But beyond the particular political orientation there are underlying motives which have remained remarkably consistent throughout."

> Youth movements have always been extreme, emotional, enthusiastic; they have never been moderate or rational. . . . Underlying their beliefs has always been a common anti-capitalist, anti-bourgeois denominator, a conviction that the established order is corrupt to the bones and beyond redemption by parliamentary means of reform. The ideologies of democracy and liberalism have always been seen as an irretrievable part of the whole rotten system; all politicians, of course, are crooks. Equally common to all youth groups is a profound pessimism about the future of present-day culture and an assumption that traditional enlightened concepts like tolerance are out of date. The older generation has landed the world in a mess, and a radical new beginning, a revolution, is needed. Youth movements have never been willing to accept the lessons of the past; each generation is always regarded as the first (and the last) in history. And the young have always found admiring adults to confirm them in their beliefs.[53]

The University and Faculty as Sources of Unrest

In the modern developed world, particularly in the United States, the conditions of university life make politics a particularly critical source of self-expression. Students are given ample opportunity to discuss and study political matters. The university, itself, in spite of its emphasis on academic freedom and on being nonpartisan, is increasingly involved in politics, as professors fulfill ever-growing roles as party activists, intellectual commentators on political events, advisers, consultants, and researchers on policy-relevant matters. Many students are thus in centers of great political significance, but have little or no share in the political status of the university. If it is to express a sense of separate identity, student politics as part of the student culture must be outside of and in opposition to that of most of the adults.

Although the student protest is directed against much of the adult world, including the faculty, any analysis of the sources of student activism, per se, must recognize that student values and political concerns are often closely related to those of the faculty. Certainly in the United States, faculties have shown by their reaction to student protest, from the Berkeley events of 1964–65 to the demonstrations against the Cambodian incursion in May and June 1970, that large segments of the professoriate and student bodies stand closer to each other in political reactions than either do to the rest of the American body politic.[54]

Intellectuals, that is, those concerned with the creation of art, culture, literature, science, and knowledge, whether academics or not, are involved with creation and innovation and are ideally partisans of the abstract and the ideal. Their occupational activities require them to value new discoveries and ideas. Originality, departure from what is established and officially accepted, is a central value in the outlook of the modern intellectual. More generally, in the tradition of the intellectual classes of Western society, there are important currents of long duration and great intellectual value which have set the intellectuals against established authority. These include scientism, romanticism, revolutionary apocalypticism, and populism. These traditions largely form the characteristic outlook of the intellectuals outside universities. Universities have been institutions established by or supported by the authoritative center of society – political and ecclesiastical – and they have been integrated into the tasks of training young persons for careers connected with the central functions of society and culture. But they, too, by their stress on scientific discipline, on creativity, and on detachment from the idols of the marketplace, have nurtured a critical attitude. Especially in the social sciences has there been a tension between society's need to affirm the dominant systems of practices and belief and the intellectual's critical attitude toward all systems.

The American university increasingly has become a major occupational outlet for many of the brightest people who seek to be innovative and free of the ideological restrictions and materialistic commitments which they believe are inherent in the corporate and professional worlds. Once liberal faculty become overtly political, their influence has tended to be self-accelerating. Evidence drawn from a variety of surveys of student attitudes indicates that colleges have a liberalizing effect on young people, particularly in areas linked to universalistic principles, racial equality, internationalism, peace, class relationships, as well as in more personal beliefs such as religion and sexual behavior.[55] Samuel Stouffer pointed out over fifteen years ago that the conservatives who attack the universities for "corrupting" young people are right from their political and moral standpoints.

But if faculty help to create a climate of opinion which presses students to the left, ironically, at least some of the sources of student malaise stem from the fact that changes in the role of the faculty have contributed to making the situation of being a student less attractive than it once was. With increasing size and greater pressures on faculty to do research, publish, and take part in extramural activities, inherently one should expect to find poorer instruction, more faculty aloofness, and administrative indifference to students. The research-oriented faculty increasingly give a larger proportion of their limited teaching time to graduate students. These activities are, of course, not new; as noted later, students and administrators have complained about faculty neglect of teaching and of students since the last century. Yet the research-consulting culture clearly spread far beyond its earlier boundaries in the "golden" age of academe which began during World War II.[56]

The very increase in the importance of the university as a center of influence and power, and as the major accrediting institution of the society, has reduced the informal influence of students within the university. The higher estates of the university, administrators and faculty, however, have sought to maintain their traditional authority and prerogatives, while reducing their own "responsibility" for the quality of the personal and intellectual lives of their students. This development is not simply or even principally a function of the growth of the university; it reflects even more the increased "professionalization" of the faculty, the extent to which "teaching" as such has continued to decline as the main identification of the role of being a professor.[57]

The changes in the roles of the faculty, their increased involvement in a national prestige system, based on evaluations of their scholarly achievements or extramural activities, the sharp increase in their income, derivative in large part from the fact that many schools are in competition for those who have or promise to attain general reputations, and the concomitant decline in faculty teaching obligations have not necessarily made for a "happier" professoriate. Faculty, like students, are in an increasingly competitive situation, one in which men see themselves being judged as to their position in national and local pecking orders. With the depreciation of the teaching function as a local source of economic reward and status, many faculty become deeply dissatisfied and anxious. Ironically, the better universities and colleges, which are increasingly competitive with each other in efforts at stockpiling distinguished scholars, are more likely to encourage such feelings among both their older and younger faculty by invidiously rewarding, often in a very public fashion, those men who are most valuable in this race for institutional prestige. Such sentiments reinforce faculty propensities to oppose the administrations of these schools, as well as the dominant values and institutions of the large society. Hence, many distinguished professors find solace in student militancy directed against the forces they hold responsible for their felt sense of status insecurity. The same faculty members who demand and secure lower teaching loads (especially after student revolts which further reduce the "bargaining strength" of the university) often tell their students that they are neglected and misused by the administration and trustees.

It may be argued that American students, as students, are subject to greater strains and fewer rewards than those of previous generations, with the exception of the Depression generation. Although the demand for "student power," for increased influence by students over the decision-making process in the university, tends on the whole to be raised by the left-wing activist group, the receptivity which this demand secures in wider circles of students may reflect an increased sense of grievance, because the more distinguished universities in terms of scholarly quality of faculty and students demand more, yet give less in the form of personal relations (informal influence) among students, faculty and administration. Thus, as in the case of workers and employees in bureaucratized industry, a sort of syndicalism has been in the offing for many decades which seeks to regain symbolically for students as a group the influence which they think they have lost individually as a result of changes in the organization of universities. Subjectively, of course, students as the "inferior" class in power and status terms would appear to have always complained bitterly about "unfair" treatment from the faculty. This has been the substance of complaint and often violent protest literally for centuries in American colleges. As Lawrence Vesey argues, there is much in the professor-student relationship which produces "class" ideology and resentment, almost without regard to variation in objective condition.[58]

One analyst of student protest, the Berkeley sociologist David Matza, has suggested that the repeated appeal of populism, of "the belief in the creativity and in the superior worth of the ordinary people, of the uneducated and the unintellectual," which has appeared in various student movements from nineteenth century Russia to the contemporary American glorification of the poorest blacks, is in part, at least, a way of attacking the moral position of their teachers.

> Among students, the appeal of populism is not simply an outgrowth of traditional radical propensities. Just as the apocalyptic mentality has a special appeal to youth, so, too, does populism. Students have a special liking for populism because it is a vehicle for an effective attack on the professional authority and a way of defending against unflattering assessment of themselves. For the radical and the bohemian, too, a belief in populism allows

students who perceive themselves as avant-garde to deflect the contrary judgments of academic elders.[59]

The unconceptualized sense of grievance with their situation, a sense which in many cases is often directed against the university, also may make many students, particularly those with a politically critical background, more receptive to political action directed against trends in the larger society. The two sources of activism thus reinforce one another; the more directly political uses campus discontent to create a set of issues around which to build a movement, while campus discontent may express itself in wider political issues. These are general aspects of student motivation to activism. There are many aspects in the situation of the group which *facilitate* mass activity, which make it easier to recruit for such action.

Facilitating Factors

Young people are more available for new political movements than adults. As new citizens, as people entering the political arena, they are less committed to existing ideologies, they have few or no explicit political commitments, they have no previous personal positions to defend, they are less identified with people and institutions which are responsible for the status quo. Inherently, they know less recent history than adults. For this current generation, as noted earlier, the key formative events in foreign policy terms have been the Vietnam war, and domestically, in the United States, heightened awareness of the oppressed position of the American Negroes.

Students are also more available because of the lesser commitments they have to their "occupational" role as compared to adults. Max Weber, many years ago, pointed out that political activity is to a considerable extent a function of the extent to which job requirements are *dispensable*. In his terms, those who could take time off from work without suffering economic consequences are much more likely to be active than those who have to punch a time clock.[60] Students (and professors) have perhaps the most dispensable job requirements of all. Students may drop out of school, may put off their studies for short or long periods, without paying a great price. They may often delay taking examinations. The numbers who dropped their books to take part in the McCarthy primary campaigns are a recent illustration of this.

Linked with this is the factor of "responsibility." As compared to other groups, students simply have fewer responsibilities in the form of commitments to families and jobs. Thus, the existence of punitive sanctions against extremist activism is less likely to affect students than those with greater responsibilities to others, or to a career ladder. Moreover, as noted earlier, students remain adolescents or juveniles sociologically, and they are often implicitly treated as such legally, particularly when they violate the law. In many societies, a number of the students involved in politically or otherwise motivated infractions are literally the children of the elite, a fact which serves to reduce the will to punish them. In addition, universities are generally run by liberal individuals who are not inclined to invoke severe sanctions against students. Students, as Daniel Cohn-Bendit has pointed out, are under less pressure to conform than other strata.[61]

Another factor which facilitates student political involvement is the physical situation of the university which makes it relatively easy to mobilize students who are disposed to act politically. The campus is the ideal place in which to find large numbers of people in a common situation. Many universities have over thirty thousand students concentrated in a small area. New ideas which arise as a response to a given issue may move readily among the students, and find their maximum base of support. Only a small percentage of these massive bodies can often make large demonstrations. Thus, from 1965 to 1967, although opinion polls indicated that the great majority of American students supported the Vietnam war – that antiwar sentiment within the group was no greater than in the population as a whole – the campus opposition was able to have a great impact because it could be mobilized. The antiwar student minority could and did man impressive antiwar demonstrations.

Although there can be little doubt that the current period of student unrest has had more impact on the body politic than any previous epoch in American history, the evidence is not conclusive, apart from the demonstrations of May and June 1970 against the Cambodian incursion, that a greater *percentage* of students have shown antagonism to the society or the university than in some earlier periods of unrest. The sheer magnitude of the educational establishment, the greater ease of communication across distances, and the presence of certain common issues, have made it possible to mobilize large-scale demonstrations. Beyond this, the introduction of the tactics of civil disobedience and confrontation, stemming in large part from the civil rights movement, has given protesters a weapon through which a small percentage of the student body can bring entire universities to their knees. And the inability of universities to handle such situations except by relying on outside force (with rare exceptions) often brought to the support of the demonstrators the majority of the campus population, both student and faculty, who were outraged by the violation of the historic norms of university autonomy, and by the sight of student-police clashes which almost never occurred without some blood being spilled.

The larger explanation for the rise of activism during the past half decade or so must lie primarily in political events: the emergence of the civil rights and Vietnam issues in a particular post-Stalinist political epoch. These gave to the more radically disposed students the issues; their social situation gave them the stimulus; and the campus situation furnished them with the means to build a movement.

Any effort, therefore, to understand the weight and impact of the activist groups must be placed within the context of an analysis of the opinions of the student population as a whole. Fortunately, a variety of surveys conducted between 1965 and 1971 permits this to be done. The next chapter reports on them.

2

Polls and Protest

Much of the discussion of the wave of protest which emerged in the late 1960s has presented it as a "youth revolt." It is important to recognize that the increasing opposition of American college students towards the war and the concomitant growth in radical-left sentiments among them does not represent an age-group phenomenon. There are other generation-units, to use Karl Mannheim's term, among American youth who have highly disparate sentiments. Idealism among a large segment of noncollege youth has been reflected heavily in a show of patriotic feelings, support for the war, and even disproportionate involvement in backing George Wallace's presidential candidacy in 1968.[1] Opinion surveys dealing with the relationship of age as such to opinion towards the Vietnam war indicate that from 1965 to 1971, those in the lowest adult age group, twenty-one to twenty-nine years old, were consistently *less likely* to oppose the war than their elders though the gap narrowed in recent years. In fact, those fifty and older were most likely to think participation in the war a mistake. This report, of course, includes both students and nonstudents, who are quite different in their views.

There is no question that young people turned against the war

TABLE 1

Percent in Different Age Groups Who Consider American Intervention in the Vietnam War a Mistake 1965–1971

NATIONWIDE GALLUP POLL RESULTS		PERCENT CONSIDERING THE VIETNAM WAR A MISTAKE		
		21–29 YEARS	30–49 YEARS	50 YEARS AND OVER
1965:	August	14	22	29
1966:	March	21	23	30
	May	29	32	42
	September	37	28	40
	November	21	30	36
1967:	May	31	34	42
	July	32	37	50
	October	43	43	53
1968:	February	40	46	48
	March	46	47	52
	April	38	46	54
	August	48	48	61
	October	44	49	64
1969:	February	49	49	57
	October	58	54	63
1971:	May	59	60	63

Source: Hazel Erskine, "The Polls: Is War A Mistake?" *Public Opinion Quarterly* 34 (Spring 1970), p. 134; and Gallup Poll release, June 6, 1971.

as the conflict continued, but so did older ones. And those fifty and over remained the most antiwar age group through to 1971. This "is even more surprising in view of the propensity of older people not to express opinions. Those under thirty averaged only about 8 percent with no opinion on the question over the years, as compared with an average of 15 percent without opinions among the fifty-and-over. This leaves positive war backing among youth even stronger than the preceding table would indicate. . . ."[2] These conclusions are based on a review of the data collected by the Gallup Poll. Two senior researchers of the Survey Research Center of the University of Michigan report that the results of their national surveys point in the same direction. "This 'generation gap' that one would have expected wherein the young oppose the war and the old support it, simply failed to appear. . . ."[3]

Student Opinion on Vietnam

The many national inquiries of student opinion since campus activities secured national attention in the fall of 1964 have documented a gradual shift to the left in the thinking of the student population, constant increases in opposition to the war, and growing expressions of criticism of the content of teaching and the internal organization of the academic establishment. The results of these surveys have also shown the increased activism of the black students, their resentments, and the heightened sympathy for their goals among the large majority of whites.

The survey data permit comparisons with dominant attitudes among noncollege youth, and with the adult population. In general, the noncollege youth have been much more conservative on domestic, foreign policy, and cultural issues than the students. There is clearly a gap in opinions and behavior between the average reaction of college students and others, but the gap is *not* a generational one; rather it is between those on and off campus regardless of age. Faculty, who have also been surveyed in some detail, are clearly much more opposed than students to militant activism and campus politicization. Yet on substantive political policy issues, Vietnam, civil rights, domestic social policy, as a group, they are fairly close to their students. Both tend to espouse as their dominant political ideology what might be described as Kennedy-McCarthy liberalism, the program of the left-liberal antiwar wing of the Democratic party. Self-identified conservatives among the students are between 15 and 20 percent; among the faculty about a quarter. Left-wing radicals run to between five and ten percent; the faculty resembles the students in this respect (see Tables 5 and 6).

The noncollege population, on the other hand, has gradually moved in a more conservative direction over the past half-decade. Increasing numbers of them identify themselves as conservatives rather than liberals, so that by 1970 many more citizens described themselves as conservatives (52 percent), than as liberals (34 percent).[4] Noncollege youth, whether over or under twenty-one, have also differed consistently from the college students. On a number of issues, not only on Vietnam, the noncollege youth have been more conservative than their campus peers and their elders. Three surveys, taken within a few months of each other, of national samples of students, faculty, and the U.S. adult population as a whole, point up the considerable differences between opinion on and off the campuses of America (Table 6).

Although massive demonstrations against the Vietnam war began in 1965 in some large high-quality schools such as Berkeley (Vietnam Day), Ann Arbor (teach-ins on the war), and Madison, the survey data, as noted earlier, indicate that the majority of students supported the war until 1968. In 1965, for example, the Harris Survey reported that only 24 percent of those with opinions on the war favored negotiations and American withdrawal from Vietnam.[5] Samuel Lubell concluded in the spring of 1966 that "two thirds of the students interviewed continue to back our Vietnam policy which is about the same proportion of support one finds in the country as a whole."[6] Another national survey of students taken by the Gallup Poll in May and June 1966, indicated that 47 percent of college youth endorsed the way "Johnson is handling the situation in Vietnam," while 23 percent disagreed because they thought the U.S. should be more aggressive, and another 16 percent opposed the President's policies for being "indecisive" or "inconsistent."[7] A Gallup survey of student opinion on Vietnam taken a year later in 1967 "showed 49 percent of students in favor of a policy of escalation compared to 35 percent who wanted military activity to be reduced."[8] Not until the spring of 1968 did the proportion of students who thought that the United States had made a mistake in getting involved in Vietnam reach 50 percent.[9] At the time, 48 percent of the public, but only 38 percent of the entire twenty-one- to thirty-year-old age group, gave the same response, suggesting the existence of a rather large opinion gap on the war between college and noncollege youth. This difference has continued in succeeding years.

Lubell, who interviewed students through the 1967–68 school year, essentially agreed with the Gallup findings that that was the year in which the campus turned against the war. Lubell credited the shift to concern over the draft spurred on by the fact that "Congress had changed the law [dropping deferments for graduate students] so that graduate students and seniors, on graduation, would be taken first." He concluded at the start of the 1968–69 school year that the unrest would grow, that "real stability is not likely to be regained until the unresolved crisis outside of the universities is broken."[10] Yet despite the increasing opposition to the war, only 7 percent of a 1968 Gallup sample of students stated that they would refuse to serve if drafted.[11]

Opposition to the Vietnam war, the perception that it was a mistake, continued to grow following the dramatic Communist Tet offensive in February, the cessation of the bombing of North Vietnam in April and the beginning of negotiations in Paris. In effect, once the U.S. government gave up the goal of defeating the Communists on the battlefield, it became impossible to prevent a steady erosion of support for the war, particularly, though obviously far from exclusively, on campus. Two Gallup samples of students taken two and a half years apart dramatically point up the change in opinion (Table 2).

Other survey organizations which compared views over shorter periods after the President's announcement about negotiations found a continuing growth in "dovish" or withdrawal sentiments. In reviewing changes in attitudes which had occurred between his two student surveys, one conducted in October 1968 and the other six months later in March and April 1969, Daniel Yankelovich concluded: "On college campuses, pacifist sentiments have spread from the more liberal students to the

TABLE 2

Proportion of Students Identifying Themselves as "Hawks"* or "Doves," 1967 and 1969 (Percent)

	SPRING 1967	FALL 1969
Dove	35	69
Hawk	49	20
No Opinion	16	11

* In response to the question: "People are called 'hawks' if they want to step up our military effort in Vietnam. They are called 'doves' if they want to reduce our military effort in Vietnam. How would you describe yourself — as a 'hawk' or as a 'dove'?"

Source: Gallup Poll release, December 21, 1969.

more moderate and conservative students."[12] Harris found that the proportion of students who, when asked whether a man's refusal to be drafted because of opposition to the Vietnam war, led them to respect him more or less, indicated "more respect," had jumped from 29 percent in spring 1968 to 48 percent in spring 1969.[13] Comparing attitudes in the fall of 1969, between late September and the end of November, during which time the two massive Moratorium and Mobilization protests occurred, the Gilbert Youth Poll reported "an increase, from 28 percent in the first poll to 43 percent in the second, among those who feel the only proper action would be 'complete and prompt withdrawal of American troops.'" A similar indication of a dramatic jump in strong opposition to the war was recorded in two polls taken by the Yankelovich survey organization. The proportion strongly agreeing with the statement "The war in Vietnam is pure imperialism" increased from 16 percent in the spring of 1969 to 41 percent in 1970, just before the Cambodian events. Those strongly disagreeing dropped from 44 to 21 percent.[14]

Yet though most students opposed the war, the survey data would suggest that a majority accepted the new Nixon administration's policy of Vietnamization as a means of getting out. The administration was able to co-opt some of the campus opposition.

Thus a Gallup survey of college students taken in May 1969 reported that when asked: "Do you approve or disapprove of the way Nixon is handling his job as President?" 57 percent approved, 27 percent disapproved and 16 percent had no opinion.[15] A second 1969 Gallup national student poll taken in the fall found that students were seemingly losing interest in the protest, though they remained heavily against the war. *Newsweek,* in reporting the survey, concluded that "the mood of the American campus is apparently undergoing a striking change: militancy and violence are in good measure giving way to passivity and personal introspection, and the revolutionary impulse seems – for a while, at least – to have largely spent itself."[16] When asked specifically what they thought "of the way President Nixon is handling the situation in Vietnam," more students (50 percent) approved than objected (44 percent).[17] The interviewing for this survey was done in October, at a time when organized efforts to mobilize campus opposition to the war were at a height – between the October 15 Moratorium demonstration and the November 15 Mobilization which culminated in a massive Washington march, the goals of which were heavily supported by the same students (69 percent).[18]

The reaction against the May 1970 Cambodian incursion, of course, produced the largest and most extensive student protest movement the United States has ever experienced. It involved more students at more campuses than in earlier years. And the survey data document the extent of participation, as well as the fact that the attitudes of students in general moved to the left, not only with respect to the war itself, but on other issues as well. Two national surveys taken during the Cambodian protest caught the full flush of this discontent. The largest one, a poll of the attitudes of 7300 students on nearly 200 campuses taken for *Playboy* by a major national opinion organization, reported that 36 percent favored pulling out "now"; 29 percent supported speeding up withdrawal; 26 percent would have continued "the administration's timetable for honorable withdrawal," while only 9 percent were still in favor of fighting for "total victory."

The Harris Poll, though presenting respondents with somewhat different alternatives, secured almost identical results. With respect to the war, Harris found that 54 percent now favored stopping the fighting and bringing the boys back home, as compared with 34 percent for a phased withdrawal, and 9 percent who wanted to expand the war.[19] This finding may be contrasted with the results of a 1965 survey of students conducted for *Playboy,* which reported that 6 percent were for immediate withdrawal, 35 percent supported continued fighting in South Vietnam, and 56 percent wanted to escalate by invading North Vietnam.[20] The antagonism to the Cambodian events naturally led to a drastic decline in student opinion of the way President Nixon was handling the war. Fifty-nine percent gave him a rating of "poor," 17 percent said fair, and only 22 percent would say pretty good or excellent.[21] Only 27 percent of the students interviewed thought the President was right in ordering troops into Cambodia.[22] And 60 percent said the action had increased their opposition to American policy in Indo-China.[23]

The increased participation in protest activities has been documented by the Harris Survey. The data presented in Table 3 clearly indicate a considerable escalation in the numbers who took part in demonstrations over a five-year period.

The same pattern of escalation of campus protest has been reported in a survey of the presidents of colleges and universities conducted during the summer of 1970 for the President's Com-

TABLE 3

Student Participation in Activism (Percent)

	1965	1969	1970
Signed Petition	72	84	87
Demonstrated	29	40	60
Picketed	18	18	29

Sources: "The Harris Survey," The Washington *Post,* March 25, 1965; "The Harris Survey," June 30, 1969; "Report of the May 1970 Harris Survey of Students," pp. 155, 157.

mission on Campus Unrest. As indicated in Table 4, the percent of schools with significant incidents more than doubled from the academic year 1967–1968 to the pre-Cambodian part of the school year 1969–1970. Strikingly, the proportion again increased by more than twofold for the protests against the Cambodian incursion. The results of this survey underestimated the extent of the protest since administrators were asked to only report on "incidents which resulted in the disruption of the normal functioning of the institution." A similar questionnaire sent to administrators by the Carnegie Commission on Higher Education concerning the May–June 1970 events inquired as to all forms of protest, including nondisruptive "essentially peaceful demonstrations," and reported that there "was some form of organized dissent on 57 percent of the campuses."[24]

One of the most striking aspects of these antiwar protests is the extent to which they reached into relatively moderate political sectors among students. Thus a nationwide study of five thousand students by two psychologists, Kenneth and Mary Gergen, taken in 1969–70, before the Cambodian incursion (sample

TABLE 4

Number and Percent of Incidents of Campus Unrest Reported by Administrators During Three Years (Number of Administrators Reporting: 1,569)

	YEAR			
INCIDENTS OF UNREST	1967–1968	1968–1969	1969 TO APRIL 30, 1970	MAY 1, 1970 TO JUNE 30, 1970
Number of Incidents	136	272	388	508
Number of Schools with Incidents	96	171	220	508
Percent of Schools with Incidents	6.1	10.8	14.0	32.4

Source: Garth Buchanan and Joan Brackett, *Summary Results of the Survey for the President's Commission on Campus Unrest* (Washington, D.C.: The Urban Institute, September 1970), Chart 1, p. 9.

somewhat overweighted to schools towards the middle and higher levels of academe) reports that "over 42 percent . . . had demonstrated against the war. . . . The data indicate that in an average group of 100 antiwar demonstrators, one might find 13 Republicans, 20 Democrats, 62 Independents, and only 5 persons who identify themselves as Radicals. The overwhelming majority of the demonstrators place a high value on traditional American ideals."[25]

The 1970 post-Cambodian incursion Harris Survey reported a heterogeneous mix as well. Thus, though almost all self-described far leftists (91 percent), and most liberals (74 percent) took part, over one third (37 percent) of the middle-of-the-road students did as well.[26]

The Spread of Political Discontent

Although antiwar protest has been the most striking feature of student activism in recent years, the survey data document the extent to which the campus has moved to the left politically over the years. From 1968 to 1970 the proportion describing their politics as radical or extreme left increased from 4 to 11 percent. More striking perhaps is the fact that in June 1970, the proportion of students who identified in this way was not much smaller than those who looked upon themselves as conservatives.

The Gergens' 1969–70 survey of five thousand students in thirty-nine schools also reported a significant shift in student general political sentiment which they linked to opposition to the war. "Over 40 percent of the sample indicate that the war has altered their political affiliation, and of these, only 7 percent have increased their commitment to one of the two major parties. The remaining 93 percent of this group [or 37 percent of the total sample] became more 'liberal,' 'radical,' 'disillusioned with party politics,' and otherwise alienated from party politics."[27]

But though there is no question of the shift to the left among the students, it is curious that the various attempts to estimate the proportion of students who are alienated or supportive of radical activism, have agreed from 1968 to the fall of 1970 on a figure of about 10 percent, of whom perhaps one third are reported to have revolutionary views. Thus in 1968, Samuel Lubell classified students on the basis of their responses to ten items and concluded that with "only one in every ten students interviewed did these ten items link up to a pattern of general revolt or 'alienation.' "[28] A Roper study in the winter of 1968–69 asked students to evaluate four basic institutions: politics, administration of justice, business and industry, and higher education. It found that "9 percent of the seniors are *very* critical of our basic institutions generally; 18 percent are *very* favorable," and while large majorities thought all four were "basically sound," the same majorities thought they "need improvement."[29]

The most comprehensive effort to specify types of responses, the Yankelovich-CBS study based on spring 1969 data, established five types: "Revolutionaries," who held all of a five-belief index affirming that the American social system is "too rotten for repair," that destroying property and assaulting police are justifiable tactics, etc.; "Radical Dissidents," who held one or more of these beliefs, but not all of them; "Moderate Reformers," who agreed with six or more statements about the need for specific reforms; "Moderates," who agreed with less than six of these statements; and "Conservatives," who held a coherent set of beliefs about the need for more law and order, the American Way of Life being superior to all others, and so forth. Among the college students, 3 percent were identified as "Revolutionaries," 10 percent were grouped as "Radical Dissidents," 39 percent were classified as "Reformers," 37 percent were described as "Moderates," and only 11 percent were defined as "Conservatives." Conversely, however, among the noncollege youth interviewed by Yankelovich, 50 percent were located in the "Moderate" category, and 21 percent were "Conservative" as defined by attitude responses.[30]

The Gilbert Youth Poll interviewed a national sample in the spring of 1970, but did not ask as explicit questions as the others, thus not permitting a direct comparison. Its results also suggested, however, that the "alienated" were still a minority, since when faced with a choice between agreeing that the U.S. form of government "needs considerable change" or that it is "just about right," 60 percent chose the latter statement.[31]

In examining the results of various national surveys of students from 1965 to 1970, it is difficult to come to any definitive conclusions concerning the depth of and enduring quality of the grievances felt by American students and their portent for continued tension between a significant portion of them and the government. The approximately 10 percent who show up as "radicals," "alienated," or "dissidents," in the surveys completed during 1969–70 may be contrasted with those who identified "socialism" (24 percent), or "communism" (6 percent) as positive terms in a 1936 Roper-Fortune national student survey. Those who advocate fundamental changes in the American system today (75 percent in a post-Cambodia Harris poll) compare with the 68 percent who favored "a revision in our attitude about property rights" in the 1936 report.[32] At the other end of the spectrum, Harris reported that in 1969 and 1970 the percentages of students who identified their politics as "conservative" were 16 and 15, (Table 5) figures which are identical with the

TABLE 5

Political Self-Identification of American College Students (Percent)

	SPRING 1968	SPRING 1969	SPRING 1970	FALL 1970
Radical or Far Left	4	8	11	7
Liberal	39	44	43	35
Middle-of-Road	33	32	26	34
Conservative and Far Right	24	16	15	19

Source: "The Harris Survey," June 30, 1969; Report of the May 1970, Harris Survey of Students, p. 3; Louis Harris and Associates, *Youth Attitudes for Life Magazine Year End Issue* (New York: November 1970), p. 65.

15 percent who told Roper in a 1936 national student survey that they felt positive about the term "conservatism."

The survey of students conducted by Harris during the "quiet" fall semester of 1970 clearly suggested that the increase in support for radical politics which accompanied the escalation in antiwar protest in 1969 and 1970 may be reversing, that the 1970s may witness a new, less radical political cycle. It is also possible that the various surveys reported on here have overestimated the move to the left which occurred during the sixties. Each of the various national polls, Gallup, Harris, Roper, the College Poll, and others have generally been based on national samples running from 1,000 to 2,000 students. There is some reason to believe that these organizations have oversampled the more selective or higher quality schools, or that their respondents on given campuses were selected using quota sample rather than probability (randomly from list of students registered) procedures. These "biases" may have resulted in an overestimation of the more radical or alienated segment. Evidence that this is so may be seen in the fact that some of the polls have greatly overestimated the membership of the Students for a Democratic Society (SDS). The largest single effort to sample American student opinion conducted by the Carnegie Commission on Higher Education with the cooperation of the research staff of the American Council on Education in December 1969 reported a more conservative student body than the other surveys did. Its weighted national sample of 70,000 undergraduates and 30,000 graduate students and 60,000 faculty members at 300 institutions found fewer on the "left" and more self-identified "conservatives" among the students than the smaller surveys (see Table 6).

A second large survey of almost 8,000 undergraduates conducted a few months later by Peter Rossi also reported a relatively moderate student population. "Politically, 40 percent of the students called themselves moderate, 32 percent liberal, 14 percent conservative, 5 percent radical, and 2 percent very conservative. . . . The students also were asked to predict things that would be im-

TABLE 6

Political Self-Identification of Undergraduates, Graduates and Faculty Compared to U.S. Population (1969) (Percent)

	UNDER-GRADUATES	GRADUATE STUDENTS	FACULTY	U.S. POPULATION	
Left	5	5	5		
Liberal	40	37	41	Liberal	15
Middle-of-Road	36	27	27	Moderately Liberal	18
Conservative	19	30	28	Total Liberal	33
				Moderately Conservative	28
				Conservative	23
				Total Conservative	51
				No Opinion	16

Source: Philip W. Semas, "Students 'Satisfied' with Education, Most of Them and Teachers Agree," *The Chronicle of Higher Education* 5 (January 18, 1971), p. 2. U.S. population figures from a Gallup survey taken in July 1969 as reported in *Gallup Opinion Index*, Report No. 50, (August 1969), p. 9.

portant to them ten years hence. Out of six choices, family life was listed as being of first or second importance by 87 percent of the students, and a career was listed first or second by 64 percent. Only 9 percent of the students listed 'community involvement' first or second among the six choices."[33]

The conclusion that only a small minority of American students have ever been alienated from the body politic is iterated in the findings of a variety of polls conducted between 1965 and 1971 which indicated considerable support for diverse aspects of American society other than those linked to foreign policy, the war, and racism. During the spring of 1965, in the first year of large-scale protest, a national sample expressed confidence in the policies of dominant American domestic institutions, particularly those linked to economic and professional elites. The majority voiced a "great deal" of confidence in the medical profession, banks and financial institutions, higher education, and big corporations. Students as a group were much less favorable to the arts, the United Nations, the civil rights movement, religion, and the labor movement, as indicated in Table 7.

Perhaps more significant than the positive responses reported in the above table in indicating how little alienation from American institutions existed among students in general in 1964–65, the academic year of the Berkeley revolt and the emergence of mass demonstrations against the war, is the very small

TABLE 7

How Students View the World Around Them; Responses to the Question "How Much Confidence Do You have in These Institutions?" (Percent)

	GREAT DEAL	ONLY SOME	HARDLY ANY	NOT SURE
Scientific Community	76	20	2	2
Medical Profession	73	22	5	—
Banks & Financial Inst.	66	29	3	2
U.S. Supreme Court	65	28	6	1
Higher Education	64	32	4	—
Big Corporations	52	40	7	1
Executive Branch of Federal Government	49	42	9	—
The Arts	46	43	5	6
Psychiatric Field	44	44	7	5
Congress	39	52	8	1
The Military	38	43	17	2
The United Nations	35	49	14	2
Organized Religion	34	46	18	2
Civil Rights Movement	33	47	19	1
The Democratic Party	22	63	10	5
The Press	20	57	21	2
Advertising	16	38	44	2
Organized Labor	13	55	29	3
Television	13	46	39	2
The Republican Party	12	53	29	6

Source: "Campus '65," *Newsweek* (March 22, 1965), p. 45, from The Harris Survey.

percentage who indicated "hardly any confidence" in the dominant economic organizations. A year later in the spring of 1966, Samuel Lubell found that 60 percent of the students he interviewed praised the role of business, while only 15 percent were critical. Lubell also reported that an unspecified majority were for "a stronger federal government but against a guaranteed annual income," and for "a more rapid extension of civil rights but against radical intermarriage." He concluded his analysis by commenting that in "their political thinking, far from being 'alienated,' the students remain basically like the rest of the country. . . ."[34]

Two surveys of student opinion in the winter and spring of the 1968–69 academic year also point up the limitations on any judgment that American college students as a stratum had become alienated from dominant institutions or the body politic. The relevant findings from a Roper survey of freshmen and seniors are contained in Table 8.

The results of the Roper survey clearly do not suggest that the bulk of American students were hostile to American institutions in the winter of 1968–69, although they had turned decisively against the Vietnam war. A somewhat similar picture of the sentiments of the national student stratum was presented in a subsequent poll completed for *Psychology Today* in the spring of 1969. This survey found that 65 percent disapproved of U.S. involvement in Vietnam, 39 percent indicating strong feelings and 26 percent mild ones.[35] On most other questions, however, they were much less critical of American institutions and policies.

The *Psychology Today* survey reaffirmed the findings of the Roper poll that the large majority of American students were not antagonistic to American institutions. The Yankelovich-CBS survey of four thousand youth, half of them in college, taken in March and April 1969, supplied further evidence that college students, though more alienated and radical than the sample of noncollege youth aged seventeen to twenty-three, still favored working within the democratic system. Though the large majority of white students agreed that America is to some degree a

TABLE 8

Attitudes Toward Four Institutions of a National Sample of Freshmen and Seniors (Winter 1968–69) (Percent)

	BASICALLY SOUND: ESSENTIALLY GOOD	BASICALLY SOUND: NEEDS SOME ASSISTANCE	NOT TOO SOUND: NEEDS MANY IMPROVEMENTS	BASICALLY UNSOUND: NEEDS FUNDAMENTAL OVERHAULING
Business				
Seniors	39	48	7	3
Freshmen	48	37	9	1
Political System				
Seniors	10	72	15	2
Freshmen	11	70	16	3
Administrative Justice				
Seniors	20	54	21	3
Freshmen	23	50	21	4
Higher Education				
Seniors	19	56	19	4
Freshmen	32	49	15	2

Source: Roper Research Associates, *A Study of the Beliefs and Attitudes of Male College Seniors, Freshmen, and Alumni,* May 1969, pp. 56, 60.

"racist nation," only 21 percent said they would welcome "more vigorous protests by blacks," 59 percent said they would disapprove of such protests. Eighty-eight percent of the white students believed that the "American system can respond effectively" to the need for change. Eighty-nine percent agreed that the radical left is as much a threat as the radical right. Close to three quarters of the entire student sample (72 percent) "believe that competition encourages excellence," and that "the right to private property is sacred," (75 percent).[36]

A fourth national survey organization, the College Poll, which

TABLE 9

Attitudes Toward a Variety of American Institutions — Spring 1969
(Percent)

	SA*	MA	DK	MD	SD
Universities:					
1. On the whole, college has been a deep disappointment to me.	4	4	2	26	56
2. The university environment has helped me find out about myself.	43	42	5	7	3
3. I don't feel I am learning very much in college.	4	13	1	28	53
4. American universities have largely abdicated their responsibility to deal with vital moral issues.	9	30	18	33	9
Social Issues:					
1. Negroes would be better off if they took advantage of the opportunities available to them rather than spending so much time protesting.	20	35	7	23	15
2. Those who knock free enterprise misunderstand what made this a great nation.	26	41	11	15	7
3. The events of 1968 prove that it is futile to work within existing political structures.	8	25	11	34	23
4. There is no point in trying to change existing political structures; if one is interested in change he must work outside these structures.	3	11	7	42	35

* SA = Strongly Agree; MA = Mildly Agree; DK = Do Not Know; MD = Mildly Disagree; SD = Strongly Disagree

Source: "A Study of the Inward Generation," Special Report published by *Psychology Today*, October 1969.

regularly queries samples of students for newspapers and NBC, also reported that the dominant mood on campus during 1968–69 was liberal, sympathetic to civil rights demands, and antiwar. Its results also portrayed a student population which was far from extremism in its views. Thus 63 percent said they believed that "the ROTC belongs on campus" during the year in which ROTC was under sharp attack from SDS and antiwar groups. When the concept of a voluntary ROTC was introduced, the proportion approving of ROTC on campus rose to almost 80 percent![37] When asked "Do you object to your university or college participating in general projects to aid the national defense" only 23 percent said "Yes," they disapproved; 76 percent indicated they had no objection.[38] Although 78 percent favored "Afro-American" courses being offered at their school, 68 percent were opposed to black student control over the selection of the faculty in these courses.[39] The College Poll also reported that over three fifths (62 percent) said they are "getting tired of all the campus unrest," 80 percent felt "that students who break the law in campus fights should be arrested and expelled."[40]

A number of national surveys taken in the spring 1970 semester before the Cambodian incursion revealed a strongly critical, reform oriented, but still preponderantly nonalienated, student population. Accompanying its increased opposition to the Vietnam war was growing support for "fundamental reform" of various major institutions. The proportions favoring such changes in institutions such as big business and the military had risen from about one third to close to half, between 1969 and 1970 in Yankelovich surveys. Yet relatively few students agreed with doing away with specific establishment institutions. Only 12 percent, for example, would have done away with the FBI, another 19 percent favored fundamental reform of the institution, while 28 would have changed it moderately, and the largest single group, 40 percent, were against any "substantial change." Only 14 percent advocated fundamental reform of the Constitution; another 2 percent would have "done away with" it; the overwhelming majority favored "moderate change" (37 percent) or "no substantial change" (47 percent). The greatest hostility was dedicated against foreign policy and racial discrimination. Thus 48 percent strongly agreed that "our foreign policy is based on our own narrow economic and power interests," and 53 percent held the same view about the statement: "Basically, we are a racist nation." In spite of these specific criticisms, only 8 percent agreed in the same antagonistic terms with the comment: "The whole social system ought to be replaced by an entirely new one; the existing structures are too rotten for repair."[41] A second national survey, the Gilbert Youth Poll found that only 16 percent stated that they thought equal rights for minority groups could not be achieved under our present form of government. Two thirds were opposed to control over business profits; about the same proportion rejected paying for medical bills through public taxation; 60 percent were against a government-guaranteed minimum income.[42] The Rossi survey found strong support for protest, since 47 percent disagreed that "laws that are unjust should be obeyed until they are changed." Conversely, a much larger percentage, 72, disagreed with the statement: "To do anything rewarding one must work outside the regular institutions of our society."[43] A study completed by Gallup just before the Cambodian incursion in late April unfortunately asked few questions which bore in any way on degree of alienation from American values. One did inquire as to whether "you think people who are successful get ahead largely because of their luck or largely because of their ability?" Only 9 percent of the students said "luck"; fully 88 percent thought that success is a result of "ability." And in spite of the widespread endorsements of the legalization of marijuana, only half the students interviewed thought that the "use of marijuana should be made legal."[44]

The obvious question arises to what extent the events surrounding the Cambodian incursion, the killings at Kent State and Jackson State, and the mass involvement in the various forms of protest during May and June of 1970 increased the alienation from the American political system. Clearly, no study made during those events could answer this question. In the heat of the reaction to these occurrences, students and others made judgments about the President and the operation of the national political system, some of which were explicitly challenged by events after the school year ended. A Harris Survey conducted in late May reported that the confidence expressed in the President's Vietnam policy or in his general activities had almost totally vanished among students as a result of these events. Thus, as noted earlier, 59 percent said his handling of the war was "poor" in their judgment; 67 percent said they thought he had not "been frank and straightforward about the Vietnam war"; more believed the military operation in Cambodia would lengthen the war (37 percent) than thought it would shorten it (21 percent); and only 19 percent accepted the President's statement that our troops would stay in Cambodia less than eight weeks. Over half (52 percent) thought United States troops would remain in Cambodia for six months or more.

Much larger proportions of students polled during this period than in earlier surveys endorsed the need for fundamental changes (75 percent), believed that demonstrations are an effective form of protest (58 percent), and felt that social progress is more likely to come about through radical pressures (44 percent), as many as thought through institutional reforms (45 percent). And while more students said that the May events had brought students and faculty closer together (54 percent) than those who said they separated them (20 percent), more of them were also inclined as seeing these events separating students and university administrations (42 percent) than bringing them together (28 percent). Most students (67 percent) believed that student protest would speed up needed changes, although close to four fifths of them (79 percent) thought that radical pressures would have their greatest impact through institutional changes rather than through efforts to overthrow the system (10 percent).[45]

Yet if the responses to these questions point up the extensive academic reaction to the Cambodian events, some other replies suggest that even at the height of the protests, student reaction expressed less than total alienation. In spite of the increased hostility to the military and the war, only 25 percent of the Harris respondents were in favor of not having ROTC on campus. Thirty-seven percent favored continuing it as a credit course, while another 33 percent supported an on-campus non-credit ROTC.[46] Only 30 percent said that individual professors should not "be allowed to undertake research projects for the military," as contrasted with 62 percent who supported their right to do so.[47] Demonstrations against companies doing defense business recruiting on campus were frequent from 1968 on. Yet even in late May 1970, only 22 percent opposed such activities, while almost three quarters (72 percent) said that companies engaged in defense work should be "permitted to recruit at college."[48] When asked by Harris *after* the Kent State killings who has been more responsible for the violence at college protests, the demonstrators or the authorities, only 17 percent replied the "authorities," an equal proportion blamed the "demonstrators," while 64 percent said "both." The survey completed about the same time for *Playboy* also inquired about responsibility for the Kent State killings, but offered respondents somewhat different alternatives. The largest group, 43 percent, agreed that the deaths were "attributable to the Nixon Administration's hostile attitude toward dissent," 38 percent thought they were an accident, "no one's fault," while 19 percent blamed the students.[49] Speaking more generally, the large majority of the Harris Survey students (69 percent) thought that "school authorities are right to ask the police for help when students threaten violence," as compared with but 21 percent who considered them wrong to do so.[50] While most of the students (52 percent) believed that it was wrong to seek help from the National Guard in such situations, almost as many (42 percent) said that the "National Guard has acted responsibly in most cases" as thought they were irresponsible (46 percent).

The most extensive investigation of a variety of student attitudes completed in the peaceful fall of 1970 by Louis Harris found, as noted earlier (see Table 5), fewer self-identified radicals and more conservatives than during the Cambodian protests in May. Unfortunately, the other questions asked by Harris were not comparable with those in his earlier study. Nevertheless, they add up to a picture of a relatively moderate and unalienated studenthood. Less than one quarter, 24 percent, had "hardly any confidence" in the ability of the "government to solve the problems of the 70s"; only one fifth, 20 percent, favored changes "to the point of socialism"; 59 percent opposed "a guaranteed annual income," 65 percent disapproved of efforts to secure "enforced racial balance through school busing"; and only 33 percent would not be willing to "work for a company that handles defense contracts." The vast majority reported "happy" family experiences. Over 80 percent said that their parents' married life had been happy, that their family had had enough money, and that their fathers had been happy in their work. Less than a third, 30 percent, indicated that they had trouble communicating with their parents.[51]

Other national surveys of student opinion taken during the 1970–71 academic year also suggest a less radical campus population. A Gallup Poll taken close to the end of 1970 reported that the "size of what is termed the 'radical left' is somewhat smaller than is sometimes believed" since only 4 percent "considered themselves to be members of the 'radical left.' " In commenting on other aspects of this same survey, *Newsweek* noted that "the vast majority of college students appears to be firmly wedded to the traditional American values. . . . Fully seven out of ten students believe there is too little emphasis today on family life. . . . the overwhelming majority of the college population still endorses the Puritan ethic as the best way to the good life. Asked whether 'hard work and effort are necessary for you to achieve personal fulfillment and satisfaction,' a stunning 85 percent answered 'yes.' "[52] The College Poll found that the proportion who said they "would marry a person regardless of race, color or creed" had declined from 71 percent in 1969 to 58 in late 1970. The objectors were mainly concerned about interracial marriages. The same organization reported that 78 percent were opposed to "forced integration of the suburbs . . . [to] help alleviate the slums of our cities." Ninety percent were against giving any special preference to black students in admission to college. In April 1971 the College Poll reported that the percentage agreeing that this is a "racist country" had declined from 58 percent in 1969 to 41 percent. In May, it indicated that 70 percent rated the FBI as "Excellent or Good." Only 10 percent gave it a "Poor" rating. A different survey group, the Campus Poll, found that 67 percent of the students thought that the leaders of the women's liberation movement were "too extreme in demands." Curiously, female students were less likely to favor the movement and more prone to think its leaders too extreme than male ones. The same poll indicated that 82 percent of students interviewed thought it "important" that the "U.S. maintain an effective military defense" (44 percent highly important). But though these responses suggest a relatively conservative studenthood, the Campus Poll also found in the fall that 24 percent agreed that "revolutionary tactics are necessary to effect significant social and political change in the U.S." It suggested that such attitudes declined steadily through the year. Thus, it reported in March 1971 that only 9.5 percent felt that "a person's disagreement with a particular law justifies his disobedience to it." In a survey conducted two months earlier, almost twice as many, 18.5 percent, had approved of civil disobedience.[53]

The findings that the great majority of American students were not alienated or sympathetic to radical causes even at the height of major, well-publicized nationwide demonstrations have also been reported for other countries characterized by major student protests. Surveys of French youth and students after the May 1968 events, perhaps the most potent student protest wave in a Western country, indicated that the great majority were opposed to a "radical transformation of society" in September 1968, four months after the great strike. Only 12 percent of a representative sample of students indicated that they agreed with this objective, as contrasted with 54 percent who said their personal concerns with reforms were limited to education, and 31 percent who were only interested in passing their exams. Subsequent French surveys provided an impression of "reasonable youth"; almost 90 percent said they were personally "happy." More recently, a survey of student opinion in the spring of 1970 at Nanterre, the suburban Parisian university at which the 1968 revolt started, which is generally recognized as the most radical school in France, found one quarter (24 percent) in favor of revolution.[54] In Italy, second only to France in the extent of the 1968 strikes, and which has had the most potent and widespread pattern of student strikes and violence in Europe during 1969 and 1970, a national student survey completed in 1969 also points up the minority status of militant student activism. As one report of this survey indicates, its results lend "weight to the hypothesis of the so-called 'silent majority.'" Only 9 percent of the student sample approved of the methods of the activists; 16 percent supported "revolution"; but when asked to state their favorite country only 4 percent listed a Communist or Third World one – the great majority gave western democratic countries with England in the lead (20 percent) and the United States second (15.5 percent).[55] The results of a 1966 national survey of Japanese students, who have had the longest history of militant, often violent, student protest since World War II, coincide with the American and European findings concerning the relative moderateness of the views of the large majority. Only 22 percent of a national sample of 1769 Japanese students disagreed with the statement "Students should not strike for political matters" (6 percent strongly); and even fewer, 15 percent, rejected the conservative interpretation that "student movements are run only by a few activists" (4 percent strongly).[56]

Attitudes to the University

The information about student attitudes towards the university also presents a mixed picture as to the extent to which structural characteristics or academic policies are a source of student unrest. A leading historian of education, Lawrence Veysey, has indicated that student complaints about the policies of faculty and administration have *always* been widespread in American academe, that they are rooted in a kind of "class tension," in the reactions of the students to being the inferior social class in the system.[57] A prominent British sociologist, Bryan

Wilson, has also suggested that "student unrest has, thus, been . . . inherent in the student situation. . . . [M]odern universities are institutions almost inviting disruption. . . . Discipline in universities was less exacting than that expected of citizens in city streets. And yet, these were large institutions, bringing together large numbers of energetic young people who experienced a relatively common circumstance that might, by a Marxist, readily be defined as 'dependent' and 'underprivileged,' imposed by an identifiable 'opposing' class of dons. Had not younger members been socialized to academic values and university allegiance, universities would long ago, have been places almost ready-made for a class struggle. . . ."[58]

The first major eruption of the current wave of student protest, that in Berkeley in 1964–1965, has been intensively studied by various social scientists. One of the earliest analyses based on interviews with Berkeley students concluded that the "data do not suggest that dissatisfaction with the education process played any role at all." Robert Somers found large majorities agreeing with statements that the administration and faculty were doing a very good educational job. For example, when asked "how well satisfied they were with 'courses, examinations, professors, etc.,' . . . only 17 percent expressed any degree of dissatisfaction." But as Somers noted, more important than the fact that the large majority were "satisfied" was the finding "that the minority of students who *are* dissatisfied with the courses, examinations, or professors are little more likely to be found among the militants than those who are satisfied."[59] A second survey of Berkeley students taken in the spring of 1965 also reported that unhappiness with the university as an educational institution ". . . was on the whole unrelated to support for the FSM."[60] The campus militants did differ considerably from those not involved in the Free Speech Movement (FSM) protest in their political ideologies. That is, what distinguished student reaction to this supposedly first great revolt against the multiversity – impersonal treatment, faculty neglect of students, and the like – was not feelings about the quality of education at the University of

California, but political ideology. The more liberal or radical a student was on general social issues, the more likely he was to support or participate in the FSM. The bulk of those who were directly involved in actual demonstrations had been active in earlier political or civil rights protests.[61] The evidence would appear to be clear that the Berkeley revolt was a politically motivated event, not an effort to change the structure of academe or its educational policies.

Robert Somers repeated much of his 1964 study four years later, after Berkeley had been the scene of continued political protest, of a growing radical student movement, and of repeated confrontations with authority, both the police and the university administration. As a result of the original protest movement and the various interpretations crediting student unrest to inadequate educational programs, the Berkeley campus had also been engaged in considerable education experimentation designed to involve students in the planning of courses, to heighten the social "relevance" of their education, and to increase personal relationships between faculty and students. The educational experience of Berkeley students should have clearly improved as judged by the criteria raised by movement-oriented critics, both faculty and students. Yet Somers found a decline over the years in the proportion satisfied with courses, etc., from 83 percent in the fall of 1964 to 69 percent in 1968. Seemingly, if answers to the surveys are taken as reflections of objective quality, teaching and other aspects of education had worsened somewhat as a result of the reforms.[62]

The trends reflected in the data from national surveys bearing on student attitudes towards the university and educational reform tend to resemble those from Berkeley. A Harris Survey conducted in the spring of 1965 during the first year of large-scale student demonstrations, which inquired into "confidence in various institutions," (Table 7), found the two institutions with lowest negative percentages (4 percent) were "higher education," and the "scientific community." As at Berkeley, the heightened national student discontent generally produced increased complaint about specific institutions, including particularly higher education. The Roper student poll conducted in winter 1968–1969, reported that 23 percent of the seniors and 17 percent of the freshmen stated that higher education was "not too sound," or "basically unsound," while only 19 percent of the seniors and 32 percent of the freshmen thought it was "basically sound and essentially good." These answers represented a considerable decline in support for higher education as compared to the Harris 1965 findings, but it should be noted that comparable changes occurred with respect to student views towards the political system, business and industry, and the system of administering justice (see Tables 7 and 8). The Gergens' 1969–1970 survey results also indicate that the increased criticism of the university is part of a general antiestablishment syndrome dictated by concern about the war. There is some indication in their analysis that draft policies and the general disruptive effects of the war on personal plans continued to play the causal role Lubell attributed to them in 1967–1968 in stimulating antiwar sentiment.

> Approximately one out of every three students has altered his career plans as a result of the war. The modal student is seeking a draft-exempt occupation, while many others indicate extreme confusion over their future. . . . In some schools, over a third of the students have altered their course of study as a result of the war. . . . More than one of every five students traces his dissatisfaction with his curriculum and rules governing student life to the war. . . . Emotional upheaval is particularly prevalent. Between 60 and 70 percent of the students have experienced increased anger, worry, and depression as a result of the war.[63]

Different studies suggest, however, that higher education has remained in better esteem among students than other institutions. The results of Roper's inquiries as to how much confidence they had in various categories of "leaders" indicated much more trust in "leaders in education" than in those in politics or other institutions.[64] Only 7 percent of the seniors replied "not much confidence" in education leaders. In another study conducted early in 1969, Yankelovich differentiated students between "practical-minded," those going to college to earn more money, who comprised 57 percent of his sample, and "forerunners," generally from more affluent backgrounds in better schools and studying liberal arts subjects, for whom college means something more intangible, including "the opportunity to change things."[65] The latter were naturally more reform-minded than the former, but both groups placed the university lowest on their list of six "areas which need fundamental reform," with the one exception that more forerunners favored reforming the universities than favored reforming trade unions.[66] A Gallup student poll taken in the fall of 1969, while reiterating the comparative findings of Roper's 1969 and Harris's 1965 results that students had less confidence in universities than had been true for four years earlier, also reported, similar to Yankelovich, that universities received the largest vote of approval among nine institutions rated by the students. The percent "favorable" to universities was 68, as compared to 56 for business and Congress, 46 for the courts, 37 for high schools, and 33 for organized religion.[67]

In spite of the growing evidence of student dissatisfaction with various aspects of the university, the largest single, statistically most sophisticated survey of American students – that conducted by the Carnegie Commission on Higher Education in December 1969 – found that "undergraduates are generally satisfied with their education." Only 13 percent "said that they were dissatisfied. . . . Specifically, more than two thirds of the undergraduates said that they were satisfied with student-faculty relations, their relations with other students, the quality of classroom instruction, the intellectual environment of the campus, and the college administration."[68] One year later, a very much smaller sample of students interviewed by Harris gave similar responses. Again only 13 percent said that they were "dissatisfied with their own education, thus far."[69]

Any increase in specific complaint about higher education between 1965 and 1970 may be linked, in large part, to the fact that the educationally dissatisfied were increasingly to be found among the politically discontented as the years of protest went on. That is, political ideology became more closely linked to educational ideology. Those students who are disposed to the left now describe the university as a bad place; more conservative students are much less hostile. This is shown conclusively both in Yankelovich and Gallup 1969 national student surveys. Demonstrators are much more disposed to think that students should have "a greater say concerning the academic side of colleges," than others.[70] The more liberal-to-left students are more likely to say that universities need fundamental reform than the more moderate or conservative ones.

These findings, of course, do not indicate anything about the predominant direction of the relationship; that is, it is possible that growing discontent with education led many students to become political protesters. While this undoubtedly occurred in many cases, a large number of studies of the social background of student activists, and of the campus population generally, indicate that there is strong intergenerational continuity in political orientations. These researches, to be discussed in the following chapter, agree with Kenneth Keniston's insightful descriptive phrase that many of the early student radicals of the 1960s were "red-diaper babies," the offspring of leftists of an earlier generation. The liberals also tended to come from liberal backgrounds. Given such evidence, it seems highly probable that the correlations between political and educational discontent reported in the various surveys are largely a result of political criticism producing a generalized antisystem point of view which includes the university. Hence, the increase in negative responses about the university over the short period 1965–1970, the growth in demands for major structural changes, have reflected the escalation of political protest, the growing radicalization of the student body, more than the worsening of the educational experience in these years.

These conclusions are reinforced by the findings of three studies of student attitudes and behavior at the three institutions which experienced the most dramatic confrontations in 1968

(Columbia), 1969 (Harvard) and 1970 (the University of California at Santa Barbara). The sit-in demonstrations and strikes at the first two, and the repeated conflicts with the police and violence at the latter, were explained in various reports as stemming from assorted educational inadequacies, or failings of the university as a "community." Yet in each instance, elaborate efforts to determine the factors which led students to participate in or support the protests indicated that as in Berkeley during 1964–65, the best predictor of reaction to the confrontations was the general political ideology of the students, while their attitude towards the university had relatively little effect. The nature of this relationship may be seen in a table drawn from the survey of Columbia students in May 1968.

TABLE 10

Relationship Between Political Beliefs and School Dissatisfaction in Affecting Support for the Goals of the Demonstration — Columbia Students, May 1968
(Figures Refer to Percent Supporting Goals)

SCHOOL DISSATISFACTION INDEX*	LEFT-RIGHT POLITICAL INDEX*			
	RIGHT	MEDIUM RIGHT	MEDIUM LEFT	LEFT
Low	5	22	59	72
Medium low	7	27	68	88
Medium high	18	36	65	92
High	10	41	79	95

* The Political Index is composed of a number of items including attitude toward the Vietnam war, black power, the Poor People's March, presidential candidates, and party support. The School Dissatisfaction Scale is formed from six items taken from Somers' studies of Berkeley students such as attitudes towards courses, impersonality as a result of size, concern for the educational welfare of the students.

Source: From a survey based on a random sample of 2,000 Columbia students completed by the Bureau of Applied Social Research. I am very grateful to Alan Barton for permission to use these and other unpublished data from his study.

It is clear from Table 10 that political orientations were much more important than educational grievances in determining the reactions of Columbia students toward the 1968 protests. In analyzing the factors related to *participation* in the sit-ins, Alan Barton found that, as in Berkeley in 1964, previous involvement in protest groups was most important. The overwhelming majority of those who took part (83 percent) had been active in earlier forms of antiwar or civil rights work. The combination of a record of activism and leftist attitudes made for a much greater likelihood of involvement in the sit-ins, than did either factor alone. Thus, the Columbia demonstrations of 1968 were clearly a result of the prior existence of activist political groups, and the fact that they occurred had relatively little to do with the assets or liabilities of Columbia as an educational institution.

Similar conclusions are suggested about the sit-in in the Harvard University administration building and the consequent student strike which occurred in April 1969. An analysis of the reactions of a sample of Harvard students conducted by Marshall Meyer concluded that the main source of support for the demonstrations, and of antagonism to Harvard, was an underlying commitment to a leftist ideology. Student respondents were classified on a nine point attitude scale from left to right. When interviewed, almost two thirds (65 percent) of those who were grouped in the two most leftist categories thought that "the takeover of the building was justified," a proportion which declined to one third (33 percent) for the next category (moderate left), and to *two* percent for those who were in the three most conservative groupings. Meyer explicitly addressed himself to evaluating the thesis that radical protest is a consequence of the failings of the Harvard faculty.

> Some critics and a committee of Harvard's overseers have concluded that loss of intimacy between students and faculty is the major source of tension. Were this the case, our data would reveal the absence of student-faculty contact and a correlation between

> leftism and the absence of contact. In fact they do not. Seventy-eight percent of Harvard students say they are friendly with one or more faculty members; three quarters talk with an instructor outside of class at least once a week; and a quarter have these interchanges more than three times a week. Moreover, there is no relationship between a student's acquaintance with faculty members and his political position. . . . This evidence [means] that attempts to promote closer relationships between students and faculty will not diminish the level of unrest though they may have other salutary effects.[71]

The same pattern is indicated by the results of an elaborate study of the factors related to the sharp escalation of protest on the Santa Barbara campus of the University of California (UCSB), which rivaled Berkeley in 1969–70 in propensity to sustain demonstrations that end in violence. Although many of the demonstrations at UCSB pressed for institutional changes, Robert Smith concluded that "the findings here indicate that dissatisfaction from the war is a major determinant of student militancy even in protests that are unrelated to the war."

> The frequency of campus protests is closely related to disaffection from the Vietnam war. When disaffection is high, campus protests are frequent. This is true even when the protests are not manifestly about the war or war-related issues. These aggregate relationships between disaffection and protest also hold true for individual students. Students who are disaffected are considerably more militant [on other issues]. This relationship is true even when a range of other test variables that independently affect militancy are simultaneously controlled. . . .
>
> At UCSB disaffection from the war provides the most powerful explanation for the change in student militancy and campus protests. This is true because the level of disaffection has increased tremendously over the last three academic years, while the levels of the test variables and the political and social characteristics of the faculty and students have remained constant. . . . It is the change in the level of disaffection that has caused the change in the frequency of campus protests and the decline in the quality of intellectual life.[72]

The fact remains, of course, that the number of protests, sit-ins, and other demonstrations dedicated to changing the university steadily increased from 1965 to 1970. This has been documented in various surveys of the issues raised in different situations.[73] University administrations and faculties have been forced to react to demands to change the curriculum, modify the forms of academic governance, reform methods of teaching, and the like. Since the groups which press for such changes usually accompany them with charges that the existing policies are a major source of student discontent, many involved with universities not unnaturally conclude that this is so, that students are being treated badly, and that if various changes are made, the discontent will disappear. But if it is true that much of the increase in complaint about the university has been a *consequence* of the growth in political unrest, then *educational reform can not be expected to reduce student unrest,* in particular those related to extramural issues. And in fact, a recent survey of over twelve hundred institutions reports that those which have made major educational adjustments, including increased student participation in governance, have *not* reduced their proneness to unrest as a result. But this is not the whole story since there is also good statistical evidence derived from aggregate data (characteristics of institutions) that the propensities of schools to experience demonstrations is related to various indicators of bureaucratic (impersonal) treatment of students. (See discussion of these and other relevant studies in Chapter 3, pp. 96–100.) It is true, however, that the university is in many ways considered the best institution by all sectors of student opinion, even though the growth in political discontent results in more disruption on campus than within any other environment. Whatever discontented students think of the relative merits and sins of the university, there is no other establishment target which can be so easily attacked and affected, giving considerable publicity, and at a minimum risk of arrest and severe punishment. This was Daniel Cohn-Bendit's message, when he stated that as compared to other strata, students had no real excuse to avoid joining in militant actions.[74]

The Overestimation of the Dramatic

The evidence presented here from the various national opinion surveys, while documenting the increased opposition to the Vietnam war and the concomitant growth in radical and critical sentiments toward social institutions (at least up to the summer of 1970), generally indicates that the alienated include a relatively small proportion of the student population (10 percent). The state of opinion on campus cannot be gauged from observing demonstrations, or even through securing estimates of such opinion from campus leaders, whether these be university administrators, student body officers, or any other set of authorities. Informants have a strong tendency to overestimate the extent of support for highly visible forms of behavior.

The general point may be demonstrated with respect to the proportions involved in drug taking on American campuses. A Gilbert national survey of youth (February 1970), asked respondents to estimate the percent of their own age group who have tried drugs. Among college students in the sample (1005), close to two thirds (65 percent) guessed 50 percent or more have tried drugs, 34 percent thought 70 percent or more have done so. The same survey found that only one third of the college student respondents reported that they had ever had any experience with a drug, marijuana or other. The proportion who were involved with regular use of drugs at the time was, of course, much smaller, just under 10 percent.[75]

This study illustrates the extent to which students, themselves, overestimate the extent to which their fellows have engaged in a form of well-publicized illicit behavior, much as students and others have exaggerated the propensity of *others* to violate middle-class sexual morality. Although there can be little doubt that the norms of the "counterculture," particularly with respect to use of drugs, have steadily gained adherents on campus from

1965 down to the present (1971), the mass media and those directly involved in or professionally working with such students have invariably overestimated the spread of drugs and other aspects of the new styles of personal expression. In a 1968 review of the literature on drug use, Kenneth Keniston concluded that such behavior was limited to a small minority of the campus population. Extensive use of drugs was to be found primarily in a small group of schools, generally the elite colleges and universities which admit the brightest students, many from liberal intellectual family backgrounds.[76] Different national surveys completed in 1969 yielded results in line with Keniston and Gilbert. Roper reported that 76 percent of the college seniors said that they had never tried marijuana, and that 96 percent had never used LSD. Only 2 percent said they use it occasionally.[77] The Gallup survey of students in all classes in November found results very comparable to those of Roper. In response to an anonymous secret ballot, 68 percent stated they had never tried marijuana, 88 percent had not taken barbiturates, and 92 percent had never used LSD.[78] The College Poll found that 62 percent denied ever taking "drugs such as marijuana or LSD."[79] The Spring 1970 Yankelovich survey reported that only 30 percent rejected outright "the prohibition against marijuana." Almost half, 48 percent, said they accepted it easily, while 22 percent stated that they accepted it reluctantly.[80] By the time of the Cambodian protests in May–June 1970, the proportion of students who told interviewers in the *Playboy* survey that they had ever used marijuana had gone over 40 percent for the first time. Yet only 13 percent said they used it "frequently."[81] A report of a poll taken by Gallup in December 1970 stressed that the percentage of students who reported having taken marijuana at least *once* had doubled between the spring of 1969 and winter 1970 – from 22 percent to 42 percent. About one student in six (17 percent) used the drug an average of once a week. But the Gallup results agree with those reported to *Playboy* that a majority were still "virgin" with respect to use of pot.[82] The Fall 1970 Harris Survey did not ask about personal use of drugs, but did inquire concerning attitudes toward the law. Only 53 percent of the college students interviewed thought that marijuana should be legalized.[83]

Although many in the older generation have an image of college students as slovenly, bearded, and long-haired, this stereotype does not jibe with the impression which Gallup interviewers formed of the national sample they interviewed in April 1969. Only 6 percent of the men had beards, and 10 percent were reported to be dressed in sloppy clothes. The interviewers judged that 81 percent of the male students and 94 percent of the females had "generally neat appearances." In the late fall of 1970, Gallup interviewers reported that close to half the students (45 percent) still had "short hair," another 23 percent had long hair which did not come over the ear. Thus, the proportion with hair that went below the ear was about one quarter of the college population, with only 7 percent among them wearing it down to the shoulder.[84] The Yankelovich survey reported that only 38 percent in spring 1969 and 30 percent in 1970 of the college youth *verbally* "reject the idea of conforming in dress and grooming." A majority (59 percent) "would welcome more emphasis on respect for authority."[85]

Since the results of these surveys are so much at variance with the conceptions of student attitudes and behavior presented by the media, and held by many students, particularly the more activist among them, and by college administrators, some may question their accuracy. The best argument for their reliability and validity is that twelve different national survey organizations varying in their method (anonymous questionnaire using different questions, or personal interview), and necessarily dealing with different samples of institutions, produce a high degree of consensus. It may be argued that the more left-disposed students are underrepresented, since in the last year or so SDS and other extreme left groups and publications have attacked survey studies of student attitudes as "pig research," serving the interests of the academic establishment. It is curious, therefore, as noted earlier, that some of these surveys would seem to overestimate the membership of SDS. For example, the Yankelovich study suggests that close to 4 percent of the student sample claimed membership in SDS.[86] Given a total student population of over seven million in 1968–1969, this would have meant an SDS membership of around 280,000. SDS, before its split at its 1969 convention, only claimed a national dues-paying membership of some 7,000, with another 30,000 involved in local chapter activities. It would seem that either the sample was drawn from institutions in which SDS is disproportionately strong, or that some sympathetic nonmembers claim membership. The argument that some who have engaged in formally illicit behavior such as smoking marijuana will not admit it to interviewers, thus resulting in an underestimation of those involved, may have some validity, but the findings of studies using anonymous questionnaires are not very different from those based on personal interviews.

The opinion surveys of American students indicate that the large majority are not sympathetic with radical doctrines and tactics; most of them seemingly are conventional with respect to appearance, use of drugs, and dedication to academic achievement and a "straight" career. Many more still fill the stadiums to cheer on their varsity eleven on fall Saturdays than take part in political rallies or demonstrations of any kind. Yet the fact remains that the anti-Establishment Youth Culture grew constantly year by year during the 1960s. Though but a small minority are radical, increasing proportions, often majorities, are discontented with the way the country is run. Perhaps no other issue has done as much to alienate American students from American society and polity as the Vietnam war. Continued participation in it convinces many that they can have no confidence in the nation's rulers, in the elites of the older generation which permit it to continue. Obviously, many factors other than the war have pointed up to the young the seeming contradiction between the potential of an affluent society and the reality of social evils such as racial discrimination and poverty. Most students took a liberal-to-left critical posture as America entered the 1970s.

The fact of predominant campus liberalism, commitment to

egalitarianism in class and racial relations, and opposition to war, explains the ability of the extreme left to set the tone in many colleges. For most students support the overt goals of most demonstrations. The majority is against the war, and, therefore, looks with some sympathy on efforts to symbolically oppose it through confrontations directed against ROTC, defense-related research, and recruiters for defense-involved corporations. The vast majority views black inequality as a crime and consequently supports to some extent sit-ins or other demonstrations dedicated to improve the position of the blacks. The majority, though not participant in the drug culture, supports the rights of others to do so. Thus, efforts to restrict the use of marijuana, and university cooperation with the police in enforcing narcotics laws are met with hostility.

Efforts to mobilize the "moderates" against the extremists usually fail because authority is seen as defending social evils or outmoded forms of authority. This is particularly true when outside force is brought to a campus to suppress a demonstration or maintain order. The resistance by the noninvolved students to such efforts is not simply a manifestation of "generational solidarity" or the affirmation of the principle of university autonomy, it is also motivated by the sympathy of the campus majority for the "objectives," if not the "tactics," of the demonstrators. To stress the minority status of the radicals or the habitual drug users does not mean that the majority has been opposed to them. The student vanguard has been powerful from 1965 to 1970 precisely because the majority of students has been politicized in a left direction by the events of the 1960s, particularly the opposition to the war.

The decline in manifest campus radicalism as reported in the polls in the academic year 1970–71 and in the use of confrontationist tactics during this period may reflect the fall-off in American involvement in Vietnam. The fact that the United States pulled out all its ground troops from Cambodia, an act unanticipated by the majority of students polled by Harris in May 1970, the continued withdrawal of American troops from Vietnam, and the sharp decline in casualties and battle news from that country, all would seem to have reduced student concern about American military policy. A report by the Urban Research Institute of campus protests in the fall 1970 term indicates that not only did protest drop off, but that it was much less likely to have involved use of violent tactics, and "that the focus of campus protest switched . . . from antiwar demonstrations to demands for minority recognition." Presumably many of these were run by black students and did not involve the white radicals.[87]

The promise of the Cambodia demonstrators to campaign vigorously in the fall elections in 1970 for antiwar candidates was not honored by the vast majority. Rather, some conservative candidates like James Buckley in New York were astonished by the turnout of conservative student activists.[88] Similar reports concerning the decline of left-wing activism stemming from the campus came in from Britain, France, Germany, Japan, and other countries.[89] It is difficult to understand what factors, the reduced war effort apart, are operating. The one common feature present in Britain, parts of western Europe, and the United States, is the end of a high level of prosperity for university graduates. Radical sociologists Milton Mankoff and Richard Flacks have noted the possibility that economic uncertainty may weaken certain forms of student protest. "The collapse of the counter-culture of the 1920s in the face of economic depression suggests that one must eschew any linear theory of societal change. The cultural revolt of the present period presupposes economic stability and affluence, conditions which, given the cyclical behavior of capitalist economics, should not be taken for granted."[90]

To some degree the change in the student mood and behavior may be a consequence of developments among the organized radical groups. In the United States and other countries as well the various extremist groups have followed a pattern of splitting and turning viciously on each other. The German SDS dissolved in the spring of 1970. The various factions of the Zengakuren in Japan spend much more energy denouncing each other than the policies they oppose. They have also used violence in such internecine struggles. In France, the assorted *groupiscules* also see those who spread false doctrine on the left as the main enemy. In the United States, SDS first divided among a number of factions, and then split into two major ones, one of which became an underground terrorist organization, the Weathermen, while the other became the student section of the dogmatic Maoist Progressive Labor Party. Fratricidal conflict in all countries meant a smaller and smaller membership, which reinforced the propensity to engage in violence, e.g., bombings, assaults, kidnappings. Whatever effect such behavior has on the policies of the political elite, it is clear that resort to such tactics discourages the more moderate elements who are sympathetic to the movement's general objectives. When each group seeks to demonstrate that it is more truly revolutionary and even violent than the other, it contributes to the growth of moral revulsion against activism among the mass. When extremist groups fling mud at each other, some of it sticks to each, and they lose what claim they had to moral leadership. Thus, in an ironic yet logical fashion, the very same factors which contributed to the increased radicalization of the student movement, to the greater influence of the extremists, have also served to undermine the political involvement of the majority. A kind of Gresham's law of extreme politics operates in which the more aggressive constantly drive out the more moderate, which means that they also press the sympathetic periphery to withdraw from politics. Kenneth Keniston has given eloquent expression to the feelings of those involved in the recent American student movement to exposure to a process that has occurred often with rightist as well as leftist extremists.

> The violent rhetoric that came to pervade the student movement could be passed off as mere talk. But when that rhetoric culminated in murder, then the members of the student movement had to face for the first time their own complicity with the very violence against which they struggled.
>
> The agony of the counterculture then, involves above all its

> confrontation, at an individual and a collective level, with its own destructiveness. In explaining the silence of this year, the sense of discouragement and despair, the feeling of embarrassment and shame are indeed important. . . . The members of the student movement gradually came to realize that if they allowed themselves to be led by their most rigid factions, dogmatism and death lay at the end of their road.[91]

To explain the changes in the predominant student mood as a consequence of specific historical events which have provided them with a different formative set of generational experiences than earlier generations does not account for the intragenerational variations. We have already seen that there is an enormous intragenerational gap between the political and social attitudes of university students and their less privileged age-mates at work in factories and offices. The statistical data presenting the distribution of attitudes and behavior among students conceals other variations which differentiate undergraduates. The eight million not only include a radical minority, they contain millions of conservatives; there are still many students who take the Protestant ethic seriously; most female undergraduates are still virgins;[92] as noted, the majority have never experimented with drugs; three quarters of the men do not wear their hair long below their ears. The many discussions of students written in recent years ignore the culture of the "squares." But a detailed examination of the factors contributing to activism should help our understanding of the general phenomenon of student protest. The following chapter deals with research on these issues.

3

Who Are the Activists?

Social Background

The major conclusions to be drawn from the large number of studies of student activism (particularly those of Kenneth Keniston and Richard Flacks) in the United States and other countries is that leftist students are largely the children of leftist or liberal parents. The activists, particularly, are more radical or activist than their parents, but both parents and children are located on the same side of the spectrum.[1] In the United States, where left-wing radical parties or consistently liberal orientations with respect to race relations, foreign policy, and socioeconomic egalitarianism have relatively little support among the less educated and poorer strata, such orientations have found the bulk of their backing among a well-educated segment of the affluent engaged in intellectual and welfare occupations, and among members of traditionally progressively disposed religious groups, particularly the liberal Protestant denominations and the Jews.[2] In other countries, in which leftist socialist and communist parties have heavy backing from workers, leftist students are more likely to come from less privileged families.

In countries as diverse as Japan, the Netherlands, Sweden, Brazil, Germany, and Britain, the available evidence would suggest that leftist tendencies secure disproportionate backing from the less well-to-do among the university student population.[3] And it seems clear, that the variation between the pattern in the United States and these other countries is related to generational political continuity. As Klaus Allerbeck puts it, these results suggest "that the affluence-radicalism correlation in the U.S. is no causal relation, but a by-product of the relations of political ideology and social stratification which are not the same in the U.S. and in Germany." What emerges from the studies of student political behavior in various countries "is the importance of the political orientations of parents for the political behavior of their children."[4] In the United States, the members of Young Americans for Freedom and other conservative and right-wing youth groups come from conservative family backgrounds.[5] Students are more idealistic and committed than their parents, but generally in the same direction.

Studies of earlier movements, both leftist ones in the United States before World War I and in the 1930s, and fascist groups in Europe, suggest a similar pattern of generational continuity. Bruno Bettelheim, who has observed the growth of student support for Nazism in Germany before 1933, and for the New Left in the United States, has commented on these similarities:

> It is mainly the children of leftist parents who become . . . student revolutionaries in our society, just as in other places and other times the children of conservative parents, under similar emotional conditions, spearheaded right wing radicalism. It was the children of conservative German parents, for example, who . . . felt a need to lay their bodies on the line for ideas their parents had only lukewarmly held . . . They felt, too, that this was a means of rebirth, a way to revitalize an ossified society, to create a new society; with little patience for the voice of reason, they asked for authenticity and confrontation. All these were the main tenets of Hitler's academic youth, as they are now those of our own student left.
>
> Thus, while the emotional constellations which make for very different student revolts are strangely similar, the specific political

> content of a student revolt depends to a large degree on the beliefs of the students' parents. For in many ways rebellion represents a desperate wish by youth to do better than their parents in exactly those beliefs in which parents seem weakest.[6]

In the United States, intellectuals, academics, writers, and so forth tend disproportionately to support the Left for reasons which are discussed elsewhere. They are predominantly liberal Democrats, or supporters of left-wing minor parties.[7] And various surveys indicate that students who are intellectually oriented, who identify themselves as "intellectuals," or who aspire to intellectual pursuits after graduation, are also much more prone to be on the left and favorable to activism than those inclined to business and professional occupations.[8]

Among both faculty and students, there are clear-cut correlations between disciplines and political orientations. On the whole, those involved in the social sciences and humanities, or in the more pure theoretical fields of science, in that order, are more likely to be on the left than those in the more practical, applied, or experimental fields.[9] Such variations, however, would appear to be more a product of selective entrance into different disciplines than of the effects of the content of the fields on those pursuing them as students or practitioners. Thus studies of entering freshmen have reported similar relationships between intended college major and political attitudes as found among seniors, graduate students and faculty.[10] Morris Rosenberg, who conducted a panel study (repeat interviews with the same people two years apart) of students, reported that political orientation proved to be a major determinant of shifts in undergraduate major.[11] A large proportion of the minority of conservatives who chose liberal (in political terms) majors as freshmen changed to subjects studied by most conservatives, while many liberals who had selected conservative majors tended to shift to fields which were presumably more congenial with their political outlook.

The relationships between academic fields and political sympathies are also linked to the finding that the leftist activists within American universities tend to come from relatively well-to-do backgrounds as compared to the student population generally. A comparison by Westby and Braungart of the delegates to conventions of SDS and YAF also indicated that the left-wingers come from somewhat more affluent backgrounds than the rightists. The majority of the latter were the children of conservative businessmen and professionals, but they included a significant proportion, one fifth, from working-class origins, a group almost unrepresented among the SDS delegates.[12] In a follow-up study which included samples of students from a number of universities, Braungart found that 39 percent of the YAF members and 17 percent of those belonging to SDS were of working-class backgrounds. Comparing members of these two groups with those belonging to the Young Democrats and Young Republicans indicated that a larger proportion of SDS members came from upper-middle-class families (55 percent) than was true of the other three groups, or of a control group of students who did not belong to political groupings.[13]

The continued validity of these relationships, as radical student protest has spread out through the campuses of the country, and has enrolled in places and strata not reached in early years, should be expected to decline. Studies of the pattern of growth of new social movements generally have suggested that the earliest recruits tend to come from different strata and political backgrounds than those who form its modal groups when it is a mass movement. In the case of the American student movement, it almost necessarily began with the scions of the relatively well-to-do, liberal-to-left, disproportionately Jewish intelligentsia — the largest pool of those ideologically disposed to sympathize with radical student action in the population. But as student activism permeated beyond its initial support group, it necessarily would have had to recruit from the less-well-to-do coming from less politicized family backgrounds and from more diverse religious orientations. The initial relationships should persist, of course, but in a weakened form.

An opportunity to test these assumptions was provided by

access to the results of a national survey of American students by the Harris poll in May 1970 during the massive protest strikes against the Cambodian incursion. Harris asked respondents whether they had taken part in demonstrations, and also to classify themselves among five political positions ranging from "far left" to "far right." The students also reported on the political stance of their parents in similar terms. Since the students described themselves as considerably more liberal than their parents, inherently most of those on the left must have shifted sharply from the political views of their parents. Thus, ten times as many students described their own politics as "far left," as used that term for their fathers' political views. Conversely, conservatives were three times as numerous among fathers as among their offspring. As the data in Table 11 indicate, most children of liberals are still liberals; many of the conservatives have moved to the left. The reports for the offspring of the far right and far left are unfortunately based on far too few cases to permit reliable estimates.

The persistence of a relationship between middle-class status and support for the far left among college students as recently as May 1970 may be seen in the results from the Harris poll presented in Table 12. The children of professionals and of white collar workers were more likely to identify themselves as far leftists than the offspring of manual workers. Those involved in business ownership or managerial tasks, whether urban or rural, however, were least likely to produce left-wingers. The differences in ideology were only loosely linked to family incomes. Nevertheless, the more well-to-do were somewhat more likely to have far left children than the very poor, while student conservatives were disproportionately to be found among those from less affluent families. Religious identification remained more closely correlated to political identification. Those who reported being Jewish or having no religious orientation were much more likely to identify with the far left than students with a Christian religious affiliation.

Though the Harris Survey suggests that the factors reported in

TABLE 11

Relationship Between Political Opinions of Parents and Students – May 1970 (Percent)

	STUDENTS' POLITICAL STANCE						
MOTHER'S STAND ON MOST ISSUES	FAR RIGHT	CONSERV-ATIVE	MIDDLE OF THE ROAD	LIBERAL	FAR LEFT	NOT SURE	TOTAL
Far Right	13	15	33	28	9	3	100
Conservative	1	27	29	34	6	3	100
Middle-of-Road	1	8	33	45	10	2	99
Liberal	1	2	9	60	24	4	100
Far Left		17		17	67		101
Not Sure	3	12	44	16	6	19	100
Total	2	15	27	41	11	4	100
FATHER'S STAND ON MOST ISSUES							
Far Right	2	11	24	40	21	1	99
Conservative	1	24	27	38	7	2	99
Middle-of-Road	2	10	34	42	9	3	100
Liberal		1	7	64	24	4	100
Far Left	16		32	10	42		100
Not Sure	2	8	26	30	6	28	100
Total	2	15	26	42	11	4	100

Source: Report of Harris Survey of Students, May 20–28, 1970, pp. 383–384.

TABLE 12

Relationship of Family Socioeconomic and Religious Background to Political Identification — May 1970 (Percent)

CHARACTERISTICS	FAR RIGHT & CON-SERVATIVE	MIDDLE-OF-ROAD	LIBERAL	FAR LEFT	TOTAL
Father's Occupation:					
Professional, Technical	15	26	42	17	100
Manager, Official, Proprietor	19	25	50	6	100
Clerical, Sales	15	27	40	18	100
Manual	15	27	46	12	100
Farmer, Farm Laborer	53	26	22	—	101
Family Income:					
$20,000 and over	14	24	48	14	100
$15,000 to $19,999	18	28	41	12	99
$10,000 to $14,999	17	25	49	10	101
$7,000 to $9,999	22	34	34	10	100
Less than $7,000	20	28	42	11	101
Religious Preference:					
Protestant	26	36	35	2	99
Catholic	20	34	41	4	99
Jewish	5	28	44	23	100
Other	13	15	54	18	100
None	4	12	55	29	100

Source: Report of Harris Survey of Students, May 20–28, pp. 389, 393, 395.

early studies of SDS and other activist groups as correlates of left-wing ideology among college were still important in 1970, the fact remains that as the movement grew it did broaden its base somewhat. The relationship between income and left-wing identification, for example, was fairly weak by 1970. Some indication of a process of change in the characteristics of student activists is indicated in the results of a study of University of Wisconsin students by Mankoff and Flacks. They contrasted the backgrounds of those students who had been "active politically . . . for three or more years prior to May 1968, when the questionnaires were distributed," and those who became involved subsequently. Their findings suggested that a change in the social class character and political family background of left student activists accompanies growth. As the movement penetrated into new segments of the student body, it recruited from less well-to-do students from less politicized families. In the Wisconsin case, the newer breed of radical supporters tended to come increasingly from those from smaller cities and apostate Catholic religious backgrounds as well.[14]

These findings jibe with what we know about the growth of new social movements generally in the body politic. Most radical movements, when new and small, tend to find their first recruits and supporters among the relatively more well-to-do and better educated, even though their program may be oriented to the manifest interests of the less privileged, and undereducated. The latter lack the psychic security and ability to work towards long-term goals which the former possess to a greater degree. When such movements grow, however, they usually secure the backing of population groups who are quite different from their early members.[15] It may, therefore, be argued that what is unusual about the growth of the American student movement is not that it has spread into diverse and less privileged student strata, but that it has done it so slowly—that the original associations between relatively privileged backgrounds and leftist commitment persist for so long.

The continuation of the "Movement's" somewhat greater appeal to the more well-to-do may be related to the consistent findings concerning the academic orientations of the left students. As noted earlier, they are disproportionately involved in liberal arts subjects (social science, humanities, and natural science in that order), and are more prone to be interested in abstract rather than practical subjects than the less politicized and more conservative students. Many studies of students in different disciplines suggest that those who major in the liberal arts subjects and have an intellectual or scholarly bent have well-educated parents, while first-generation college students of working-class origins tend to be vocationally oriented in a narrow sense.[16] They are more likely to be found among those preparing to become engineers, businessmen, and the like. They come disproportionately from that segment of the less well-to-do which is strongly oriented towards upward mobility and the values of the privileged. Their strong concentration on professional objectives, plus the need of many of them to hold a job during school term, also results in these students being less available for political activities than those from more affluent families. These findings may help to explain the fact that colleges attended by large numbers of less well-to-do students, apart from blacks, were less likely to be strongholds of left-wing groups during the 1960s and 1970 than those which educated the scions of the upper-middle class.

Not surprisingly, the black student activists do not resemble the white militants in their social background and aspirations. As suggested earlier, their principal objectives are not to change the fundamental character of the society or to engage in espressive personal protest, but rather to improve the position of the blacks within the larger society generally, and inside the university in particular. Although to achieve their objectives they often find it necessary to engage in militant, sometimes violent forms of protest, their goals are similar to the instrumental ones of the less privileged, sometimes racist, white youth. They want a better life, more money, a job with higher status, social dignity. The black student activists are less aspiring for personal advantages than other black youth, seeing themselves as leaders of their people, but they clearly differ from the white activists. A study of 264 black student activists in fifteen colleges and universities in 1969 indicated that the blacks came from much poorer families than the whites. Only 11 percent had college graduate parents. While most white activists are undecided about future careers, 76 percent of the black militants "said they were fairly certain!"[17]

The political reputation of certain schools, therefore, may be linked to sources of selective recruitment and the resultant political orientation of their students. Those with a large number of well-to-do Jewish students, or currently, with the rise of Negro militancy, of black students, have tended to be centers of activism. High-level liberal arts institutions with an intellectual aura attract students oriented to becoming intellectuals. Thus we may account for the pattern of student protest at schools like Reed, Swarthmore, Antioch and others. The best state universities, as judged in terms of faculty scholarly prominence, e.g., California, Michigan, and Wisconsin, are also schools which have become the most important centers of confrontationist politics. These schools attract a disproportionate number of intellectually oriented students, including many Jews. The same finding occurs among predominantly black colleges and universities in studies of factors related to protest participation among their students.[18]

Generally, the greater the proportion of students from high socioeconomic status (SES) homes, the greater has been the rate of participation. The association may be explained by other variables that are related to the proportion of high SES students. For instance, schools of high quality generally have a higher proportion of students from high SES backgrounds and also have higher rates of student participation.

Participation in the 1970 Strike Wave

Two surveys of student participation in antiwar protests in the spring of 1970, one by Mary and Kenneth Gergen and the other by the Harris Survey, reinforce the conclusion that the general set of correlates associated with activism had not basically changed. The Gergens secured data from a national sample of 5,000 students, both before and during the Cambodian protests. The demonstrators were predominantly "from a prosperous home . . . ; their parents have in the main, gone to college, and most frequently their fathers are either professional men or are in the higher echelons of business." They were disproportionately Jewish, or of no church affiliation. "The bulk of the protestors attend nonsectarian colleges which are rated as 'moderately selective' to 'very selective' in admissions policies. . . . The major field of interest for the protestor is the social sciences, where 40 percent concentrate. One fourth are in the humanities, and only 15 percent major in natural science."[19]

The Harris poll of student behavior and opinion during the protest wave against the Cambodian incursion also differentiated among respondents with respect to many of the factors which had been investigated in earlier studies of activism. It distinguished the kinds of academic backgrounds which were more or less likely to have led students to participate in the demonstrations. Eighty-five percent of those interviewed reported that demonstrations had taken place at their schools. Fifty-eight percent of the students at schools which had demonstrations indicated that they had taken part. This means that about half the college population in the United States (49 percent) actually were involved in protests during the Cambodian incursion. The relevant characteristics of those so engaged at schools with protest are reported in Table 13.

The findings of the Harris poll conducted during the 1970 national strike wave on the whole are surprisingly comparable to the results of studies dealing with characteristics of left-wing ideologists and activists. They do not permit, of course, any statistical specification of the relative effect of the different factors in a multivariate context, since all that is available is the percentage distributions.

The very low rate of participation of the self-described Protestants is quite difficult to explain. In part, it is linked to the low involvements of those at denominationally controlled schools, and of Southerners. Other data in this survey indicate that the children of farmers are far more conservative than those from other occupational backgrounds, and almost all of them are Protestants. The low rate may also reflect the fact that many birthright Protestants who become radicals report their religion as "none." Family political background (mother's stand "on most issues") clearly has a considerable impact on the availability of students for protest activities. What is perhaps more impressive than the variations among the different background traits is the extent to which protest had spread during May and June of 1970 into environments which had previously been unreceptive, such as relatively low-quality schools, or those controlled by religious denominations. Southern students remained resistant, but even among them, 38 percent of those in schools that had protests, report personal involvement in them.

Perhaps the most interesting finding included in Table 13 is the difference in the behavior of white and black students. Fewer of the latter were at schools which had protests – presumably these were largely segregated black colleges in the South. But even among students who were at demonstrating institutions, black students were less likely to have taken part in these actions than whites. This discrepancy in racial behavior was not a function of greater support for the war among the blacks. If anything, the Harris data indicate that the black students were more hostile to the conflict than the whites. Fully 72 percent of the blacks thought President Nixon was doing a "poor" job in handling the war as compared with 58 percent among the whites; 65 percent of the blacks would bring the soldiers home as soon as possible, while only 52 percent of the whites had the same opinion. The black students also reported a greater propensity than whites to having engaged in protest activities *before* Cambodia. Thus 41 percent of the former and 29 of the latter had been on a picket line; and 31 percent of the blacks and 24 percent of the whites had visited a public official.[20] The Yankelovich-CBS survey completed in the spring of 1969 pointed to similar racial differences. Black students in general were much more critical of the war and the social system, and more supportive of demonstrations and of militancy than whites. (Parenthetically it should be noted that noncollege working youth, including the blacks among them, were *much less militant* or critical of various policies and institutions than the white college students. The black working youth, who of course comprise the large

TABLE 13

Background Characteristics Related to Participation in Protests or Demonstrations During the Cambodian Incursion — May 1970

<table>
<tr><th></th><th>PERCENT PARTICIPATED IF SCHOOL HAD PROTESTS</th><th>PERCENT AT SCHOOLS WITH PROTESTS</th></tr>
<tr><td>Region</td><td></td><td></td></tr>
<tr><td>East</td><td>71</td><td>90</td></tr>
<tr><td>Midwest</td><td>54</td><td>88</td></tr>
<tr><td>South</td><td>38</td><td>63</td></tr>
<tr><td>West</td><td>67</td><td>99</td></tr>
<tr><td>Size School</td><td></td><td></td></tr>
<tr><td>10,000 and over</td><td>67</td><td>94</td></tr>
<tr><td>3,000–9,999</td><td>47</td><td>82</td></tr>
<tr><td>Under 3,000</td><td>57</td><td>69</td></tr>
<tr><td>Type School</td><td></td><td></td></tr>
<tr><td>Public</td><td>58</td><td>85</td></tr>
<tr><td>Private, Nondenom.</td><td>69</td><td>83</td></tr>
<tr><td>Denominational</td><td>44</td><td>79</td></tr>
<tr><td>Admissions Standards</td><td></td><td></td></tr>
<tr><td>Above Average</td><td>69</td><td>94</td></tr>
<tr><td>Average</td><td>60</td><td>94</td></tr>
<tr><td>Below Average</td><td>49</td><td>72</td></tr>
<tr><td>School Class</td><td></td><td></td></tr>
<tr><td>Freshmen</td><td>61</td><td>85</td></tr>
<tr><td>Sophomores</td><td>62</td><td>83</td></tr>
<tr><td>Juniors</td><td>56</td><td>82</td></tr>
<tr><td>Seniors</td><td>54</td><td>84</td></tr>
<tr><td>Major Subject</td><td></td><td></td></tr>
<tr><td>Humanities and Social Sciences</td><td>68</td><td>85</td></tr>
<tr><td>Natural and Physical Sciences</td><td>59</td><td rowspan="2">82</td></tr>
<tr><td>Other (Professional Schools)</td><td>45</td></tr>
<tr><td>Race</td><td></td><td></td></tr>
<tr><td>Black</td><td>51</td><td>64</td></tr>
<tr><td>White</td><td>59</td><td>85</td></tr>
</table>

TABLE 13 (*continued*)

	PERCENT PARTICIPATED IF SCHOOL HAD PROTESTS	PERCENT AT SCHOOLS WITH PROTESTS
Sex		
Male	61	83
Female	55	84
Father's Occupation		
Professional and Technical	64	87
Manager or Proprietor or Official	58	80
Clerical, Sales	64	90
Manual	60	79
Farmer, Farm Laborer	20	39
Family Income		
$20,000 and over	63	86
$15,000 to $19,999	60	82
$10,000 to $14,999	77	66
$7,000 to $9,999	54	77
Less than $7,000	51	69
Religion		
None	80	94
Other	66	92
Jews	73	90
Catholics	60	82
Protestants	36	71
Ideology		
Far Left	91	97
Liberal	74	88
Middle-of-Road	37	79
Conservative and Far Right	14	69
Mother's Ideology		
Far Left	80	86
Liberal	69	87
Middle-of-Road	62	84
Conservative	51	80
Far Right	49	78

Source: Report of Harris Survey of Students, May 20–28, 1970.

majority of black young people, repeatedly rejected the use of aggressive protest tactics, often by large majorities, while the black college students were the most militant of the four youth groups, i.e., white college, white noncollege, black college, black noncollege).[21]

The indications that black college youth are militantly antiwar, but were relatively low in participation in the anti-Cambodian incursion demonstrations, can probably be explained as a consequence of the growing gap which exists between black and white students. The black students tend to abstain from protests led by white radicals or liberals. They keep their distance even when they agree. But the fact that they are visibly non-present at white-run antiwar rallies clearly does not imply a lack of opposition. The evidence from a variety of investigations definitely indicates that black college students are much more discontented than whites.[22] And they are much more likely to continue to press for major changes when the Vietnam war ends. Since the far left as well as the more liberal white students are disposed to back race-related demonstrations, the probabilities are great that the major campus issues once the war ends will be linked to civil rights.

Determinants of Protest-Proneness

The evidence available differs as to whether the propensity of a given institution to sustain protest is largely a consequence of the type of students who are attracted to it, or is also a function of the treatment which students receive from the faculty and institution in terms of values and personal relations. Faculty surveys strongly indicate that the more intellectually prestigious a school in the United States, the more liberal-to-left the political outlook of its faculty.[23] Seemingly, therefore, students from more intellectual cultural and political backgrounds — liberal to left — attend schools where such orientations and values are reinforced by their teachers. Thus, it has been argued by some that a sufficiently large enrollment to provide a critical mass for impressive demonstrations and the appropriate type of student body should result in a politicized campus under present conditions, almost without regard to the administrative policies pursued. The case for this thesis has been supported in a number of research publications. It was initially sustained statistically by Alexander Astin in a study based on a sample of thirty-five thousand students in 246 schools in the 1967–68 school year. His analyses were designed to estimate the relative importance of student and institutional variables. He concluded:

> The proportion of students who participate in demonstrations against either the war in Vietnam or racial discrimination can be predicted with substantial accuracy solely from a knowledge of the characteristics of the students who enter the institution. . . . Environmental factors seem to be somewhat more important with respect to protests against the administrative policies of the college, although student input characteristics still appear to carry much more weight than environmental characteristics in determining whether or not such protests will occur.[24]

A number of subsequent studies dealing with questionnaire data and incidents of protest from later school years have all agreed that sympathy for student activism, involvement in demonstrations, and propensity of institutions to sustain protests, have been correlated with size and quality of institution, plus various student characteristics, particularly those associated with a liberal-to-left family political orientation. For example, in dealing with protests which occurred during 1968–1969, Astin and Bayer reported that given the same type of student body, large universities are more likely to have demonstrations than smaller ones.[25] Hodgkinson analyzed reports for 1230 institutions secured in 1968–1969, which dealt with whether they "had experienced an *increase* in student protest and demonstrations during the last ten years."[26] He also found that the more scholarly committed schools, as indicated by the highest degree awarded and research involvements of faculty, were most inclined to have had an increase. Size also was closely associated with tendency to sustain protests. The range of difference ran from 88 percent for those with more than twenty-five thousand students to 14 percent for schools with less than one thousand enrolled.[27]

Two independent surveys of the characteristics of institutions involved in the May 1970 protests against the Cambodian incursion also reiterated the results of the earlier studies. The Carnegie Commission on Higher Education and the President's Commission on Campus Unrest, each sent out questionnaires to the presidents of all colleges and universities (the government one also wrote to the chairmen of faculty senates and of student governments) inquiring as to the nature, extent, and "causes" of demonstrations. The Carnegie study found that the more selective the student body and the larger the institution, the more likely it had been to have had a significant protest activity. Identical results were reported by the staff of the President's Commission.[28]

Many of the respondents to the President's Commission questionnaire, particularly the student body presidents, suggested that increased involvement of students in university governance would reduce the likelihood of major outbreaks in the future. These assumptions were challenged by Hodgkinson's findings that "an increase in student control in institutional policy making" did not appear to reduce the rate of protests; if anything, the "reverse would seem to be more likely." He reached the conclusion "that tinkering with structures may not be any long-term solution to problems of student protest . . . [since] There are quite clearly protest-prone students and protest-prone faculty."[29]

Many of these results, of course, can be interpreted to reinforce the argument that the basic factor accounting for more activism at larger schools is not impersonality, bureaucracy, but the presence of a "critical mass." Kenneth Keniston and Michael Lerner in defending this thesis at length pointed out that actually "there are *fewer* protests per 10,000 students at large universities than at small ones." Using American Council on Education data for 1968–69, they indicated that in four year colleges, there were

2.63 protests *per* 10,000 students in schools with less than 1,000 enrolled as compared with but .69 *per* 10,000 in schools with more than 5,000 students on the campus. And they concluded that the reason for the relationship between size of institution and demonstrations is that "there is more of everything at larger institutions. Larger campuses are also more likely to have chapters of Young Americans for Freedom (a right-wing group), literary magazines, science clubs, fraternities, and massive football rallies. The obvious explanation is that, compared to small colleges, large universities have more students available for almost everything. Not surprisingly, they have more and bigger protests as well." They deduced, therefore, that "the main reason some campuses experience more and bigger protests than others is that these campuses admit more of the kinds of students who appear 'protest-prone.' "[30]

There is a growing body of evidence, however, that schools play a role as centers of activism beyond what may be explained by the characteristics of their students. It may be suggested that the political traditions and images of certain institutions help to determine the orientation of their students and faculty, and, more generally, that protest-proneness is related to the way colleges treat their students.

In the United States, Madison and Berkeley have maintained a record as centers of radicalism. The University of Wisconsin image goes back to before World War I – the strength of progressive and socialist politics in the state contributed to its political aura. Berkeley is a particularly interesting case in point. The San Francisco Bay Area has a history dating back to the turn of the century as being among the most liberal-left communities in the nation. Various data pertaining to the Berkeley campus since the end of World War II point up the continuity of that university as a center of leftism. Berkeley was the only major institution in the country to sustain a major faculty revolt against restrictive anti-Communist personnel policies in the form of the loyalty oath controversy of 1949–50.[31] The data collected by Paul Lazarsfeld in a national opinion survey of the attitudes of social scientists, conducted in 1954 to evaluate the effect of McCarthyism on universities, indicated in an unpublished analysis that the Berkeley faculty members were the most liberal of any of the schools sampled in this study, a pattern which subsequent events suggest continued into the sixties.

In 1963–64, the year before the celebrated Berkeley student revolt, San Francisco Bay Area students received national publicity for a series of massive successful sit-in demonstrations at various business firms — designed to secure jobs for Negroes. Prior to the emergence of the FSM protest, the Berkeley campus probably had more different left-wing and activist groups with more members than any other school in the country. The vigor and effectiveness of the Free Speech Movement must in some part be credited to the prior existence of a well-organized and politically experienced group of activist students. A study of the six hundred students who held a police car captive in the first major confrontation of the affair in October 1964, reported that over half of them had taken part in at least one previous demonstration, and that 17 percent indicated they had taken part in *seven or more*.[32] Since the Berkeley revolt, Bay Area activists have continued their leading role, by major efforts to disrupt the operation of the Selective Service, by conducting two of the four most publicized student demonstrations of 1967–68, and in six major confrontations during 1968–69. During the protests against the Cambodian incursion in 1970, large segments of the Berkeley faculty and students again took the lead in efforts to "reconstitute" the university in classroom-based efforts to end the war and "the social conditions which made the war possible," which involved giving regular grade credit for participation in election campaigns and other political activities.

It is interesting to note that in analyzing the factors which explain why the Free University of Berlin "is the Berkeley of West Germany," that is, the leading center of militant student activism, Jürgen Habermas, a leading sociologist who also happens to be a strong supporter of left-wing politics, points to causal factors in the background of Berlin, which strongly resemble those present in Berkeley in 1964. First, the Free University has been the most liberal one in the country, that is students have had more "extensive rights and powers" than elsewhere. "Second, the composition of the student body, as shown by empirical studies, favors politicization owing to selective immigration from West Germany." Those students who seek to escape West German conscription, more likely on that score to be leftist, can do so by moving to West Berlin. "Third, the proportion of politically conscious and liberal-minded professors at some of the Berlin faculties is, in my estimation, considerably higher than at universities in the Federal Republic. Hence, students in Berlin have always been able to count on the solidarity of a group of their professors."[33] Thus, Professor Habermas argued that the basic reasons for a heightened level of political disturbances and violence at the Free University were clearly not a consequence of its relative educational deficiencies, but rather that, as at Berkeley, it attracted many more radically disposed students and professors than other universities.

The efforts to argue or demonstrate that the protest-proneness of institutions of higher education are solely a function of the presence of a critical mass of left-oriented students would seem, however, to exaggerate the case. In a more recent detailed analysis of data on campus unrest for the 1968–69 academic year, Astin and Bayer reported, that holding other factors constant, those institutions with fewer protests "have environments characterized by a high degree of concern for the individual student." The protest-prone schools were those in which "students and faculty had little involvement in class, [and] students were not on warm, friendly terms with the instructor," and had "an environment which lacks cohesiveness (measured primarily by number of close friendships among the students) . . . ." Astin also reported using 1969–70 data that "the size of an institution and its emphasis on graduate work seem to be causally related to the emergence of protests, even after adjustments are made for differences in student characteristics."[34] Blau and Slaughter, in a survey of the relationship between propensity to sustain demonstrations and various characteristics of over a thousand schools, came to similar conclusions relying on 1967–68 data. They found that school size, indicators of student intellectual ability, impersonality (as reflected in the extent to which a school uses computers for administrative purposes), capacity for intellectual innovation as indicated by the presence of new fields of learning, and willingness to give the students the right to evaluate teacher performance, were each *independently* associated with student protest.[35]

The various studies of the institutional correlates of student activism in the 1960s thus suggest the importance of three sets of factors: (1) size, insofar as it may be regarded as a source of the critical mass, the number necessary to sustain a protest movement and demonstrations; (2) bureaucratization, or degree of impersonal treatment of students; and (3) the politically relevant or predisposing characteristics which students (and faculty) bring with them to university. These findings, though as yet incomplete and tentative, and varying considerably for different types of political protest, do offer some solace to those who would seek to reduce the severity of demonstrations by following a policy of "counter-bureaucratization." It should be noted, however, that the extant research would still indicate that greater administrative flexibility has less of an effect on propensity for activism than factors linked to size or student characteristics. Whether or not a student is a radical, or demonstrates against racism or the Vietnam war, would appear to result much more from his social background and orientations than from the way he is treated by his university.

In stressing that involvement in leftist student activism is to a considerable degree a function of the general political orientation which students bring to the university, it is not being argued that major changes in attitude do not occur, or even that conversions rarely take place. Universities clearly do have an important liberalizing effect so that there has been a significant shift to the left. This even occurred during the "silent fifties." A considerable number of students in the late 1960s have been much more radical in their actions and opinions than earlier postwar generations of American students, or than their parents. The larger events which created a basis for a renewed visible radical movement have influenced many students to the left of the orientation in which they were reared. Many students of liberal parents have felt impelled to act out the moral imperatives implicit in the seemingly "academic" liberalism of the older generation. Political events, combined with various elements in the situation of students, pressed a number of liberal students to become active radicals.

Kenneth Keniston and William Cowdry conclude from a survey of Yale that the students "most likely to hold radical beliefs *and* act on them" are those whose fathers have similar social and political values to their own. Those who hold radical beliefs, but are not active politically, are more likely to report that their fathers are unlike themselves.[36] The principal predisposing factors which determined who among the students would become activists, therefore, existed before they entered the university.

However, if we hold pre-university orientation constant, it obviously will make a difference which university a student attends, what major he chooses, who his friends are on the campus, what his relations are with his teachers of varying political persuasions, what particular extracurricular activities he happens to get involved in, and the like. The relationships between the orientations which students form before university and the choices they make after entering which help maintain their general political stances are only correlations; many students necessarily behave differently from the way these relationships would predict.

Clearly, conversions, drastic changes in belief, in political identity, do occur among university students, as among other groups. During a period in which events shift the larger political climate to the left or right, young people, with fewer ties to the past, are undoubtedly more likely to change than older ones. There is also a special aspect of university life which enhances the chances that certain groups of students will be more likely to find satisfaction in intense political experience. Various studies suggest that mobility, particularly geographic mobility, where one becomes a stranger in an unfamiliar social context, is conducive to making individuals available for causes which invoke intense commitment.

Thus new students, or recent transfers, are more likely to be politically active than those who have been in the social system for longer periods.[37] Local students, or those relatively close to home, are less likely to be active than those who are a considerable distance from their home communities. In Berkeley, Madison and other university centers, the activists have come disproportionately from the ranks of the migrants, and of recently arrived new students.

Psychological Research

Some of the research by psychologists seeks to go beyond the analysis of factors which seem to have a direct impact on political choice. Psychologists have also sought to account for varying orientations and degrees of involvement by personality traits. Thus they have looked at such factors as variations in the way different groups of students have been reared by their parents, i.e., in a permissive or authoritarian atmosphere, as well as investigating family relationships, student intelligence, sociability and the like. Such studies have reported interesting and relatively consistent differences between the minority of student activists and the rest of the student population. These widely heralded findings are unconvincing, in large part because few of the extant studies hold constant the sociological and politically relevant factors in the backgrounds of the students. For example, Richard Flacks, and Westby and Braungart, report that leftist activists tend to be the offspring of permissive families as judged by child-rearing practices, and of families characterized by a strong mother who dominates family life and decisions.[38] Conversely, conservative activists tend to come from families with more strict relationships between parents and children, and in which the father plays a dominant controlling role. To a considerable extent these differences correspond to the variations reported in studies of Jewish and Protestant families. Childhood rearing practices tend to be linked to sociocultural political outlooks. To prove that such factors play an independent role in determining the political choices of students, it would first be necessary to compare students *within* similar ethnic, religious and political cultural environments. Efforts to do this by Lamar Thomas, dealing with the children of politically active parents from both ends of the political spectrum, found no relationship between activism and permissiveness among students, when parental "cause-orientation" was held constant.[39] Jeanne Block and Norma Haan, while agreeing that the extent of parental permissiveness is not associated with activism, did find that activists are likely to come from families in which parents stressed training for independence. Block and Haan attempted to control for the effect of religion, to test a suggestion of mine that some of the differences in child-rearing backgrounds between activists and conservatives may reflect ethnic-cultural variations. Although Block and her colleagues concluded that their results "undermined" this hypothesis, they appear very inconclusive since they report on extremely small percentage differences between a group of thirty-eight "conventionals" and thirty-five "activists," who are non-Jewish.[40] It is, therefore, still difficult to conclude that socialization experiences, as such, have an independent causal effect, that is independent of family values which bore relatively directly on politics. Thus Kenneth Keniston, in summing up the recent evidence bearing on the earlier critique of mine which raised this question, concluded:

> . . . the issue cannot be settled with only the evidence at hand. In all probability, several interacting factors are involved. On the one hand, it seems clear that *if* children are brought up in upper-middle-class professional families with humanitarian, expressive and intellectual values, and *if* the techniques of discipline emphasize independence and reasoning, and *if* the parents are themselves politically liberal and politically active, then the chances of the child's being an activist are greatly increased, regardless of

factors like religion. But it is also clear that these conditions are fulfilled most often in Jewish families. And there may be still other factors associated with social class and religion that independently promote activism; for example, being in a Jewish minority group that has preserved its culture in the face of opposing community pressures for centuries may in some way prepare or permit the individual to take controversial positions as a student.[41]

Thus far student protestors have been discussed as if they were a relatively coherent group of activists who, though varying in their ideas as to how to reconstruct society, agree in rejecting the polity and culture. They should, however, be differentiated into two groups, the radicals and the renouncers, segments which are often confused with each other because, on the surface, their behavior, their antiestablishment beliefs, their total rejection of the system, often seem the same. Yet in a real sense, the radicals are closer to other protestors such as the Wallacite white youth or the black militants, since all three are basically concerned with *owning* Western industrial society. The renouncers are essentially interested in *disowning* Western society. The terms "renouncer" or "renunciation tendency" are clearly inadequate, yet they are useful, for it would be a definite mistake to describe this tendency as "radical" or "revolutionary." In fact, in its rejection of much of the modern world, including the use of, and products of, large-scale technology and urbanization, it is much closer in outlook to many classic conservative or reactionary doctrines. One reason why it has been difficult to analyze the renunciatory tendency apart from the other forms of militant student protest is that there is, in fact, considerable overlap between the radicals and the renouncers. Many students move back and forth between them. Many radicals engage in renunciatory styles of dress and personal behavior. Most renouncers agree with the specific antisystem activities of the radicals.

The distinction between the radical and renunciatory tendencies among youth, or in society generally, is, of course, related to comparable distinctions drawn in other analyses. The sociologist David Matza has suggested that deviant behavior among youth may take one of three forms, delinquent, bohemian, or radical. All three are "specifically antibourgeois," i.e., reject private property relations. Delinquency, however, "seems most pronounced among that section of youth which terminates its education during or at the end of high school. Radicalism and bohemianism, particularly in the United States, are apparently enmeshed within the system of higher education." The bohemians, as Matza uses the term, those who are "opposed to the mechanized, organized, centralized, and increasingly collectivized nature of modern capitalism," come close to the concept of the renouncers.[42] The psychologist Kenneth Keniston has similarly differentiated student deviants between the "alienated," who are apolitical, romantic and aesthetic in their orientation, and the "activists," who are political, humanitarian and universalistic.[43]

More recently, another sociologist, Alvin Gouldner, has pointed to the emergence within the protest movement of the "psychedelic culture," which "differs profoundly from the protest movements and 'causes' of the 1930s, however politically radical, for psychedelic culture rejects the central values to which *all* variants of industrial society are committed. . . . [It] resists . . . routine economic roles whether high or low, inhibition of expression, repression of impulse, and all the other personal and social requisites of a society organized around the optimization of utility. Psychedelic culture rejects the value of conforming usefulness, counterposing to it, as a standard, that each must 'do his thing.' In short, many, particularly among the young, are now orienting themselves increasingly to expressive rather than utilitarian standards, to expressive rather than instrumental politics. . . ."[44]

The distinction between the politically radical and the culturally renunciatory protestors suggested here has not been made in most of the sociological research literature on student activism. Some psychologists, however, have attempted to isolate differences between "hippies," "nihilists," habitual drug users, and political radicals, analyses which come close to differentiating between the renunciatory and radical tendencies. These indicate that the renunciatory group is involved in some sort of generational conflict, of rejection of traditional or conservative views of their parents, while the political radicals come from the liberal-left family backgrounds. Both groups, of course, share a radical rejection of the conventional society. As Kenneth Keniston has described the difference:

> [the political radical tends to follow] the pathway of identification. Both father and son are described as expressive, humanitarian, and idealistic. The son identifies with his father, although the son is usually more radical. Such sons are very likely to be radicals in action as well as in beliefs. . . . There is, however, clearly a second pathway to radical beliefs, though less often to radical actions: the pathway of rejection of identification. Such students describe themselves as expressive, idealistic, and humanitarian, but describe their fathers as distinctly *not* any of these things. They are rather less likely to be politically active, more likely to adopt an apolitical or "hippie" style of dissent, and, if they become involved in political action, more likely to fall within the "nihilist" group.[45]

Jeanne Block and her colleagues have pursued similar differentiations between "activists" – those disillusioned with the status quo, involved in antiestablishment protest *and* supporting programs and policies designed to do something about "pain and poverty and injustice" – and those "dissenters" who are also involved in antiestablishment protests, but who do not seek to change the policies and institutions they object to through positive action. Activists differ from dissenters in evaluating their relationships with their parents more positively. The dissenters tend to describe a "conflicted, unsatisfying parental relationship," one which presumably precipitated or justified a break with family social values.[46]

Studies of committed drug users among students also indicate that they differ from those who express their antagonisms to society more through organized political activities than through expressive forms of personal deviance in similar ways to those reported above. Richard Blum concluded that "families with greater divergency of opinion, more distant relationships to the children, and more unresolved parent-child interpersonal crises seem to be those which generate the drug explorers."[47]

But if the psychological research does suggest that those engaged in renunciatory activities are disproportionately recruited from the ranks of individuals with histories of family conflict and personal difficulties, a number of analysts of left-wing political activists have reported that "the findings on activists are reasonably consistent in showing that on the average, they are good students and are psychologically 'healthy'. . . . They can also be close to their families rather than rebellious and can reflect intellectual, humanistic, and democratic ideals fostered in the home."[48] As one study summed up its findings, "few college students in general can match the positive development of these personality characteristics that distinguish student activists from their college contemporaries."[49] Many writers and researchers dealing with the background and values of student activists have continued—up until 1971, at least—to elaborate on these supposedly positive traits of the active protesters.

These reports on the psychological "health" of left-wing militants pose an interesting problem in the sociology of knowledge, for a number of other studies and evaluations of the research literature have pointed for many years to the fact that almost all the analyses of student activism which conclude that the left-wing militants exhibit "superior" attributes are based on comparisons with the student body as a whole, rather than with activists of other ideological persuasions. A 1966 review of the extant studies pointed to the evidence that conservative activists, as well as those involved in student government affairs, possessed some of the psychologically healthy traits assigned to the campus militants.[50]

More recent efforts to systematically compare various groups of involved students refute the thesis that leftist activists are the noblemen of the campus. The psychologist Larry Kerpelman explicitly set out to analyze the psychological traits of different groups of students on a number of campuses: "left activists, middle-of-the-road activists, right activists, left nonactivists, middle-of-the-road nonactivists, and right nonactivists." He concluded that "characteristics that have been identified with left activists . . . characterize the involved generally . . . All student activists, no matter what their ideology, are less needful of support and nurturance, value leadership more, are more socially ascendant and assertive, and are more sociable than students who are not politically active."[51]

Similar conclusions with respect to consistency of political action and ideology were reported by Cowdry and Keniston in their study of a random sample of 1968 Yale seniors. They found when comparing the characteristics of students who were for or against the Vietnam war that those whose actions (signing or refusing to sign an antiwar petition) were consistent with their beliefs about the war were more like each other than either resembled the "inconsistent" antiwar group.[52]

A somewhat different study designed to test the assumption that "militant radicals" were psychologically healthier than moderates and nonmilitant conservatives, also found it necessary to reject the assumption that radical students are psychologically "healthier."

> There were statistically significant differences between the student types on four of the six personality measures: Authoritarianism, Dogmatism, Paranoia and Personal Efficacy. Militant radicals were the least authoritarian and the least dogmatic while nonmilitant conservatives were the most authoritarian and the most dogmatic. These findings supported the view of student radicals as "healthy" personalities. On the other hand, militant radicals were most paranoid and least efficacious. Clearly, if one assumes that it is more desirable to be lower on paranoia and higher on efficacy, these findings do not fit the "healthy" personality thesis.[53]

Various early surveys suggested that left-wing activists were superior academically to other students. This finding has also been challenged since a comparison of various analyses indicate that the alleged superiority of the leftists is based on *"self-reported* grade-point averages," but that surveys which compare the *"actual"* grades reveal no differences.[54] Left activists seemingly have a propensity to "perceive themselves as ranking higher . . . than they are in reality."[55] These findings that left-wing activists, such as members of SDS or participants in sit-ins, do not have higher grades than other students may seem at first hand to contradict the previously reported relationship between school academic quality and propensity to sustain demonstrations. In fact, it does not. The latter linkage is derived from the relationship in America between intellectuality, as reflected in cultural tastes and occupational preferences, and political liberalism. Schools which are strong in the liberal arts, the nonprofessional subjects generally, attract students from relatively well-to-do, high culture-oriented and politically liberal families. They tend also to be better qualified for admission to the more selective colleges. The more prestigious a school, therefore, the more likely it is to have a significant segment of its student body predisposed to sympathetically support militant protests. But *within* such institutions, the available data clearly indicate that those who are deeply involved in radical activity resemble those active in other groupings in terms of scholarly achievements. In general, those who have the psychic energy to be active, whether as conservatives, moderates, or leftists, tend to be somewhat more qualified academically, than passive students.

Reports on the as yet scanty research on the characteristics of activists, as distinct from opinion survey results concerning the supporters of leftist activism in the student population as a whole, suggest in other countries also that the small group of committed militants may differ considerably from the population which sympathizes with their general political orientation. Thus, although leftist students and sympathizers with militant radical groups tend on the average to be of lower socio-economic status than the student body as a whole in various countries in Europe and Japan, reports from France, Germany and Japan indicate that the activist core group tends to resemble those in the United

States, in being disproportionately composed of the children of men engaged in intellectually linked high status professions, particularly academe itself. Presumably being of a high status, intellectually oriented, left-leaning background provides the political predisposition, the family support, and the psychic security, in a university environment, to engage in radical protest. The less privileged supporters of radical ideas in these countries remain close to their family values but, like their more conservative status compeers in America, are too involved in trying to secure vocational benefits from their university experience to be active in politics.

The reports that American left activists have more "democratic values" than other students have also been challenged by the results of a study which attempted to test a hypothesis of mine regarding the source of the reported positive traits. It appeared that "their ideologies rather than their true sentiments . . . are dictating the answers . . . [that] leftists who have demonstrated intolerance and authoritarian behavior traits in practice may still give voice or pencil to liberal values in principle."[56] Miller and Everson report that their findings show "a remarkable fit with the Lipset thesis (and understandably somewhat disconcerting to the authors of this paper). We cannot reject the Lipset model. In fact, it provides the best fit of any model tested."[57]

Many scholars in this field have generally ignored the contradictory evidence and methodological inadequacies of studies purporting to demonstrate the greater academic success and healthier personalities of left-wing activists. Given the sharp discrepancies in research data, it becomes obvious that we must ask why. Curiously, the most insightful explanation for the bias has been suggested by an investigator, Richard Blum, who himself has given expression to the positive stereotype. Blum points out that there is a correspondence of interests and values between the intellectual community and the protesting students.

> The importance of adjustment, of curiosity, of social criticism, and of "progressive" sociopolitical doctrine, as well as an

> emphasis on . . . spontaneity in relationships, and on being antagonistic toward traditional authority, are likely to be found in the social sciences and mind-studying trades, or espoused by their members, as well as by the liberal students. Consequently, when these students and clinicians undertake to evaluate today's left and/or drug-using students, they are often looking at people much like themselves . . . [Their] "liking" reactions [for these students] probably reflect preferences for people acting more as . . . [they] thought people ought to act . . . The danger is that the evaluation may be positive only because of the charm of the young people without the investigators' recognizing the grounds for their reactions and without coming to grips with either fundaments or implications of student behavior. We are posing the problem of investigator indentification with his subjects, of "countertransference," in which it may be — as some of the students contend — that the young are admired because they act out the fantasies of their frustrated elders. The corollary danger is also acute and is commonplace. When conservative people offer their more negative evaluations . . . many university and professionally based people reject outright what the "reactionaries" have to say.[58]

As the 1960s drew to a close, a second factor entered overtly to affect the selection of research topics and the way in which research results are presented. With increasing polarization on campus, many of the more radical activists concluded that no useful function could be served by their cooperating with social science inquiries concerning student activism. Empirical research was defined as "pig research," as inherently a form of counterinsurgency, regardless of the political values of the scholars involved. Two major national studies of student behavior, one conducted by the American Council on Education and the other by the Carnegie Commission on Higher Education, were frequently attacked in the left-wing student press, and students were urged not to cooperate, not to permit themselves to be interviewed. At least one major analyst of student protest, the Santa Barbara sociologist Richard Flacks, who had been active in SDS as a student and who has remained an active radical as a faculty member, announced at the 1969 session of the American Sociological Association on student activism, that he no longer would do empirical studies of student activists, since his experience had convinced him that establishment forces made use of his work in spite of his intentions. Another equally creative sympathetic student of student radicalism, Kenneth Keniston, raised the issue of the unhappy political consequences of reporting unpalatable facts about radical students in the context of a review of a book on the Harvard demonstrations of 1969 written by Steven Kelman, the national chairman of the Young People's Socialist League, which was strongly hostile to SDS and the Harvard militants. Keniston was sharply criticized by sociologist Dennis Wrong, for this position.

> Reviewing Steven Kelman's account of student politics at Harvard, *Push Comes to Shove,* Kenneth Keniston concedes the validity of Kelman's charge that the SDS radicals "are undemocratic, manipulative, and self-righteous to the point of snobbery and elitism," but then observes that although "Kelman's angry book is written almost entirely to those on his Left . . . his book will mostly be read by those far to his Right, and it will be used (much against his wishes) to provide further ammunition for the Reagans, Mitchells, and Agnews in their politically profitable war against the alienated and radical young". . . .
>
> [O]ne finds Keniston clucking his tongue over Kelman's "exposé of the dirty linen of cultural revolutionaries and political revolutionaries in Harvard SDS," as if the only important consideration was what the right-wing neighbors will say.[59]

The political values and concerns of scholarly researchers are not the only element which may produce variations in research results. Studies concentrating primarily on activists which attempt to distinguish the social and psychological traits of students of different persuasions are also confronted by special analytical problems. Whether or not students direct their extracurricular energies into politics is strongly linked to political orientations. Studies of student bodies in different countries indicate that those on the left generally (and the small group on the extreme right) view politics as an appropriate and even necessary university activity.[60] Committed morally to the need for major social changes, leftists feel that the university should be an agency for social change; that both they and their professors should devote a considerable portion of their activities to politics.

Conversely, however, the less leftist students are, the more likely they are to disagree with this view, the more prone they will be to feel that the university should be an apolitical "house of study." Liberals and leftists, therefore, are much more likely to be politically active than moderates and conservatives. A relatively strong conservative stance will not be reflected in membership or activity in a conservative political club. This means that on any given campus or in any country, the visible forms of student politics will suggest that the student population as a whole is more liberal or radical leftist than it actually is. Since conservative academic ideology fosters campus political passivity, one should not expect to find much conservative activity.

Presumably it takes a lower threshold of political interest or concern to activate a liberal or leftist than a conservative. One would deduce, therefore, that the average conservative student activist should be more of an extremist within his ideological tendency than the average liberal. Hence a comparison of campus activists of different persuasions should find a greater share of extremists among the conservatives than among the liberals.

The Conflict Continues

Students, as the discussion in the next two chapters suggests, have more often than not contained an unruly minority, ready to protest whatever offends them, within or outside the university. It can be strongly argued that the circumstances of their being a "privileged" group which give them the psychic security to act are also among the factors which make their activism possible. It can be argued on the same grounds that a politically inactive student population is a cause for greater misgivings than an active one. The fact remains, however, that a large part of the group of self-identified "radicals" in the American movement which began in the mid-sixties have been close to total alienation from the rational and the political world. The overwhelming majority of them do *not* belong to any of the numerous "small c" communist groups which dominate the organized New Left and maintain some links (though often very nebulous) to philosophical and tactical doctrines of Marxism-Leninism. They belong, in fact, to the renunciatory rather than the radical tendency. The anarchist Paul Goodman, whose writings were a basic text for many of the Berkeley activists of 1964–65, and who was invited to teach at San Francisco State, with the students voluntarily paying the bill, wrote at the end of the decade with troubled concern about the future of the movement with which he once almost totally identified. As he points out, many students had isolated themselves from any ability to communicate about reality.

> There was no knowledge, but only the sociology of knowledge. They had so well learned that physical and sociological research is subsidized and conducted for the benefit of the ruling class that they did not believe there was such a thing as simple truth. To be required to learn something was a trap by which the young were put down and co-opted. . . .
>
> Inevitably, the alienated seem to be inconsistent in how they take the present world. Hippies attack technology and are scornful of rationality, but they buy up electronic equipment and motorcycles, and with them the whole infra-structure. Activists say that civil liberties are bourgeois and they shout down their opponents. But they clamor in court for their civil liberties. Those who say that the university is an agent of the powers that be, do not mean thereby to reassert the ideal role of the university, but to use the university for their own propaganda.
>
> Though each one is doing his thing, there is not much idiosyncracy in the spontaneous variety. The political radicals are, as if mesmerized, repeating the power plays, factionalism, random abuse, and tactical lies that aborted the movement in the thirties. And I have learned, to my disgust, that a major reason why the

young don't trust people over thirty is that they don't understand them, and are too conceited to try. Having grown up in a world too meaningless to learn anything, they know very little and are quick to resent it.[61]

Others on the left have noted the strong similarities between the action-oriented segments of their movement and the extreme right. The national New Left weekly, *The Guardian,* in reporting on a meeting of the National Youth Alliance, an overtly racist advocate of Right Power violence and an offshoot of "Youth for Wallace," commented: "Contemporary commentators often lump the extremes of right and left together. Indeed, despite obvious differences there were striking similarities exhibited . . ."[62] Some sections of the movement have gone even further to point up the close resemblances between some groups on the New Left and the original youth-oriented Fascist party of Benito Mussolini. An editorial in *The Campaigner,* published by the New York and Philadelphia Regional SDS Labor Committees, stated : "There is a near identity between the arguments of anarchists (around the Columbia strike movement, e.g.) [that is, Mark Rudd and his followers who became the Weathermen faction] and Mussolini's polemics for action against theory, against program."[63]

An article in the same magazine argued:

> It is an irony of history that certain New Leftists today would be quite at home with Mussolini's radical polemics . . . We must look to historical precedent in order to reveal the dangers inherent in certain New Left rhetoric today. . . . [Mussolini] fought for the idea that the revolution would be decided in the streets. . . . Similarly, fascism celebrated youth as a class. "Giovenezza" was the official Italian hymn to youth; similar examples are found in Nazi propaganda. The image of youth was extended to attack on the "older" capitalist nations, the "old," effete parliamentary bureaucrats.

The authors of this article go on to point to other similarities, including the evolution of the ideas of Georges Sorel, the French syndicalist theoretician, "the spiritual leader of those Italian syndicalists who produced the fascist movement. 'Purgative violence,' so recently repopularized by the writings of Frantz Fanon, played a central role in the revised [fascist] syndicalist theory."[64]

Perhaps more significant than this criticism by one SDS faction of another is the fact that a detailed analysis of the ideology and behavior generally of the current wave of new radicalism by Irving Louis Horowitz, the literary executor of C. Wright Mills and radical authority on revolutionary thought, came independently to similar conclusions.

> This is the first generation in American society, at least in this century, to combine political radicalism with irrationalism. . . .
>
> The current style of radicalism is abrasive, physical, impatient and eclectic. . . . This moralistic style is a ready handmaiden to the "totalitarian democracy" that the historian Jacob Talmon spoke of. It is a fanatic attempt to impose a new social order upon the world, rather than to await the verdict of consensus-building formulas among disparate individuals as well as the historical muses.
>
> [T]he modern Left movement . . . is not so much an attack on the world of ideas as it is an attack on the idea that reason is the only modex of knowing. The suspicion is that reason is an ideology that teaches us to stand between two extremes, unable to act. This identification of liberalism with the spirit of judiciousness and prudence is precisely why liberalism, at the psychological level, continues to be the main target for radical jibes. . . .
>
> *Fascism returns to the United States not as a right-wing ideology, but almost as a quasi-leftist ideology,* an ironic outcome that Sorel anticipated in his own writings when he celebrated Mussolini and Lenin as if they were really two peas in one pod.[65]

The sociologist Peter Berger, who has been active in the peace organization SANE as well as in various antiwar protests, also reports that as a European emigré, "observing the [American] radicals in action, I was repeatedly reminded of the storm troopers that marched through my childhood in Europe." Trying to understand this emotional reaction, he found that Old Left (Communist) activists did not produce this feeling in him, although he was opposed to them. He was forced to conclude that the New Left has strong similarities to facism which is lacking in the Old Left.

> What is specifically fascist about this ideology?
>
> A movement characterized by its negations rather than by a positive vision of the future: The new radicals take it as *ipso facto* evidence of counterrevolutionary intellectualism if one asks specific questions about their design for the future . . . The basic counter-position is between "the movement" *(die Bewegung,* as the Nazis called themselves) and "the system" *(das System* . . .) – the one absolutely noble and embodying the wave of the future, the other absolutely corrupt and representing nothing but decaying stasis. . . . Liberal democracy is a sham and, indeed, is the principal enemy. . . . Rationality is nothing but manipulation on behalf of "the system. . . ."
>
> The clearest symptom of the continuity of . . . themes is the mystique of the street. I recall a recent scene I watched on television, a group of students chanting rhythmically, "The streets belong to the people" – and the almost physical shock, as I remembered, at this moment, the opening lines of the second verse of the "Horst Wessel Lied," the anthem of the Nazi movement: "Die Strasse frei den brauen Bataillonen . . ." – "Clear the streets for the Brown battalions. . . ."
>
> The political cult of youth: How, in the midst of all the glorification of youth that surrounds us today, could one forget that the anthem of Mussolini's Italy began with the invocation "Giovinezza, giovinezza, primavera di bellezza . . ." – "Youth, youth, springtime of beauty. . . ."?
>
> The totalization of friend and foe, and the concomitant dehumanization of the latter: Again, linguistic usage is highly instructive here. Anyone who remembers the Nazi use of *Saujuden* (Jewish pigs) should stop to reflect about the human implication of the current usage of the term "pigs."
>
> Finally, the assurance of the radicals that they represent a mystical "general will," even though it is undiscoverable by empirical means. . . . This elitism is particularly repulsive in

> view of the democratic rhetoric. . . . In fact, the new radicals are not only contemptuous of the mechanisms of liberal parliamentary democracy; they are fundamentally contemptuous of *any* procedures designed to find out what the people want for themselves. . . .
>
> If one adds up these themes, one is confronted by an ideological constellation that strikingly resembles the common core of Italian and German fascism. Indeed, one is drawn to the conclusion that the concepts and interpretations drawn by many contemporary radicals from Marxism are grafted upon a body of motives and perspectives on the world that have nothing to do with Marxism.[66]

The parallelisms which Berger draws between major sections of the New Left and the fascist movements of the twenties and thirties are, of course, startling, precisely because they strike home. But the question must be raised to what extent this common ideology and tactics have comparable roots. As Berger notes, the Italian fascist party glorified "youth." Before the seizure of power it was, in fact, largely an antisystem youth party. Few leaders other than Mussolini were over thirty. Many of its activists were students. The German Nazi movement was somewhat different, but again, it should be noted that its earliest centers of strength were the universities. The Nazis captured control of the national German student organization and of the student councils in the bulk of the universities by 1931, before they had anything like comparable strength in any other stratum. As in Italy, their activists were young men.[67] Where youth is unrestrained by being part of an adult party or organization, it is probable that youth's variant of radicalism, whether rightist or leftist, will take on the violence-prone elitist orientations noted by Berger and the others.

Writing close to sixty years ago, the young undergraduate socialist Randolph Bourne, perhaps the most impressive young radical intellectual the United States ever produced, discussed at length the characteristics of youth in politics. Much of his analyses and descriptions of the collegiate youth before World War I are prescient of Berger's harsh descriptions, although Bourne himself was largely positive.

> Youth can never think of itself as anything but the master of things. . . . Its enthusiasm for a noble cause is apt to be all mixed up with a picture of itself leading the cohorts to victory. The youth never sees himself as a soldier in the ranks, but as the leader, bringing in some long-awaited change by a brilliant *coup d'etat*. . . .
>
> The youth of today are willful, selfish, heartless, in their rebellion. They are changing the system blindly and blunderingly. They feel the pressure, and without stopping to ask questions or analyze the situation, they burst the doors and flee away. Their seeming initiative is more animal spirits than anything else. . . .
>
> It is a fallacy of radical youth to demand all or nothing, and to view every partial activity as compromise. Either engage in something that will bring revolution and transformation all at one blow, or do nothing, it seems to say. . . .
>
> Radical youth is apt to long for some supreme sacrifice and feels that a lesser surrender is worth nothing. But better than sacrifice is efficiency! It is absurd to stand perplexedly waiting for the great occasion, unwilling to make the little efforts and to test the little occasions, and unwilling to work at developing the power that would make those occasions great.[68]

But Randolph Bourne's complaints about some of the traits of the radical youth of his day were only reiterating ancient descriptions of the tension between youth and authority. Much of this was known, at least as early as Aristotle, who said:

> [Youth] have exalted notions, because they have not yet been humbled by life or learnt its necessary limitations; moreover their hopeful disposition makes them think themselves equal to great things—and that means having exalted notions. They would always rather do noble deeds than useful ones: their lives are regulated more by moral feeling than by reasoning. . . . All their mistakes are in the direction of doing things excessively and vehemently. . . .
>
> [T]hey love too much, hate too much, and the same with

> everything else. They think they know everything, and are always quite sure about it; this, in fact, is why they overdo everything.[69]

In essence what Aristotle and more recent commentators on the values and attitudes of youth have said is that youth lacks restraint. If political behavior can be seen as a combination of impulse and restraint, then young people are much more likely to press for the attainment of seemingly positive ends, and to ignore the extent to which the means used shape the ends which are achieved. Restraint, in essence, involves curbs on the means one uses to secure what one wants. And as Earl Raab and I have noted in our analysis of right-wing extremism, "Democratic commitment can be seen essentially as a matter of restraint." The Bill of Rights is couched in the language of restraint: "Congress shall make no law . . ." It is the essence of extremism in politics to eliminate restraint, to conceptualize the struggle as one between absolute good versus absolute evil, thereby justifying the use of any tactics.[70] Political socialization in democracy involves learning about restraints, about means-ends relationships, as well as about how to secure objectives. It must develop a political superego, which limits the uninhibited desire to destroy those in the way. And the greater propensity of youth for the "ethic of absolute ends" as distinct from the "ethic of responsibility" discussed earlier is another way of saying that youth politics are more likely to reflect impulse than restraint. It also is another way of indicating that youth are more prone to favor change, reform, radicalism of all varieties, than older people. Youth-based movements, therefore, whether of the left or right, should have major elements in common.

This point may again be illustrated by reference to extreme right-wing movements. In 1968, many in the noncollege segment of American youth showed their propensity to go to political extremes in defense of their values by disproportionately backing George Wallace. All opinion polls agreed that in various stages of his campaign up to and including Election Day, Wallace secured more votes from the twenty-one- to twenty-nine-year-old group than from older age cohorts. He was also heavily backed according to opinion surveys among high school youth, particularly those of less well-to-do parentage who had no plans for a college education. Postelection surveys continue to point up Wallace's youth appeal. A Gallup Poll taken in March 1971 found that 20 percent of the new eighteen-to-twenty-one-year-old voter group preferred Wallace to Nixon or Muskie and Humphrey. Among the over-twenty-one electorate, Wallace's support was much less, 13 percent.[71] Since relatively few college students prefer the Alabaman, this means that his following among the under-twenty-one-year-old noncollege electorate is more than 25 percent.

Within the Wallace movement itself, the youth segment, which formed the independent group, the National Youth Alliance, after the election, turned out to be much more overtly racist, pro-violence, and antidemocratic than any other outgrowth of the American Independent Party.[72] The young former Wallacites, in effect, went to the extreme of their tendency. In so doing, as various New Leftists noted, they resembled the New Left. *The Guardian* reported:

> [NYA] leaders hit hard at the establishment, the liberals and their elders for botching up the country. "We are more antiestablishment than anyone. . . ."
>
> The alliance attacked the "criminal politico-economic system of maintaining full employment and buying votes by intervention in alien wars. . . ." The alliance warns rightists of the consolidation of corporate concerns. . . .
>
> The NYA resembles the New Left also in seeing its primary constituency as young workers and college students. It "vowed" to forge a "revolutionary" alliance of students and young workers to crush the left, stem the "liberal" tide and save a dying republic.[73]

These rightist youth, unlike many of their elders in the Wallace movement, but like the New Left, openly proclaim their opposition to conservative economic principles and "bourgeois values."

> We do not concern ourselves with the intricacies of economic conservation. We shall never deny what is needed to those who need it. . . . Those who seek to put bourgeois values over the hopes and aspirations of the people are enemies of the Right Front.
>
> The NYA hopes to unite all American youth in a movement for peace, progress, and the restoration of the rights of the American people.[74]

The Alliance even makes some of the same complaints about American higher education that New Leftist students have uttered. "You are no longer the individual you thought you were; but are now a mere number in a file. . . . Your English professor hardly shows up for class."[75]

The NYA has contempt for George Wallace and many other rightist leaders for adhering to the rules of the political game. They proudly announce their belief in racial inequality by wearing buttons with the mathematical symbol of inequality. They denounce the Jews, Negroes, American Indians, and all other nonwhite races as inferior. They call for teaching the superiority of the white race in "white studies" courses.

The emergence of right-wing extremism among youth is not limited to the American defenders of segregation and white supremacy. In Germany, where the radical right-wing National Democrats secured more electoral backing (4.6 percent) in 1969 than the left-wing movement supported by the New Left students (0.6 percent), "it seems that the young people have infused the [rightist] movement with new strength."[76] A year later, a report on German undercover investigations among right-wing groups reported over half the participants in rightist confrontations "belonged to the younger generation. This response of young people to nationalist agitation is partly an expression of backlash against left-wing supremacy among politically conscious German youth."[77] In France, *Le Monde* reported that "extreme right-wingers are on the move again. . . ."

> The fact that students and young people predominate in these new far-Right movements explains the injection of fresh ideas

> into the shopworn theories of fascism, elitism, and totalitarianism. . . .
>
> Since the May 1968 student-worker revolt in France, certain groups of young right-wingers have been rivaling the Left in condemning the consumer society and the industrial bosses. . . .
>
> Unyielding nationalism is one of the main planks of a rather small group calling itself Action Nationaliste, which draws most of its support from students at the Institute for Studies in Political Science. . . .
>
> Far-Right activists usually do not bother to conceal their taste for violent action and mystery. The Mouvement Jeune Révolution, for instance, revels in secrecy. . . . MJR, like the other extreme right-wing organizations, attracts rightists who "want to do something."[78]

In Italy, second only to France in the extensiveness of student protest in 1968, right-wing extremism in the form of a revived fascist student and youth movement is now again powerful. "Squadrismo," militant violent fascist bands, now operate on some campuses, particularly Rome. "As a fixed fact there seems to be a good deal of truth in the view of those who see the rebirth of youthful neosquadrismo" as springing from the so-called "trauma of the future." Their program has been described as "a bomb underneath the institutions."[79]

The emotive movement of the 1960s is not the first American student expression of sharp discontent with the university and society. Although probably the most powerful one, since, though a minority, it is based on a campus population of close to eight million, it has been preceded by many others which have played a role in changing the university, politics, and cultural practices. Whether one despairs or rejoices about the activities of the current generation-unit of renunciatory youth, any effort to evaluate it must rest not only on comparisons with youth and extremist movements in other countries, but some knowledge of the previous comparable activities of American students is necessary. The next two chapters turn to this effort.

4

Historical Background: From the Revolution to World War I

Many of the explanations for the emergence of student political and cultural protest during the 1960s discussed in Chapter 3 suggest that this event is causally related to structural changes in the university system, or in the ways in which Americans bring up their youth. Thus some writers have pointed to the presumed educational deficiencies derivative from increased university size, or greater concern for research than for teaching. Others have accounted for student patterns of cultural renunciation (drugs, hair, dress, freer sexual practices, etc.) as a consequence of increased parental permissiveness, the unwillingness of adults to discipline children. Some interpretations stress the gravity of the problems facing the nation, especially the Vietnam war, the inability to fulfill the promises of equality made to blacks, and the various ecological pressures stemming from industrialism, metropolitanism, and population pressures, in undermining the legitimacy, the "title-to-rule," of the dominant social institutions.

While all of these factors would seem to have some relationship to the expansion of student unrest, placing the analysis of student activism in comparative and historical perspective challenges the interpretations which seek to account for its current American phase by reference to unique national patterns. Clearly the present wave of student unrest has affected universities and countries in all parts of the world, underdeveloped, Western European, and Communist. Student protest movements have been more widespread and involved a larger proportion of the university population in countries as varied as France, Japan, South Korea, Indonesia, Czechoslovakia, Poland, Senegal, Argentina and Mexico. I have dealt with various aspects of student activism in other countries elsewhere, and do not want to repeat these discussions here, except to note that the similarity in patterns of behavior found in so many different cultural, familial, educational environments suggests that many of the contemporary America-centered interpretations are at best incomplete.[1]

The broad structural explanations, which stress the uniqueness of aspects of the contemporary scene, are also largely stated in absence of any consideration of the history of American campus activism. Much of what has been written is based on the assumption that American students have been quiescent until recently, presumably because their educational experiences were relatively good. In fact, the historical record reveals previous periods in which important segments of the college population have engaged in campus violence, in cultural and sexual experimentation, and in political radicalism. Earlier efforts to explain developments have frequently been stated in almost identical terms with those given for current events. Both in the last decades of the nineteenth century and in the 1920s, many writers urged that the increased emphasis given to research and extramural service activities by faculty resulted in inferior education and consequent student resentments. Similarly, the widespread demand for increased "student power" in the 1890s, and the innovations in cultural and sexual behavior and the disregard for law exhibited by many collegians in the 1920s, were both credited by contemporary analysts to the changes in the American family system, particularly the decline in parental authority. In calling attention to these and other similarities between the interpretations of the past and the present, I am not arguing that any of them are necessarily wrong. But clearly any effort to understand the sources of student behavior in a given time and place must be rooted in a general understanding of the factors in the social situation of university students which encourage particular modes of behavior among them generally, as well as knowledge of the way in which different segments have acted over time and place.

Groups dedicated to change either within society, or more commonly within the university have been relatively frequent among the undergraduate population. There are many explanations, obvious and less obvious, offered particularly in recent years for the special qualities of these students. To summarize generalizations made in the preceding chapters, various elements in their situation – their exposure to familial, religious, and social ideals presented in an absolute fashion, their relative lack of experience with the conflicting pressures derivative from varying value obligations or role demands, the insecurities stemming from being marginal men, in between the security and status derived from their family, and the obligation to find a mate, career, and status of their own – press them to see more clearly and purely the imperfections in university and society. On the other hand, they are freer than other segments of youth as well as older generations to act without concern for consequences to themselves or those close to them. They are footloose, in between engagements so to speak, and with considerable energy to use up. And whatever outlet any particular group of them chooses to use, the ecology of the university – the easy communication among those on a campus – makes it possible for all predisposed in a given direction to find one another, to mobilize that minority of students who are in agreement. Out of their new awareness as members of an intellectual community, out of their detached and advantaged position, students are better able than most of us to recognize the flaws, the inconsistencies around them, and can afford to be offended by them. Sometimes their horizons are limited to the institutions that are close by, the universities themselves, as in much of the nineteenth century; in periods of broad social ferment, however, the world and its problems are their oyster. These statements are as valid for an avant-garde unit of the American student population ever since the beginning of the Republic in 1776 as they are for those of any other nation, as a brief examination of their behavior over time demonstrates.

Protest and Violence on Campus: From the Revolution to the Civil War

The first record of American students as a protest group may be found in the annals of the American Revolution. As Richard Hofstadter points out: "In nationalist and colonial revolutions college and university students have always played an aggressive part, and to this the American college students were no exception."[2] Samuel Eliot Morison quotes a member of the Harvard Corporation writing in the early 1770s that the students "are already taken up with politics. They have caught the spirit of liberty."[3] The celebrated educational historian W. H. Cowley has described the general reaction of students to the Revolution.

> All of the nine existing colleges either closed down or greatly limited their operations because most of their eligible students had joined the militia or the Continental Army, but more relevant here are instances of students frustrating the British and discomfiting Loyalists. Two such illustrate these numerous harassments: Harvard students drove out of Cambridge the tutor who directed British troops to Lexington and "the shot heard round the world"; the soapbox harangues and the pamphlets written by an eighteen-year-old Kings College undergraduate named Alexander Hamilton helped arouse the mob that, despite his pleas against violence, three weeks later forced President Myles Cooper to seek refuge on a British warship bound for England.[4]

For a half century after the Revolution, students recurrently engaged in protests, some of them quite violent in character, directed *against the universities* for various deficiencies. G. Stanley Hall noted a seven-year-long Harvard outbreak beginning in 1790 against the examination system, and "more serious rebellions" in 1807 and 1830.[5] He also recorded similar events in other universities, and the presence among many faculties of "a fear that the whole student body is capable of being united and arrayed in organization against their authority."[6] Morison concluded: "The typical student of the early seventeen-nineties was an atheist in religion, an experimentalist in morals, a rebel to authority."[7]

At Harvard a series of strikes and other demonstrations occurred in the late eighteenth and early nineteenth centuries against bad food. Many students were expelled, actions which often led to new and more intensive protests. In 1818, four students were dismissed for throwing crockery during a food riot. "Their classmates chose to fight the tyranny of the administration, and, led by young Emerson and many sons whose fathers' names are still remembered as great patriots of the American Revolution, they rallied round the rebellion tree."[8] Emerson was suspended for his role in this affair. In 1823, over half the senior class was expelled shortly before graduation. During that year there had been explosions, the dropping of inked water on tutors, etc. In 1834, the resort to the power of the public authorities by President Quincy to punish riotous students, then as now considered a violation of university norms, brought a drastic reaction from the students comparable to the events of 1969 when police were summoned to Harvard Yard.

> Then, hell broke loose! Quincy had violated one of the oldest academic traditions: that the public authorities have no concern with what goes on inside a university, so long as the rights of outsiders are not infringed. The "black flag of rebellion" was hung from the roof of Holworthy. Furniture and glass in the recitation rooms of University were smashed, and the fragments hurled out of the windows. The juniors, led by Ebenezer Rockwood Hoar, voted to wear crape on their arms, issued a handbill with an acute dissection of the President's character, and hanged

> his effigy to the Rebellion Tree. A terrific explosion took place in chapel; and when the smoke had cleared, "A Bone for Old Quin to Pick" was seen written on the walls. A printed seniors' "Circular," signed by a committee who were promptly deprived of their degrees, gave their version of the Rebellion in language so cogent that the Overseers issued a forty-seven-page pamphlet by Quincy to counteract it. . . . Quincy never recovered his popularity.[9]

At Princeton, according to Harry Bowes, student of the history of student rebellions, "following a rebellion in 1806 half the students were expelled. . . . This dealt the college a blow which impaired its usefulness for over a decade. Six rebellions equally violent occurred from 1800 to 1830. During one riot, the students gained possession of the college buildings and defied authorities to try and enter them."[10] On another occasion, after three students were expelled, "for several days Nassau Hall resounded to the report of pistols and the crash of bricks against doors, walls and windows."

Yale also had frequent rebellions culminating in "The Great Rebellion" of 1828, which resulted in the "rustication from the college of some forty students." The University of Virginia, following Thomas Jefferson's enlightened policies, gave its students more freedom than other schools. The university established a plan "under which a board of six student 'censors' would assist the faculty in maintaining order." A series of riots in 1825 undermined the effort. "Three former presidents of the United States who had administered the nation for twenty-four of its thirty-six years [Jefferson, Madison, and Monroe] sat on the Board of Visitors when it met to restore peace, but not even their knowledge and prestige could breathe life into a scheme of self-government that collided with the deeply embedded tradition of student contumacy."[11]

The College of South Carolina is cited in the literature in this field as a more typical example of a Southern school which underwent frequent riots and other disturbances, many protests against poor food and compulsory commons. In 1822, President

Cooper of the college wrote to Thomas Jefferson that "Republicanism is good, but the rights of boys and girls are the offspring of Democracy gone mad."[12] Parents frequently intervened to get a harsh punishment revoked.

Jefferson himself wrote in a letter to George Ticknor of Harvard on July 16, 1823: "The insubordination of our youth is now the greatest obstacle to their education. We may lessen the difficulty, perhaps, by avoiding too much government, by requiring no useless observances. . . . On this head I am anxious for information of the practices of other places, having myself had little experience of the government of youth."[13]

No analysis has been made of the backgrounds of the students who caused trouble in those days. Morison, however, indicates that at the beginning of the nineteenth century, as much later, the sons of the well-to-do were the discontented, while those from less privileged backgrounds took delight in their opportunities to benefit themselves. "If the college atmosphere seemed oppressive to young scions of rich mercantile families, it was Elysium to boys . . . who came up to Cambridge from poor or provincial surroundings after a hard struggle to qualify."[14]

Dormitories were deliberately established at various schools as a means of giving students "a common experience under the protective shelter of the faculty's guiding hand. . . . Group living was supposed to develop self-respect and group responsibility." However, as Bowes points out, the dormitory "also brought students into close proximity usually under poor [living] conditions . . . it was a hatching ground for pranks and plots. In general, dormitories helped to create an atmosphere that invited frustration, peer conformity, and crime."[15]

Although much student "indiscipline" in the first half century after Independence revolved around local college issues, underlying a considerable part of it was resistance to the efforts of the schools to impose a traditional uncritical religious outlook on undergraduates receptive to the intellectual challenges to orthodox Protestantism. Bowes notes that "the 'college fathers' . . . strongly associated the spirit of liberty and self-reliance with infidelity and godlessness. . . . [On one occasion] a number of Princeton students celebrated a triumph over the faculty by breaking into the Presbyterian church, removing the pulpit Bible, and burning it. The leader of the senior class claimed to be an atheist and stated that Godwin's *Political Justice* was his bible. His attitude was quite popular during this period of American history."[16]

The conflicts over the right of the college to impose its religious views and practices on the students were to some degree linked to the domination of most schools by conservative, often clerical, groups of trustees, presidents, and faculty. According to Earnest, in "the early days of the Republic the teaching, except in a few Southern colleges under the influence of Jefferson, was mainly Federalist," in politics, and theologically orthodox.[17] Conversely, Sister M. Kennedy indicates "Deism made rapid inroads among the college students of the day. Disrespect for authority, a sense of impermanence, and liberal theological ideas were heightened and spread by the Revolution. When the intellectual repercussions of the French Revolution reached the United States, skepticism and infidelity became rife and were accompanied by greater rowdyism in the colleges."[18] Many clergymen attributed student unrest to the "vogue of infidelity, Jeffersonianism, and rationalistic philosophy."[19]

The student opposition to rigid discipline within the colleges, as well as to the religious control over them and to the dogmatic beliefs enunciated by many of the colleges, did not constitute generational conflict per se. Rather they reflected and were allied to the liberal forces in the outside world led by Jefferson. These stressed the need for greater freedom from institutional control within the clerically dominated institutions of higher education, as well as the need for a totally voluntaristic religious system in the society as a whole. Morison reports that many of the conflicts within the Harvard Board of Overseers were along party lines, with the Federalists supporting strict authority and the Jeffersonian Republicans arguing for student rights.[20] In the larger polity, many of the Jeffersonians argued that the state was obligated to provide services for its citizens seven days a week – that it could not deprive non-Christians of their right to receive mail on Sundays. In 1810, Congress passed a law providing for the Sunday delivery of the mails. The issue of Sunday activities was to remain a major one for some decades.[21] In 1830, a Senate committee report, authored by a future Vice-President, Richard Johnson, stated explicitly that in the United States religion and irreligion had equal rights, and that laws proclaiming that the government should not provide services on Sunday would work an injustice on irreligious people or non-Christians, and would constitute a special favor for Christians as a group. The report enunciated in unequivocal terms: "The constitution regards the conscience of the Jew as sacred as that of the Christian, and gives no more authority to adopt a measure concerning the conscience of a solitary individual than that of a whole community. . . . If Congress shall declare the first day of the week holy, it will not satisfy the Jew nor the Sabbatarian. . . . It is the duty of this government to affirm to *all* – to the Jew or Gentile, Pagan, or Christian – the protection and advantages of our benign institutions on Sunday, as well as every day of the week."[22]

Such sentiments, of course, outraged the Evangelical Protestant segment of the community. The Anti-Masonic party, which swept through the more isolated rural areas of the North in the late 1820s and early 1830s, in many ways represented the first major backlash movement directed against the cosmopolitan educated elite who were corrupting traditional values through their power over politics, the media, and the cultural and intellectual centers. It identified the Masons, the Jacksonians, and the deistic intellectuals as anti-Christian. Campus religious liberalism, therefore, was involved in one of the major conflicts of the day.[23]

Bowes concludes his discussion of the period from 1790 to 1830 by saying that student behavior reflected "the growing liberalism of the age, a liberalism which was impatient with puritanical restraint and in some cases with religion itself." The universities tried "to crush what they termed as irreligious, immoral, and disorderly behavior," but failed. He suggests the internal conflicts resulted in "a deterioration of creativity, good scholarship, and inspirational teaching."

Although the succeeding epoch, from 1830 to 1880, witnessed fewer conflicts over discipline, much occurred which also had a contemporary air about it. President Quincy of Harvard "was plagued with the problem of nonconformity of dress by the students."[24] Quincy himself, as an undergraduate, had insisted in 1818: "Resistance to tyrants is obedience to God." He led a forbidden rally around the "Rebellion Tree," and was suspended by President Kirkland for this action.[25] In mid-nineteenth century conflicts with students, the police are described by Bowes as "often guilty of needless brutality and lack of tact."[26] In defense of the police it should be added that the "students make it a point to wantonly insult and exasperate the peelers [police] on every occasion when it can be done with safety."[27]

At the University of Virginia, which had started with more trust in student self-government than any other school in the country, "fear of student violence kept the faculty on edge." But when the boys organized an independent military company and announced that they would resist the "tyrannical movements of the faculty" which ordered them to remove all arms from the campus, the teachers in 1836 out of desperation or boldness ordered a substantial number of expulsions. Two days of rioting ended in compromise: the appearance of the militia upheld the majesty of the law and the retreat of the faculty readmitted the offending students. Ironically, the professor who engineered the compromise was shot to death by a student four years later.[28]

It is difficult to generalize concerning the political and social sentiments of American students in the Jacksonian and pre–Civil War periods. One American, C. A. Bristed, who graduated from Yale in the late 1830s and then went on to study for five years at Cambridge University, during which time he also visited continental universities, concluded "that the majority of highly educated young men under any government are opposed to the spirit in which that government is administered. Hasty and imperfect as the conclusion is, it certainly does hold good of many countries. . . ." Bristed went on to argue that the typical student "sees the defects in the government of his country; he exaggerates them with the ardor of youth, and takes that side which promises to remedy them, without reflecting at what cost the remedy may have to be purchased."[29]

If American students in the 1830s and 1840s were critical of a mass electoral democracy from a conservative-elitist stance as Bristed suggests, they did little actively to foster this viewpoint. During this period, however, a number of abolitionist clubs appeared on various campuses. The University of Michigan had a secret organization devoted to smuggling runaway slaves into Canada.[30] The Amherst abolition society included one third of the student body before it was banned in 1835. Other schools with such societies included Dartmouth, Franklin, Hamilton, New York, Williams, Union, Western Reserve, Illinois, Oberlin, Marietta, Miami University (Ohio), Kenyon, and many others. Many of these campus groups secured public, and thereby historical, attention because efforts were made during the 1830s to deny their right to exist. "[I]t appears from a study of the cases that the infringements upon freedom of opinion in Northern colleges arose less from fear of the ideas of the [student] abolitionists than from distrust of the *agitative and apparently radical methods* they employed." The administrative opposition disappeared, since with "the penetration of abolitionism into the upper levels of Northern society and with its entrance into politics and the church, antagonism to its discussion in Northern colleges quickly lessened."[31] Some elite northeastern schools such as Princeton, Harvard, Yale and Pennsylvania had large Southern enrollments and their administrators sought to avoid internecine warfare on campus. The occasional college straw vote I have run across indicates overwhelming backing for the Republicans in 1856 and 1860.

There is some indication that Southern students were more aggressive in fostering their regional point of view than their Northern compeers. Cowley reports that students often joined "in molesting anti-slavery visitors from the North and the rare

Southerners who expressed even mild doubts about the sanctity of slavery. In 1856, for example, University of North Carolina students burned in effigy and threatened to tar and feather a professor who supported the newly organized Republican party. In the same year University of Virginia students cheered when their alma mater presented Preston Brooks with a cane like the one he used on the floor of Congress to beat Charles Sumner into invalidism."[32]

After the Civil War, many "disorders in Southern universities . . . resulted from student membership in such organizations as the Ku Klux Klan." The Klan and other white supremacy groups were strong in a number of universities and used terror tactics against campus opponents and Negroes.[33]

Much of the intramural tension in this period, however, did not relate to any political issue. Essentially, students exhibited often in fairly violent fashion resentments against the faculty which were comparable to those expressed a century later. A recent sophisticated history of the American university reports:

> [A] personal relationship [between faculty and students] had seldom existed in the past, and least of all in the mid-nineteenth century. The barrier between teacher and student loomed, if anything, far higher. . . . it had . . . been revealed by riots, the throwing of stones at professors' houses, and in at least two cases by actual murder of a professor. At Dickinson College in 1866, "students regarded the faculty as a species of necessary evil. . . ."
>
> [C]ollege students betrayed many of the symptoms of a deeply disloyal subject population. Why else would oaths of allegiance have seemed appropriate for the students at Yale during the sixties and seventies? Or why would the freedom of students to congregate in large groups sometimes be inhibited by regulation? (e.g., at Harvard in 1871).[34]

Student Power and Radical Politics: The Interbellum Years

The period from the end of the Civil War until the turn of the century witnessed few politically related campus activities, other than efforts to support one of the two major party presidential candidates. There is some suggestion in the historical literature that if political protest was absent among the students of this era, romantic renunciatory, anticommercial and anti-industrial-civilization sentiments were present. "[C]ontemporary observers of the college scene, including those who studied freshman themes for the content of their ideas, agreed that the college student of this period placed high regard upon veracity, frankness, honesty, and such virtues, while opposing hypocrisy and sham." One student editorial in 1872 in a national paper for undergraduates, proclaimed Hamlet as the one character who suggests the ideal of students, for he was "the noble-hearted friend, pure, chivalrous."[35]

This choice of Hamlet as the ideal of American undergraduates a century ago is particularly appropriate for, as Erik Erikson points out, he is "an abortive ideological leader," who exhibits in Shakespeare's portrayal the special identity problems and need for commitment of introspective youth. He "is the morbid young intellectual of his time, for did he not recently return from studies at Wittenburg, the hotbed of humanist corruption, his time's counterpart to Sophist Athens and to today's centers of learning infested by existentialism, psychoanalysis—or worse? . . . He is estranged from the ways of his country . . . and, much like our 'alienated' youth, he is estranged from and describes as 'alienated' the overstandardized man of his day, who 'only got the tune of time and outward habit of encounter.' . . . He abhors conventional sham and advocates genuineness of feeling." And Hamlet's appeal lies precisely in the fact that he is a figure who epitomizes the inherent tragedy of idealistic youth, "that his fidelity must bring doom to those he loves, for what he accomplishes at the end is what he tried to avoid at first. He succeeds in actualizing only what we would call his negative identity and in becoming exactly what his own ethical sense could not tolerate: a mad revenger."[36]

The students of that long-past American age not only sought to identify with heroic and tragic figures, they also expressed their renunciation of the corrupt modern world in the practice common among Yale students in the late 1860s, who "often indulged in primitivistic idylls, camping out for a week or two on lonely islands in the Long Island Sound . . . living after the manner of the primitive savage, the independent barbarian. . . ."[37] In their romantic enthusiasms, these American students resembled the much more full-blown renunciatory groups of German youth who formed the extensive Youth Movement before World War I.[38]

Student demonstrations revived on an extensive scale in the last two decades of the century. They were largely directed "against the doctrine of *in loco parentis*." Student newspapers demanded that the college "should adjust itself to the liberal changes in the structure of the American family." The *Williams Argo* argued that "Few parents would attempt any such government of twenty-year-olds as do colleges of their students."[39] At a number of schools in this period students forced through public "trials" of their president and secured the removal of many of them. Lincoln Steffens described a successful uprising at Berkeley during his freshman year (1885) there.

> One evening, before I had matriculated, I was taken out by some upper classmen to teach the president a lesson. He had been the head of a private preparatory school and was trying to govern the private lives and the public moral of university "men" as he had those of his schoolboys. Fetching a long ladder, the upper classmen thrust it through a front window of Prexy's house and, to the chant of obscene songs, swung it back and forth, up and down, round and round, till everything breakable within sounded broken and the drunken indignation outside was satisfied or tired. . . . [The president] was allowed to resign soon thereafter. . . .[40]

Students were sometimes instrumental in naming new presidents. Lewis Feuer points to various examples of faculty support for student protest against college administrations and suggests: "Ambitious faculty men who allied themselves with student uprisings found a new avenue for upward mobility."[41] The rebellious students, though expressing a high degree of alienation from their institutions and faculty, showed little interest in national politics, especially of a radical or reform kind. Analysis of campus straw votes indicated that all "over the United States (except, of course, in the South) college students recorded an overwhelming preference for the Republicans. This was true both in the Midwestern land-grant institutions and on the East Coast."[42]

The one source of a politically related controversy during this period was the requirement of the Morrill Land Grant Act that universities benefiting from it must provide compulsory military training. Many students in state universities, those primarily affected, strongly objected to military drill. The University of Wisconsin paper, the *University Press,* argued in 1870 that the American tradition opposed militarism. The most violent protest among the many hurled against such activities occurred in 1886, when students attempted to sabotage the program by breaking in and stealing the stocks and barrels of one hundred muskets.[43] Tensions derivative from the existence of military drill precipitated major student protests at the University of Illinois in 1879–1880, and again in 1889–1891. In both instances, the struggle ended with the resignation of the president.[44] These conflicts, like later ones, resulted in student activists generalizing their antagonism to the power of the faculty and regents. Thus, in 1880, a student paper, the *Vindicator,* "lashed the entire Faculty for twisting truth and using power unjustly, and boldly ridiculed individual professors." It described a typical regent as "a man who builds his house of cheap bricks, bought at reduced rates, on pretense they are for state purposes, and then denies it before a committee of the legislature."[45] During the second conflict, a student paper argued: "It seems inconsistent in this age and country to educate young men and women in republican sentiments and at the same time attempt to govern them by a set of laws in the making of which they have no voice at all. . . ."[46]

Demonstrations against compulsory military drill in state universities apart, almost all of the student protests of the late nineteenth century were manifestly directed against the shortcomings of the institutions as schools, around the issues of discipline, curriculum content, administration power, due process, student self-government and the like. "Disaffected young men rebelled through boycotts, strikes and demonstrations. . . . Frequently the most promising students led the agitation."[47] Then, as now, according to Feuer, they occurred "not in the universities where students were from the lower classes but in the schools of the more well-to-do, not in the universities where the sciences and the practical arts were pursued but in the colleges of the liberal arts." He went on to suggest that class origins made the difference.

> The class origin of the students, indeed, was a decisive factor in their unrest, but in a way precisely opposite to what a Marxist would expect. The Michigan or Illinois [non-protester] . . . came from a home where life's struggle was real and keen; he came to a state university because it was virtually free; often he worked his way through college; he chose his courses with an eye to his livelihood. . . . When the obstacles of life are genuine and concrete . . . then there are no surplus energies available for generational revolt.[48]

If the period of student protest in the first quarter of the nineteenth century witnessed the rebellious students pressing for values which they shared with adult Jeffersonians, the widespread demonstrations of the last quarter often involved a shared concern with the faculty for a change in university governance. This was also a period of faculty revolt against the absolute power of college presidents.

> Throughout the 1880s and 1890s . . . professors began increasingly to identify themselves by academic discipline or as members of a separate, professional class. One sign of this new faculty solidarity was the unprecedented frequency with which faculties as a whole openly opposed their presidents. Another sign was the professors' success in having faculty positions rearranged by intellectual disciplines, or departments, rather than individual chairs whose incumbents . . . were responsible only to the president. Yet a third sign was the unprecedented growth that occurred in the formation of professional societies during these years.[49]

Articles published in a variety of magazines read by the elite, the *Nation,* the *Critic,* the *Atlantic Monthly,* the *Forum* and others, contained frequent articles by professors and others concerning the problems of higher education. They dealt with sources of student unrest, the relationship between research and teaching, academic governance, faculty salaries and the like. It was generally recognized that higher education was in a stage of change and crisis. The emphasis on teaching and close faculty contact with undergraduates was attacked as a source of student discontent. It is interesting to note that even before the Civil War, student unrest was explained by "a growing [faculty] minority [as resulting from] . . . the faulty methods of teaching and the uninspiring content of instruction. A small contingent of Americans who had studied at German universities came home to insist that power was better exercised over subjects than over subject schoolboys, that a contribution to philology was far more significant than a contribution to student manners, that the whole emphasis of the college should be shifted from discipline to scholarship."[50] Shortly after the war, the Ann Arbor undergraduate paper, the *University Chronicle,* complained that "the University was not on a par academically with most Eastern universities and ought to admit it." It criticized the university for appointing too many faculty "without tested reputations."[51] These demands for scholars were advanced in much stronger and more general terms as a response to the turmoil of the latter part of the century.

An editorial on "College Discipline" in *The Critic* of July 30, 1881, raised the question why "American youths in college behave worse than . . . German youths." Its explanation for lesser student indiscipline was "the German policy of non-interference by faculty with students" supposedly derived from the fact that German professors were primarily dedicated to research. And both to improve "real learning in American colleges," and reduce student unrest, the editorial writer of *The Critic* argued:

> It must be borne in mind that the modern specialist gains no reputation by merely appropriating the knowledge of the past in

> his branch of study; one must continually question Nature and push back the boundary of darkness which on all sides surrounds him. He must mark out a new path of investigation and arrive at new results. The ideal professor is not the mere pedagogue who sits at his desk hearing recitations. . . . The time has evidently come for the return of the latter type to his proper sphere and the establishment in professorial chairs of zealous [research] specialists.[52]

A German psychologist turned Harvard professor, Hugo Münsterberg, argued in the same vein some years later: "A young scholar ought to devote himself to special problems, where he can really go to the sources; instead of that our young instructor has to devote himself to the widest fields, where it is impossible to aim at anything but the most superficial acquaintance."[53]

Faculty defenders argued that excessive emphasis on teaching made for dull lecturers who bored their students and impelled them to dislike their college. In an article published in 1894, "Research The Vital Spirit of Teaching," G. Stanley Hall argued that "excessive teaching palls and kills." Exciting teachers are men whose knowledge "is fresh from the sources, and not second- or third-hand."[54] Münsterberg was to make a similar point:

> The young man who has to conduct twenty "recitations" a week, and to read hundreds of examination books, and to help on the administrative life of the place, begins by postponing his scientific work to the next year, and the year after next, when he shall be more accustomed to his duties. But after postponing it for a few years more his will becomes lame, his power rusty, his interest faded.[55]

Since college presidents and trustees supposedly were primarily interested in assuring that the faculty spent most of their time with students, an objective which some protesting students resented as much as those faculty who sought more time for research, Hall, though a new university president himself, called for faculty self-government. "[The] ideal university . . . is sure to need a larger academic policy shaped more by the faculty, who can be best trusted with the interests of science if their quality is once well established."[56]

Important segments of the students and the faculty were demanding greater freedom, more right to participate in government. A variety of student senates or councils were established for the first time. Undergraduates were allowed to take part in disciplinary committees or boards at a number of schools. These seeming triumphs had some real consequences in the elimination of areas in which colleges claimed the right to act *in loco parentis*. The experiences with shared power through student self-government was much less successful, however, than the increase in faculty influence at major schools.

> But though the students begged loudly for a "New System" when they were without it and complimented themselves on the prospect of running the college, once student government was a reality, the undergraduates lost much of their enthusiasm. There had always been something fraudulent in the idea of student *government*. Students did not, and could not, literally govern the college. The idea of student government was most often a proposition administrations tried to use to harness the rebellious energies of undergraduates. *The Bowdoin Orient* expressed typical disillusionment when it editorialized of Bowdoin's Student Jury, a system colleges throughout the East were clamoring to imitate: "The students do not desire to govern themselves nor is there any logical reason why they should be expected to do so. The faculty is given the authority and the faculty cannot delegate their responsibility." To the *fin de siècle* undergraduate, independence meant freedom from faculty interference in his extracurricular organizations. . . . Students discovered that they did not want to take over the colleges, but rather to insulate themselves from its demands. The grandest independence American students could conceive was their outright rejection of faculty, trustee, and alumni pleas to make a face-saving gesture before the public and reestablish the famous Senate.[57]

The awareness that student participation in the governance of universities involves co-optation rather than shared power, links critics of the campus scene of the 1890s with those of the 1960s. This was not the only similarity that may be found in the writings of the two periods. Then, as now, men differed as to the significance of student indiscipline. Some argued that it was the work of a small minority who did not really represent the feelings of, or the problems concerning, the great majority.

Thus a Harvard professor, N. S. Shaler, in a discussion of "The Problem of Discipline in Higher Education," contended in 1889, in terms prescient of many articles concerning the contemporary student population, that the considerable "public remark as to the evil behavior of Harvard students" was occasioned by the extreme actions of two to three percent which are well publicized, and "carry alarm into the households whence come some twelve hundred normally well-behaved young men."[58]

The controversies among faculty, administrators, and others, as to how to handle the disruptions on campus also resembled current debates. Men differed all during the nineteenth century as to whether to follow Jefferson's advice to reduce external controls and punishments as a means of reducing student hostility, or that of President Josiah Quincy of Harvard who resorted to calling the police and to trying to enforce civil law within the university.

The norm, accepted in many foreign countries, that universities are autonomous and that the police should not be called to intervene in intramural disturbances has always had strong support in the United States, particularly among students. Francis Wayland, pre–Civil War president of Brown, argued that campus unrest would be ended by subjecting students to the same civil penalties and external police power as the rest of society. He pointed out that he had "known college officers to take very great pains to shield students from the consequences of their violation of municipal regulations."[59] Discussions in the public press made the same point during the upheavals of the end of the century. An article by a professor in *The Forum* in 1887 concerning "College Disturbances" stated that they were in some part a result of the notion "that a different code of honor, morals, duty, and conduct belongs to college life from that which attends common life . . . that a college community is to some degree exempt from common obligations and responsibilities. . . . Students – many, not all – act upon the assumption, and the public in too many cases practically concedes it. Practices condemned and punished by the common and statute law are looked upon as allowable . . . in college."[60]

The German emphasis on research and graduate training gradually began to spread among the leading schools. By 1902, Johns Hopkins University, founded as a research oriented graduate school, was celebrating its twenty-fifth anniversary, and was regarded as a great university. Woodrow Wilson, then a professor of politics at Princeton, read an address to President Gilman in which he emphasized the new ideal.

> [Y]ou were the first to create and organize in America a university in which the discovery and dissemination of new truths were conceded a rank superior to mere instruction, and in which the efficiency and value of research as an educational instrument were exemplified in the training of many investigators. . . .
>
> You also first recognized the importance of publication as a function and a duty of a modern university, and by your demonstration of its feasibility and value you set a quickening example which has been widely followed.[61]

Although many academics agreed with Woodrow Wilson that reducing the teaching load and increasing support for research were good for education, these changes were followed by articles in the press which voiced the sentiment of administrators, trustees, and some protesting students in contending that research was interfering with adequate instruction and consequently made for student unrest. An article in *The Educational Review* in 1895 complained that "most young college professors are more concerned with their subjects than with their pupils." Charles Ramsey argued:

> In the zeal for special research which . . . has become the ideal aim of much college instruction, it has come about that only the

> most brilliant scholars are chosen to be instructors, regardless of their lack of more strictly professorial preparation and experience. As such instructors are usually promoted, this in turn has also become the ideal method of recruiting professional ranks.[62]

The Nation editorialized in 1900 on "The Decline of Teaching," arguing that it resulted from the fact that it "is the making of books, and not the training of the young in habits of thought and work, that holds out to the teacher of to-day the main promise of reward." *World's Work* suggested in 1901 that research and teaching ought to be separated, that the two interfere with each other. "And in most of our universities the teaching of youth has become less efficient than it once was, and surely less than it ought to be, because of the too common effort to unite it with original research."[63]

An article in *The Atlantic Monthly* in 1902, while recognizing that talented professors ought to be encouraged to engage in creative scholarship, "to explore the farthest boundaries of human knowledge," strongly argued that the passion for research resulted in the neglect of other professorial duties by the large majority who were not genuinely creative.

> Yet the college teachers who really make original contributions to human knowledge are few in proportion to the total numbers engaged in the profession. The passion for scholarship, like that for poetry, does not always imply a corresponding power for production; and because we are glad to release some picked man from the common social obligations and services, and bid him Godspeed upon his adventures, it does not follow that a similar freedom may be claimed by those who stay at home.[64]

Seven years later in the same magazine, Abraham Flexner presented what was to become the classic story illustrating lack of concern for undergraduate teaching.

> I took occasion, not long ago, to ask a college dean who was the best teacher in his institution. He named a certain instructor.

"What is his rank?"
"Assistant Professor."
"When will his appointment expire?"
"Shortly."
"Will he be promoted?"
"No."
"Why not?"
"He hasn't *done* anything!"[65]

A comprehensive and highly praised survey of the operation of *Great American Universities,* published in 1910, generalized following a discussion of the situation of students at Harvard concerning the absence of concern among faculty for undergraduates.

> Here is the weak point of all the great colleges, and even of the smaller ones — the lack of personal contact between teacher and student. It is not due to the influx of an overwhelming number of students because the faculty has generally grown in proportion or more. It is partly due to defective organization and partly to the development of a new school of teachers, who detest teaching, who look upon students as a nuisance, and class work as a waste of time.[66]

The current debates concerning the multiversity, dealing with the involvement of professors in extramural organizations, reiterate points made at the turn of the century. Some welcomed the participation of faculty in such activities; others saw them as interfering with scholarly and teaching duties. The description in any case is familiar.

> [A] newer type of college professor is . . . everywhere in evidence; the expert who knows all about railroads and bridges and subways; about gas commissions and electrical supplies; about currency and banking, Philippine tariffs, Venezuelan boundary lines, the industries of Puerto Rico, the classification of the civil service, the control of trusts. . . . [The] college professor who represents the "humanities," rather than the distinctly

> scientific side of modern education, is likewise brought closer to the public than ever before. The newspapers report — and misreport — him. Editors offer him space to reply. Publishers weary him with appeals to write textbooks. . . . The professor's photograph . . . assaults your eye in the marketplace. The college press club and the university's bureau of publicity gives his lecture dates in advance. The prospectus of your favorite magazine bids you inspect his literary qualifications as well as his thoughtful countenance. *Who's Who in America* informs you of the name of his second wife.[67]

Then, as now, participation by professors in political affairs led to their being denounced. Turn-of-the-century comment sounds extremely contemporary.

> Within a twelvemonth college teachers have been openly denounced as "traitors" for advocating self-government for the Filipinos. In many a pulpit and newspaper office, last September, it was declared that the utterances of college professors were largely responsible for the assassination of President McKinley. . . . One must admit that a good many college professors have taken the Irish members of Parliament as their exemplars, and are boyishly pleased if they can merely obstruct the business of the House. Miss Evelina Burney once wrote of Sir Philip Jennings Clerk, "He is a professed minority man." This type of man is familiar in academic circles.[68]

This period also witnessed the first large group of academic freedom cases. A number of schools sought to fire controversial professors. The emergence of the "controversial" academic was, of course, not a coincidence. It stemmed from the shift in the conception of the professor from teacher to researcher, "from conserving to searching." Insofar as research, innovation, frontier knowledge began to gain status within academe, faculty members were occupationally motivated to reject the values and lore of the past, to assume that the knowledge and agreed wisdom of the present was tentative, that "tradition was mere opinion and experience, but that opinion improves as society ages and that experience grows stale with senescence."[69]

The growth in explicit reformist political concerns among the faculty and in the intellectual community generally after 1900 was to be paralleled among a small minority of students who became involved in socialist politics in the form of the Intercollegiate Socialist Society (ISS) formed in 1905. By 1908, a conservative English visitor, Alexander Francis, was impressed that the spread of socialism in America had deeply penetrated the intellectual and student worlds.

> If . . . the term "intellectuals" covers all who have had a college career, a considerable number of them may be said to have professed socialism. Socialist societies have established themselves at the universities; and Secretary Taft, speaking at Yale, referred somewhat scornfully to these "dreamers and impracticable thinkers at the universities of this country who would abandon the system lying at the base of modern society." Well, youth everywhere is prone to be full of impetuosity and self-confidence, at once purblind and bold; and in its state of half-culture, undergraduate youth is peculiarly apt to seize with enthusiasm upon a general principle, regardless of its limitations or relations to other principles. But I met not a few professors who hold and teach socialistic doctrines; and it is significant that most, certainly the most extreme, of these have positions in colleges and universities which have received large pecuniary gifts from millionaires.[70]

The young socialist Randolph Bourne, while still an undergraduate at Columbia in 1912, generalized in the same fashion concerning the spread of socialism among undergraduates and the role of the faculty at the leading American universities. "Settlement work and socialist propaganda . . . are now the commonplaces of the undergraduate." And he went on to argue that these tendencies were clearly a function of the university, for "his education, if it has been in one of the advanced universities, will have only tended to confirm his radicalism. . . ." The younger teachers, particularly, rejected traditional values, and Bourne called on the dedicated undergraduate to "ally himself with his radical teachers in spirit and activity. . . . The college thus becomes for the first time in American history a reorganizing force. It . . . now finds arrayed against it, in spirit at least if not in open antagonism, the churches and the conservative molders of opinion."[71]

David Shannon reports that "in the great upsurge of progressivism and radicalism just before World War I, the ISS had chapters in sixty colleges and universities. There were chapters in the major New England colleges, most of the state universities outside the South, and the most prominent Protestant denominational colleges."[72] The ISS had about two thousand dues-paying members, among a national college population of under four hundred thousand in 1912–13. For comparative purposes this may be placed alongside the claim of SDS of six thousand dues-paying members out of a national higher education population of close to seven million in 1968–69.

Once socialism entered the university, student protest enunciated a set of ideological themes and action concerns which have continued down to the present. Upton Sinclair, one of the organizers of the ISS, used the "factory" analogy in his analysis of the operation and function of the university.[73]

John Reed, a founding member of the Harvard Socialist Club, left behind two autobiographical essays which were published long after his death. The first was written in 1912, shortly after his graduation, while the second was drafted five years later. His description of events and ideology has a strong modern ring:

> What's wrong with Harvard? Something is the matter. Numbers of letters from alarmed alumni pour into President Lowell's office every day, asking if Socialism and Anarchy are on the rampage among undergraduates. . . . Old graduates shake their heads mournfully and agree the place is going to the dogs. . . .
>
> [The] group that founded the [Socialist] Club were Fabians, that is, they believed in "permeating" the University with the doctrine which they stood for. . . . The idea was to stir up

> criticism, revolt, discussion, opposition, not only of the present state of things in the outside world, but of the state of things at Harvard. They wanted to make undergraduates take sides on every issue that concerned them; to learn what they wanted to learn, and demand of the Faculty that the "dead wood" among the teachers be cleared away. . . .
>
> So Lippman and MacGowen, the inner circle of the Socialist Club, deliberately planned to get control of every organization that would help them, or at least to be represented therein. . . . They set themselves enthusiastically to become accomplished dialecticians, indomitable arguers, to be able to talk, and talk well, on any subject that might be brought up. . . . [T]he Harvard Socialists turned their theories upon themselves, determined to work them out at Harvard University. . . .
>
> [W]ithin half a year, the active enrolled members of the Club amounted to fifty, with about twice as many more interested. . . .
>
> Many of the professors and instructors had become interested in the various undergraduate movements . . . the Socialist Club received the warm sympathy and support of the great William James, of Professor Adams, of Professor S. B. Johnson.[74]

The Harvard Socialist Club, like its campus successors in the Student League for Industrial Democracy in the 1920s, the American Student Union in the 1930s, and the SDS in the 1960s, took as one of its tasks, improving the conditions of Harvard cafeteria and cleaning workers. The radical group organized in 1908 also set a precedent followed by the others in later decades for campaigning on local off-campus issues, particularly with reference to housing conditions in Cambridge and Boston.

Writing in *The New Republic* in 1916, Randolph Bourne argued that intellectual and student radicalism had become too popular for their own good. "The real trouble with middle-class radicalism today is that it is too easy. It is becoming too popular. . . . Let the college man or girl . . . join the Intercollegiate Socialist Society or some similar institution, and discover how discouragingly respectable they are." He sounded like some contemporary older left critic of the New Left when he criticized these groups for being "full of the unfocussed and unthinking," and argued that they could most effectively serve the radical movement "by being fiercely and concentratedly intellectual. This is something these organizations have so far failed to do." Bourne went on to urge that "intellectual radicalism should not mean repeating stale dogmas of Marxism. . . . The young radical today is not asked to be a martyr, but he is asked to be a thinker, an intellectual leader." However, Bourne noted that many of the young socialists of his day dropped away when they failed to make contact with the working class. "The young radical soon learns to be ashamed of his intellectual bias, and after an ineffectual effort to squeeze himself into the mind of the workingman drifts away disillusioned from his timid collegiate radicals."[75]

Bourne indicated support for social reform and socialist causes that went considerably beyond the narrow circles of the dues-paying members of the ISS, much as support for the New Left during the late 1960s was more extensive than the two thousand five hundred to seven thousand members claimed by SDS in different years. Another indication of this pattern was suggested at the most conservative of Ivy League institutions, Princeton, by F. Scott Fitzgerald, in his description of life there before the United States entered World War I.

> In his last years at Princeton, Fitzgerald noted that the students around the small tables in the Nassau Inn "began questioning aloud the institutions that Amory and countless others before him had questioned so long in secret." They discussed sex and socialism, and the "social barriers as artificial distinctions made by the strong to bolster up their weak retainers and keep out the almost strong." In "a fury of righteousness" one hundred men resigned from their clubs.[76]

Between 1914 and American entry into the war, there was considerable antiwar activity involving both socialist and campus peace groups. A poll of eighty thousand students in May 1915 on "the question of introducing military drill" in colleges, found that sixty-three thousand voted against it.[77] Opposition to military training in the form of ROTC was, of course, to continue to be a major feature of student activism in later periods, viz., the mid-twenties, the 1930s, and most recently in the late 1960s.

The early twentieth century demand by many college students for relevance, for the opportunity to apply their values in social betterment, met its greatest fulfillment, however, not in radical or antiwar politics but in the participation in settlement work, in direct contact with the poor in the urban slums. Thousands of students and young graduates threw themselves into staffing the rapidly growing number of settlement houses. By 1911 there were 413 of them, three-quarters of which had been formed since the turn of the century. They involved twenty-five hundred residents and another ten thousand to fifteen thousand student volunteers.

> In America, settlements came as an exciting release to the feelings of purposelessness that had frustrated so many college graduates. . . . Settlements in this country were . . . protests by students against learning that was never put to use. . . .
>
> The settlement movement . . . offered students the chance to put the collegiate ideals to work in these cities, just then beginning to dominate national life, and spread their problems across the country. . . . To the early settlement leaders it seemed inevitable that students should predominate in the movement. . . . To Jane Addams it was plain that young people led the reform because they were the ones to feel most fully the lack in their own lives that came from being estranged from the active part of the nation. . . . Students would go into cities ultimately because only there could they save themselves from atrophy. It was their defense against the kind of deterioration into irrelevance that had so frightened their elders in the elite.[78]

Although the settlement house movement clearly involved many Progressives and liberals, it should be noted that some of the most prominent leaders of it, people like Jane Addams, Lilian Wald, and Mary Simkhovitch, were socialist supporters. The outlook of the movement struck an English student visitor in 1908–09 as involving the assumption that "there is no such word as 'cannot' in the lexicon of youth," and that his "favorite motto is 'Do it right now.' Acting on these principles, he is dealing with the vast social problems that beset him through the agency of the various Settlements. . . ."[79]

An analysis of the backgrounds of those active in settlement work points up the similarities among young people who choose the path of reform and transformation of the situation of the poor in different epochs.

> Most settlement workers came from families that were moderately well-to-do. The fact that they were able to enter settlement work at all, especially during the early years, was often an indication that they did not have to earn a living.
>
> . . . Whatever their occupation, many of the parents were actively involved in reform or concerned with aiding the poor. . . . There were some who entered a settlement against their parents' judgment, but the majority inherited a tradition of service. . . . In some cases they felt they were rebelling against their parents, but more often they were translating an inherited impulse to fit a new situation and a new generation.[80]

Campus criticism threw up another wave of protest against pre–World War I American society, the Young Intellectuals. The very term was used to mean a critic of society. As Henry May points out its "origins were partly socialist; the intellectual to the Marxists was the bourgeois who repudiated his class."[81] The groups who so identified themselves came from two streams, midwesterners, and graduates of Ivy League colleges, particularly Harvard, Yale and Princeton. Like those involved in the ISS and settlement houses, "most of these young radicals came from secure upper-middle class families, and for this reason were eager to like and admire the poor, especially, the urban poor, especially the recent immigrants."[82] They flocked to New York, and took up their cause, particularly that of the Jews, who lived in abysmal crowded slums in the midst of extreme wealth.

> The Young Intellectuals . . . turned the conventional hierarchy upside down. Anglo-Saxons, repressed and bigoted, were at the

> bottom of the scale; at the top were the Italians, the Slavs, and above all, the Eastern European Jews of the East Side. Writers of Puritan ancestry like Hutchins Hapgood, earnest radicals like Ernest Poole, who was studying Yiddish, found an endless satisfaction in the quarter's crowded streets. . . .[83]

The Young Intellectuals, like many of the student socialists from whose ranks they frequently came, found the electoral activities of the growing American Socialist Party prosaic and boring. Like their compeers in the future, they were attracted to militant tactics, including violence.

> Where the left wing of American socialism merged with the I.W.W., the Young Intellectuals found a . . . focus for their loyalty. Syndicalism attracted them because of its appeal for direct action and also its European intellectual prestige. . . . Anarchism, the noblest of radical dreams, attracted many of the Young Intellectuals. . . . The anarchist movement, with its drama of bombs and spies, outrage and espionage and persecution, had furnished subjects for Dostoevsky, Henry James and Joseph Conrad.
>
> . . . The anarchism of Emma Goldman and Alexander Berkman appealed deeply to the Young Intellectuals. For one thing, Russia, and particularly Russian radicalism, had great prestige. Furthermore, the anarchist leaders hated the halfway measures and compromise goals of current progressivism or majority socialism. Their morality, like their courage, was absolute. They attacked bourgeois culture, marriage and religion as well as government. In the face of public hatred, they refused to give up their belief in the propaganda of the deed. Destruction must be justified by the establishment of a new reign of individualism and brotherhood, mystically combined.
>
> . . . [Another] revolutionary cause which greatly interested the Young Intellectuals . . . [was] the revolt in sexual morality. . . . Neither socialism nor feminism necessarily implied sexual radicalism. . . . Yet the left wing of feminism and revolutionary socialism could come together. . . .[84]

The élan of the various student-based movements, both political and settlement house, was destroyed by the war. Their adherents divided sharply as to whether to support or oppose America's entry, a conflict which continued even after the declaration of war. With minor, though distinguished exceptions, the campus threw itself wholeheartedly into "making the world safe for democracy," and had little time left for other causes.

Any evaluation of the campus-based movements which emerged after 1900 must first recognize that they did not constitute an independent youth or student revolt against the older generation, whether on campus or off. These were also the years of a growing Progressive and Socialist movement which culminated in the large third party votes received in 1912 by Theodore Roosevelt (27 percent) on the Progressive party ticket, and by Eugene V. Debs (6 percent) running as a Socialist. The Socialist Party received over 900,000 votes and had close to 125,000 members in that year. Both the Intercollegiate Socialist Society and the settlement house movement were campus expressions of the same tendencies which inspired mass support for reform and radicalism in the population as a whole. The rapid growth of the industrial cities with their teeming immigrant slums, their corruption and their high crime rate, shocked the sentiments of many middle-class Americans, including a large proportion of their children away in college.

The college faculties, as Francis and Bourne reported, undoubtedly contained many sympathetic to these efforts for social change. The settlement houses "were enthusiastically supported by most of . . . [the] idealist professors."[85] There are no reliable data concerning the politics of college faculty as a group before World War I. One study which dealt with faculty attitudes toward religion did, however, suggest that they were more liberally or radically disposed than has generally been assumed. James Leuba, a psychologist, studied the religious beliefs of randomly selected samples of the membership of the sociological, psychological, and historical societies, and of scientists listed in *American Men of Science* in 1913–14. He reported that the majority in each group did not believe in God or immortality. Although religious and political beliefs are clearly separate, a variety of studies, including some of faculty opinions in the last two decades, indicate a high correlation between religious and political outlooks. Irreligious people are much more likely to have liberal and left-wing views than believers.

There are no comparable data for the nonacademic portion of the population before World War I. The religious census data, however, report that 55 percent of all persons fourteen years of age or older were actual *members* of religious denominations during this period. Leuba was able to compare academic and nonacademic members of the American Sociological Society, and found that the academics were more likely to disdain religion. Perhaps more significant was his finding that the more distinguished professors were much more irreligious than their less eminent colleagues.[86] This result coincides with much more recent survey studies of academic politics which also suggest that academic prestige is associated with more liberal-left views.[87] Seemingly, before 1914, sizable groups of American academics, particularly the more scholarly and creative among them, located disproportionately at the more distinguished schools, were out of step with conventional social opinion. Then as now, therefore, the children of the elite attending such institutions were involved in an intellectual milieu in which a liberal outlook held sway. Those students who sought to act out the implications of such orientations in political clubs like the ISS, or through participation in settlement houses, were not in revolt. Rather, as Randolph Bourne argued, they were probably conforming to the dominant values in the liberal arts in the leading schools.

Leuba collected comparable data on the religious beliefs of students which unfortunately are not as representative of larger populations as his surveys of different groups of scientists and social scientists. He secured 927 questionnaires from "all the students of a number of classes belonging to nontechnical [liberal arts] departments of nine colleges of high rank, and [from] two classes [78 answers] of a normal school." He found that 56 percent of the men and 82 percent of the women in this nonrepresentative sample believed in "a personal God." Less than 10 percent rejected belief in any concept of God. Leuba concluded from these and other data that "considered all together, my data would indicate that from 40 to 50 percent of the young men leaving college entertain an idea of God incompatible with the acceptance of the Christian religion, even as interpreted by the liberal clergy." The rate of unbelief "increases considerably from the freshman to the senior year in college." These findings are clearly less significant than those concerning the faculty, but they do lend weight to the assumption that a substantial minority of American students may have been receptive to radical or progressive ideas before World War I.[88]

The wave of activism and protest among the pre–World War I young was not blamed solely or primarily on the failings of the university, or the teaching of the faculty. Then, as during the 1920s and 1960s, spokesmen for the conventions located the decline in the morality of youth on societal changes which had undermined parental authority. Cornelia Comer bemoaned the effect of the media and the decline of religion and family discipline, which resulted in a *culte de moi* among the affluent young.

> How can anything avail to refine children whose taste in humor is formed by the colored supplements of the Sunday paper, as their taste in entertainment is shaped by the continuous vaudeville and the motion-picture shows? . . . While most vaudeville performances have one or two numbers that justify the proprietors' claim of harmless, wholesome amusement, the bulk of the programme is almost inevitably drivel, common, stupid, or inane. . . . "I don't approve," your fathers and mothers say anxiously, "but I hate to keep Tom and Mary at home when all the other children are allowed to go." . . . In the wrack of beliefs, your parents managed to retain their ingrained principles of conduct. Not knowing what to teach you, they taught you nothing wholeheartedly. . . . If you are agnostic-and-water, if you find nothing in the universe more stable than your own wills—what wonder?
>
> . . . [As a result] when these young people adopted a philosophy, it was naive and inadequate. They talked of themselves as "socialists."[89]

Two months later, the Columbia junior Randolph Bourne wrote a reply to this attack on the soft character of the badly brought up young radicals. In it, he agreed that home discipline had broken down, but he drew a different conclusion. The youth of his generation could see more clearly precisely because they were freer than previous ones from allegiance to outmoded beliefs. "Having brought themselves up they judge utility by their own standards." He also credited their exposure to the output of the mass media for broadening their horizons. "In an age of newspapers, free libraries, and cheap magazines, we necessarily get a broader horizon than the passing generation had. We see what is going on in the world, and we get the clash of different points of view, to an extent which was impossible to our fathers." And as a result of not having been indoctrinated by an older generation which was certain of its values, Bourne argued that his generation has "retained from childhood the propensity to see through things, and to tell the truth with startling frankness."[90]

5

Historical Background: The Twenties Through the Fifties

If the campus had been a recurrent source of indiscipline, illegal pranks, and unrest, there is no real evidence that any major segment of the student population was alienated from society and polity in the first century and a half of American national existence. But a major generation-unit had its watershed in the 1920s, which Henry May has described as the "decade when the fragmentation first became deep and obvious . . . a period in which common values and common beliefs were replaced by separate and conflicting values."[1] Walter Lippmann referred to the "vast dissolution of ancient habits" in the 1920s.[2] It is not surprising that old habits were dissolving. All of the changes which had been gathering in America, and which are usually described under chapter headings such as "technology," "urbanization," and "mobility," seemed to be coming to a visible head in the 1920s. The 1920 census was the first in which the urban population exceeded the rural population. In the thirty-year generation span since 1890, the number of Americans living in cities of half a million or more had tripled from four to twelve million, while the total population had not doubled. The number of people engaged in manufacturing had doubled. There were millions of people in new jobs, places and proximities.

Education was also spreading out among the American population. The limitation of college training to a small elite was coming to an end. The number of college-age youths attending college shot up from 4 percent at the turn of the century to 12 percent by the end of the 1920s. At the same time, America was beginning to turn the corner of its nineteenth century innocence and euphoria. Basic premises were being laid open to question by the general jarring loose of old associations, marked by the dramatic trauma of World War I.

This state of dissolution lent itself to a revival of the kinds of political protest which had characterized the prewar radical movement of students and young intellectuals. A Marxist analyst, Martin J. Sklar, has recently pointed to the ways in which the strains of the 1920s produced a visible and significant group of radicals among the latter.

> [T]he young intellectuals were conscious of themselves as a distinct group arrayed against the bourgeoisie, its ideology, its values, and its society, . . . Abstractly at first, and increasingly in more specific political terminology, the young intellectuals identified with the industrial proletariat and with the dispossessed generally. They presented themselves as partisan, in varying degrees to socialism. . . . The young intellectuals' outlook assumed that working men and women, and especially the young among them, given the opportunity, would recognize and assert the same objectives as their own, a fuller, richer, deeper personal and social life where work might increasingly become a self-expressive activity. . . .[3]

The moral breakdown also lent itself to another kind of disaffection, which often expressed itself in political terms but was really of a quite different quality. It involved not so much an optimistic passion for social betterment as a disillusioned rejection of the total set of classical rational assumptions on which American and Western society had rested. An identifiable generation-unit of youth began to share this disaffection with a growing class of writers and intellectuals, much the same phenomenon as was to recur in the 1960s.

Similarly to the 1960s, the dominant intellectual spokesmen of anticapitalist criticism came from the children of the affluent whose main concerns were not economic, but cultural and moral. They condemned the class from which they sprang for "dullness, stupidity, aggressiveness in commerce, conformity to the remnants of traditional morality, and a moral opportunism, linked with certain blind convictions about the economic status quo." Many of the students and young intellectuals seized on the Freudian analysis of the sources of moral conformity. Their favorite term to characterize the society was *repression,* predating the influence of Marcuse by four decades.

> For the young men and women of the period the word served as a convenient label for all their grievances against society. It was their feeling that the absurd, exorbitant moral demands which society had made upon its victims had culminated in a national neurosis. Repression became the American illness. With little or no thought of personal responsibility . . . they decided that any force was evil which stood in the way of a full, wholesome, primitive expression of natural impulses. . . .
>
> The idea of repression was soon enough applied . . . to American history and sociology. If repression was a national illness, then all social and moral forces which had led to the neurosis of an entire people must have had this object, to repress the natural life of a people, to shut off the natural satisfaction of healthy desires as the price paid for achieving economic and industrial success. . . .
>
> The proper reaction . . . was to defy [the Puritanical social] . . . code, to act in deliberate scorn of it, and to experiment as much as possible with sexual matters prohibited by it. In some cases this defiance of Puritan morality acquired the characteristics of a primitivism, an attempt to point out the great happiness of people [particularly lower-class Negroes] who were not brought up in terror of sex and who therefore lived a normal, happy, casual life.[4]

The campus-based radical movement was initially in bad shape to take advantage of the disillusionment which characterized some students and many intellectuals. Wartime repression and postwar anti-Bolshevik hysteria had undercut the civil liberties of radicals on and off campus. Socialists and Wobblies were jailed, and professorial opponents of the war were fired. The radical movement first split over the issue of support or opposition to the war. It divided again concerning its reaction to the Russian Revolution and over the efforts to create a Communist party within the United States. Conservatives, on the other hand, moved increasingly towards justifying a repressive stand to prevent the revolutionary wave from reaching American shores. Many in the business and conservative communities argued publicly that college faculties were honeycombed with Communists and Socialists. In February 1919, Edward L. Doheny, an oil millionaire, announced that a "majority of college professors in the United States are teaching socialism and Bolshevism. . . ."[5] In 1921, Vice-President Calvin Coolidge wrote a series of articles on "Enemies of the Republic" in *The Delineator*. His first one dealt with the activities of "Reds" in colleges. The breakdown in the political order which disturbed him was a consequence in part of the fact that "college faculties rebel at the authority of presidents and trustees."[6] And in an introduction to Coolidge's articles, the editor of *The Delineator* proclaimed: "Better a sane hewer of wood or drawer of water in one's family than a University graduate who has nothing more than antagonism to contribute to the service of society."[7] Harry Haldeman, the founder of the Better America Federation of California, commented that his organization was "having students of radical tendencies watched."[8] A study conducted by the ISS of "Freedom of Discussion in American Colleges," reported in 1920 that "an increasing number of schools were (1) prohibiting outside affiliations for political groups, (2) placing increasing restrictions on speakers, and (3) censoring the faculty's right to express liberal opinions."[9] Partly as a reaction to such pressures, the ISS changed its name to the League for Industrial Democracy (LID).

Various campus clubs dropped the name "Socialist Club" in favor of varying titles such as "Social Science Club," "Social Problems Club," "Politics Club" and assorted others.

Such pressures seemingly did not reduce the scope of campus radicalism, since the LID found large audiences for the speakers it toured across the nation. Right-wing attacks seemingly stimulated the more liberal minority to react sharply to the severe postwar repression, to industrial ills, and to militarism.

Antiwar, progressive, and socialist clubs, which invited controversial speakers to the campus, sprang up around the country. As Earnest notes, the issues of free speech occasioned serious controversies in many colleges. "Students demanded the right to hear all sides of every question; conservative alumni, trustees, and citizens objected to colleges becoming a forum for radical views." The Handlins report the spread of "underground student newspapers – *Gadfly* at Harvard, *Critic* at Oberlin, *Proletarian* at Wisconsin, *Saturday Evening Pest* at Yale, and *Tempest* at Michigan – [which] demanded not only the right to ask critical questions but also the right to give the answers."[10]

The renewed wave of meetings, demonstrations, and discussions of campus radicalism led some older intellectuals to once again perceive socialism as the prevailing undergraduate mood. Writing in May 1922, George Santayana reacted strongly to its presence:

> [The] sophomores . . . have discovered the necessity of socialism . . . [They] all proclaim their disgust with the present state of things in America, they denounce the Constitution of the United States, the churches, the Government, the colleges, the press, the theaters, and above all they denounce the spirit that vivifies and unifies all these things, the spirit of Business. Here is a disaffection breaking out in which seemed the most unanimous, the most satisfied of nations; here are Americans impatient with America. . . .
>
> I have made a severe effort to discover, as well as I may from a distance, what these rebels want. I see what they are *against* – they are against everything–but what are they *for?* I have not

> been able to discover it. This may be due to my lack of understanding, or to their incapacity to express themselves clearly, for their style is something appalling. But perhaps their scandalous failure in expression, when expression is what they yearn for and demand at all costs, may be a symptom of something deeper: of a radical mistake they have made in the direction of their efforts and aspirations. They think they need more freedom, more room, a chance to be more spontaneous: I suspect that they have had too much freedom, too much empty space, too much practice in being spontaneous when there was nothing in them to bubble out.[11]

Santayana was not alone in voicing complaints about the orientations of the students of the twenties in terms which resemble the agitated outcries of faculty in the sixties. Thus an Oberlin sociology professor argued in 1922: "Youth is dogmatic. . . . The enthusiasm of youth may appropriate socialism or free thinking instead of the traditional faith, but it is likely to have the zeal of religion, and call bigotry, liberalism."[12] C. Hartley Grattan, a well-known professor of English, complained bitterly in 1925 that students judged literature on political rather than aesthetic grounds.

> The students . . . tend to applaud contemporary writers because they are rebels, not because they are artists. . . . And consequently students tend to neglect really fine writers whose rebelliousness is not so apparent, or but a minor part of their work. . . . Then, too, sympathy for a particular social attitude leads to the acceptance of bad but congenial writers, and the rejection of good but incongenial ones. . . .
>
> What the college student needs to guard against more than anything else is the tendency, in reaction to an even greater stupidity, to accept all that is new as good, and all that chimes in with his social attitude as best.[13]

Some indication of the renunciatory concepts advanced by the more radical students may be found in the effort of the editor of *The New Student*, Douglas Haskell, to present the policy of his paper. *The New Student* was the predominant expression of student activism in the 1920s. It was published regularly as a national paper and magazine, once every fortnight through the decade, supported by subscriptions around the country. In many ways, Haskell presented an approach to society and knowledge which was close to that which was to disturb Paul Goodman about his students at the end of the 1960s.

> We do not believe it is any longer possible for the American college to give an education to its students but we still believe it is possible for students to get an education for themselves in American colleges. . . .
>
> With all respect to the older generation, some of us become more and more certain that they cannot feel the chaos as we do. . . . Spiritually, this is an age of ruin – of nausea. We suspect that many of our elders retain the nineteenth century belief in science and knowledge. We cannot share it. We need a faith. . . . At least we know what must go.
>
> Mechanization must go.
>
> A certain scholarly, scientific attitude must go. The values for which we are searching do not seem susceptible of proof, of capture by the "scientific spirit." The faith, the assumptions on which science rests are lacking, hence there are no "social sciences." Moreover we need to look ahead; and creative thought is different in kind from mere knowlege. . . .
>
> We cannot even accept the leadership of the younger [faculty] men. The forces of decay are so strong that we cannot trust a cocksure psychology or a "radical" sociology any more than we could the old hand-dried economics. . . . [although] we still find inspiring friends among our teachers, little as most of these have to give us. . . .
>
> We suspect that there are many individual students who do not care to join organized groups, who nevertheless have ideas better than do many leaders of organizations. Often the sanest imagination belongs to the pure in heart who are not even conscious of any revolutionary tendency. These people should be kept in touch with one another.
>
> Through *The New Student* we are trying to arrange an interchange of ideas between them. . . .[14]

The largest single protest group was probably the Student Christian Movement (SCM) which urged "the correction of such social matters as child labor, industrial strife, poverty, and above all war." W. H. Cowley estimates that the SCM enlisted about 5 percent of the undergraduate population, and that in sum, "during the twenties approximately one student in ten joined a group or groups devoted to examining broad societal problems. . . ."[15] A statistical datum pertaining to the strength of moderate radicalism or progressivism may be found in the results of a presidential straw vote conducted in 120 colleges and universities in 1924 which reported that 14.5 percent of the 51,457 students who completed ballots supported Robert LaFollette, the third party candidate of the Progressive and Socialist parties. This may seem like a large left-wing bloc, but LaFollette secured 16.6 percent of the national vote. The percentages received by the three presidential candidates in this campus poll corresponded closely to that which they secured among the general electorate. Thus Coolidge captured 58.6 percent in the straw vote and 54 percent among electors, while Davis, the Democratic candidate, had 26.9 percent on campus, and 28.8 percent in the nation as a whole.[16] These results would suggest that the campus population strongly resembled the adult world in its politics, that in the conservative Republican twenties, students were also predominantly conservative Republicans. Although this empirical generalization is undoubtedly true, it is important to note that the undergraduate population of this period comprised about 10 percent of the age cohort, as contrasted with close to 45 percent today. This meant that the students were largely from families whose conservative Republican propensities were far higher than that of the general electorate. Hence it is likely that the campus support for LaFollette represented a shift to the left among students as compared with their family politics. Some slight evidence for this thesis may be found in the report of the campus poll which indicates that in a number of colleges, Coolidge's support was lower among seniors than among freshmen, while LaFollette's increased.

A year later, a leading newspaper, the New York *World,* editorialized concerning the "revolt which is going on in colleges and universities all over the country" in terms which indicate that a significant minority of students were involved in various activities. The *World* credited *The New Student* with a major role.

> Revolt against what? That is a little hard to say. In one college there is a revolt against stupid courses, in another against abridgement of free speech, in another against the cheap commercialization of the endowment drives, in another against official interpretations of American history. Always there are the same symptoms: the outlaw student paper, with its devastating satire and cartoons; the speeches, the meetings, the reprisals by the faculty, the mutterings of discontent in the student body. The revolt has been growing for two or three years now; in a loose sort of way it is organized, for it has a magazine, *The New Student,* which circulates widely, and is given over to recording its spicy doings. It has reached such proportions that it cannot be disregarded. . . .[17]

Organized campus protest in the mid-twenties revolved around the issues of peace and the Sacco-Vanzetti case. The disillusionment with the last war brought considerable support for the movement to reduce the scope of the Reserve Officers Training Corps (ROTC) on various campuses. "In 1925, a tremendous agitation began against compulsory military training. . . ."[18] The pages of *The New Student* reported incident after incident on campuses throughout the nation of demonstrations against compulsory military training.

The most important single issue arousing leftist sentiment among intellectuals and students in the mid-1920s, however, was the Sacco-Vanzetti case. The conviction of these two immigrant anarchists for murder in 1921 resulted in a crescendo of protest among liberals and leftists around the world. Gradually, a large proportion among those so inclined became convinced that the majesty of the American juridical and police system had been deliberately mobilized to execute two innocent men. The conflict between the protesters in the American intellectual world and the powers enlarged the cleavage between the two to the point where each was ready to believe the worst about the other.

> Thus when writers and professors begin to voice . . . doubts, it seemed to many conservatives only another proof of dangerous radicalism among the intellectuals. And the writers and the professors, bringing out fact after fact which showed the prejudice and perjury involved in the conviction, came increasingly to feel that the leaders of business and government were not interested in evidence but only in teaching the radicals the brutal lesson that there was no room for dissent in America.[19]

Since the trial took place in Boston, Harvard was much involved in the protest on both faculty and student level. President A. Lawrence Lowell chaired a three man committee appointed by Governor Fuller, which concluded that the two anarchists were guilty. "The case . . . emphasized the dichotomy between the professors and the powers that ruled the academic community. . . . The socially and politically aware members of the academic community were imbued with a deep distrust and hostility to the conservative elements . . . in the church, business, and government. . . . Many a student who knew nothing about the trial of Socrates became deeply stirred over that of Sacco and Vanzetti. . . . [T]housands of them came to believe it important to know more about shoemakers and fishpeddlers."[20]

Much of the activity against ROTC, the execution of Sacco and Vanzetti, American military intervention in the Caribbean, and a myriad of other issues reported during the 1920s in *The New Student,* seemingly involved white students in the more prominent universities and colleges. Schools like Harvard, Dartmouth, Yale, Wisconsin, California, appear frequently. In this respect also there has been seeming consistency in the sources of collegiate activism. Another group which was to figure prominently in the activism of the late 1960s also entered the campus unrest scene during this decade, the Negro students.

As during the 1960s, campus protest by black students cannot be viewed primarily as an outgrowth of their situation in the university. The decade of the twenties was also marked by racial violence, most of it initiated by whites; but Negroes fought back, killing whites in Chicago and other cities, using guns in the black belt in the South. The concept of the "New Negro" who would stand up and demand his rights emerged. Black nationalism which called on the Negro to "reject whiteness, to see the beauty of his own skin" became a major tendency.[21] Marcus Garvey, who totally rejected white culture, became the head of the largest Negro political organization that had yet appeared, the Universal Negro Improvement Association, one which was much bigger than any of the current black power groups. He proposed that Negroes leave the corrupt white civilization and go to their homeland in Africa.[22] Negro writers gave voice to the new militancy in novels, plays, poetry, and belligerent anti-white articles. It is not surprising, therefore, that Negro students also exhibited some of the aggressiveness. Contemporary description of Negro unrest in the twenties points up the relationship between economic security and the potential for campus disturbances.

> The recurrence of disorders ranging from summary expulsions of individual students to wholesale student strikes in Negro colleges will tell even the most casual observer that something is radically wrong. . . . One thing is certain: The Negro student is not what he used to be.
>
> . . . [S]tudent strikes have come to be regarded as an unavoidable and periodic liability of the white college. Not so the Negro college. . . . Economically bound by almost impregnable fetters, the Negro student had no time for anything but the acquisition of a meager education. . . . [H]e was generally so poor that what leisure time was his had to be spent working at odd hours. . . . Then came the War. With it came a tremendous betterment of the economic conditions in the southern Negro home. More students came to college. Fewer found it necessary to work their way through school. The radio, the newspaper, the moving picture, the spread of liberal ideas, and the *élan vital* of the Negro Renaissance developing into the concept of the "New

> Negro," all conspired to send to the threshold of the Negro college a new type of student, wholly unprecedented.
>
> There were strikes at Fisk, at Hampton Institute, [three] at Howard . . . at Kittrell, at St. Augustine, and at Knoxville College. There have been revolts almost equivalent to strikes in nearly every Negro college in the South. These were obviated in many instances only by wholesale expulsion of large parts of the student body.[23]

A recent study of the 1927 Hampton Institute strike basically agrees with the earlier account. Edward Graham notes that by the winter of 1927, "Student strikes had already reached epidemic proportions at Fisk, Shaw, Howard, Lincoln (in Missouri), Florida Agricultural and Industrial Institute and elsewhere." The Hampton strike, which demanded a better faculty and a relaxation of parietal rules, was broken and many students were expelled. Those most deeply involved serving on the Protest Committee were drawn heavily from among the superior students in intellectual and leadership-ability terms. Success at other schools and in subsequent careers indicated that those who had led the strike were "probably one of the most talented groups ever to leave a college or university campus."[24]

On the campus the rejection of the prewar past was most widely expressed through new forms of personal behavior: short skirts, freer relations with those of the opposite sex, violations of the law banning alcoholic beverages. Kinsey has documented one aspect of the break in statistical terms in his report that a big jump in the proportion of females with premarital sexual experiences occurred in the 1920s.[25] Seemingly, the proportion did not increase again, at least among college students, until the 1960s. Earnest, in his history of college life, concludes that this period witnessed a general break with the conventional verities, even among the large apolitical and unintellectual majority.

> Thus without intellectualizing it, a host of boys and girls in the early 1920s instinctively knew that the platitudes about honesty, democracy, chastity and religion did not represent the truth

about American life. They knew that kikes and wops and niggers were outside the pale – in fact, many of the college students agreed that they should be. . . . With the coming of prohibition they knew of the liquor in country-club locker rooms or in the family cellar. . . . What the defenders of the established order overlooked was that the youth has an instinctive hatred of bunk.[26]

The result was a revolution in manners and morals. This was evidenced by new dress styles, the open flaunting of sex and liquor, and the strong objections voiced to conventional religion. But the avant-garde elements among intellectuals and students not only rejected the traditional mores; they also expressed their renunciatory tendency through general opposition to rational political society – not just the pathology but its very concept. This is sometimes difficult to perceive, because the range of expression was so broad. There was nihilism, sheer bohemianism, Dadaism, whose motto was: "I do not wish to know whether there have been men before me."

A . . . revulsion against civilization broke out . . . in the black humor of the Dadaist movement. . . . Dadaists gave lectures from within diving helmets to the sound of clanging bells and held exhibits in public urinals. Their assaults on a victim-public were exactly like the "happenings" reinvented here in the mid-sixties. . . . Dadaism took its slogan "destruction is also creation" from Bakunin, and its poetics from Rimbaud.[27]

In reviewing campus culture during this period, Oscar and Mary Handlin conclude that rebellion "became a conventional student posture." They also describe a dominant mood reflecting a radical rejection of the past in terms both of ideology and personal behavior.

Intellectually, it took the form of a call for liberation "from the entanglement of mere traditional authority and provincial prejudice" and for the discard of the millstones of "dead formalism in religion, and narrow thinking in social relations." The de-

> mands were peremptory: "Saccharine Sunday-school religion, blatant Fourth-of-July patriotism, inherited class bias – all must fall." A pronounced shift in patterns of personal behavior expressed the same impatience with institutional restraints. The lost generation – self-proclaimed – flaunted its interest in sex and whiskey in defiance of the Puritans and of the prohibition laws and provided a compelling model for college youth.[28]

But though their elders who had gone through the war often referred to themselves as the "lost generation," the students of the twenties went far beyond them in rejecting tradition. For the first time in America, the concept of the generation gap, of the sharp difference in values between the young, particularly the college students and their elders, appeared as a general notion. And interestingly, then as during the late 1960s, age thirty was taken as the dividing point.

> The greatest gulf, however, was that between generations. Parents, and faculty members over thirty, found the younger generation incomprehensible, while youth regarded their elders as either hopelessly incompetent or as pious hypocrites. Probably never in American history had two generations found it harder to communicate. One of the characteristic lacunae in the work of F. Scott Fitzgerald is the absence of characters over thirty. . . . In an introduction to a collection of Fitzgerald's short stories, Malcolm Cowley explains this gulf on the ground that "the elders were discredited in their [the younger generation's] eyes by the war, prohibition, by the Red scare of 1919–1920, and by the scandals like that of Teapot Dome."[29]

Recognition that an important part of the college population had rejected the traditional values of the society resulted, in each affected period, in an analytical literature which tried to specify what went wrong. "Why is the Younger Generation so different?" One such effort by a journalist resembles both earlier and later writings in stressing social changes which reduced the "sense of parental responsibility." Urbanization, John Gavit argued, brought about a sharp reduction in time spent by parents with children, a reduction in "the sense of responsibility to neighborhood public opinion and standards," and a greater involvement in formal pleasure-seeking activities by the parents. In addition, many of the older generation who advocated "law and order" and condemned sexual immorality and radicalism were engaged during the decade in "openly flouting the Constitution and the law in the matter of Prohibition." And Gavit concluded:

> People, young and old, whose home experience has given them no standards, or no self-control with which to enforce such as they have, always go to pieces when superimposed restraints are lifted. . . . There is no absurdity more futile than that of saying to a young person: "Do not follow my example; do what I *say*." . . .
>
> Whose fault is it if the young people are coming to college with the most casual ideas of purpose and responsibility? The lamentable characteristic of the typical college student is not that he has "radical" convictions, but rather that he has so poor an outfit of convictions on any subject.[30]

Writing at the end of the twenties, Christian Gauss, dean of the college at Princeton, pointed to the general pattern of protest "against restraints – against all rules and regulations," and the widespread demand that "the colleges be turned over to the students and be run by undergraduate committees." He argued that since such behavior could be found around the country on highly different campuses, the explanation could not be "merely collegiate," that the student reactions must be "the reflections of some underlying condition in the country at large."[31] And he found the answer in the rapid rate of social change which produced what a writer in 1970 would call "future shock."[32] The youth of the twenties were faced with a long list of "inventions and conceptions which began to affect our way of life after 1900."

> We can repeat only a few of them here – such as the long-distance telephone, wireless, jazz, bobbed hair, brain storm, the bootlegger, the hijacker, the airplane, the airship, antitoxins, the

> flapper, camouflage, propaganda, the automobile. . . . The most popular amusement to-day is the cinema; it, too, has had its effect. The boy or girl who comes to the college, and who has been attending the movies for the past six or eight years, has seen far more life than the ordinary undergraduate of 1895 ever dreamed of. . . .
>
> We have changed our world from top to bottom, and where things have changed so rapidly, society is usually in for a long and often painful process of adjustment.[33]

Much of the efforts by those concerned with higher education, both academics and students, to explain campus discontent in the twenties, however, like those of the sixties and early seventies, did not focus on extramural social tensions and technological changes, but rather placed the blame on the presumed failings of the educational system, itself, to do a good job of teaching and relating to undergraduates.

A committee of Dartmouth seniors submitted a report to the president of the college in 1924 informing him of needed changes. They objected strongly to "the impersonal relationship between teacher and student, the present classroom, lecture-hall, and final examination system of education." They proposed to replace classroom activities by freeing the students to learn through independent reading in all subjects, such as the social sciences and humanities, in which there are a variety of points of view. The professor's role should be to discuss the books after the students have read them, not to lecture at the students or to impose an overly integrated point of view.[34]

Attacks on teaching methods and the lack of close relations between faculty and students tended, then as in more recent years, to be linked to the growth of universities. Thus *The Daily Nebraskan* complained that "the University has grown immensely" and "classes are now so cumbersome . . . that personal contact is impossible."[35] The editors of *The Vagabond* of Indiana University noted with dismay: "In all our institutions of higher learning there is a tendency toward Gigantism, the worship of Bigness, which regards the success of the school as proportionate to its enrollment, the acreage of the campus . . . and number of men on the faculty."[36] A Wisconsin professor eloquently portrayed the grievous lot of the undergraduate in the large state university of 1920, in terms which sound like Mario Savio talking of Berkeley in 1964.

> The student is admitted by thousands, registered by a vast clerical machine, assigned to courses, divided into sections, lectured to, quizzed, tested, examined; he is warned by his instructor, warned through his parents; . . . he is limited in the number of his semester hours, limited in his elections, limited in his "student activities," limited in his social life; he is recorded, card-indexed, filed, questionnaired, statisticized, and his documentation is kept in a safe.[37]

The concern for better teaching and more personal contact between faculty and students was not limited to criticism about the size of the universities or classes. The discussion begun in the latter decades of the nineteenth century about the effect of increased emphasis on research on teaching filled many pages in the 1920s. Essentially the specific arguments and proposed solutions were much the same as those advanced earlier and which continue to be proposed today. Thus Frank Spaulding argued that "great teachers" have almost totally disappeared because in "appointments and promotions the primary question is not how successful the man is as a teacher, but what has he done in research in his subject, what has he published?"[38] In his 1925 presidential address to the Modern Languages Association, William Neilson complained that graduate education is planned "for the production of scholars, hardly at all for the training of teachers."[39] Writing in 1928, Addison Hibbard of the University of North Carolina reported that "probably at no time since the beginning of higher education in America has the criticism of our colleges and universities been so general and so bitter as it is today." This was largely because of the lack of interest in teaching, which he blamed not only on the greater rewards for research but on the considerable growth in rewards in terms of publicity and outside income: "Extracurricular service—popular lectures given by faculty members, field research, help of one kind or another to outside organizations."

> Professors are great makers of textbooks in or out of their field—and students in their classes keep on buying them. Teachers of science serve the State and private corporations in countless ways: the psychologist and penologist are advisors to State departments; sanitary and civil engineers give advice to one commission or another; the geologist and forester advise on conservation and mineral deposits; public health measures take the time of the university medical staff; the United States government now and then calls for a man to serve in one capacity or another; this corporation or that asks for chemical analyses of some of its by-products; State legislatures ask that surveys be made; . . . [P]rofessors gain a reputation in a field and are called upon for commercial lecturing; magazines, newspapers, publishing houses urge men to write of their specialities.[40]

The president of Hibbard's university, Harry W. Chase, who had earlier presided over two other universities, argued persuasively in 1924 in terms that had been used a generation before him, and which were to be used half a century later, that the emergence of a national research-oriented professorate had created a "new" problem of loyalty for the university.

> [I]t seems to me that individual faculty members today are less deeply rooted in the soil of the institution they serve, less complete in the identification of their interests with its development, less concerned about it as an institution, than were the men who came into university faculties a generation ago. . . . [W]e have lost something of the deep sense of personal attachment of an earlier day. And this loss seems to me to constitute an important problem for those who are concerned about the most effective functioning of universities.[41]

The solution to the problem of the "truant professors" was to enhance the status of teaching as such, in particular by creating new highly paid "superprofessorships," not for research competence but for men proven "preeminent *as a teacher.*" The young Robert Hutchins in his inaugural address as president of the University of Chicago in 1929 addressed himself to the same dilemma, how to get first-rate teachers who stuck to the classroom. He, too, advocated higher salaries. He also proposed, however, that the graduate departments of his university undertake "to devise the best methods for preparing men for teaching." He intended to place "a new responsibility upon the departments, that of developing ideas in college education."[42]

The most popular explanation for inadequate teaching, for faculty involvement in research and consulting activities, and for inadequate resources, among radicals of the 1920s, both students and others, was the control of the university by reactionary trustees, almost all of whom were big businessmen, who could determine the internal decisions through the absolute campus power of their appointee, the president. This thesis was presented in elaborate detail, campus by campus, by Upton Sinclair, in his book *The Goose-Step,* widely circulated among undergraduates of the decade. Yet some radical intellectuals closely acquainted with the workings of the university tried to challenge this simplistic approach, much as was to occur with respect to the revival of such interpretations in the 1960s. The *Freeman* magazine, then one of the most important liberal-radical organs, ran a series of articles on problems of higher education during 1922–23, directed in part to clarifying these issues. In discussing the role of the president, Somnia Vana argued that "nothing could be further from the truth," than the image of the all-powerful role of the president who could prevent heresy and intimidate the faculty. A new president "finds a mesh of academic rights, titles, and privileges before him. . . . His chief business is to raise money by collecting it from those who have it." He is expected to remain outside of academic issues, particularly if they affect policies within departments. Any interference by him with "departments is usually hotly resented." In terms which closely resemble Clark Kerr's analysis of the behavior of the president in

The Uses of the University, published over forty years later, Vana argued that the president's principal function is "constantly mediating among contending academic interests," that he must have "a talent for manipulation." The difficulty with reforming academe, argued this 1920s student of American university life, was not that it was controlled by the reactionary affluent, but that there were within it so many vested interests protected by "all kinds of customs, laws, compacts, understandings, agreements, promises, and obligations, created by years of conscious, unconscious, and subconscious operations. It is a vast, magnificent, and historic tangle. About all that the mighty gentleman who presides over it can do, is to stand on a height above it and squirt perfume on the ensemble."[43]

Cultural Conformity: The Thirties Through the Fifties

The emergence of a pattern of seeming renunciation of the behavior of their elders by an important segment of the college generation was curiously inhibited by the Depression of the 1930s. As noted earlier, two radical sociologists recently suggested: "The collapse of the counter-culture of the 1920s in the face of economic depression suggests that one must eschew any linear theory of societal change."[44] That traumatic event did, of course, stimulate major political changes among both students and intellectuals.

"Straw polls" taken on college campuses each presidential election year point to a marked shift from the 1920s to the 1930s. They show that the G.O.P. had a substantial majority among students in the twenties, but lost this position in 1932 and 1936; the Socialists received 18 percent nationally in 1932. Of course, these straw polls are not reliable estimates of the opinions of the campus populations since they dealt with returns from a small, self-selected number of colleges and students. (The 1936 returns, for example, were based on ninety-two colleges and 80,590 ballots out of a student population of more than one million.) A recent report on the results of various academic surveys of student political attitudes on assorted campuses at different times in the 1930s concluded that "students expressed more liberal views toward economic planning and change than their counterparts before the Depression and this liberalism increased during the four years of college attendance. Polls repeatedly showed that President Roosevelt was held in high regard among the younger generation." *A Literary Digest* poll of college students across the nation in 1935 found that those who replied favored Roosevelt's policies by two to one.[45]

The American Student Union, formed in 1935, as a coalition of Socialists, Communists, and liberals, was to report twenty thousand members out of a student population of over one million, clearly proportionately much more than has ever been claimed by all the radical student groups in the hectic 1960s. In April 1934, twenty-five thousand students were reported to have taken the Oxford Pledge against participation in war during the student antiwar week. By April 1935, 185,000 students were counted as participants in such demonstrations. Peace Day or Peace Week demonstrations in the late thirties are reported to have included several hundred thousand students.

A comprehensive academic study of the student movement of the early thirties, that by George Rawick, concludes that it "received its major impetus from the antiwar movement." Polls of students indicated that the strength of pacifist feeling was much greater than the following of the organized groups. Thus in one Ohio college sample in 1932, one third of the students said they would be conscientious objectors in a future war; and one quarter reported they might take that position; while only 41 percent said they would definitely go if drafted in a war. In 1933, a national poll of seventy colleges found that 39 percent of those queried stated they would not take part in any war, while 33 percent said they would fight only in the event the United States was invaded. A larger, more systematic, though still inherently unrepresentative poll of student opinion on foreign policy issues was conducted by *The Literary Digest* in 1934–35. Ballots were returned by 112,607 students out of the 318,414 who received them. The large majority of those who replied took a strongly peace-oriented position. Thus, 82 percent said they would not bear arms if the United States were involved "in the invasion of the borders of another country"; 63 percent disagreed that "a national policy of an American navy and air force second to none is a sound method of insuring us against being drawn into another great war"; 91 percent favored "government control of armaments and the munitions industry"; and 82 percent supported "the principle of universal conscription of all resources of capital and labor in order to control all profits in time of war."[46]

As in the 1920s and the 1960s, a second major set of concerns was "free speech." "It is significant that amongst the chief issues of contention [during the 1930s] was the student's right to political activity at all: bans on speakers, censorship of student newspapers, punishments for demonstrations, were frequent *causi bellicum*."[47]

The Communists, who were particularly influential in the leadership of the American Student Union, the American Youth Congress (with a claimed membership of affiliated groups including over five million youths), and the Southern Negro Youth Congress (claimed membership of five hundred thousand youths), lost most of their influence by 1940 as a result of shifts in the party line related to the Soviet Union's foreign policies.[48] The Young Communist League itself reported a membership in 1939 of twenty-two thousand youth, student and nonstudent.

The Communists and the various student and youth groups which they eventually dominated kept the potentially alienated within the political system. The CP, following the international Popular Front line of the Comintern, insisted on supporting Franklin Roosevelt, the New Deal, the Democratic Party, and an aggressive anti-Fascist foreign policy. These policies, together with involvement in the campaigns to organize workers by the CIO, attracted the largest portion of college dissenting youth, who could thus link a super-rational ideology with support for the underdog in the form of unorganized workers, persecuted Jews, and the Loyalists in the Spanish Civil War. And the rational in-system politics of the Communists and the liberals, who were encouraged to remain so by the CP, discouraged any thrust toward cultural innovation. Ironically, then, the very considerable power of the Communists within intellectualdom and the student movement severely weakened the pressures towards renunciation of American culture and polity. The dominant "radical" group held back the formation of a generation-unit which would have rejected the premises of Western political society, then being undermined by the greatest depression in history.

> The Communists set the tone for the student movement of the thirties . . . because they had the advantage of numbers, because they offered the weak the impression of strength, and because they had a church which no one else could match. They offered in short an available escape from the reality. Most students, of course, managed to bear reality quite well enough to be apathetic about any avenues for escaping it. The Communists were a tiny fragment of the whole, but they were a majority of the committed. To reject them meant to surrender even the illusion of strength and condemn yourself anew to that alienation which had moved you to commitment in the first place.[49]

Although the Communists were always a relatively small group on and off the campuses, many individuals passed through the movement, particularly in the 1930s, and again during the period of the American alliance with Russia in World War II. Estimates of the number range as high as 750,000 different individuals. "Party members stayed for short periods; they might be active for shorter periods, and a good many didn't even pay their dues regularly."[50] What makes the figures concerning large rapid turnover within the CP particularly relevant for an analysis of student politics is that the overwhelming bulk of those who joined were of college age. "The peak age appears to be 18–23. In fact a majority of the rank and file have not only joined but have left the party by the time they are 23. The late teens seem to be an especially susceptible time."[51] It seems clear that "the proportion of party members who have been to college is very high. Even more striking is the great number of graduate degrees among them."[52]

Given the findings that the Communists were heavily composed of people recruited from those who attended college, it is not surprising that the membership, particularly during the period of massive recruitment in the 1930s, was heavily white collar and professional. Party leaders who were committed to building a proletarian party frequently expressed their dismay at this fact, and sought to get students and college graduates to take jobs as manual workers.[53] The family backgrounds of the party members resembled those reported for New Left activists in the 1960s.

> They have been brought up, in general, in comfort and often in luxury. They are the children of professional men or more than usually successful businessmen, bankers and ministers. In fact, the Communist Party in America seems to be such a highly educated, non-manual laboring group that at times there would seem to be more rejoicing in its headquarters over the recruiting of one common laborer than over ten Ph.D's.[54]

The Communists also resembled the current student activists in "that a large proportion of its members were of Jewish origin."[55] Parenthetically it may be noted that attitude surveys among college students during the 1930s which sought to locate the correlates of liberal-left to conservative beliefs generally reported comparable results to those of the 1960s. The more liberal students tended to come from relatively well-educated professional families disproportionately Jewish or irreligious, and tended to major in the social sciences.[56] "A definite linkage with father's and mother's political attitudes was established, not supporting the view that student radicalism is primarily a protest against parental conservatism. . . . The most striking factor . . . was the rather high correlation between college scholarship and radicalism. . . ."[57] The strength of the latter relationship led Gardner Murphy and Rensis Likert to try to answer the question: "Why is the bookish student more radical?" They concluded that modern intellectualdom and radicalism are closely related.

> The answer lies in a study of the modern temper. The whole whirl of the first third of the twentieth century is definitely a radical whirl, and this is particularly true of the postwar period. To be bookish in this era has meant to steep oneself in the disillusioned gropings of postwar thinkers, most of whom, from philosophers to lyricists, are clearly "radical" in the everyday sense of striving to find a new base for the relations between men. . . . The literary groups to which these men belong, the day-by-day conversations in which they train one another to think and to feel, are full of the modern doubt and disquietude, and, even more frequently, of the modern challenge and rebellion. To be bookish today is to be radical. . . .
>
> This is our theory, and it is nothing more; but it is supported by many straws of evidence. We . . . note that "books" are the one thing *besides parents* that are credited by [radical] students with consistent and powerful influence, and that radicals make mention of books and magazines more frequently than conservatives do, as factors to be underscored in the shaping of their attitudes. If our hypothesis is correct, the preferred courses of radicals will be those which emphasize wide reading as against those emphasizing laboratory work, mathematical calculation, or the acquisition of practical skills. A glance at Tables 34 and 35 [in the Murphy-Likert book] will show that the courses meeting this specification, such as philosophy, psychology and English literature, yield the expected results.[58]

Clearly the New Left of the 1960s recruited activists from the same social pool as did the Communists and other radicals of the 1930s and early 1940s. In fact there is some evidence to suggest that the activists of the 1960s, born for the most part in the 1940s, are to an extent the actual children of radicals and fellow travelers of the earlier generations.[59] Given the educational, occupational and cultural background, it is likely that the overwhelming majority of their children went to university. And studies cited in Chapter 3 report a family history of political activism and a left-liberal ideological outlook in the background of the contemporary crop of collegiate radicals.

While there can be little question that the decline of renunciatory tendencies and the failure of campus radicalism can be blamed in large part on the Communists and their effort to gain support for the Soviet Union's foreign policy, the one comprehensive effort at a national representative sample (1220) of college youth, conducted for *Fortune* in the spring of 1936, documented both the decline of the cultural renunciation which had characterized the twenties and the limited appeal of political radicalism. Concern with their economic future brought a yearning for security, for a job with tenure. *Fortune* worried that the students were too willing to do what they were told to get and hold a job, and raised the question, "Are good corporation heads made out of tractable material?" It found that the "family as such is no longer an object of derision, as it was in the early twenties. Fathers and mothers are listened to once more. . . . Deference to the advice of father is part of the general yearning for security among the young." Politically, there had been a sharp shift to the left, as compared with the surveys of campus opinion in the mid-twenties which had found Republican majorities. By the mid-thirties, "liberals and democrats. . . . form the thick equatorial bulge of the [campus political] turnip. . . ."[60] An examination of the unpublished detailed report of the survey does indicate that many of the students did favor structural changes. Close to one quarter (24 percent) of those interviewed, when asked about various terms which "suggest ideas toward which you feel sympathetic," picked "socialism" as a positive term and 6 percent said "communism," as contrasted to 15 percent for "conservatism," 45 percent for "liberalism," and 2 percent for "fascism." Over two thirds indicated that they favored changes in the Constitution to enable people "to live comfortably . . . even if this means a revision in our attitude about property rights." Yet close to 90 percent indicated their belief that "there are plenty of employers who will give you satisfactory promotion in due course if you work hard and learn your job well."[61]

Fortune's reporters who visited many campuses were impressed with the relative weakness of the organized radical groups. The politically active and concerned are described as numbering at most between 5 and 10 percent. The exaggerated image of campus radicalism is sustained because the "college newspapers are often far to the left of the undergraduate bodies." In this respect, of course, the sixties resembled the thirties. There are other comparable patterns which are an outgrowth of similar peakings in the cycle of concern for political reform in the two decades. The college athletic and fraternity type social events lost appeal in favor of a more positive concern for relevance in courses. "Students have been flocking to history, economics, and sociology courses. . . ."[62]

Radical political activity in the 1950s was notable by its absence. Liberal and left student organizations either passed away or existed with tiny memberships and small agendas. A number of conservative campus groups acquired considerable publicity in the national media, as supposedly representing the new campus mood.

Why was there such political quiescence on the campuses during the 1950s? Many who have written on the problem have suggested that it reflected the coercive pressures on the adult world, particularly faculty and other intellectuals, imposed by the various aspects of the phenomenon known as McCarthyism. Professors were fired at a number of institutions for refusing to take loyalty oaths, or for failing to answer charges that they had been or still were members of the Communist party. Relatively little was done to defend the civil liberties of those charged with being Communists, in part because few of them ever tried to defend their rights to be Communists or radicals. Rather the tactic that was followed – of "taking the Fifth Amendment," of refusing to answer questions concerning political beliefs or memberships on the grounds of possible criminal self-incrimination –

made a civil liberties defense based on the First Amendment right to hold and espouse unpopular beliefs difficult. The issue in most cases became a detective story one; was the individual under attack actually a Communist, not whether he had a right to be one. In all previous periods of repression of radical opinion, those involved had vigorously defended their right to be political radicals, and by so doing had created *causes célèbres* around which others could rally. In addition, the first four years of the fifties, 1950–1954, were not only the era of repressive McCarthyism which intimidated many; more importantly they were the years of the Korean War, of a war perceived as having been started by an invasion of a non-Communist state by a Communist one. Wartime sentiments and pressures presumably also held critical sentiments in check.

But the interpretations which see the low ebb in student and other forms of radical activism as a response to repression are inadequate, since much the same pattern occurred among the students and intellectuals of Western Europe and Canada. Polls of student opinion in Britain revealed conservative majorities. The London School of Economics, once the principal stronghold of radicalism in the British Isles, was frequently described in this period as having become conservative or at least apolitical. Canadian students and intellectuals, clearly out of McCarthy's reach, showed close political resemblance to their American brethren. *The Canadian Forum,* the Canadian magazine which most resembled American ones like *The Nation, The New Republic,* or *The Progressive* in its outlook, and which had been outspokenly socialist in its sympathies during the 1930s and 1940s, became increasingly critical of socialism as an ideological outlook during the 1950s. In many European countries, socialist parties modified their programs so as to eliminate references to the class struggle or to the traditional goal of a socialist society, with little or no opposition from their intellectual or campus supporters.

The left-disposed segments of the students of the 1950s were caught up in a political era that inhibited deep political commitments and political activism. The experiences of the 1930s, and the behavior of the Communist states both internally (overt anti-Semitism, new purge trials), and in foreign policy (the Czech coup of 1948, the Berlin Blockade, the North Korean attack) made them, as well as their intellectual elders, suspicious of simple answers to complex problems. Fear of the aggressive power of monolithic Communism played the same role in the late 1940s and the 1950s that fear of Nazism had played during the late 1930s and early 1940s. The "lessons" preached by the Communists to other radicals during the 1930s were applied to Stalinism. To resist the totalitarian threat, liberals and non-Communist leftists, in effect, adopted the tactics advocated by the Communists to fight fascism against Stalinism, namely to concentrate on defeating the expansionist enemy, even to the point of sharply reducing criticism of the status quo in one's own country. For a second time, Western intellectuals accepted a defensist rather than a critical posture. Few proposed radical answers to current domestic problems, and still fewer were raising any important questions about inequality, poverty, or power. The students under these circumstances turned inwards. They became concerned with their psyches, their personalities, and their feelings. The fact that *The Catcher in the Rye* was a collegiate best seller in the 1950s should occasion no surprise.

Yet it would be a mistake to reach a conclusion from the presence or absence of an activist campus minority in any given period concerning the viewpoints of the student population. Clearly, the behavior of the very small minority of politically involved or avant-garde oriented students at any point in time must not be taken as typical of the attitudes and values of the generation cohort. During the 1920s, in spite of the concentration of attention on those engaged in cultural revolt, and the increase in premarital sexual relations from approximately 15 percent to close to 30 percent of the female population reported by Kinsey, studies of religious attitudes of college students revealed a commitment to religiosity among the great majority. The national poll of campus voting preferences in 1924 found that the large majority of the students participating in this straw vote were for Calvin Coolidge. The 1936 *Fortune* poll pointed up the minority status of the radicals of the thirties.

If it is proper to stress the unrepresentativeness of those who set the dominant mood on campus during the 1920s and the 1930s, it should also be noted that there was considerable student support for unpopular views during the 1950s, even though there was relatively little action. Thus a national survey of a sample of male college students taken in April to May 1952 revealed considerable opposition to the Korean War. Thirty-three percent expressed outright opposition, 19 percent were uncertain, and 48 percent favored our policies in Korea. Less than a fifth (19 percent) stated that they never had felt the war "is not worth fighting." Only 10 percent indicated that they would like to serve in the military.[63] To place these results in perspective, it should be noted that a majority of American students still supported the Vietnam war as late as 1967.

Evidence that the dominant mood in academe was not conservative even during the height of McCarthyism and Eisenhower Republicanism may be adduced for both students and faculty. The most comprehensive analysis of student opinion in the early fifties found that liberal opinions were more prevalent the higher the class in school, suggesting the liberalizing effect of the university.[64] A survey of faculty opinion in October 1956 reported disproportionate backing for Democratic and leftist third party presidential candidates in the 1948 and 1952 elections and in vote intention in 1956. In 1948, Harry Truman received 50 percent of the academic ballots, while Henry Wallace, the Progressive candidate, and Norman Thomas, the Socialist, took about ten percent. In 1952, when Eisenhower was sweeping the country, Adlai Stevenson received 54 percent of the professorial vote, and various left minor candidates had two percent. In 1956, the Stevenson percentage among faculty rose to 60 percent.[65] Since propensity to support liberal or left candidates varies with discipline and with school quality — the liberal arts fields, particularly the social sciences, and the more prestigious schools, as noted earlier, are more liberal — the support for Stevenson or left-wing candidates was undoubtedly much higher in the major centers of academe. A comprehensive survey of the opinions of social scientists completed in 1955 revealed that the Republican candidates in 1948 and 1952, Thomas E. Dewey and Dwight Eisenhower, took only 28 and 34 percent of the vote. The overwhelming majority of the social scientists supported the academic and political rights of Communists and other radicals in the midst of McCarthyism.[66] Since backing for these views and for political liberalism and radicalism increased with quality of university, it is clear that the more intellectually oriented students of the 1950s were in an environment in which prestige was associated with opposition to conservative views.

Perhaps the most telling report concerning the mood on the American campus during the 1950s are the conclusions reached in a book by a conservative, M. Stanton Evans, concerning the conservative revival during the decade. In general, Evans emphasized all the evidence from pre-election straw votes, formation of conservative clubs, and student reactions to various issues, to point up the magnitude of right-wing strength. The evidence clearly pointed to the greater political conservatism among the campus population during the early and mid-fifties as compared with the previous two decades. Eisenhower had widespread student support. Yet all during the period, sizable minorities expressed attitudes toward the role of government, welfare, and foreign policy, which can be best described as left-liberal and even socialist. And in summing up the results of various opinion studies made during the fifties, Evans concluded that the dominant student mood "is permissive, antireligious, and relativist in the realm of ethics; statist in the realm of politics; anti-anti-Communist in the *sui generis* crisis which grips our age. In a word, it is liberal."[67] These conclusions, it should be noted, were derived more from studies of the late fifties than from the early years, and may help to explain the rapid growth of civil rights, antiwar and leftist activism in the following decade.

A summary of the findings from various surveys of student opinion completed during the 1950s compared the characteristics associated with liberal or left social attitudes in that decade with those found in the studies of the 1960s, reported in Chapter 3, and concluded "that liberal or left students in each decade are recruited from similar sociological reservoirs,"[68] as were those of the 1930s. That is, those on the left side of the ideological division were more likely to be in the social sciences or humanities, to be Jews rather than Christians, to report higher grades, and to come from Democratic rather than Republican family backgrounds.

This brief survey of American campus discontent and politics is not designed to prove any general thesis concerning the cyclical sources of such behavior. The repeated periods of student unrest and political activism have given rise to various efforts to account for a given wave of protest. The similarity in causal analysis among them is striking. Most commonly, commentators assume that the contemporary discontent is a consequence of a structural trend, which has had as its inevitable results the contemporary state of affairs. From Cornelia Comer writing in *The Atlantic Monthly* of February 1911 to the editor of *The New Student* in October 1923 to Margaret Mead and Kenneth Keniston, in 1970, writers have pointed to the ways in which new and rapidly changing modes of communication and technology have upset standards, have reduced the influence of older generations, and have led students to look for new values and to support radical change.[69] The analyses of the changing characteristics of the university which presumably result in student unrest also have repeated themselves, often using identical explanations for close to a century.

Two studies of published material dealing with the role of the professor, one comparing articles from the 1890s to the late 1930s, and the other comparing turn of the century comment with those made in the late 1940s and 1950s, demonstrate this continuity in detail.[70] Veysey's analysis of the *Emergence of the American University* before 1910 argues that student complaints about faculty have been continuous and similar under varying conditions and teacher-student ratios – the small nineteenth century college or the large research and graduate-oriented university, the lecture or the tutorial system. He points up comments suggesting an inherent "class" tension between students and faculty and administration.[71] Given the presence of discontent, commentators have indicated comparable intra- and extramural causes. The campus-located causes take the form of inadequate teaching – overspecialized (or underspecialized), irrelevant to personal or social concerns, impersonal (although there was a time when relations were viewed as too close) – and also, at least since Jefferson's day, too tight institutional control. The solutions have also been similar. A multitude of articles written from 1900 to 1970 have called for greater rewards to teaching as compared to research, for special graduate programs to train college teachers, for a degree other than the Ph.D. for those who prefer to teach, for various programs which would end the lecture system, for more freedom for students to choose their courses and programs of concentration, for more generalized and socially relevant courses, for senior professors to teach elementary classes, and for greater student participation in the governance of the schools.

Off-campus factors are presumed to have resulted in a much higher degree of permissiveness and resultant lack of emphasis on basic morality than was experienced by the previous generation, as a result of larger social adjustments which have undermined basic beliefs. These usually have been the result of changes in the media, leisure activities, and pace of transportation: first, the rise of the penny press, the silent movies and vaudeville; later, radio and the automobile; and currently, television and the jet plane. Each older generation is convinced that the rate of change which has occurred in the last decade or two is the greatest in the history of mankind, that it has upset moral values, and that, consequently, young people have become more likely to follow their impulses or new pure ideals than at any previous time. If any solution has followed from such diagnoses, it has been to urge a speedup in the pace of political responses to the new moralistic demands of young people and to give them more of a share in the decision-making system.

The explanations for student unrest which focus on specific historical events also have in common an insistence that the experiences faced by a given student generation represent the greatest challenge to the American Creed that has been experienced in modern times. Thus, the radical wave before World War I was viewed as a response to the rapid growth of crowded, corruptly run cities, inhabited by hordes of immigrants living in abysmal poverty close to fantastic wealth. And in fact, the immigrant ghettoes of the East Side of New York were much more densely inhabited than the slums of Harlem today. The spread between the income of day laborers and the untaxed wealth of the *nouveaux riches* industrialists was also much greater than at present. Governments did almost nothing to aid the unemployed and poverty-stricken, who also were proportionately more prevalent than currently. The period from 1870 to 1914 did witness immigration at a rate of over a million a year, much of which was settled in the urban slums. There can be little doubt that the Progressive, Socialist, and settlement house movements, all of which were represented among the campus population, were an earnest of the tensions created by the gap between the nineteenth century American ideal of a society of independent yeomen, and the reality of the machine-run immoral dirty city.

The generation which came of age during the 1920s was also convinced that history had dealt a body blow to the American dream. The promises of the war to end wars, "to make the world safe for democracy," proved to be hollow. The immediate postwar era was characterized by a wave of political repression against dissenters, the passage of immigration restriction legislation which was nativist in intent, and specifically designed to limit Catholic and Jewish migration, violent race riots in many cities, the rise of the multi-million-membered Ku Klux Klan, legislative efforts to prevent the teaching of evolution in many states, and the dismal failure of the Prohibition Amendment, as large segments of the middle class and their college-student off-spring openly violated the law by patronizing racketeer boot-leggers to get their liquor.

The collapse of economic institutions, widespread bank-ruptcies, evictions from farms and homes of those who could not pay their mortgages, and from 15 to 20 million unemployed, all gave the students of the 1930s a set of domestic experiences strong enough to undermine faith in American institutions. Abroad they witnessed the seizure of power by the Nazis in Germany, the revival of religious persecution on a scale not seen for centuries, the expansion of totalitarian rule through force and war in Austria, Czechoslovakia, Ethiopia, Spain and China, with little opposition from the United States or other democratic countries. And the promise of Communism turned to ashes with the state-created famines of the early thirties, the purge trials and large-scale imprisonments in concentration camps of the late thirties, and the ultimate conclusion – collaboration between Hitler and Stalin to eliminate the independent states between their borders – an event which precipitated World War II. The youth of the thirties, too, could and did cry out that no other modern genera-tion had their experience of such a series of catastrophic value-challenging events.

Post-World War II generations have obviously seen much to make them query the worth of the larger social system. World War II, like World War I, left in its wake more extensive authoritarian regimes. The nuclear bomb, and the emerging cold war, meant all those who have come of age since 1945 have lived under threat of annihilation. Hot wars in Greece, Korea, the Middle East and Vietnam, made concern for peace a constant interest. Poverty in the underdeveloped world and at home was raised to mass consciousness. The struggle of the blacks in the United States for equal rights reached a level of intensity prob-ably not matched at any time since the Civil War. The failure of the United States to defeat a small impoverished Asian enemy undermined the American self-image that its foreign policy is designed to further the right to self-determination. Once again a major segment of American collegiate youth demonstrated their disgust at the failures of the society by various forms of personal and political protest.

The response of the alienated youth of the late 1960s to the changes and events they have experienced is undoubtedly greater and more intense than occurred in the earlier periods of this century. In part, the difference is produced by greater numbers, nationally, as well as on given campuses and in particular areas. Given almost eight million students in institutions of higher education in 1971–72, the small percentage of the thoroughly alienated constitute a much larger absolute mass base for aggressive student protest than has ever existed in any country at any time. The Boston metropolitan area, for example, has about 250,000 students in fifty-five colleges. Some of the protest groups, both white radicals and black militants, recruit from all over the metropolis for demonstrations on a given campus.

The willingness of discontented Americans to violate the law, to use confrontation tactics, and even on occasion to resort to violence, is not new. The students of the early nineteenth century engaged in serious campus violence. Labor movement organizers and radicals blew up buildings and used dynamite to gain their ends around the turn of the century. Blacks and whites fought each other with guns in the early twenties. During the 1930s, striking workers occupied factories in massive industrial sit-ins, while militant farmers brought their guns to prevent foreclosure sales at neighboring farms.

It is difficult to evaluate the severity of the recent pattern of polarization as compared to past waves. Clearly higher education has been affected more severely than at any previous time. The concentration of disaffection and alienation among students and younger faculty in the best universities and colleges of America has had an impact far beyond the campus. They are regarded by many who do not agree with them as the voice of their generation, a role which gives them considerable influence on those sections of the elite which are oriented towards the intellectual and university communities. Regardless of how small or disorganized the various radical groups are, there still is a "movement" today which includes the hundreds of thousands who read the "underground press," attend demonstrations and rallies, and give close moral support to the more violent militants.

The escalation of protest on the left and the right during the late 1960s does not necessarily mean a renewed period of growth in political polarization, or even its maintenance at a high level in the 1970s. As noted earlier, there is no doubt that both activism and radical sentiments declined considerably during the 1970–71 academic year. As David Riesman pointed out in his commencement address at the University of Pennsylvania at the end of the year, this change may reflect a new phase in the "recurrent cycles of activism and withdrawal" which have characterized student behavior. The brief look presented here into the history of campus-related unrest and protest should force us to be humble both about our ability to understand and to predict waves of discontent. Heightened social, political, or educational tensions seemingly bring a number of academic, societal and political reactions which reduce the sources of particular crises. Marxists in their historical analyses of revolutionary strategies have been well acquainted with the ebbs and flows of their potential strength. Marx, Engels, Lenin, and Trotsky each pointed up the necessity for revolutionaries to moderate their tactics during conservative tides, to avoid giving reaction the excuse for repression by the "adventurist" or "putschist" tactics of the left.

But whatever the future of the current wave, this American record does lend support to those explanations which stress the inherent potential of students as the most available social base for innovative forms of cultural behavior and aggressive political action dedicated to the attainment of "absolute ends." It reinforces the conclusion that the student population is the most volatile and most easily mobilizable of all social strata. Whether, and how, and for what causes it is mobilized will depend on specific events, on changes in the larger climate of opinions and custom within intellectualdom and the polity and society generally. Foremost among the forces in the adult world which affect student reactions is the faculty. Some analysts have even argued that faculty discontents and policies are at the heart of student reactions.[72] But this relationship, even between faculty and student radicals, is not a simple one. The following chapter turns to a discussion of some aspects of this.

6

Faculty and Students: Allied and in Conflict

The descriptions of student activism in the 1960s, as well as over the previous century and a half, have indicated an alliance between student and adult protest. The early nineteenth-century undergraduate opponents of orthodox theology found support from the Jeffersonians on the Harvard Board of Overseers as well as in other institutions. Student abolitionists were allied to older activists in the movement. The waves of student rebellion against parietal rules and the absence of student government in the last two decades of the century were clearly linked to the changes in the role of the faculty which led many professors to demand more intramural power and freedom. The various types of student political protest from the Intercollegiate Socialist Society of the first decade of the present century down to the Students for a Democratic Society of the 1960s were each, in turn, related to trends in the adult world, particularly among faculty. In a real sense, therefore, student rebellion has not been a generational revolt, but rather has represented the undergraduate contribution to social and political tendencies which have been present within each age group. The students, for reasons discussed earlier, have frequently been the most militant, the most extreme, the least disciplined, the most uncompromising segment of the ideological grouping of which they have been a part, but it is rare that any student movement has occurred without counterparts in the larger intellectual world.

Faculty participation in stimulating or supporting current student unrest has been documented in various surveys conducted by the American Council on Education. A comprehensive analysis of demonstrations which occurred at 181 institutions during 1967–68 found that faculty were involved in the planning of over half of the student protests which occurred. In close to two thirds of them, faculty bodies passed resolutions approving of the protests.[1] Faculties have clearly been bitterly divided on the issues involved in campus unrest, but a detailed investigation of the sources of faculty political involvement points to predispositions among professors to sympathize with student activism, as well as to the existence of basic tensions between student radicals and faculty supporters which result in faculty backing being short lived for student protest on any given campus.[2]

Intellectuals, who, as noted in the first chapter, are concerned with creation and innovation and are partisans of the abstract and the ideal, have a predominant sympathy for causes and ideologies which reject the status quo in their particular society and wing. Such orientations need not be political, and they may be right-wing or left-wing. Daniel Patrick Moynihan has advised Richard Nixon that since "about 1840, the cultural elite have pretty generally rejected the values and activities of the larger society. It has been said of America that the culture [the intellectual elite] will not approve that which the polity strives to provide."[3]

This comment of Moynihan's errs on the side of being too parochial. Similar judgments concerning the inherent tendency of the intellectuals to oppose the system have been made at different times by writers as diverse as Joseph Schumpeter, Robert Michels, Karl Mannheim, Reinhold Niebuhr, Sidney Hook, Richard Hofstadter, Lewis Coser, Richard Flacks, and many others. One hundred years ago, Whitelaw Reid, then the new young editor of the New York *Tribune,* presented what has become a frequently expressed thesis concerning the relationship between the academy and the rest of the elite, one which resembles Bristed's 1840 statement concerning the oppositional tendencies of students discussed in Chapter 4.

> Exceptional influences eliminated, the scholar is pretty sure to be opposed to the established. The universities of Germany contain the deadliest foes to the absolute authority of the Kaiser. The scholars of France prepared the way for the first Revolution, and were the most dangerous enemies of the imperial adventurer who betrayed the second. . . . While the prevailing parties in our country were progressive and radical, the temper of our college was to the last degree conservative. As our politics settled into the conservative tack, a fresh wind began to blow about the college seats, and literary men, at last, furnished inspiration for the splendid movement that swept slavery from the statute book. . . . Wise unrest will always be their [the scholars] chief trait. We may set down . . . the very foremost function of the scholar in politics, *To oppose the established.*
>
> . . . As for the scholar, the laws of his intellectual development may be trusted to fix his place. Free thought is necessarily aggressive and critical. The scholar, like the healthy redblooded young man, is an inherent, an organic, an inevitable radical. . . . And so we may set down, as a second function of the American scholar in politics, *An intellectual leadership of the radicals.*[4]

And most recently, the most significant conservative in American academe, Milton Friedman, has approvingly quoted an unpublished manuscript of his equally conservative economist colleague, George Stigler, to the same effect as Whitelaw Reid:

> The university is by design and effect the institution in society which creates discontent with existing moral, social and political institutions and proposes new institutions to replace them. The university is, from this viewpoint, a group of philosophically imaginative men freed of any pressures except to please their fellow faculty, and told to follow their inquiries wherever they might lead. Invited to be learned in the institutions of other

> times and places, incited to new understanding of the social and physical world, the university faculty is inherently a disruptive force.[5]

Much of the discontent during the last decades of the nineteenth century was expressed as conservative disdain for the crude materialism of *nouveaux riches* businessmen and the vulgarity of taste in democratic society. Increasingly, however, during the twentieth century, the critical stance of the intellectuals, including first the social scientists and later the humanists within the university, took the form of a predominant sympathy for antiestablishment, liberal-left positions. Opinion studies, the earliest of which date back, as noted in Chapter 4, to before the First World War, indicate that American academics as a stratum, have been much more likely to express liberal opinions in religion and politics than other strata. They have lent disproportionate support to atheistic, antiwar, civil rights, civil liberties for deviants, liberal Democratic, and third party causes.[6] Given this relatively consistent outlook among the pacesetters of the academic and intellectual world, it may be argued that faculties should have shown much more support for student protest than in fact emerged. A look at some of the reasons for faculty opposition may help explain the growing tension between faculty and student activists.

The most obvious and important source of division in faculty response is linked to variations in faculty roles. Professors clearly differ in the extent to which they are involved in creative, intellectual, scholarly, and hence critical functions, as contrasted with teaching, professional, and applied activities. Most faculty employed in the twenty-five hundred institutions of higher learning in America are primarily teachers, not scholars, and hence more dedicated to the passing on of the existing tradition, not the enlargement or critical rejection of it. Second, disciplines vary in the degree to which they are "intellectual." The more intellectual fields, those more dedicated to the value of knowledge, art, basic research, as valued goals in themselves — the liberal arts fields – tend to recruit or produce practitioners on both the student and faculty level who are sympathetic to antiestablishment reform or radical positions. Conversely, the more practical fields, such as engineering, education, business, and agriculture, include on all levels the more conservative.

Given the relationship between intellectual creativity, commitment to innovation, and political criticism, it is not surprising that a variety of surveys indicate that the most successful scholars in all fields, those most dedicated to research and to national intellectual activities rather than teaching and local campus affairs, tend to be the most liberal or left-wing members of academe. This pattern results in a high correlation between the academic quality of institutions and faculty predilection for liberal-left politics.

The particular disciplines and universities which have the highest proportion of students inclined to the left politically and involved most heavily in campus demonstrations are the same ones whose faculty members have the most sympathy for the values and causes espoused by the students. Hence, as we have seen, the "gap" between student and faculty political orientations, like that between parents and their offspring, is relatively small. The liberal-left children of liberal-left parents study subjects and are in colleges where teachers are also among the more left-disposed among American academe.

Analyses of faculty opinion agree that the most important single determinant of attitude toward given campus demonstrations, or student activism generally, has been personal political outlook. The more liberal-to-left a professor is on wider social and political issues, the more likely he is to support radical student activities. The principal factors modifying this generalization are the related ones of age and longevity at a given institution. Within the same political category, e.g., faculty holding radical or liberal opinions, the older ones and those who have been at a given school longest are least likely to back campus demonstrations or locally relevant campus demands.

But, most student activists, even the more moderate among

them, sharply challenge the description of their faculty as a critical, antiestablishment group sympathetic to the same ideals as themselves. For in spite of the initial endorsement through faculty-meeting resolutions of the objectives of given campus protests, the activists find a lack of commitment to the endeavors of student protest movements even by those faculty who *are* intellectually oriented, critical of the status quo, and liberal-left in their political ideology. A study of opinions of a sample of social science faculty who had signed various advertisements against the Vietnam war validated the impressionistic complaints of the activists, for only 21 percent of this group of antiwar professors indicated that they approved of the student demonstrations that had occurred at places like Columbia, Cornell, Harvard, and San Francisco State.[7] These liberal-left faculty seem to justify the charge levied by many student activists that the faculty, like their parents, are hypocrites, that they do not act in ways congruent to their proclaimed beliefs.

It becomes necessary for the liberal faculty to explain themselves to their students. The conservatives will obviously oppose the politicization of the campus from the left, but theirs is not a relevant objection to leftist students. There are important reasons why scholars have opposed politicization, regardless of their political ideology, which derive from the very nature of scholarship. And just as it is possible to argue that a critical antiestablishment stance is inherent in the functions of the intellectual and the university, it is also possible to urge that the university cannot accomplish its task if it becomes a center of political advocacy. This is a view not easily or normally understood by morally concerned, politically dedicated students.

Politics and scholarship are highly different types of human activities, even though many scholars are also political actors and some men shift from a political to an academic career or vice versa. Many radicals fail to recognize the major differences between scholarship (both teaching and research) and politics (relevance). Both activities also involve the same types of actions, namely, writing and lecturing. Many academics, of course, are experts in policy-relevant fields and may be called upon to advise policy makers. Yet, in spite of the considerable overlap in activity and concern, the differences between the roles are greater than the similarities.

The political activist, whether a member of SDS or a leader of the Republican party, is expected to be an advocate. One of his major tasks is to mobilize support behind his group or party. To do this, he presents a point of view which emphasizes all the arguments in its favor, which ignores or consciously represses contradictory materials. In a real sense, the political activist is like a lawyer, whose obligation is to make the best case possible for his client. Inherent in the effort to gain a following and to win power is the need to simplify, to insist that the policies fostered by the group can eliminate evil, can gain the goals of the group, whether these be the ending of a war, the elimination of corruption, the end to depression or inflation, law and order in the cities, the end of poverty, the elimination of ethnic-racial discrimination, social equality, religious morality, mass participation, and so forth. The political leader who points out that life is complicated, that he is uncertain about the way to end practices which his group regards as evil, will not last very long in the role. Political leadership calls for decisiveness, for the ability to make decisions quickly on the basis of limited knowledge, with the awareness that there is a good possibility that the action will be wrong.

Scholarship, clearly, emphasizes the opposite characteristics. Ideally, or normatively (which by definition means major discrepancies from any given practice), those involved will be concerned with careful and extensive studies of the broad range of human knowledge. A scholar should consider all existing points of view and all available evidence before reaching a conclusion. He is expected to take his time in coming to a definitive conclusion before publishing his findings as knowledge. One of the worst things that can be said about an academic is that he publishes too quickly, that he rushes into print before he has exhausted the possible areas of inquiry. A scholar is normatively required to present contradictory evidence, to point to any methodological weaknesses in his materials. In attacking a research problem, he is initially required to complicate the issue, to introduce as many factors as appear at all relevant. Thus scholars writing on issues of race relations, equality, poverty, inflation, foreign policy, war, etc., tend to emphasize the indeterminate character of knowledge in these fields, the fact that the evidence rarely justifies any simple cause and effect relationship.

The dialogue between the scholar and the activist must inevitably be one in which the former undercuts the will of the latter to act, if he remains in the academic world. Or conversely, if the scholar takes to the hustings, he must cease being a scholar. There are, of course, considerable areas of overlapping usefulness. Any good political leader will want to have as much information as possible about a given topic before he makes a decision. He may call upon the scholar for policy-relevant research, which he wants to be cautious, to err, if at all, on the side of complexity and conservatism. The politician will often still have to make a decision, which assumes an ability to predict consequences with great probability, even when the extant knowledge implies a very low order of predictability about outcomes of different policies. Ironically, in his use of the scientific policy-adviser, the politician, therefore, is not looking for originality, but for "safety." He calls upon the scholar in much the same way as he might ask an engineer to plan a new bridge. The latter will always put in a great safety factor to make sure the bridge will not fall down. For this reason, the most brilliant and prestigious scholars may not make the best policy advisers. For the highest rewards in intellectual life are generally given for originality, for new ideas, for theoretical breakthroughs, not for valid replications, for proof that an existing proposition is valid.

The scholar, even when concerned with applied politically relevant problems, is committed to the notion that visible forms of behavior which can be described in common sense layman's terms can be better understood as the product of a complex set of underlying relationships which must be treated analytically in an effort to synthesize such linkages. A variety of seemingly disparate behaviors can only be identified as having common causal elements through use of abstract theoretical models. Hence science will insist that a cure for cancer will never be found if everyone interested in the disease becomes a surgeon; rather that an ultimate solution requires basic research on genes, cellular growth patterns, body chemistry, and so forth. Concern with racial tensions does not mean that every social scientist should concentrate on attacking racism or documenting its punitive character in economic, psychological, or sociological terms; it also requires detailed investigations into the underlying processes which make discrimination a characteristic of every multi-group society, of the functions of intolerance, of its effects on the abilities of those subject to discrimination to interact effectively, and so forth. The scholar involved in basic research will often deliberately separate himself from any substantive (policy-relevant) problem so as to be free to look for more abstract levels of generalization. This point has been made effectively by the radical historian Christopher Lasch, who finds the work of Erving Goffman on stigma and "spoiled identity" particularly useful in analyzing the behavior of leaders of Negroes and other socially oppressed groups:

> Goffman deliberately excludes the race problem from his analysis of "spoiled identity," on the grounds that established minorities do not provide the best objects for an analysis of the delicate mechanisms surrounding the management of stigma. . . . At the same time an understanding of face-to-face relationships drawn from quite a different perspective throws unexpected light on certain aspects of race relations – notably on the role of "professionals." As Goffman notes with his usual acuity, traditional fields of study such as race relations are areas "to which one should apply several perspectives"; and "the development of any one of these coherent analytic perspectives is not likely to come from those who restrict their interest exclusively to one substantive area."[8]

These differences between scholarship and politics are particularly significant for the social sciences, and to a lesser extent for the humanities, since matters of academic concern in these disciplines are often also political policy issues. As has been noted, many students who take social science courses or decide to major or do graduate work in these fields often do so because of the subject matter, because they see ways of enhancing their political objectives. Hence the interest of many students in these disciplines is not that of the scholar but of the politician, of the political activist. Such an interest is clearly a valid one, much as is the interest of the pre-engineering student in physics, or the premedical candidate in biology. But the activist-oriented social science student often wants his research-involved professor to join him in his efforts to gain social change by immediate political activities.

If students do not understand these differences between scholarship and politics, they must be taught them. But since most students will not become scholars, there is no reason why we should expect or try to force them to accept scholarly values for themselves. They should be encouraged to be as political, as relevant, as they wish *outside* the classroom. The demand for relevance is a political, not a scholarly demand. When students demand "relevant" courses, they are asking for courses which involve advocacy, or which see the faculty members acting as policy advisers. Efforts by faculty to be "objective" in courses which bear on politics are often regarded as forms of escaping from an obligation to fight evil, or even of supporting the system. And the committed activists, regardless of ideological stance, regard any claim to objectivity as pretense, as an effort to conceal the ideological commitments, the value preferences, and the biases which all men have.

Many social scientists, on the other hand, will argue that precisely because their fields touch so directly on politics and are involved with subjects about which they, like all aware men, have strong feelings, it is important to try to separate their values from their research *as much as possible*. The effort to engage in objective scholarship is clearly much more difficult in the social sciences and humanities than it is in the natural sciences.

This stress on the problems of scholarship in the social sciences and humanities does not mean that any such thing as objective or value-free scholarship occurs in any pure or absolute sense. Practically every major writer on these methodological problems has recognized that personal values, variations in life experiences, differences in education and in theoretical orientation, strongly affect the kind of work which men do, and their results. Such differences enter first into the choice of problems, then they affect the variables dealt with, the rigor with which they explore alternative explanations for given phenomena, and the like. Max Weber, who is frequently credited with being the major exponent of value-free, politically neutral scholarship in the social sciences, clearly enunciated the impossibility of such work. He argued, in fact, that the concept of ethical neutrality was spurious, and that those who maintained this "spuriously 'ethical neutral' " approach were precisely the ones who manifested "obstinate and deliberate partisanship."[9] He stated unequivocally that all "knowledge of cultural reality, as may be seen, is always knowledge from particular points of view."[10] He pointed out that the "significance of cultural events presupposes a value-orientation toward these events. The concept of culture is a value-concept. Empirical reality becomes 'culture' to us because and insofar as we relate it to value ideas."[11]

Weber was a highly political individual. He was an active partisan, wrote and spoke as a politician, intervened directly and often in political matters. He stressed that every professor had a personal "party-line." Because of this, and even with his general recognition of the role of personal values in affecting what we see as problems and facts, and his deep political involvements, he insisted that teachers and scholars were all the more obligated to try to be as objective as possible in their teaching and scholarship. A teacher, knowing something about his own political biases, should consciously try to negate them in class by presenting more materials contradicting his opinions than supporting them. He should make his values manifest to those who read his works or listen to his lectures. As a teacher, he must set

> . . . as his unconditional duty, in every single case, even to the point where it involves the danger of making his lectures less lively or attractive, to make relentlessly clear to his audience, and especially to himself, which of his statements are statements of logically deduced or empirically observed facts and which are statements of practical evaluation.[12]

As a methodological precept, Weber suggested that scholars should be more disposed to accept as valid findings which challenged their values and preconceptions than those which agreed with them. Clearly, he assumed that scholars, regardless of their efforts at objectivity, will be prone to recognize results and deductions which indicate they are right rather than the opposite. Hence, if science is to progress, particularly the strongly value-laden social sciences, great care must be exerted to reduce the impact of personal preferences on research results. The ultimate test, however, of scientific validity is the exposure of research results to the community at large. Any given scholar may come up with erroneous results stemming, in part, from the way in which his values have affected his work. But the commitment of scientists to objective *methods* of inquiry, the competition of ideas and concepts, will heighten the possibility of finding analytic laws which hold up regardless of who does the investigation. "For scientific truth is precisely what is valid for all who seek the truth."[13]

These are complicated methodological issues which have concerned scholars for many decades. They are not issues which should be of any great interest to the politically involved, students or others. Yet the politically concerned students live in the university. It is their home, their political base, and they, not unnaturally, want others in the institution to join them as allies in their morally justified political efforts to eliminate evil. Faculty who seek to deal with politically relevant matters in any "objective" fashion, who refuse to engage in advocacy, who point up the complexities involved in any causal treatment of the subject, necessarily become enemies; they are seen as partisans of the status quo who, if listened to, reduce the commitment to moral action.

The argument against overt political involvement by the university or the faculty as a body must also be dealt with. Karl Marx himself included as a plank in the program of the revolutionary movement: "Government and church should . . . be equally excluded from any influence on the school."[14] This issue is linked to the historic struggles of universities to free themselves from clerical and state control. In demanding and securing freedom from such controls, the university argued that its members as individuals must be free to come to any conclusion about topics relevant to religion or politics. In turn, it implicitly committed itself *officially* to ignore religious and political commitments in making appointments to its faculty, or in its formal policies. This meant that a university could appoint men who agreed with one political or religious point of view, who were liberals, atheists, radicals, or conservatives, as long as they never spoke out as a corporate body on such issues. In the United States, conservatives like William Buckley, Ronald Reagan, and others have argued the need for political balance, that is, for more conservative professors to reduce the predominant liberal-left dominance within liberal arts faculties in major universities. Others denounce the university faculty for being disproportionately composed of agnostics and atheists. And today, they are joined by student radicals who argue that more radicals should be named to academic appointments.

The university can only fight off such renewed demands by political and religious groups by insisting that the only formal criteria for appointment be scholarly, and that, even if this results in a faculty weighted toward any given side in extramural conflicts, the university and its faculty do not use their corporate prestige as a weapon in such extramural conflicts. Of course, such a formal position does not mean unpoliticized or neutral universities. That is impossible. But as Robert Wolff, the Columbia philosopher who co-authored *A Critique of Pure Tolerance* with Herbert Marcuse and Barrington Moore, points out, the myth of the apolitical university, though a myth, serves to protect unpopular minorities, that is, radicals. To insist that the university make manifest its politics would "have reactionary rather than progressive consequences. . . ." As a radical he argues against pressing the faculty to vote on political issues:

> [T]he politicization of the university invites . . . the ever-present threat of pressure, censorship and witch-hunting by conservative forces in society at large. The universities at present are sanctuaries for social critics who find it very hard to gain a living elsewhere in society. Who but a university these days would hire Herbert Marcuse, Eugene Genovese, or Barrington Moore, Jr.? Where else are anarchists, socialists and followers of other unpopular persuasions accorded titles, honors, and the absolute security of academic tenure? Let the university once declare that it is a political actor, and its faculty will be investigated. . . . It is a bitter pill for the radicals to swallow, but the fact is that they benefit more than any other segment of the university from the fiction of institutional neutrality.[15]

Barrington Moore, perhaps the most radical American sociologist, has defended the idea of a politically open university, not only on the grounds of political utility, but also as a basic principle.

> Nevertheless the general situation does create a dilemma for those of us who find ourselves in passionate opposition to the general drift of American society—a position often reached with uneasy astonishment. As students and teachers we have no objective interest in kicking down the far from sturdy walls that still do protect us. For all their faults and inadequacies the universities, and especially perhaps Harvard, do constitute a moat behind which it is still possible to examine and indict the destructive trends in our society. . . . The faculty's overwhelming commitment to free speech in the university community is part of this

moat, perhaps its most important part. To attack it heedlessly is irresponsible and self-defeating. That is so not merely because we who are vehemently opposed to many basic trends in American society may badly need its protection from time to time. The principle is important in its own right.[16]

The need to separate formally the political concerns of scholars as citizens from their academic role was held up at the convention of the American Historical Association in Washington at the end of December 1969 by three prominent historians who have attested to their personal involvement in dissident politics. The leaders of a fight against a resolution which would have placed the association in formal opposition to the Vietnamese war were Eugene Genovese, H. Stuart Hughes, and C. Vann Woodward. Genovese, who is probably the leading Marxist historian in the United States, lost his position at Rutgers University five years earlier because of his open advocacy of a victory for the Viet Cong. Hughes, who has been president of the peace organization SANE for many years, ran for United States senator from Massachusetts on a third-party peace ticket. Woodward, the leading historian of the South, has spent considerable time in civil rights activities. He was also prominently involved in the early meetings which established the Socialist Scholars Conference some years ago. These three men successfully argued, in opposition to the proposals of the "radical caucus," that the historians were morally obligated not to confuse scholarship and politics. They felt that radicals must defend scholarly institutions from politicization, even when these efforts came from young leftists.

Both Hughes and Genovese have published strong statements emphasizing their belief as political dissenters in the separation of politics and scholarship. Thus Hughes states:

The social wrongs that may be committed by the university, such as being a bad landlord or aiding the "military-industrial complex," are not to be corrected by turning it into a social service institution. There are other institutions better equipped to do that. If you lose the "ivory tower," you've lost the university. . . .

Just because a minority of conformist professors corrupted our universities through their tie-in with the "military-industrial complex" . . . just because one minority misbehaved is no reason for us, the opposing minority of dissenters, to turn around and do the same. . . .

The present need, then, is for de-politicization rather than re-politicization. . . . The task is to de-politicize connections with the right, rather than to re-politicize from the left. . . . If we don't do so, we will experience a polarization of the faculty and the campus, and wherever this has happened, whether under the auspices of the right or of the left, the result has always been a lowering of intellectual tone and the near-impossibility of teaching controversial subjects such as contemporary history.[17]

Genovese, himself a recent victim of political persecution, like Wolff stresses his belief that leftist student efforts to dominate the university will result in rightist control.

The pseudo-revolutionary middle-class totalitarians . . . support demands for student control as an entering . . . wedge for a general political purge of faculties, a purge they naively hope to dominate. . . . But they may very well help to re-establish the principle of the campus purge and thereby provide a moral and legal basis for a new wave of McCarthyism. The disgraceful treatment of Professors Staughton Lynd and Jesse Lemisch, among many who have been recently purged from universities by both liberal and right-wing pressure, has already set a tone of renewed repression, which some fanatical and unreasoning left-wing militants are unwittingly reinforcing. . . .

Universities must resist the onslaught now being made against them by superficially radical bourgeois students who have exploited the struggle over black studies programs to advance their own tactical objectives.[18]

It is important to recognize, as both Hughes and Genovese also point out, that many of the faculty, administrators and trustees who now would emphasize the inherent need for university autonomy against pressures from leftists manifestly to combine politics and scholarship have contributed to the current situation. Since the 1930s, the American university has increasingly become a major center of political involvement. Many faculty have engaged in applied, policy-oriented research, and have not taken care to separate their academic from their policy-adviser role. Professors and institutions have lent their prestige to "establishment" as well as other causes. Universities, through their choice of politically involved men to receive honorary degrees and other indicators of esteem, have implicitly endorsed the value of the work which these men have done. And if the name of the university is used in ways which have clear political consequences, it is difficult to now argue that leftist efforts to use the university should be ruled out, even though they may involve more overt forms of politicization. The argument that the defenders of the status quo can be more subtle in their politically relevant endeavors clearly has merit. Now that the issue of politicization and university autonomy has been joined again, there is a clear need to think through the rationale behind the involvement of academe as such in nonacademic concerns.

Writing as a radical critic of society and the university, Noam Chomsky carries the argument further by pointing out to student activists that they are pressing the university to live up to standards which no institution which operates within a given inequalitarian social system can do.

> Consider, for example, the matter of government contracts for research. . . . [T]here is little doubt that government research contracts provide a hidden subsidy for the academic budget, by supporting faculty research which would otherwise have to be subsidized by the university. Furthermore, it is quite probable that the choice of research topics, in the sciences at least, is influenced very little by the source of funds, at least in the major universities. It is doubtful that scientific education can continue at a reasonable level without this kind of support. Furthermore, radical students will certainly ask themselves why support from the Defense Department is more objectionable than support from

capitalist institutions, ultimately, from profits derived by exploitation – or support by tax-free gifts that in effect constitute a levy on the poor to support the education of the privileged. . . . [The university] cannot free itself from the inequities of the society in which it exists.[19]

Chomsky goes on to argue in terms similar to those of Robert Wolff that radicals must defend freedom of inquiry within the university, including the right of faculty to "work on counterinsurgency" if they so choose, for once the principle of interference with research is introduced, it is likely in the long run to legitimate repression of radical ideas. The leftists, in other words, have an interest in protecting the right of their campus opponents even to do research which is paid for by oppressive forces involved in atrocious activities. As Chomsky puts it:

> One legacy of classical liberalism that we must fight to uphold with unending vigilance, in the universities and without, is the commitment to a free marketplace of ideas. . . . Students are right to . . . point out . . . [that] access to funds, power, and influence is open to those who undertake . . . work [on counterinsurgency], but not, say, to those who would prefer to study ways in which poorly armed guerrillas might combat an enemy with overwhelming technological superiority. Were the university truly "neutral" and "value-free," one kind of work would . . be as well supported as the other. The argument is valid, but does not change the fact that the commitment is nevertheless undertaken with eagerness and a belief that it is right. Only coercion could eliminate the freedom to undertake such work. Once the principle is established that coercion is legitimate, in this domain, it is rather clear against whom it will be used. And the principle of legitimacy of coercion would destroy the university as a serious institution; it would destroy its value to a free society. This must be recognized even in the light of the undeniable fact that the freedom falls far short of ideal.[20]

From his experience in universities, Chomsky argues that the university as it now exists "is highly decentralized and rather loose in its structure of decision making and administration, hence fairly responsive to the wishes of its members." He suggests that much about the university which radical students dislike "results not from trustee control, not from defense contracts, not from administrative decisions, but from the relatively free choices of faculty and students." Hence he feels that various proposals for "restructuring of the university" will not eliminate the ills which bother the radicals, but rather are "likely to have the opposite effect, namely, they may lead toward a system of enforceable regulations that may appear democratic on paper but will limit the individual freedom that exists. . . ."[21]

Barrington Moore has also pointed out that students in fact do have a great deal of power in the contemporary university. He, therefore, calls on the students to use the traditional methods of scholarly discourse, and warns that reliance on rigid and dogmatic tactics will have less effect in achieving radical ends within the campus.

> Directly and indirectly the students in a university, especially the best students, have a tremendous influence on this general climate of opinion. If imponderable, this climate is probably the most influential single factor in determining individual decisions in a university and thereby deciding what the university really is. Naturally the faculty plays a decisive part as well. But I wonder if the students actually realize how much influence they do possess. . . . I have yet to know a scholar who did not respond in some fashion to the flow of written and oral arguments presented by good students. This situation provides the most significant opening for students who respond critically and negatively to the world about them. If they come to the faculty rigidly and dogmatically prepared to defend radical positions at all costs, they will get nowhere and defeat their own purposes. The consequences of this rigidity are often a tragic waste of essentially fine human materials. On the other hand, if they come in some degree prepared to be convinced as well as to convince, and if they are also willing to do the hard work necessary to demonstrate their intellectual mastery of the evidence, their impact can be enormous.[22]

The issues of university governance, as far as they involve student participation, also relate in part to a comparable set of concerns about politics and scholarship. Since the students in the social sciences and to a lesser extent the humanities are the most radical, the demands for student participation have generally been raised most in these fields. These areas, however, are not only the most politically relevant, they also differ from the natural sciences in that judgments concerning methodological issues and research competence remain highly subjective. There is almost no recognized piece of research, or scholar, in these disciplines whose distinction is not controversial. With few exceptions, it is quite possible to argue that any given work is either methodologically inadequate, that it is following a sterile approach, and/or that its weaknesses stem from biases which have led the researcher to ignore important factors and to come to erroneous conclusions.

In these less precise fields of scholarship, the more committed individuals are to a political role, as distinct from a scholarly one, the more likely they are to judge scholarly work by its presumed political consequences. Obviously such factors, and other sources of personal values as well, affect the way in which academics evaluate each other, regardless of age or institutional status. But in a politicized era, those who have not been fully socialized to the norms of the academy, who are more wont, as students, to feel the primacy of politics, will look for political allies among their professors. Not accepting the worth of the particular discipline in the same terms as its professional practitioners, being less disposed to believe that most scholars try to be objective, students will be more prone to want the university to act in directly political terms than will professors. In dealing with curricular matters, they will be less likely to respect the need for abstract theoretical, methodological, or "basic" fields which do not deal directly with social problems than their elders. An increase in "student power" in matters of faculty appointments or curriculum, therefore, almost inevitably means greater politicization in the methodologically soft disciplines.

There are important arguments against student involvement in the selection of faculty or the research program of other scholars which go beyond the particular issue of politicization. If all intellectuals, including professors, are obligated to stress innovation and creativity according to the standards and logic of their fields, then the questions of who shall take part in a given creative field or what kinds of work shall be considered important cannot be put to a vote of anyone. All intellectuals are in the same position as an artist or serious composer. Talented people will consider the judgments of their audience, of those who buy their paintings, of museum directors, for the reactions of the consumers of their creative product will determine their income. But no creative intellectual worthy of that name will consciously subject the direction of his work to the decision of the marketplace. In any case, innovators, creators, are by definition deviants, who explore unanticipated areas. If students are allowed to vote on the choice of faculty (they should, of course, be consulted), they, like other laymen, will favor what is currently popular. Even in the social sciences, some fields of current "relevance" such as urban studies were of little interest to students during the 1950s. Fellow intellectuals know that they cannot dictate what others should do. Thus, many faculty see the struggle to maintain the rule that only professionals may vote on new members as part of the historic effort of intellectuals to maintain or gain their freedom from interference by patrons, by those with consumer power. A case against student interference with the work of the professor has been effectively made by the British sociologist Ernest Gellner, who himself has been a severe intellectual critic from the left of dominant trends in his discipline.

> What is worrying about the student part of the [New Left] movement is its occasional illiberalism. However libertarian its members may be about legalizing marijuana, they do sometimes put forward proposals such as the student control of "what is taught and how." It does not occur to them that the implementation of this proposal would not involve the *transfer* of power

> from one set of people to them, but the *institution* of control where none exists at present. . . . [A]t least in British universities, teachers . . . are safe and free to teach what and how they wish, and the students, who also complain, not without cause, of the quality of teaching, know that there is very little control of teachers. Those who demand control by themselves over "what" is taught do not seem to realize the enormity, not of giving *them* control, but of instituting control *at all,* or rather, of replacing the present "sociological" controls, working through indirect pressures which can be defied without excessive difficulty by anyone really wishing to do so — by formal and, presumably, enforced controls. The present pressures are limited in their effectiveness precisely because they are held to be illegitimate: they can only operate in camouflage, and this hampers them. But the rebels wish to institutionalize and legalize the controls which *they* would impose, and thus nothing would inhibit *their* effectiveness. They do not seem to have pondered the institutional implications of their proposals. What is to happen to teachers who disobey their instructions? One can only wonder whether they *do* know what they are saying, and are profoundly illiberal and totalitarian, or whether they do *not* know what they say, and the proposal is merely part of . . . general invertebrate thinking.[23]

As I noted earlier, ever since the time American faculty began to turn increasingly to research, there has been a perpetual argument of the relative advantages for teaching and intellectual life of varying emphases and encouragement to research or teaching. The thesis that research interferes with teaching, that undergraduates are being short-changed as a result, was present by the beginning of this century. Suggestions that universities establish teaching doctorates which do not require a dissertation as a means of upgrading undergraduate teaching also date back to that period. The "neglected" undergraduate has been a favorite article topic for well over three quarters of a century. And such writings have pointed to the pressures on professors to engage in extramural activities for almost as long. Thus the eminent professors of earlier decades were accused of neglecting their university duties for the lecture circuit and for writing financially lucrative textbooks or articles for magazines or the popular press.

The issue of teaching versus research, however, did not take on a political character until recently. In fact, if any deduction concerning the ideological correlates of those on different sides of the question may be identified, it is that the conservatives have favored more teaching. The links between intellectuality and political liberalism discussed earlier clearly point in this direction. Conservatives have defended the teaching function of the university that seeks to preserve the classical ideal, to stress the need to absorb the wisdom of the past, the "great books," not to create new knowledge. The pressure to make the university a center of research and innovation has more frequently come from those imbued with the idea of progress, of social change.

Student movements, however, insofar as they represent the "class" sentiments of students, have perceived professors primarily, if not solely, in their role as teachers. They want more time from them. And they have seen grades as mechanisms of social control, as means of getting them to conform to the authority or whims of the teacher. The leftist students have added to this criticism the idea that grades help maintain the "capitalist" emphasis on competition, on the "rat race," on the struggle for success, rather than on learning for its own sake.

The faculty, of course, also divides on these issues. Many younger professors in recent years have accepted the doctrine that research is often self-serving careerism. Some resolve to devote their careers to teaching, to working with students. Those who disagree with this position argue that an emphasis on teaching can be a way of escaping from being judged in the necessarily highly competitive intellectual world. It has also been suggested that a stress on teaching as the primary function of the academic job makes the task of "succeeding" easier. There is less strain in devoting oneself to lectures and discussions with students than in seeking to produce research which is regarded as first-rate.

There would appear to be an "interest" factor in this discussion which is partially generational. The older, more "successful" faculty, who have acquired academic distinction through their research, have an obvious reason for defending the existing system, including the ways in which support has been distributed. Those who have "failed," or are too young to have succeeded, are more prone to stress the virtues of teaching. Yet the inherent requirements of an intellectual career will press many younger faculty to seek jobs which facilitate their concentrating on research and writing. Presumably, it will be precisely those who are high in intellectuality, in scholarly competence, and hence also in political liberalism or radicalism, who will want this. As a group, at the moment, they are clearly in a cross-pressure situation. They, in effect, are the one group in academe who are pressed to resolve the dilemma between degree of emphasis on teaching or research in their own behavior.

Thus far, there is little evidence that the increased concern for undergraduate education which is manifest in the myriad of articles, books, national commissions, and local campus surveys has, in fact, changed the dominant practice of the American academy. Some years ago, the Israeli sociologist Joseph Ben David suggested as a general proposition concerning American academe that any event which reduces the attractiveness of a given university to retain or attract faculty would necessarily result in an increase in the bargaining power of faculty vis-à-vis the administration. A major internal crisis or a change in the ecological environment of a campus meant that the university had to pay more to gain or maintain a high level faculty. His first example was Berkeley after the loyalty oath crisis of 1949–50. He suggested that the cut in the pre-oath teaching load, three courses a semester, six a year, to a four or five course a year load, together with a rapid increase in upper-range salaries, which occurred soon after the oath fight, reflected the need of the university to improve faculty working conditions and income, to make up for the negative image. A similar sharp drop in teaching load and increase in salaries which occurred at the University of Chicago in the late fifties and early sixties seemed linked to the decline in the attractiveness of the neighborhood surrounding that school. And Joseph Ben David, who happened to be a visiting professor at Berkeley during 1964–65, the year of the Berkeley revolt, predicted similar results from that event. History has seemingly validated his prediction. The teaching load at Berkeley which is under the control of departments has been reduced since 1965 in many departments, particularly in the politically vulnerable, and, therefore, competitively less attractive, social science fields.

Few observers of the Berkeley scene who have commented in detail on the various experimental programs designed to improve the quality of undergraduate education there have noted that the biggest change in faculty-student relations is less faculty classroom contact with students than before. Crisis, as Joseph Ben David suggested, means greater bargaining power for faculty, and faculty use such power to reduce their teaching obligations. A similar set of events followed on the Columbia sit-in and student general strike in the spring of 1968. Until that event, the normal teaching load at Columbia was three courses a term; since then, it is two courses. Thus, though many, probably most, of the faculty at these and other institutions honestly believe that they are more interested in and dedicated to teaching since the emergence of student protest in 1964–1965, the evidence as reflected in time given to students at major American institutions does not bear them out. The reasons are obvious, and no amount of moral advocacy that is not accompanied by a change in the reward structure will affect practice. As Jencks and Riesman put it:

> There is no guild within which successful teaching leads to greater prestige and influence than mediocre teaching. . . . No doubt most professors prefer it when their courses are popular, their lectures applauded, and their former students appreciative. But since such successes are of no help in getting a salary increase, moving to a more prestigious campus, or winning their colleagues' admiration, they are unlikely to struggle as hard to create them as to do other things. Indeed, good teaching can be a positive handicap in attempting to meet other payrolls . . . for the able teacher finds students beating a path to his door and leaving him

> little time for anything else. If he is really committed to research he may well find that the only way to make free time is to remain aloof.[24]

It is important to recognize that the teaching issue is one in which the student activists can expect more support from administrators, trustees, alumni representatives, and politicians than from the faculty of major universities. The former are much more disposed to view the university as a school, are more concerned with the way it treats the students than are the professors. The highly competitive, nationally oriented research faculty are seen by the administrative classes of the university in much the same way as the radical students see them, that is, as self-centered, self-serving individuals, who are using the university to benefit themselves, and who give as little as possible to more campus-centered activities.[25]

Alex Sherriffs, special consultant to Governor Ronald Reagan on higher education, sounded like a radical student in a discussion of the activities of the University of California faculty:

> Frustrated, normally idealistic youngsters . . . come up against a faculty which teaches less – and I mean less – than five hours a week. It's symbolic to the kids. If you've got a big name, you're too busy for them. . . . A guy who's an excellent teacher is looked on with some suspicion [by other faculty] as a guy who couldn't make it. They still play the foundation game. That's how you get your grants and your secretary and your prestige. And when they [the faculty] have to cut the budget, they cut out pupils every time. That shows their priorities.[26]

The same criticism of the university faculty has been made up and down the state by Governor Reagan himself. In addition to attacking the radicals on the staff, whom he sees as a small minority, his major explanation for student unrest is what Clark Kerr once called "the faculty in abstentia":

> "Young men and women go to college to find themselves as individuals," the Governor declared in the speech that has be-

come a kind of educational testament. "They see the names of distinguished scholars in the catalogue and sign up for courses with the belief that they will learn and grow and be stimulated by contact with these men. All too often they are herded into gigantic classes taught by teaching assistants hardly older than themselves. The feeling comes that they're nameless, faceless numbers on an assembly line – green cap at one end, cap and gown and an automated diploma at the other."

And on and on the Governor goes with his paraphrase of the FSM, including such classic complaints as the priority of "publish or perish" over concern for teaching and the desire of the students to have someone "know they're there."[27]

A similar political lineup on issues such as these occurs among the faculty. As has been noted, the less research-oriented faculty tend to be more politically conservative and locally oriented in terms of campus affairs, and more concerned with teaching as an institutional function. They, too, deprecate what they consider to be the exaggerated emphasis and rewards given for research. They are the people who staff the committee system, who assist the deans, who keep the place going in normal times. (In a national survey of social science faculty conducted in 1955, Lazarsfeld and Thielens found that conservatives are more disposed to be department chairmen and to be active in campus affairs than liberals, even when age is controlled.)[28] Hence when student groups raise the teaching-research issue, they are likely to confound the basis for faculty political cleavage. The "conservatives" and the establishment agree with them while the more research-oriented "liberals" will, if they honestly speak their minds, be more likely to disagree.

The same apparent "contradiction" exists with respect to outside involvements as consultants for government agencies or business firms. The radical students assume that both sets of institutions are reactionary, and presumably those faculty who are involved with them have "sold out" and should be among the more conservative members of the faculty. But in fact a 1966 national faculty survey conducted by the National Opinion

Research Center indicated that professors who had *never* worked for extramural organizations, whether business or government, were most disposed to *back* government policy on Vietnam. Those who had served government were most opposed to the policy.[29] An even stronger relationship between having been called in as a consultant to business and political liberalism was indicated in the Lazarsfeld-Thielens study of social scientists' reaction to (Joe) McCarthyism. Holding age constant, those who strongly favored academic and civil liberties for Communists and other unpopular minority dissidents were most likely to have been consultants for business. At every age level, the "clearly conservative" had the lowest level of involvement with business.[30]

The "missing" intervening variable in both sets of findings, presumably, is that the most successful scholars are the ones called on to consult, and, as indicated by many surveys, academic success, regardless of how measured, is correlated with degree of leftism in political attitudes. The same results should obtain in any estimate of the relationship between involvement in Defense Department research and political liberalism, or even opposition to the Vietnam war and other American foreign policies. Since the Defense Department has been the largest supporter of basic (non-policy oriented) research in the country, it is likely that its grants have been given largely to the most prestigious scholars in various fields, therefore to the most liberal. This presumed relationship may explain the fact that many of the most prominent faculty radicals and opponents of the Vietnam war have not backed opposition to Defense Department support of basic research when this issue has been raised by student radicals. At Harvard, Berkeley, and MIT, for example, the most radical member of the faculty in terms of public utterances in each case has been a long-term client of the research agencies of the Defense Department.

These differences between the student activists and many of the faculty who stand relatively close to them in general political philosophy or ideology can be conceptualized in another way. Students, including, or especially, the radicals among them, want the university to retain the characteristics of a school and the faculty to behave like teachers in lower levels of education. Many students seek teachers who will tell what they think about life generally. They will see, in professorial claims to seek objectivity by introducing contradictory material, an evasion of their responsibility to take a stand. The faculty, particularly at universities which are major centers of research, who are themselves committed to a life of productive scholarship, see higher education and the role of the professor as highly differentiated, in which teaching is only one of the activities.[31] Florian Znaniecki, in his analysis of the role of the intellectual, pointed up the distinctively different functions of the university and the school:

> . . . [T]he school of higher learning performs the specifically social function of an educational institution only because its main activities are not social but scientific, do not aim to contribute to the maintenance of the social order but to the maintenance of knowledge as a supersocial domain of culture supremely valuable in itself. . . . The school of general education, on the contrary, as an institution of the modern society serves directly the maintenance of social order — whether it be a traditionally static order or a more or less dynamic new order.[32]

It is important to note in Znaniecki's distinction that he describes the institution which advocates radical change and the one which supports the status quo as both being primarily schools rather than scientific organizations. Michio Nagai has pointed out that the teacher-student relationship in the school is one of a parent-substitute to a child, which tends to become particularistic. The teacher in nonuniversity education is expected to consider all aspects of the child's life. He suggests that "the reasons why it is so difficult to establish professional standards for teachers may be found in the diffuseness of the function of the teacher. . . ."[33] Thus, the school is characterized particularly by the diffused content and method of instruction in it as distinct from the highly specialized university.

Given the assumption that schoolteachers have diffuse authority over pupils and that they have a particularistic relationship with them, it follows that the method of teaching, the very role of the teacher in the classroom and in personal discussions must be different:

> While the university professor has authority over the student only in a restricted area of human activity, the schoolteacher . . . has authority over children in many aspects of their lives. . . . The task of the teacher, unlike that of the professor, is not only to teach how to learn science, but how to live.[34]

It may be argued that when the activists criticize the educational system today, they seek to retain the status of pupil and to have teachers rather than to be students of university professors. Although their demand is now couched in terms of the faculty taking an activist position in support of radical social change, it is a demand that their professors act like their schoolteachers, that they take part in "bull sessions" in which they discuss the totality of human experience, not simply their subject matter. In 1971, radical philosopher Michael Novak was to report that the need of the underprivileged for grades helped to end the experiment in unstructured public higher education in Old Westbury.

> . . . [B]lacks and Puerto Ricans often operated as the most conservative educational forces; desiring grades, clear standards, written assignments, sequences of courses, a firm structure of authority and tests. . . . (They wanted) courses that would get them into law school, graduate school and the arts. "Old Westbury is an interlude for us," one said. "If that degree doesn't mean something, we go back to the streets."[35]

The argument concerning grades also cuts across the usual left-right dimensions, although in recent years it has been raised largely by student activists.[36] Radicals see in the power to grade an instrument of coercion which prevents the free interchange of ideas and opinions between faculty and students. The fact that a meritocratic grading system has been seen as an instrument of freedom by those from underprivileged backgrounds is foreign to them. Felix Frankfurter, who came to Harvard Law School from

CCNY as an immigrant Jewish youth before World War I, never got over his awe at the democratic implications of the rigorous grading system:

> What mattered was excellence in your profession to which your father or your face was equally irrelevant. And so rich man, poor man were just irrelevent titles to the equation of human relations. The thing that mattered was what you did professionally.[37]

As Frankfurter saw the situation, the alternative to a rigorous grading system had to be reliance on faculty "personal likes and dislikes, or class, or color, or religious partialities or antipathies. . . . These incommensurable things give too much room for personal preferences and on the whole make room for unworthy and irrelevant biases." The young Randolph Bourne, socialist scion of Anglo-Saxon higher status, also argued in similar terms before World War I: "Scholarship is fundamentally democratic. Before the bar of marks and grades, penniless adventurer and rich man's son stand equal."[38]

The general issue is how much and under what conditions institutions of higher learning should reflect in their internal structure the different norms and orientations of the worlds of the school and scholarship. In this respect, we meet again a congruence between the Left and the Right. The leftist students agree with many conservative critics of the university. Both want the university to be a school. The Left, however, desires a school which will favor radical social change, while the conservative politicians and alumni want a school which will defend the status quo. Neither wants an institution which is dedicated to subject all simple propositions, all explanations, all reforms, to the test of scientific validity. For in essence the university is the enemy of simplification. The norms which must govern a university make of it a qualitatively different environment than a high school. In shifting from the status of high school pupil to university student, youth must adjust to a highly specialized and segmented system in which their professors will be men for whom undergraduate teaching is necessarily only one of a number of functions, and not even the most important one in the better institutions.

It is essential that those concerned with university life recognize that universities are not schools, that the norms which govern scientific activities are quite different from those which characterize schools. The approach of science and of the university has been analyzed in formal analytical terms by Talcott Parsons and Robert K. Merton. The values they specify describe the "role structure of the scientist" (Parsons) and "the cultural values and mores governing the activities termed scientific" (Merton) in terms which are in variance with the involvement of faculty in indoctrination, in preparation for life, and with the total personality and character found in the school.

Merton emphasizes the neutral, objective, disinterested, and skeptical values inherent in the scientific process. Parsons similarly points out that the ethos of science, which includes functional specificity (professional specialization) and achievement orientation as well as those activities mentioned by Merton, has "above all become embodied in the university as its principal institutionalized frame." These guiding values imply that professors have no general claim to superior knowledge, but must combine organized skepticism and universalism (treatment of all according to impersonal criteria) in their application of objectivity to their specific area of expertise with an understanding of the boundaries of their professional abilities. Further, both men stress that while scientists must conduct themselves commensurate with these values, nonscientists, including students, must reciprocally respect the scientist's inviolable rights in his own field.[39]

These value orientations which are inherent in the scientific ethos contain liberal-left political implications and call for emphasizing the role of the student as apprentice scholar, not as the pupil of a Mr. Chips-type teacher, whether radical or conservative. The values of science emphasize the need for a free society operating under the rule of law. State interference to guarantee that science adheres to a party, national, or religious line, or that scientists are not free to criticize each other, makes for bad science. The stress on universalism, on functional specificity, on achievement orientation, implies opposition to those aspects of stratified societies which limit equality of opportunity. For science, trained intelligence, not family background, race, or wealth, must be the primary quality associated with status and social rewards. Hence, as noted earlier, the more committed an academic to scientific research, the more likely he will oppose those aspects of the social system which appear to perpetuate inequality of opportunity.

Some of the same elements of the scientific ethos which press men in a liberal and left direction politically, also, of course, include the action imperative to treat students in a highly specific, meritocratic manner. To advance scientific knowledge means that all qualified youth must be encouraged and rewarded, but that little reward (or attention) should be given to the unqualified or to the less able. Science is inherently concerned with locating and rewarding the aristocracy of talent. Anyone familiar with the norms of major centers of graduate study in the liberal arts fields knows that this is the way they operate. The faculty are only interested in graduate students who seem to have the ability to make major contributions to knowledge; the inadequate among them are regarded as out of place in such departments. And such values which must be present in major graduate and research centers inevitably inform the treatment of undergraduates in the same institutions. (It may be noted that the leading state universities such as Berkeley or Madison which do not have as highly selective undergraduate admissions policies as the major private institutions, but which maintain an elite research-oriented faculty, have created the optimum condition for fostering neglect of the undergraduates.)

The differences between graduate school university faculty and those at four-year colleges are also to be found among the colleges. Jencks and Riesman have detailed the way in which the ethos of graduate education has affected the entire character of

American academe.[40] In an earlier study, Riesman and Gusfeld have shown how undergraduate schools vary in faculty and student orientation with respect to the different concept of the college they sustain. Some of the consequences of the distinction attempted here between the school and the research institute, graduate-training role of the university, and between the pupil and the student roles open to undergraduates, were developed by Riesman and Gusfield in their analysis of the differences in the activities of undergraduate institutions. They distinguish between the "adult-forming" and "youth-prolonging" aspects of higher education by noting that by using adult standards of performance, universities "weed out" the childlike students. In a limited sense, the highly specialized professor also provides a model of one possible adult role. However, the instructor who views himself less as a specialist and more as a member of a broad intellectual subculture seeks to preserve youthful traits in his students and tends to remain young himself, ". . . young in the sense of being rebellious, open, uncommitted to specific authoritative roles. Correspondingly, they are much less eager than their more didactic colleagues to induct the students into a particular speciality; what they want of them is a greater playfulness, a release of inhibitions imposed by the parochial past and the looming vocational future – in other words a moratorium."[41]

It may be argued that the traits of science enunciated by Parsons and Merton and of "adult-forming" educational functions specified by Riesman and Gusfield are relevant to scientific research and the work of research institutes but not to colleges and universities. The latter are primarily educational not research organizations. Hence the application of scientific traits to the college properly has made for student dissatisfaction and unrest. This argument, made by both students and politicians in authority over universities, clearly is quite valid. Much of what is done in the American system of higher education is closer in function to the work of high schools than it is to graduate centers of education and research. The courses usually taught in lower division, in the freshmen and sophomore years, in most colleges and universities are extensions of high school work, if they are not in fact courses identical to those given in many high schools. Elementary work in languages, in mathematics, in English, in a variety of other subjects, is not on the level of university courses in the sense in which the university has developed in Oxford and Cambridge, in Germany, and elsewhere. The university in much of Europe has ideally at least been closer in requirements to the American graduate school than to the undergraduate college. The *Gymnasium, lycée,* grammar or public schools in Europe cover many of the courses which in this country are included in colleges or universities. The first university degree in Europe is a specialized degree, often in one subject, requiring a thesis. The doctorate is the only degree given in Germany, northern Europe, and many Latin countries. (It is more akin to the American master's degree than the Ph.D.)

As a result of the growth of the research function, American institutions of higher education today are torn between being schools and graduate research centers. When we think of the intellectual or scholarly status of a university, we think of the prestige of its faculty as researchers, not their abilities as teachers. The supremacy of the research function over teaching as a source of institutional status is inherent in the fact that scholarly recognition is a national, often international phenomenon, while the reputation of a man as a teacher is local, limited to people only associated with his campus. Hence, although relatively few institutions are major centers of research, probably the majority of students attending four year degree-granting colleges are in institutions in which the faculty is held to the requirement that they engage in productive scholarship, that they be judged for salary, rank, and local prestige by their presumed research rather than teaching merits. A study of the role of the teaching assistant at major universities indicates that a considerable amount of lower division instruction in such institutions is given by graduate students who are devoting most of their energies to getting a doctoral degree.[42]

Students and faculty are properly in a confused state with

regard to their respective roles. As the importance of the research function for the larger society increased (very few professors were expected to be researchers in the nineteenth century and few were), the more prestigious professors in the centers of graduate training and research took on a variety of activities in addition to research and teaching. A relatively small segment of the American professoriate has been asked to serve as consultants for government, industry, political parties and international agencies. The same men are in demand for extramural lectures, articles, books and editorial consultation. They are invited to participate in the increasing number of international conferences made possible by the jet plane and foundation funds, which are often genuinely necessary to facilitate rapid communication of research results and new ideas. While few schools have separated the graduate from the undergraduate faculty, the number of graduate students increases rapidly. Research in many disciplines now involves the administration of substantial funds and the coordination of the work of various colleagues and assistants. All of these tasks have been added to the work of undergraduate teaching, which was the primary, usually the exclusive, task of professors in the major institutions in the nineteenth century.

To put the whole matter another way, the leading universities and professors have been accumulating more tasks, while they continue to do their old one, undergraduate teaching, as well. These institutions and faculty are judged for eminence and the rewards which go with high status by their research output. The reports on the relative status of academic departments and universities which have been prepared for the American Council on Education and other bodies, and which are made much of by the press, administrators, and faculty themselves, are ratings of these departments as graduate schools, as centers of research, not ratings of undergraduate teaching. This increased pressure on faculty at such institutions for differentiated involvements and the lesser time given to undergraduate education should make the university world an increasingly less happy place for both faculty and undergraduates.

And as we have seen, both the leading faculty and the students at institutions with the highest admission standards tend to be among the most rebellious politically. The political rebellion stems from factors other than the tensions inherent in institutional and faculty role conflict, but a liberal-radical political ideology and "job dissatisfaction" should reinforce one another. The upshot of many politically motivated campus disturbances has been an attack on the governance or other aspects of the university as a place in which to work or learn.

The emphasis on the internal governance of the university to which many faculty and student activists have turned as a "solution" to the problems of higher education seems to be misplaced, as Chomsky suggests. More faculty work, more committees, only make the situation worse. In previous crises, efforts to democratize university government resulted in involvement in "busy" work (committees) of the less research-involved, also more conservative faculty, once the original crisis which activated the concerns of the younger and more liberal-left faculty ended. The increased "democratization" (more elected faculty committees) thereafter increases the importance of the role of the more conservative and scholarly less prestigious "committeemen," since they can claim to be the elected "representatives" of the faculty rather than the appointed consultants of the administration. In effect, faculty elections often serve to give populist legitimacy to locally oriented, relatively conservative professional faculty politicians, who rise to the "top" because the "cosmopolitan," more research-involved liberal faculty see campus politics as a waste of time in normal periods. In a period of renewed crisis, the elected spokesmen of the faculty, chosen before the troubles, usually differ greatly in their political orientations from the dominant faculty mood. The general situation has been well described by William Roth, a leader of the liberal minority on the Board of Regents of the University of California:

> The rhetoric of faculty governance, however, betrays the usual cultural lag. Through an intricate structure of senates, assemblies,

> and committees, it maintains the pretense of a self-governing community of scholars. The inaccurate word is "community," for its members are more concerned with doing their own thing than with the general welfare of the particular society which nourishes them. Traditionally, the professor does not want to be bothered by problems of governance. If out of sudden guilt, rage, or embarrassment, he occasionally rises in protest, he soon lapses again into his own affairs. When there is a dramatic, albeit often symbolic, issue to be confronted, the faculty turns out en masse. But the day-to-day business of university government that must be carried on is left to a small minority of concerned people – the scholarly bureaucrats and politicians.[43]

Student participation on a representative basis, as a minority of a campus-wide faculty-student senate, is not likely to give the bulk of the student body any sense of increased participation or involvement. All that they get out of such reforms is the opportunity to vote once a year.

In terms of sheer educational satisfaction, or optimal personal adjustment, there clearly is no "right" form of higher education for everyone. The diverse pluralistic form of American universities and colleges has as one of its advantages the opportunity for students and faculty to sort themselves out, to try to find the best type of school for their personalities and talents. Unfortunately, of course, such a choice is not available to most people.

There does seem to be a set of problems calling for reform stemming from the multiplication of tasks handled by faculty as individuals and by universities as institutions. Differentiation, separation of functions, has been the pattern of response in all institutional life as tasks have multiplied. In the Soviet Union and other communist countries, the research-institute graduate-training set of activities is conducted separately from that of undergraduate teaching. Japan is planning to separate graduate work from other forms of higher education. These alternative systems clearly have liabilities of their own. But if the recent wave of politically induced discontent within the American university is to have any useful function for the life of the university itself, there is a clear and present need to examine the need for, and the possibilities of, a restructuring of the system into a variety of component parts. One important possible reform would be to vary considerably the types of state supported higher education available, as California has done to some extent. This should be combined with much greater encouragement than now exists for students to "try out" different varieties of schools by making transference among institutions easy.

This counsel does not imply the necessity to separate research and teaching. It does suggest, however, the need to recognize and not be afraid to state that a genuine university should not have the attributes of a school in the sense used earlier in this chapter. If a university is to educate for adulthood, it cannot be concerned with continuing to be a *gemeinschaft*, a community which resembles an extended family. Students must learn that intellectual life is complicated and difficult, that professors are also scholars who do not have the time to hold their hands or spoonfeed them with intellectual nourishment. The scholar must share with the student the tentativity of knowledge, his uncertainties about his conclusions, his self-doubts, and his triumphs. The student must be prepared to challenge the findings of his professors, after he has learned the methodology of the field, as another seeker of truth. To communicate the complexities of knowledge to sharp questioning minds is essential to the process of intellectual clarification. Scholarship requires dialogue, controversy, not only among established men in the same field, but with students as well. Those who would turn universities into schools or into research institutes are seeking to escape the intramural conflict by an easy capitulation. The primary function of the university is scholarship, which includes rigorous education, not politics or therapy. This means, of course, that there can only be a relatively small number of universities which have severe standards for faculty and students, although there will be thousands of accredited institutions of higher education.

7

Some Political Consequences of Student Activism in Comparative Perspective

The rise of student protest movements since World War II has been more extensive and more important than in earlier periods. Students played a major role during the 1950s in overthrowing or weakening regimes in the underdeveloped and communist worlds. Thus, student movements were important in the revolts against Perón in Argentina in 1955, against Pérez Jiménez in Venezuela in 1958, in different protest movements in South Korea and South Vietnam during the 1950s, in India, Japan, and many other countries. They helped initiate liberalizing movements in Poland, Hungary, the Soviet Union, and China in 1955–1956. During the 1960s, of course, student protest spread to the developed countries of Europe and the United States.

These movements have a great deal in common in tactics and political style. Student culture is a highly communicable one — the mood and mode of it translate readily from one center to another, one country to another. Yet it would be a mistake to try to interpret the seeming phenomenon of a worldwide student revolt as a response to common social conditions or as an effort to secure a common objective. The sources of student protest must be differentiated among different types of societies: underdeveloped systems, authoritarian regimes, mainly Communist, and the economically developed democratic societies.

The Third and Communist Worlds

In various underdeveloped countries and new states of the third world, the sources of intellectual and student protest may be found in the wide gap which exists between the social outlook of the educated younger part of the population and the more traditional, less educated, older age groups. The gap between the social and political expectations engendered within universities, and the reality of underdeveloped societies, motivates students and intellectuals to accept ideologies which define the status quo as unacceptable and seek drastic institutional changes so as to foster modernization, i.e., the values of the "advanced" societies. This gap is reinforced by the fact that the very logic of the university imposes values of achievement, competitive standards of merit, which are frequently in conflict with the traditional, particularistic values both of the controlling elite and the population at large. Thus, the intellectuals and students of Eastern Europe in the nineteenth century rejected the institutions of their own societies as backward compared to those of France and Britain. Chinese "returned students" in the early years of this century favored the overthrow of the backward Manchu dynasty so as to catch up to the West.

Although the principal source of ideological tensions within such societies involves the conflict between "modern" and "traditional" values, a conflict which opinion surveys suggest is largely linked to differences in education and age, such differences are often tied to positions on international issues. In much of the underdeveloped world the opposition to existing domestic elites and social-cultural-economic systems for being involved in and responsible for national backwardness, is accompanied by support for the Communist model as an example of a successful effort to break through the restrictions on development and modernization. Since the existing social system is often allied internationally with the United States, the student opposition movements tend to associate the symbols of the United States, capitalism, the free world, with the conservative elites of their own society. Opposition to domestic traditionalism and liberalism becomes translated into support for some form of leftism which in international terms means opposition to the United States. Hence, in large measure, leftist student activism in most of the underdeveloped world is a force against any alignment with the United States. It is, however, not necessarily a force for support of the Soviet Union.

The leftist student groups differ considerably from country to country, and in recent years there has been an increasing growth of "third force" revolutionary organizations which are both anti-American and anti-Soviet. Some tend to be Maoist, others identify in a very loose way with Trotskyism, a few are explicitly anarchist. There is a tendency to take over a variant of what has come to be know as the New Left ideology, that is opposition to all power groups. But regardless of the differences among the leftists, there can be little question that the focus of their hostility in international terms is the United States. This opposition has become intensified with the escalation of the Vietnamese war since 1964. In large measure opposition to American intervention in Vietnam has become the predominant political issue of many of the left-wing groups.

There is one major variation among the different underdeveloped countries which relates to the image and role of the governing power concerned, i.e., whether it is viewed as leftist or not. The political movements of students in countries which are aligned to the Soviet bloc have often opposed Soviet policy.

Two outstanding examples of this phenomenon occurred in Indonesia under Sukarno and in Ghana under Nkrumah.[1] In both of these countries led by pro-Communist leaders, the students took a position in opposition to the regime, arguing in favor of increased liberty within the universities and political life generally. Their advocacy of greater freedom and their criticism of various actions of the regime led them to foster the ideologies of democracy and certain kinds of liberalism. In a sense, the general proposition may be advanced that the most activist student groups tend to be opposed to the existing regime, and consequently take on a political ideology in opposition to it. The situation in the various Communist countries is, of course, a case in point.[2] Where student activism has developed in Communist societies it is critical of the existing regime as oppressive and also critical of its international orientation. To some degree in Eastern Europe, the oppositionist students have favored withdrawal from the Warsaw Pact, have shown signs of being pro-Western, and have taken up the issue of Communist-Israeli relations as a symbolic one. The students in Poland and Czechoslovakia have been strongly in favor of Israel.

The sources of the tensions between the regime and the university and intellectual life which are conducive to student activism in Communist countries are somewhat different from those in the third world. As in the underdeveloped countries, there is an inherent gap between some norms which are an aspect of university and intellectual life, namely, academic and intellectual freedom, and the structure of society. Intellectual and scientific life requires freedom. To simply mouth Party truth, or to limit the problems which one studies or the conclusions which one reaches, to those which are authorized by the regime, places a basic strain on intellectual activity. Lenin and the Bolsheviks, of course, distrusted intellectuals precisely for this reason. It is antithetical for an intellectual simply to be a publicist or spokesman for a given system. Intellectuals, as noted earlier, place a premium on originality as a source of status, and originality means rejecting the verities of the present and past. Hence there is a predisposition among those involved in the world of the intellect, whether inside or outside of the university, to resist authority on such issues, a strain which becomes manifest during periods of crises. One of the most dramatic examples of the strength of such values among intellectuals and students under Communism surfaced during the brief "hundred flowers bloom" period in China in 1956. The relaxation of controls by the

Maoist regime produced a sudden outburst of critical speeches and statements on the campuses of the country which denounced the government for inhibiting free speech, research, and teaching, and for maintaining an absolutist state. Many of these criticisms pointed to Titoist Yugoslavia as an example of a Communist state which supposedly allowed freedom and which followed an independent policy with respect to the Soviet Union.[3]

Improvements, i.e., a relaxation of controls, serve often to stimulate increased criticism of the system among those who take the values of freedom seriously. For new generations of Eastern European (or Spanish) university students, the fact that there is more freedom than in Stalin's day, or than three years ago, is an ineffective argument. They only know that the present system is not free, that the present rulers are repressive even if they happen to be men who pressed for more freedom a few years earlier. Thus, once the issue of freedom is joined in authoritarian states, we may expect students and intellectuals to fight to drop the existing restrictions, a struggle which can lead either to greater liberalization, or a return to absolutist controls, as recent Czech, Polish and Spanish history unfortunately demonstrate.

The Developed Democracies: The United States and Europe

On the basis of the analyses of the sources of intellectual and student protest in the third and Communist world, it would seem that radical student activism should occur less frequently and be less prevalent in the developed democracies of Europe and the English-speaking states. Since modern industrial societies are largely characterized by their support for a universalistic ethic of merit, of freedom, and of scientific and intellectual creativity and originality, there should be diminished tension between the values of the world of intellect and the larger society. This would be true even recognizing that the universities still place a greater emphasis on egalitarianism and the free competition of ideas than do other institutions. It is worth noting again that the current wave of student unrest in the United States arose as a response to the one issue, race relations, in which the United States has retained an aspect of premodern traditional caste values, which are basically at odds with the norms of a democratic industrial society. Anti-imperialism, that is, opposition to colonial rule, is another example of student identification with the explicit values of democratic society against its own practices. Previous to the emergence of American student protest, the largest post–World War II upheaval in the Western world was occasioned by French student support for the FLN in the Algerian war. The protest against the Algerian war involved many thousands of students, who engaged in fairly drastic measures to sabotage the war effort.[4]

There is, however, another source of the tension between political intellectuals and modern academe, which though not new, is one which has only recently been recognized as a source of political resentment. It involves opposition to the trend toward the growth of hard social science and expertise, the decline of diffuse intellectualism in the social arena. The differentiation of social science knowledge into distinct fields of technical expertise has sharply undermined the role of the humanist intellectual who has traditionally claimed the right to comment on and influence public policy. This phenomenon may be seen most strikingly in economics. Economists now contend that many of the decisions about economic policy require technical knowledge beyond the competence of the informed layman. And as the other social sciences have extended their spheres of competence, and have become more systematically empirical and quantitative, they also question the ability of laymen to understand the factors which affect educational achievement, child-rearing practices, international relations, and the like.

Increasingly, the expert tells the general intellectual that the particular matters under discussion are simply too complicated, too technical, for them to be influenced through advocacy of relatively uncomplicated solutions associated with a particular ideological bent. Those who seek to reform society in some specific way find themselves up against arguments supposedly derivative from specialized scholarly knowledge. And commitment to the increasing importance of social science and specialization reinforces the ideology of the "end of ideology," i.e., the position that ideologically dictated positions are basically irrelevant, that governmental decisions should increasingly reflect expert knowledge, a position which was put strongly in John F. Kennedy's speech at Yale in the spring of 1963.

These trends have contributed to the rise among left intellectuals and students of a kind of "intellectual *poujadisme,*" a backlash opposition to systematic and quantitative social science, to large-scale social research, to the very conception of the utility of efforts at objective scholarship in policy-relevant fields. Many intellectuals react to the emphasis on social science and the concomitant belief in gradualism, expertise, and planning with a populist stress on the virtues of direct action against evil institutions and practices. They attack the involvement of the university in policy matters as inherently corrupting the values of pure scholarship and intellectual freedom. The negative reaction to the application of academic expertise to politics, which ironically may be found among many natural scientists who are laymen in fields of race relations, stratification, foreign policy and the like, has reinforced the hostility of activist students to the "complicating" social scientists.

The intellectual *poujadiste* reaction is, of course, related to a much older and continuing source of conflict between intellectuals and the power structure. This is the tension between the patron or consumer and the intellectuals. The latter tend to view work which is oriented toward the demands of the marketplace, rather than to the intrinsic logic of creativity, as corrupt. Such criticism has taken two forms, a conservative or rightist one which views democracy as a mass society in which intellectual elites are pressed to conform to the low taste of the public, and a leftist one which sees the source of the corruption in the power held by those who buy and distribute intellectual products, i.e., business or government. The conservative critique has in recent years been absorbed in many countries into the left-wing one.

The view that there is an inherent conflict between the values of intellectuals and those of the marketplace has sustained an anticapitalist ideology among many humanistically inclined intellectuals, one which also affects students preparing for such pursuits.

The Return to Domestic Politics

In Chapter 1, the case was made that the revival of student activism in the United States and other Western countries was fostered by the breakdown in the image of a monolithic internationally unified Communist enemy. Polycentric communism, faced with its own forms of internecine conflict, undercut the rationale inhibiting sharp criticism by left-inclined intellectuals of the social inequities and bad policies of their own societies. Although the Vietnam war became the principal moral issue of the late sixties, in a sense during the decade the Western world returned to a more "normal" political environment in which the main focus of intellectual and student politics has been domestic opponents. The domestic system, including the educational system itself, is held up to criticism for not living up to the ideals fostered by the society. This process has become increasingly evident on both sides of the curtain. The rise of a critical intelligentsia and a New Left student body in the West is a reflection of the change.

The current political scene increasingly resembles that which existed before World War I, in that relatively prosperous conditions have given rise to a growing radicalism. In that earlier age, the mood of liberals and progressives about social change was much more optimistic, in spite of the fact that the socialist movements campaigned against the possibility of international war; there was no real expectation that the prolonged period of peace, economic growth, and the expansion of democracy dating from the 1870s would end. Rather as the economic situation improved, the left, socialist, anarchist, and progressive forces continued to grow, and intellectuals criticized their domestic systems for various internal inequities and inequalities. The first student socialist movements in the United States, Germany, and France date from the period 1900 to 1914. They operated, however, within a much smaller and more elitist student body than at present, and had less impact on society.

It may also be worth recalling again in this connection that students and intellectuals were involved in highly visible activist opposition movements in the underdeveloped countries, particularly in Latin America and parts of Asia, during the 1950s, long before the emergence of university-based opposition movements in the developed states. Anticommunism and cold war ideologies were much weaker in these states. Hence they were less subject to ideological constraints on their propensities to attack the status quo in society or university.

The growth in student opposition during the 1960s was in large measure identified with a left-wing critique of the social welfare planning state in the Western democracies. The available data on the backgrounds of student activists in a number of countries, discussed earlier, suggest that many of the leaders (though not the followers) are the children of relatively affluent, liberal or left-wing parents. They have been reared in progressive households to accept the ideology of equality, democracy, helping the poor, and the like. Their parents represent that part of the elite of their generation who reacted radically to the events of the Depression and the anti-fascist conflict. Right-wing radical critiques of the existing society have to a certain extent been outmoded by the discrediting of fascist doctrines and the reduction of right extreme movements to forms of *poujadisme* based on the outlying provincial declining areas of different societies. The politicized university students have the values of modern egalitarian democracy. That small minority of them who were impelled to be activists often concentrated the fire of their attack on domestic ills.

This domestic concentration, however, has resulted – in foreign policy terms – in a criticism of international collective-security anti-Communist alignments as outmoded and unjustified. The New Left is sympathetic to movements in other countries seeking social change in an egalitarian direction, which means, in the underdeveloped world, Communist or pro-Communist movements of the Castro, Hanoi, Maoist varieties. Since the United States can obviously be identified as a force seeking to maintain the status quo in the underdeveloped countries, as well as a source of support for its own conservative social system, the student left, as noted earlier, is inherently sharply anti-American and against the American alliances. It simply does not accept the underlying theses which justify both alliances such as NATO and SEATO, and the opposition to revolutionary pro-Communist movements.

The Vietnam war with direct armed conflict and intervention by the United States has, of course, exacerbated the extent of the opposition to the United States. The common theme justifying alliances among the student left in different countries has been opposition to American foreign policy. This fact, however, should not lead us to underestimate the extent to which these movements are really primarily domestically oriented or directed against local power structures and universities and the political parties and culture. These are the revolts of activist youth against the older generation in power in their own country. They have the effect, however, of also being a revolt against the system of international alliances and against America's role in the world.

In the Eastern bloc countries, of course, as noted earlier, these revolts are directed to some considerable degree against the system of alliances among the Communist countries. There, the alliance is also a power system in that the Soviet Union keeps control over other countries through it. But basically youth on both sides of the curtain are seeking to reform or revolutionize their own societies and they are opposing the main power to which their country is linked, which they see as a source of support for the status quo at home and abroad. In short, it is the fact that the cold war has declined, that the basis for the system of alliances is no longer as strong as it once was, that made a new international youth movement possible.

The movement which arose in the 1960s differs in a number of significant ways from earlier student movements. As compared to the previous ones, it has almost no relationship to adult organizations. Student and youthful leftist groups, before World War I or during the interwar period before World War II, were to a large extent the youth or student affiliates of adult political parties. They usually were more extreme in their ideology than the adult organizations, but essentially their conception of how to get social change in their country was through their adult party coming into power or increasing its influence. This meant that the primary tasks of the youth group were to recruit support and train leaders for the adult organization, and also to provide the mass base for demonstrations. Insofar as the adult groups were involved in parliamentary activities and tactics, the student groups were as well.

This pattern may still be seen today in the activities of the young Communists in various countries, that is the youth or student sections of the pro-Russian Communist parties. In the West and in many underdeveloped countries, the pro-Russian Communists tend, where possible, to rely on the use of parliamentary and pressure-group tactics. Their student groups also follow the same procedures, essentially the traditional legal methods of demonstrating, striking, picketing, and the like.

Most of the non-Communist left-wing student movements in the underdeveloped states of Latin America and Asia also retain an instrumental orientation towards social change in their own country. That is, they believe in the possibility of progressive social change through policies designed to foster economic development, education, land reform, and political democracy. To achieve these objectives, they favor placing a new adult group in power. Similarly, the student activists in Eastern Europe are concerned with concrete reforms, usually of a political nature.

The student left of the Western democracies, however, is in a postreformist phase. The New Left youth groups initially rejected almost all political parties. For many of them the political parties of the left, both Socialist and Communist, were parties of the parliamentary establishment. They identified these groups as supporters of the domestic or foreign, i.e., Russian, status quo. They saw no adult organizations as genuinely revolutionary, as genuinely resistant to the major trends of the society which they oppose. Hence an international revolutionary movement of students and youth emerged which expressed in almost pure unadulterated form the ethic of absolute ends. They were almost completely uninhibited and uncontrolled, politically, since they had no relations to parties and organizations which had some sort of interest in adhering to the rules of the game and which accepted the need for compromise. Their politics were more expressive than instrumental. The New Left groups also had no clear concept of any road to power, of a way of effecting major social change. They were ready and willing to use tactics which violate the normal democratic game.

It is notable, however, that these tendencies which dominated activist student politics during the 1960s began to change by the end of the decade. In spite of the massive publicity they received and the occasional major demonstrations led by New Leftist groups, particularly in May and June 1968 in France and other parts of Europe, the New Left clearly failed to build a new mass movement and to reach allies outside the campus. Since 1968, most of the European groups have declined greatly. To repeat points made in Chapter 2, the German SDS officially dissolved as a national organization in the spring of 1970. The French groupings are bitterly factionalized and ineffective. The American SDS lives on at the beginning of the 1970s as a shadow of its past self. After a disastrous set of splits, what remains is, in effect, the student section of the Maoist Progressive Labor Party. The Young Socialist Alliance, affiliated to the Trotskyist Socialist Workers Party, was generally recognized by the end of 1970–71 as the largest left-wing youth group, and it has little more than a few thousand members. As noted earlier, American opinion polls were recording a drop-off in the percentage of students identifying themselves as radicals and an increase in conservative backing on campus. Everywhere from California to France and Scandinavia, the New Left parties have secured tiny votes, from one to three percent. The effect of such defeats has been to turn some New Left militants to terrorist tactics as in France and Italy, much like the Weathermen in this country, or to expressive forms of personal protest, of secession from society.

The bulk of the left-inclined students, however, have not followed such forms of despair. Rather, the majority turn passive and the more activist increasingly seem to return to the dominant leftist parties, Communist or Socialist, e.g., in France to the Communists, in Germany to the Social-Democrats. They often do so with the intention to press these parties to support a pure form of communism or socialism. But insofar as these parties operate within the parliamentary and electoral system, the student activism of the 1970s may, in effect, become the radical wing of the more moderate left movements. The same tendency may be seen in the United States in the participation of students in peace- and reform-oriented electoral campaigns.

Assuming a continuation of present trends, both international and domestic, it may also be assumed that the phenomenon of Western student activism is not a temporary one, although it should have peaks and declines. Specific issues which enable the extremist minority to mobilize strength outside their own ranks will result in increased extraparliamentary actions, but such support will largely drift away as specific issues disappear or lose salience.

One example of this phenomenon was the decline of activism after the Algerian war in France. The antiwar movement was very much like the one in the United States today against the Vietnam war. Once the war ended, however, in 1962, the mass support for an activist French student movement fell greatly. This event, of course, cannot be separated from the general decline of political activity that occurred under De Gaulle in the same period, but it does indicate the way in which changing political events can affect the movement, that we are not necessarily dealing with a secular pattern.[5]

A somewhat similar development occurred in Britain in the

late 1950s. The concept of a New Left arose in Britain at this time, seemingly as a reaction against both the Labour and Communist parties. The New Left youth and student movement which emerged in many of the universities was largely concerned with cultural critiques of the larger society rather than with demonstrations, although many of its members were also involved in the Campaign for Nuclear Disarmament. The subsequent electoral victory of the Labour party under Harold Wilson, who was then identified as a left-wing Labourite, sharply reduced the appeal of the British New Left, and it declined during the first few years of the Labour rule.[6] It regained strength, in some part fostered by the impression that the Wilson Labour Government was a failure, that it was conservative in practice. By 1970, however, the largest group of left-inclined students campaigned in the party's ill-fated battle for reelection. And since then, as on the continent, radical British students have shown more concern to build the left wing of the Labour party than to sit-in university buildings.

The Short-term Effects of Student Activism

What has been the effect of this wave of student protest on the politics of the respective countries? The answer clearly is not a simple one. On one hand, the powerful student movement is a force pressing the moderate left and the Communists to move further to the left, to become more militant in order to secure the support of the students. Many adult radicals have begun to identify with the student movement, and this, too, presses on the left parties. Many student demonstrations have been interpreted as reflecting the existence of genuine academic grievances. Various efforts have been made to appease these concerns, particularly by university reform, and occasionally by extramural reform.

On the other hand, the irresponsibility of some of the student movements, their willingness to rely on extraparliamentary, illegal methods, their proclamation that their goal is the revolutionary overthrow of society, their resort to street violence, also have created a backlash among the more moderate and conservative and established parts of the electorate.

In France, the student revolt has had one obvious political consequence; it has given the country its first majority party government in history, one which is right-wing. Thus, it may be argued that student demonstrations strengthen the conservatives within the body politic, that they help place conservatives in power or increase their majority. Such contentions also have been made about California politics and United States politics generally. The Berkeley disturbances were credited with having played an important role in electing Ronald Reagan in California in 1966. The Chicago demonstrators helped elect Nixon in 1968.

The counterproductive character of confrontations with the adult public was brought out strikingly by different surveys of reactions to the battle between Chicago police and antiwar demonstrators at the 1968 Democratic convention. A nationwide Sindlinger telephone sample survey taken soon after the conflict reported overwhelming support for the behavior of the police. A national voting survey conducted by the University of Michigan Survey Research Center two months later found that only 19 percent thought "too much force" had been used against the demonstrators in Chicago; 25 percent said "not enough force," and 32 percent indicated the police had employed the "right amount of force." More significantly perhaps, only 36 percent of McCarthy supporters and 29 percent of Kennedy backers criticized the police for using "too much force." The antagonism to the Chicago demonstrators carried over to antiwar protest generally.

> On a feeling thermometer running from zero to one hundred degrees, 35 percent of the respondents . . . rated "Vietnam War Protestors" at zero. By contrast, the next coldest group – "Liberals" – were rated zero by 5 percent of respondents. One must return to the 1964 Survey Research Center election study to find two groups received more coldly than protestors – the Ku Klux Klan and the Black Muslims.[7]

During the Cambodian incursion in May 1970, the campus demonstrated its antagonism to the war through massive strikes and other forms of protest. Yet, the opinion polls revealed that the electorate as a whole, though overwhelmingly opposed to the war, declared, in a Gallup Poll taken late in May, that the most important problem facing the country was campus unrest.[8] And a variety of opinion surveys completed before the November 1970 state and congressional elections indicated that various politicians who had taken a strong stand against campus unrest gained thereby. Evidence of such reactions, and the scurrying to cover among many liberal Democratic candidates who felt the need to condemn student protest, led Sam Brown, the organizer of the student-based McCarthy campaign in 1968 and of the national antiwar Moratorium movement in the fall of 1969, to write a bitter analytical article in the August 1970 issue of the *Washington Monthly* which strongly argued that much student protest was counterproductive.[9]

Perhaps the most dramatic examples of the negative effect of being identified with student activism on the fortunes of major electoral parties occurred in the Japanese election in December 1969, and in the Finnish one in March 1970. The Japanese Socialist party, which is dominated by its left-wing China-oriented faction, strongly opposed the efforts of the Liberal-Democratic government to enact strong campus control measures, and of the student affiliate of the Communist party to prevent disruptive forms of student protest, while cooperating with efforts at campus reform. In the elections, the Communists gained greatly, while the Socialists lost a third of their seats. In a statement evaluating the election results, the Communists credited the Socialist defeat, in part, to the party's "trailing behind the Trotskyite anti-Communist gangs of thugs and the blind followers of Mao Tse-tung," that is, the militant student groups.[10] In Finland, the coalition Popular Front government of the Communists, Social Democrats and the Center party, supported by a small New Left oriented party, acceded to the demands for increased student power of the Finnish Students' Union. The

Center party Minister of Education brought in a bill to reform the university by providing for heavy student participation in university governance, a proposal strongly opposed by the Professors Union. The March elections, fought on this issue, brought about the greatest shift in votes ever experienced in Finland. The Center party lost over a quarter of its seats, and the more conservative Countryside party, formed to fight it, captured eighteen seats, a gain of seventeen. The New Left TPSL also lost all of its seven seats; the Communists declined greatly, while the party which had most strongly opposed the students' demands, the Conservatives, was the big winner.[11]

The picture, of course, even in electoral terms, is not clear-cut. In Italy, the 1968 national and 1970 provincial elections did not produce any change, although the 1971 provincial elections witnessed startlingly large gains by neo-Fascists. In Germany, the Social Democrats gained in 1969, but they were openly hostile to the SDS, and the small radical leftist party which backed the campus militants took .6 percent of the vote.[12] In general, it seems apparent that one effect of extraparliamentary youth politics in the 1960s was to reinforce the electoral appeal of the conservatives.

The sharp cleavage between the views of university students in the United States and other countries and those of the population is not solely, or even primarily, a function of a "generation gap." As noted earlier in Chapters 2 and 3, young people as such have furnished disproportionate strength to the candidacy of George Wallace, and have *not* been more heavily opposed to the war than older age groups. The gap *within* the youth, the conflict among generation-units, has been greater than that *between* different generations. This conclusion is brought out sharply by reactions to the use of force at the 1968 Democratic convention. Among white respondents, the percentage agreeing that "too much force" was used against the demonstrators was 14 for those who had not graduated from high school, 20 among high school graduates, 32 for those with some college, 50 for college graduates, and 63 percent for those with a graduate degree. Among college students, the proportion was highest, of course, 67 percent.[13]

A similar gulf between student and nonstudent, predominantly working-class, youth with respect to attitudes toward radical change in the political and cultural spheres is indicated by surveys in other nations. Thus the report on a 1969 Italian survey of two samples of youth (17–26), national and university student, indicates that 34 percent of the national sample and 44 percent of the students favored major social changes; 12 percent of the first group and 16 percent of the second agreed that a complete revolution was needed.[14] The picture in Germany based on 1968 surveys of students and youth (18–25) is even more striking. Forty-three percent of all youth as contrasted to 7 percent of students agreed "one should not tolerate criticism towards one's fatherland from foreigners." Fifteen percent of the former and 60 percent of the latter disapproved of capital punishment. Less than a third (29 percent) of the youth sample believed in the right to strike and demonstrate if the public order is endangered, while the majority in two student surveys (54 and 62 percent) agreed with the right. Similar differences occurred with respect to a variety of questions dealing with democratic attitudes, tolerance for opposition, and the like.[15] In Japan, where surveys of students show significant majority sympathy for socialism, a survey in June 1970 of manual workers indicated that those under twenty-two years of age were quite conservative, much more in fact than the older workers. The survey reported that "35.8 percent of the young versus 27.4 percent of the older workers felt a capitalist social system was the best for Japan, while 11.7 percent of the young and 22.3 percent of the older workers preferred a socialist system."[16] A Brazilian survey completed in 1964 just before the military coup d'état indicated that workers generally and young workers, in particular, were "much more conservative than students. . . . The differences between young workers and students are much greater than the differences between young workers and older workers."[17]

The findings of surveys such as these point up the dilemma of activist student movements. While the campus population, both student and faculty, are generally sympathetic to the specific objectives of many demonstrations, and are, therefore, prepared to identify with the protestors in clashes with the police, the general population, including nonstudent youth, are not. Consequently, the provocative tactics often deliberately designed to precipitate violent clashes with the police gain them support within the university community, but alienate those outside, including the workers and other youth. And the practical consequence is to strengthen considerably conservative political tendencies among the electorate.

The strengthening of the Right may actually have also contributed to maintaining the foreign alliances with the United States. Since the conservative parties, France apart, are the more pro-American, collective-security-oriented ones, this paradoxically could have the opposite effect to what the students themselves are striving for internationally. This outcome, however, is not a necessary one.

The dominant political groups in various countries are concerned with maintaining domestic tranquility. Consequently, they should be interested in reducing the size of opposition student movements, and will try to avoid giving the activists any justification for engaging in violence against the government. Many politicians see foreign policy issues as a major source of annoyance for their students. Former German Chancellor Kiesinger explicitly credited the Vietnam war with being responsible for the growth of a violent German student movement and for the alienation of many German youth. Whether he was right or wrong is irrelevant; what is important is that he saw it this way. In Japan, which witnessed a strong New Left–type student movement before the phenomenon occurred in the United States and Western Europe, student opposition to international alliances with the United States, while not upsetting them, has had the effect of reducing the public commitment of the Japanese politicians to such alliances. The United States has withdrawn forces to avoid student protests.

In evaluating the cost to the nation, or to the government and political forces, of a given international policy, those in power have had to count as one of these costs an increase in street opposition to the government, a decline in respect for law and order. Should the other forces pressing for maintenance of the alliance weaken, one may therefore assume that the rise of an activist student movement will become a force for isolationism. If a politician must choose between internationalism and isolationism and if he feels that the international consequences of the choice have become less important, he may opt for the isolationist course to gain domestic tranquility, to maintain law and order, to reduce emotional opposition.

The continuation of the Vietnam war has, of course, made international relations a major source of emotional tension. For those opposed to the war, any alliance with the United States may be perceived as an alliance with murderers, with those who are killing a small country. In the absence of the war, the issue of whether a given country remains part of NATO or has a mutual security treaty with the United States still may remain an important issue for debate and controversy, but presumably will not provoke as intense a set of reactions.

Generation Differences: The Long-term Effects

In the long run, the most important effect of the current wave of student activism on foreign policy may reflect the outcomes of differences in outlook toward politics among different age groups or generations. The experiences which have sustained a strong commitment to the Western alliances are an outgrowth of the struggles against fascism and Stalinism. As noted earlier, Munich, the Hitler-Stalin Pact, the 1948 Czech Coup, the Korean war, the Hungarian Revolution, are all ancient history to the generations which have come of age during the 1960s. Adults often find it hard to understand the extent to which relatively recent events which occurred before a given group of youth reached political and intellectual consciousness simply are not salient to them.

A major consideration of the consequences of political events on a society requires the specification of the role of political generations. Many analysts of politics and cultural styles have stressed the extent to which the concept of the generation must be used as an independent analytical one. The thesis underlying this type of analysis indicates that people tend to form a defined frame of reference in late adolescence or early youth within which they fit subsequent experiences. That is, the first formative political experiences are most important.

A number of scholars have attempted to trace through the participation of different generations in the politics of various nations. They have pointed to the way that workers who came of age during the Great Depression have continued to react to issues of unemployment, economic security, and the like, ever since. The Depression youth, as adults, have been much more likely to be concerned about the welfare state than earlier and subsequent generations. Similarly, as noted earlier, many who were concerned in their youth with foreign policy issues stemming from fascist or Communist expansionism have continued to react along lines stemming from such issues more recently. It is easy to visualize how such processes operate. A small increase in the current unemployment rate will shock someone who has experienced the Depression, while it might not even be noticed by someone who has not. The Soviet Union's military action in Czechoslovakia should have more effect on those who remember the Czech coup or the Hungarian revolution as a major experience of their political youth than those who do not. The events which surround the entry of a generation into politics may continue to have their impact on national life for many decades after these events are forgotten as topics of political discussion, particularly through determining the conceptions of the governing and intellectual strata.

In foreign policy terms, the United States apparently created an isolationist generation out of the events of World War I and the immediate years thereafter. This generation as it grew older, remembering the way it had been "fooled" in World War I, resisted steps toward intervention during the 1930s. Conversely, however, the young people of the later 1930s and early 1940s learned that isolationism and neutralism had led to the rise of fascism and World War II. They presumably have shown up as a much more interventionist group.

To a considerable extent, the contemporary political leaders of the United States and many other Western countries are people who came to political consciousness at a time when foreign policy issues involving the containment of fascism or communism were most salient. This generation of political leaders and their supporters did not need much convincing to react militantly to Communist threats. In this connection it may be important to point out that the United States Government did not feel it necessary to justify the decisions concerning Vietnam taken by Presidents Eisenhower, Kennedy, and Johnson, by exposing the domestic inequities of the North Vietnam regime, its use of force against its own people, or of the terror tactics of the Viet Cong.

This policy was dictated in part by the desire of each administration to keep the United States role in Vietnam as limited as necessary to prevent a Communist takeover in the South, to restrain the pressure of the "hawks" who sought to escalate the war, and thus to risk its widening far beyond the borders of Vietnam. But the reluctance to undertake any significant propaganda campaign in support of the war was also in some part a reflection of the fact that, to those older men in charge of the American information policy, there seemed to be no need for elaborate justifications of efforts to prevent a Communist takeover in another country. All Americans, they thought, recognized that communism is an evil social system, and hence could be expected to back this latest episode in the struggle to contain it.

The internal conflict which developed in the United States over the war illustrates the phenomenon of the generation gap as well as any event that can be presented. For youth, the new generations of college students, the past evils of Stalinism constitute events which have little relevance to the immediate present.

European communism no longer can be identified with Stalinist oppression, with the slaughter of the innocents, or with monolithic power.

Thus, different generations have reacted to a different sense of the nature of, and the political potential of communism. Though those who have dictated American policy in the past decade have been aware of the changes in the Communist system as much as the younger people, there can be little doubt that the variations in the reactions of the generations reflect the fact that the older know from personal experience the potential for evil in communism, while the younger ones only know it as words in the history books. It is perhaps inevitable that they should react quite differently to arguments concerning the need to resist a Communist movement in another country.

The same situation, of course, exists in other countries. It is perhaps more strikingly illustrated in Berlin where until the Berlin Wall, there was considerable support for strong anti-Communist policies among all groups in the city, including the students. The Free University of Berlin, in fact, was founded by refugees from communism. But the Berlin Wall was more successful than those who planned it could have expected. They built it in order to prevent people from leaving East Germany. But by so doing, they destroyed the past relationship to, and function of, West Berlin for East Germany. West Berliners, including students, no longer talk to people who have fled communism. For the Berlin youth communism exists in a society with which they have little contact, while there are many things wrong with the society in which they live. And the student movement of West Berlin, once primarily concerned with the East, is now mainly concerned with changing the society of West Berlin and West Germany.

Recognition that there are generational differences in outlook is not simply relevant to an analysis of any given contemporary scene. For the most important thing about generations is that they may persist. Consequently, any effort to evaluate the consequences of the present political revival of student militancy must include a consideration of its potential impact on future events. Some years ago a private Japanese opinion study of the attitudes and political beliefs of younger members of the Japanese business executive stratum, those under forty, revealed that the majority of such executives had become much more moderate politically over the years, but they still voted for the Japanese Socialist party. Seemingly, the majority of Japanese youth who go to universities, particularly the better ones, become supporters of some brand of Marxism or radicalism. And they continue to identify with the Left for many years after most of them go to work for bureaucratic industry or government, entering ladders which can lead them fairly high up into the Japanese elite.

The Japanese data bear directly on the maxim discussed in Chapter 1: "He who is not a radical at twenty does not have a heart; he who is still a radical at forty does not have a head." This statement expresses a generally expressed consensus that youth may be irresponsible and radical, but as they get older they become more responsible and conservative. There can be little doubt that there is considerable validity to this generalization. The Japanese data, however, indicate that although most Japanese young radicals become more moderate in their opinions and their actions as they get older, many of those who become business executives remain on the left politically, adhering to various doctrines of socialism and, in the Japanese context, anti-Americanism.

Assuming this study is accurate, it suggests that Japan may be moving into a period in which it will have an elite which does not believe in the system which it operates. This more radical elite may not do anything to change the system, but their beliefs may affect the way they react toward radical pressure on them from other groups, as well as their view of new issues as they occur. In a history of czarist Russia, written in 1910, Bernard Pares devoted about two hundred pages to the political activities of the intellectuals and students of the czarist empire.[18] He discussed in great detail the fact that the students were radical and antiregime. Pares, however, then stated that these activities did not mean very much, since the students after graduating went to work for the bureaucracy or entered other sections of the elite and thus became supporters of the system. There is little data on what former Russian radical students did in later years, but clearly there is some possibility that there is some relationship between the radicalism of the Russian students and the weakness of the elite in 1917.

Currently, in the United States, the elite of a more radicalized student generation is gradually moving into the lower and sometimes even the upper rungs of important parts of the society. For example, in the university, in journalism, in other aspects of the communications industry, and in various government agencies, observers have noted that the youthful members of the staffs tend to be much more radical in their reaction to the functions of the organization than older hands. As in Japan, it is probable that many of them retain important parts of the opinions which they formed as students. In spite of the coercive pressures on them to conform which come from participation in the bureaucracy, some aspects of their environment may continue to support their youthful opinions. It is possible, therefore, that the current generation of radical university students will continue to affect the larger body politic in many countries ten, twenty, or even thirty years from now. Their elites may contain a much larger proportion of liberals or leftists than they now do. They may also include many whose image of the United States and its role in the world will be quite different from that of earlier generations.

As another illustration of this process, it may be noted that some analysts of the contemporary American university scene have argued that one of the factors contributing to increased student activism today is the presence on university faculties of many whose political attitudes were formed during the New Deal experience, the Depression, or the struggle against fascism. University faculties are much more liberal or even leftist than they ever have been in the past. It is noticeable that a visibly significant number of senior American university faculty members today are individuals who took part in student movements — liberal and radical politics — during the thirties and early forties. As noted earlier, the current generation of student activists are often the children of people who were active in radical movements in the earlier period. In a sense, these studies indicate that generations sometimes may even appear twice, first in their own right, and second through their influence over their children, who are given a set of ideals which they then try to activate, ideals which stem back to the conditions of their parents' formative political years.

This emphasis on the persistence of political orientations formed in youth does not belie the fact that many, if not most, people do change their beliefs as they grow older and become involved in the responsibilities of career and family, or simply are exposed to a variety of new experiences which may undermine the convictions of their youth. Thus, though the generation of the 1930s has thrown up visible reminders of the effects of the Depression, it is also true that opinion surveys from the 1950s and 1960s indicated that the majority of college graduates of the 1930s had become relatively conservative and usually voted Republican. This fact should be placed alongside the report of the first national survey of American students made in 1936 (see pp. 184–185 in Chapter 5) that most of them were liberal Democrats, that 24 percent identified socialism in positive terms, as contrasted with but 15 percent who were favorable to conservatism. Seemingly most students who had been radicalized in the mid-1930s had given up such views by the 1950s. The conflict of the generations is not simply or even primarily a conflict among generations that have had different formative experiences, it is also a conflict between the young and the older. This conclusion is dramatized by the finding that those who went to college in the conservative, silent, apathetic, conformist, (Joe) McCarthyite 1950s turn out to furnish a higher proportion of voters and supporters for liberal and left candidates and political positions in the late 1960s and early 1970s than do the older alumni of the 1930s, the years of the Red Decade, the Great Depression, and the struggle against fascism. Viewed in the mass, the college experience has not created "generations" which have continued to display distinctive political commitments. It is likely that the college cohort that passed through the radical and activist campus politics of the late 1960s will not behave as one either, although, like the cohort of the 1930s, they will probably throw up a visible group of intellectual and organizational leaders who will retain a radical position.

A change in views is inherent in the differences between college communities and those in society at large. Colleges are encapsulated communities. Their students have been abruptly removed from the various constraints of their parental family experience, and placed in an environment in which peer group pressures are especially intense and pervasive. For four years they inhabit this world apart, a remarkably homogeneous and unstratified society, in which the dominant elite, the faculty, is considerably to the left of any other in the larger society. After graduation, however, most – even today when the number rejecting affluence, a "careerist" outlook and the regular occupational system is far greater than ever before – reenter the highly differentiated social system and take part in an affluent middle-class life in job, family, and community. As we have seen, the intellectual legacies of college are by no means lost, particularly for those who remain within the intelligentsia occupationally after leaving school – but the intense pressures of the encapsulated community which make for the distinctive and wildly fluctuating bodies of student political opinion are for most removed as abruptly as they had been introduced.[19]

How the cohort of the late 1960s will behave politically in the long run will, of course, be affected by factors other than those associated with aging. The larger political situation may press them to the right or left. But all the available evidence strongly suggests that as they grow older they will become *relatively* less receptive to new change-directed thrusts than those who follow them through the university. That is, even though American politics and morals may continue to "liberalize" over time, the relative relationship of the older to the younger remains "conservative." In this sense, societies like our own, which have a built-in process of enormous social change, also always have a generation gap of some magnitude, particularly between those living in the encapsulated, experiment-oriented campus, and those outside.

No society should find it remarkable that a segment of its student population should be involved in activist student politics that is directed militantly against the status quo. It can be strongly argued, as C. Wright Mills argued, that students are the one group who will continue to supply recruits for such causes, even when no other stratum is available.[20] A completely inactive student body is a much more curious phenomenon historically than one which is involved to some degree in activism. Any efforts to analyze the future of politics, whether on the domestic or international scene, will ignore the students at the peril of being in error.

Part Two:

Passion, Pot and Politics

by Gerald M. Schaflander

Dedication

To: Bill Creed, Hilary Schifrin, Griselda Brown, Edwin Rothschild and those special marginal ambivalents – with whom I have hopefully bridged the generation gap.

To: Malcolm X, Medgar Evers, John F. Kennedy, Martin Luther King, and Robert F. Kennedy – tragic victims of violence; whose assassinations have made the task of nonviolent social change more difficult; whose leadership is sorely missed in the democratic conflict for power in America.

To: Charles Merrill – whose overall support was and is constant and invaluable.

To: Justin, my two-year-old son, who undoubtedly will "shape up" the aforementioned MAs when he hits campus in September, 1986.

To: My wife, Vicky – who played her multiple roles with warmth and insightful understanding.

Gerald M. Schaflander

8

Marginal Ambivalents

Professor Lipset has analyzed the sources and history of radical student activism, which today involves up to 5 percent of the student population, and the existing tension between faculty and radical students. It seems appropriate now to record and analyze the political, drug and sexual behavior of a prototypical group of liberal-moderate students who make up 30 to 40 percent of the national student population. These students, whom I shall call marginal ambivalents, are generally opposed to university administrators, a majority of the faculty, and the radical-left activists.

Against the background and theoretical framework of radical student activism, as delineated by Professor Lipset, we shall now observe the marginal ambivalents as they grapple with value conflicts and strategic and tactical decisions, sometimes opposing, sometimes following, often redefining their differences from the radical student activists.

Parents and opinion leaders must begin to understand and differentiate just what is happening to the various stratified types of college students in the broad spectrum of the United States college population, which numbers eight million.

The following chapters are primarily about those college students, MAs who are concerned, humanistic, often studious and intellectual, unorganized, moderate politically, groping and confused. Their instincts are hesitant and their actions minimal. Their values are changing, ambivalent and contradictory.

This section is *not* primarily about the hippies, the New Left, the radical activists or the alienated who together make up only 10 percent of the total college population.

Nor is this section about the "jocks" – the fraternity and sorority clan which comprises about 30 percent of all college students. Greek brothers and sisters are, for the most part, eager to move to the suburbs to promote and propagate the values and goals of a technologically affluent, materialistic, driven, white middle-class society.

This is a documentary and sociological analysis of the values, ideas and fears of the marginal ambivalents. Hopefully, it is a prototypical, representative report of a cross section of these students, who number in all about three million. Which way these MAs turn politically and socially might well determine the future of American politics.

The MAs are the chief object of the left-radicals' future recruitment. In the last analysis, it is the MAs who have to be radicalized if the extremists are to flourish.

It is from the MAs that the dorm leaders, student government leaders, and most of the service and tutoring leadership evolves. It is precisely for this reason that one must stratify, separate, and thoroughly analyze the MA students, since they are and will be the balance in the battle over the resolution of the university crisis.

The MA students are discontent with most of their parents' values. However, they also reject most of the values and actions of the hippies and the New Left. Generally, they understand and agree with Jules Henry's analysis of the United States and its technologically driven culture:

> Ours is a driven culture; driven on by its achievement, competitive, profit and mobility drives and by the drives for security

> and a higher standard of living and expansiveness . . . all generated by the culture.[1]

The MAs love their parents and would feel guilty if they hurt them. They don't want to instigate the traumatic or psychologically disturbing scenes that are inevitable when they oppose their parents. Most of these MA students do not openly defy or rebel against their parents or authority figures in general. Yet they often harbor deep internal conflict because they want to love and respect their parents and continue to have a warm relationship with them while simultaneously they desire to be free and liberated from their parents' values and emotional hold over them.

Many of the MAs' values are only partially formed as they grope for an explanation for what is happening in Vietnam, in the ghettoes, on the campuses, and within themselves — as they question their own identity, sexuality, acceptability, maturity and future goals. Many of these half-formed values are based on peer-group interaction, legitimation and approval. These peer-group values are predominately conflicting with those of their parents and the culture.

The MA students don't identify with most of the hippies' extreme behavior vis-à-vis sexual promiscuity, dirty, antique-neuter clothing, hair styles, and excessive drug and pill experimentation. And they don't identify with the New Left's political extremism *re* certain anarchistic and totalitarian tactics in abusing the rights of other students, faculty and administrators on campus. Neither, however, are they vocally in outright opposition to or violently repelled by the hippies and New Left as are most of their parents. They just don't feel personally threatened by New Left and hippie behavior.

They understand what bugs the hippies and the extremists of SDS; they tolerate their noisy, conspicuous, and active dissenting, but are *not* as uptight and extreme in their own behavior; they occasionally join the hippies and the New Left in broad free speech, civil liberties, or antibureaucracy protests; but essentially they reject them.

Just to make a buck, work in a large corporation, be secure, have a nicely furnished house in the suburbs with a two-car garage and live bureaucratically conformist lives like their parents is simply not enough for most of the MAs. But they are hesitant in breaking with their parents and frightened if they don't. They are petrified that they will be co-opted, enveloped into a "right" marriage and go the way of all flesh – the path of least resistance. And some undoubtedly will.

The central conflict for the marginal ambivalents is how to become free and liberated from their parents. They don't want to break with them completely, but they do want to be able to make independent decisions affecting their own lives.[2]

This book then, is also a serious warning to MA students to liberate themselves now, no matter what the cost!

If this liberation is not accomplished, there will probably be little relevant, democratic social change in the United States in the near future. C. Wright Mills was brilliantly perceptive when he observed that "private troubles and public issues are inextricably joined together."[3] If the majority of MA students are unable to free themselves from their personal ambivalence – their private hangups which prevent them from moving towards an independent personal career – they will never be able to join together with other students, teachers, artists, scientists and professionals in an effective coalition to challenge the political and cultural status quo. Only when they are liberated from their parents' conformist values and fears and anxieties can they ever engage in group political action to effectuate social change.

Let's be clear. Only through the political process are war, welfare, taxes, education, pollution, poverty, civil liberties and civil rights decisions made – decisions which irrevocably determine our lives.

The MAs' parents are perpetuating, not challenging, the cultural and political status quo. These parents, mostly middle class and upper middle class, scarred from the Depression and obsessively driven to economic and social security, have a deep, pervasive and vested interest in continuing the driven-value system dominant in our culture.[4] The parents are driven to motivate their own children to *their* standards, their values, and never fit their own behavior to their children's (the students') developing needs, growing desires and peer-oriented values. And yet, the parents of most of these MA students are often frustrated, unhappy, and dissatisfied with their own marriages and unfulfilled private lives. The children often serve as an unconscious mechanism for parents who are trying to relive and redo the failures and frustrations in their own lives. They now have a second chance to be young again, to correct or protect their kids from assumed negative pitfalls, to live vicariously and indirectly through their own children's lives. So, under the guise or facade of love, children nauseously and repetitively hear the dreary plaint:

"We are only doing this to help (prevent, guide, protect and save) you. . . ."

And the grinding, unceasing pressure to "shape up, settle down (or) in, listen to us" – "we've lived years longer and know what's right and best . . ."

Compounding these middle- and upper-middle-class parental value hangups is the increasing acceleration of bureaucracy in every institution in American life. (The six major institutions are: the military, the economy, the polity, religion, the family and education).[5] Largescale, dehumanized, computerized organizations saturated with rules and regulations are the mushrooming, overwhelming and rigidified way of life for most Americans.

The middle-class parent is thus inevitably driven to bureaucratically socialize and prepare his child to compete, to get along, to role-play, to win (gracefully, of course), and to stand out from the crowd. But never, never must anyone be so different and so unique that he will be seen as a threat to smoothly running groups and organizations; to the commonly accepted, homogenized and bureaucratic values of the large institutions in the adult society.

The middle-class parent's ambivalence is matched by the child's – when he is socialized to be popular and well-liked by his peers whose values are constantly in conflict with his parents' values. He is taught to win (he must win) the approval and respect of his peers; but the child is also fearful of losing the approval and love of his parents. His peers often smoke pot (marijuana) and chide, put-down, and ridicule him if he doesn't join in. His parents, on the other hand, are terrified that he'll be caught breaking the law. They fear and dread the embarrassment, bad publicity and social disapproval of their friends. Forbidden fruit is dangled before our MA in enticing forms – while the parents and adult society say absolutely no.

And it is the same with sex, signing petitions, joining demonstrations, and preparing for adulthood, careers and marriages – as I shall attempt to document.

The needs and desires of MA college students clash most sharply with the values, fears and anxieties of their parents at the level of the students' last and final preparation for adulthood, marriage and careers – college life. This documentation and analysis of college students is aimed at achieving scientific insight into the interactions between a statistically representative cross section of young, middle-class MAs as they come to grips with and relate to two major institutions in American life – education and the family.

Following the impact of urbanization, postindustrialization, and bureaucratization (with the accelerating growth of a technological-worshipping, expanding and expansive middle class), we must look searchingly at the MAs as they approach the turning point of their lives – the end of adolescence in the last year or two of college. We look at them at that stage in history when the United States Government is fighting the most unpopular war in American history – the immoral and illegal intervention in a civil war in Southeast Asia; when the black-white polarization in the major cities of the country threatens a civil war;[6] at a time of United States technological superiority unmatched in the world; when our streams and air are polluted, unbreathable, and unswimmable; when the traffic jams in the cities are unmanageable; when the housing in lower-class sections and ghettoes is unlivable; when whites are moving out to suburbia to avoid black and brown minorities, and away from inadequate teachers and schools, thereby lowering the city tax base at precisely the time and point when proliferating social services are necessary to expand and improve the lot of the desperate and starving urban and black underprivileged; and finally, at a time when the sons and daughters (the MAs) of the affluent middle class are seriously questioning the tone, style and substance of "conspicuous consumption" suburban life. Simultaneously, their parents, covert and overt racists (Kerner Government Commission Report conclusions) are preventing minority groups from partaking in the materialism of suburban American life which the minorities so desperately want. Ironically, the white middle-class students are either rejecting or questioning these materialistic values.

At this critical juncture, the 1968 assassinations of the Reverend Martin Luther King and Senator Robert Kennedy – charismatic spokesmen for nonviolent, antiwar, egalitarian and progressive social change – have brought into boiling focus the conflicting passions and generational value conflicts in the culture.

Many of the Black Nationalists and the Old and New Left see this society and culture as a monolithic, syncretic power structure totally unresponsive to the needs of the poor, underprivileged, creative and innovative.[7] They see nothing good; everything is totally rotten. They dream of Africa, Che, Mao, Ho, Fannon, Algeria and Fidel without realizing the unparalleled political freedom in the United States, the unfettered right of free speech and assembly, the right to choose our own representatives in primaries.

The MAs on the other hand understand that there isn't a spark of political freedom in the Soviet Union, Spain, China, Portugal, Cuba, Greece – or in the left- or right-wing dictatorships around the globe. They see internal fratricide in Nigeria and the Congo as well as that externally imposed by us in Vietnam and the Dominican Republic.

The MAs see that there is no magic or utopian system or dialectic panacea to solve their own or the world's problems.

They see rigidified bureaucracy just as mechanical, rampant, choking and undemocratic in the technological-industrialized Soviet Union as it is in the United States.

They see no easy economic or social solution to their own, France's, Czechoslovakia's, India's, Peru's, or China's problems. But what does seem apparent to the MAs is that we have a unique kind of political freedom in the United States. It allows for a chance to participate and work for a new kind of politics – like the McCarthy campaign for the Democratic nomination for the presidency – and a chance to develop and articulate alternative political choices. It was the students who helped bring the Johnson administration down[8] within the political process. For it's within the polity that all decisions that affect all American lives are made. It is this tough, pragmatic reality that the left-white and supranationalistic black students and their extremist supporters totally misunderstand.

The MAs while struggling for liberation from their parents must learn quickly and in turn teach the new politics to their parents and future colleagues.

For it is the unbelievable ignorance of how politics works in American life that hinders the personal growth and social maturation of students. It is the feeling of ignorance, of social and political powerlessness, of loneliness, of "what can *I* do?" that permeates the consciousness of most adults, and particularly the MA students. It is the absence of educative knowledge as to how the American political system works; the lack of experience in actually overturning the political professionals (as in the New Hampshire and Wisconsin McCarthy victories in primary fights); the lack of feeling of personal and political involvement and relevant craftsmanlike participation in the mainstream of American political life which has hindered change and caused passivity. If more MAs were experienced in working to change things – policies and representatives who are answerable to voters – it would promote the needed changes within the democratic process.

Which way the MAs turn or move at this crucial juncture, therefore, has more than sociological or research significance. These MAs may well be the last and best hope for nonviolent, peaceful, democratic change. They have not yet made their deal with life. They have not yet settled down. They have not yet dropped out or turned off American society.

As to predictions and prognostications about the MAs, here's the consensus that may portend their future:

The real student revolt by the vast majority of college students is just beginning.[9] The significant, relevant student dissenters to the hypocrisy, cant, role-playing, and double standards of adult, middle-class American life are just starting to coalesce into new forms of democratic social action. The McCarthy campaign had a profound effect on tens of thousands of students. They saw that they could help bring LBJ down; could help bring the United States to the Paris peace table. At the Chicago Democratic convention they saw that they could influence over 40 percent of the vote for a strong, antiadministration, anti-Vietnam peace plank; could unseat the racist Mississippi delegation; could obtain the support of half the Georgia delegation; could bring down the century-old unit rule and open states like Texas to insurgent Mexican-Americans – progressive representation; and they saw this accomplished after only six full months of political work. All was *not* lost at Chicago. Kennedy, with McCarthy's help, surely would have been elected President, would have ended the Vietnam war, and would have restructured the ghettoes – had he not been assassinated.

The open dissent against bureaucratic middle-class America, not just by hippies, but by clean-cut, solid and responsible young men and women (MAs), is just around the corner.

The forms it will take are being actively debated by the students. It probably will encompass the form of delayed marriages and many more graduate school careers where the draft permits.

It probably will take the form of many more students running for political office; first in wards and precincts, and then in primaries for community, state and congressional offices.

The students will undoubtedly flock into the black, Mexican-American and Indian ghetto and barrio communities to help organize massive infant and child care and new educational centers for deprived and dispossessed infants and children.

They will probably study to become psychologists, sociologists, psychiatric nurses, recreational leaders, teachers, doctors, lawyers and community organizers, and will undoubtedly put these skills to work at a community level where they are deeply needed. Community development corporations[10] should be flourishing soon and these MAs will try to work as equals, not as colonialists or as guilt-ridden subordinates, appeasing and genuflecting to minorities in a reverse master-race charade.

They will absorb more and more of their own educational expenses through work-study programs or through part-time jobs which will complement their part-time studying in content and time. Many of the MAs will choose to study and work near lower-middle-class areas where Jewish and Catholic populations predominate like New York City, Chicago, Boston, Los Angeles, San Francisco, Cleveland, Philadelphia, Baltimore-Washington, and Detroit, where the overwhelming black-white housing and educational conflicts erupt and where, also, the key delegates and key city, state, and national delegate voting power exists in American political life.

Inevitably, they believe, there will be infinitely more group-dating and group-working.

Substance and content will probably replace the temporary and glittering worship of style, form, and cool, cool, role-playing.

Cosmetics, padded bras, jewelry and absurdly tight and sexually manipulative clothing will be discarded by most of the females.

Bikes and small motor scooters will probably replace cars as basic transportation.

Girls will refuse dates if they don't like the guy, will go out with other girls on Saturday nights and won't be afraid or ashamed to admit they just don't have a date. Guys, too, will start facing reality. They will stop trying to constantly prove their virility by pushing and forcing and trying to exploit their dates sexually. They won't have to brag about how far they went, and the mechanical, "plumbing" aspect of sex in the back seat at the passion pit may soon be a thing of the past.

There will be an increasing number of virgins waiting for the right guy and marriage, without guilt; and, an increasing number of truly warm, loving relationships where couples will make love out of a genuine affection and deep mutual respect.

And there will be infrequent abortions since safer contraceptive pills and intrauterine devices will be openly dispensed and used more freely by those who want to have children only when they're emotionally and financially able to bring up a family.

There will be less and less reliance on drugs as emotional and social crutches. Also, pot will be legalized.

There will be much more group child rearing at integrated, infant and child care centers organized and run by young marrieds; and women will combine career and mother and wife roles with increasing skill and with the approval of their husbands. Men will genuinely admire their wives as they make contributions to social and political life.

Finally, college institutions will have to be radically restructured. Freer parietals (visiting rules in the dorms), pass-incomplete grading, and student-faculty control of the total institution will be necessary before the universities choke to death in rigidified sludge, or the extremists paralyze the daily life of teachers and students.

The MA students should begin openly to take on the revolutionary hippies and New Left as they will increasingly see them as irrelevant and ineffectual. They will take over the college papers, the former preserve of the Left, the jocks and the Greeks.

The MAs will inevitably start to date, marry and have children with all minority, ethnic and religious groups, particularly those of different origin. Ethnocentrism, chauvinism, and religio-tribalistic-nationalism will be condemned and shunned so that a truly integrated and egalitarian culture will be built in the rhetoric tradition of the aborted American Revolution.

Yes, I believe that the MAs will do many of these things and accomplish these social changes. And I admit that I am idealistically ebullient and optimistic. But is there any other way that can guarantee any future for all of us?

In the following sections I will examine the current values and attitudes of students toward three key processes or behavior patterns: *passion, pot* and *politics.* These three areas have the most impact on students today, are given the most attention by the media, and are the most disturbing and confusing to the older generation. Students are not a monolith, and as a singular group they do not have the same singular attitudes toward sexual behavior, drug usage and politics, as some chroniclers and analysts of university students proclaim. The data that I have collected, I believe, will indicate that the attitudes of MA college students in relation to these three areas differ sharply from the attitudes of the hippies, and the radical-left types. The following sections will also attempt to develop a common theme connecting the MA values and attitudes in all three of these areas – as contrasted to the radical-left-hippie values and attitudes as a common theme in all three areas.

Before examining the data, it is appropriate to indicate the primary sources of this data and the method used in collecting, recording and evaluating it.

The typology of prototypical students I have drawn is based on data collected from over two hundred students with whom I have come in close contact between 1965 and 1970. In getting students to reveal honestly their innermost feelings, attitudes and behavior toward such sensitive issues as sex, drugs and politics, the survey questionnaire technique by itself seems to me to be inadequate, and frequently, inaccurate. It was my close personal and organizational contact with these students in a variety of different conflict situations, both on and off the campus, that put me in a unique position to record the highly personal data that follows. The method I used to record this data was primarily the tape recorder.[11]

Some of the tapes were made via a lavalier mike which I wore under my shirt. Some were made with a mike openly revealed on top of my desk or car seat while engaged in two-, three- and four-way debates and arguments. Some were recorded by hidden hip mikes, powered by portable batteries, unknown to students arguing and fighting. But in every single case, I revealed that conversations had been taped for scientific research and disclosure—*after* they had ended. I made it very clear that all names and identities would be protected and obscured, if I found the data content to be valuable and usable. I reiterated that I wanted honest, truthful, uninhibited data. And I stated that data obtained unobtrusively, sometimes even unknowingly, often could be the most significant. Finally, I said I would not publish the data if the recorded information derived from particular MAs was not agreeable to them. If they did not want the data to be a part of scientific research, I would, of course, delete that individual or portion—and in some few cases, I did eliminate a certain individual's contributions—or parts thereof. But I never played back or showed written reproductions of conversations to any of the MAs, except two people. Those two had to give permission for their material to be used on a local college FM radio station, for an edited, transcribed show which I prepared. I wanted their specific editing and comments about this material.

These representative MA students, however, were never interviewed by me in the old, structured, controlled questionnaire type of survey-research methodology. This method was too artificial, inhibiting, and often blatantly inaccurate for my purposes. I wanted to secure the data in a more naturalistic, institutional conflict situation—whenever and wherever possible.

It was possible for me to do this because first, these representative MAs were my students, and studied with me in and out of class as I tried to connect theory with practice in the real world. Second, they joined me in organizing various groups and institutions to battle other groups and institutions in an attempt to democratically effectuate social change.[12] I acted with them in specific, real-life struggles against bureaucracy and tape-recorded many of our natural interactions as they studied me, I studied them, and together we studied and analyzed opposing groups and institutions.[13]

The analysis that flows from these studies is derived from the actual human successes and failures in building and interacting within new or ongoing institutions by sociologically involved observers.

These observations, tools for analysis, are of the raw data and resources emanating from role and value conflicts, and between policy-making leaders and colleagues, not just participant-observers; from a concerned decision maker, not just a detached, sterile, and neutral observer.

The fundamental question then is: Would students open up to an outsider-researcher? Would they ask for direction to competent, private psychiatric help, or seek abortion, draft, and drug advice from adults who preach, disapprove, judge and measure them, or would they open up to adults who work with them, side by side, as political and organizational equals?

This data is socio-documentary history as it was lived by me, my students and colleagues.

It is as true, honest, accurate and scientific as I could possibly record it as an imperfect human being.

The recording of any data must be coldly accurate and scientific; particularly, the action and interactions. But personal involvement, evaluation, and analysis of data must, of necessity, be partially biased and subjective. Only if one is a charlatan and fraud would he twist, distort, and eliminate the vital recordable facts of institutional life. Analysis and strategic recommendations are entirely a separate thing, however. It is how one uses the data and interprets it that is up for debate and conflicting analyses. This unique, scientific approach towards collecting the data[14] should be accepted just as survey-research, punch-recorded questionnaires are presently accepted as a methodological means to an end . . . truth!

The students, their peers, and parents who read this section will be the final judge (in the last analysis) of the book's accuracy.

Confrontation

9

Passion

A. S. Neill, the controversial, brilliant British educator, and author of *Summerhill* and *Freedom, Not License!* has said, "Sex is a natural part of every human's life. If it doesn't come out fully and naturally . . . it will come out in other suppressed, negative and bitter forms."[1]

The menstrual period for girls, swelling of the breasts and new curves in the hips and legs; the advent of boys' wet dreams, penis erections at the sight or thought of attractive females, and change of voice, are all natural signs of the beginning of physical maturity and the battle MA students have with raw and basic passion.

The mass media, peer pressure, and parental anxieties all titillate and prod the curiosity of most sixteen-year-olds about the opposite sex. By the time most teenagers arrive at college, the bulk of the controls that society imposes upon them has begun to unravel.

The curiosity, excitement, and growing lust to explore and consummate the increasing passion that arises in most male-female dating interactions, climaxes in the junior and senior years at college.

Most parents and adults are bewildered and confused by the change in talk and behavior of the MAs concerning premarital sexual behavior.

It is the contention of the overwhelming majority of MAs that a new and significant sexual revolution has taken place. All the evidence from anonymous votes in my Marriage and The Family classes; all the private discussions with my students; the constant observation and overheard confessions, lead me to the inescapable conclusion that Reiss,[2] Bell,[3] and others, are drastically behind the times and ultraconservative in their analyses and studies of premarital sexual behavior.[4]

In short, the data I have accumulated points to over 65 percent of all female college students engaging in coital intercourse; over 75 percent of other females (technical virgins) regularly petting to orgasm; and 90 percent of males having premarital sexual experience. Almost every student knows of a key friend or roommate who has either been pregnant, had an abortion or taken pills to induce bleeding before the eighth week. Over 95 percent of all college students talk freely and knowingly about every aspect and value conflict concerned with premarital sexual behavior.

Why? What are the reasons? How has it happened? What does it mean?

Using as little sociological jargon as necessary, it seems important to review quickly the historical trends and sociological patterns that have slowly and now, suddenly, helped create a new, passionate, sexual behavior revolution amongst marginal ambivalents on college campuses.

First came the revulsion at planned, family-arranged marriages (peaking early in the 1920s) which were traditional. The sweep of the romantic love ideology, fostered by radio, movies, and fiction, created the first break in the sexual revolution (during the thirties and early forties).

Then came the feminist movement with women becoming more aggressive and fighting for their rights. They moved off the pedestal and into the arena of human conflict and struggle for full identity and power. As females became more independent economically, as they moved into the labor and work force (World War II), they became less sheltered and more emancipated in every aspect of their personality and behavior.

The move from rural America into cities as a result of industrialization made it easier to live freely, anonymously and privately in urbanized industrial centers. The decline of the traditional family authority and the lessening of kinship family controls flowed from urbanization. And the breakdown of church and small-town community and familial controls inevitably followed.

Finally, the proliferation of the automobile served to replace the horse and buggy in more ways than transportation. The car became the private and away-from-home place to be alone with your date; to explore freely the intimacies of sex away from prying eyes and familial and community controls.

Now, for the present scene.

The Kinsey reports shocked the country in the fifties by showing a huge discrepancy between the values most adults expressed and their actual sexual behavior. Books, articles and TV discussions swept the country as value conflicts came out in the open and sex became a familiar topic. The old sanctions and fears slowly subsided as honesty and integrity became the adolescent catchwords for the new morality.

Then came Pope John and the talk of new encyclicals leading to international tension and conflict over potential Catholic birth control policy revisions.

Finally, came the mass-marketing breakthrough of the pill. A great many women began to use the pill and planned parenthood organizational growth boomed, supported by fears of the population explosion.

And so, with this brief socio-historic background, we move to the actual breakdown of the evidence of the generational value conflicts and personal ideologies of the MAs as they live and expand this premarital sexual behavior revolution.

The twenty-three representative MA students (primary source

of key data) range in age from twenty to twenty-four. Five are black, five Catholic, five WASP and eight Jewish. Ten are males and thirteen are females. They were the most representative and generally prototypical of the more than two hundred MAs I recorded in depth.

The colleges they attended are: Harvard, Radcliffe, Northeastern, Brooklyn College, Smith, Amherst, Duke, Chatham, New School for Social Research, Boston University, Middlebury, Tufts and San Diego Junior College.

These colleges are extremely varied in peer and environmental influences. They include: big city (New York, Boston); stay-at-home (Brooklyn College, Northeastern); Ivy League–New England (Harvard, Smith, Radcliffe); Little Ivy (Amherst, Middlebury, Tufts); metropolitan-private (New School for Social Research); West Coast junior college (San Diego); lower third of top third cosmopolitan out-of-town (Boston University); top Southern private (Duke); Midwest, private, women (Chatham).

So, private and public; small town and big city; day and night; coeducational and all-girl; high, middle and average in academic prestige; East, Midwest and West Coast geographically; stay-at-home, commuter and live-away are some of the differential, cross-section categories represented by the thirteen colleges.

Most of these twenty-three MAs differ vastly from one another. In manner, style and personality, in intellectual capacity and perceptiveness, no two are identical or similar. I have tried to integrate their collective biographies with a brief, analytical social history of the times – a social-psychological analysis of character meeting social structure (particularly in the "Politics" chapter of this book). I have highlighted those value statements and those repetitive behavior patterns that are common to the lives of all twenty-three MAs. And, inevitably, I present them as far more homogeneous than they really are.[5]

Clarke and Trow, Schuman and Stanfield, Warren and the College Student Questionnaires (a hundred and twenty thousand students) all have delineated in differing interpretations the wide diversity of student characteristics. Richard Peterson attempted to synthesize all these student diversities in a model typology which seems to fall close to the breakdown I have observed over a two-year period.[6] The Peterson typological stratification of students follows – with specific indications of where the MAs fit into this typology. It's particularly appropriate to again note here the stratification differentiation of students before introducing "Passion" data.

1. VOCATIONALISTS: students training for a specific occupational career, i.e., engineering, business; working-class background.

2. COLLEGIATES: commitment to popularity, play, sex (Greek brothers and sisters); anti-intellectual, conservative politically, conformist and "other-directed."

3. PROFESSIONALISTS: born of upper-middle class professional parents; private high school or prep school; geared to enrollment in postgraduate professional school (law, medicine, government); cool, seldom excited by issues and ideas; conservative to middle-of-road, oriented toward status quo.

4. RITUALISTS: lack of commitment to anything; from lower socio-economic strata; below average academic aptitude; uninterested in either academic or collegiate environment, pushed into college (as "thing to do," near home, easy to get into).

5. HIPPIES: promiscuous utilization of drugs, sex; estrangement from American values and institutions; pessimistically apolitical; temporarily or permanently withdrawn from society and ordinary pressures of college life.

6. LEFT-ACTIVISTS: personal involvement in action; directed at reforming some facet of American life; parents prosperous, liberal in outlook; highly intelligent; non-career-oriented academic interests center in social sciences and humanities; passionate sense of outrage at hypocrisy, injustice, wrongdoing; have courage to act (or psychological need or hangup for excitement). One half of this group is nihilistic and revolutionary; *other half worked for McCarthy* (the marginal ambivalents).

7. INTELLECTUALS: oriented toward ideas and networks of ideas irrespective of the curriculum; concerned with questions of interest to intelligent men everywhere; philosophers or historians; parents middle or upper class; highly individualistic; liberal politically (but rather cool or unemotional about it); aestheti-

cally sensitive; motivation for grades not noticeable (marginal ambivalents).

8. ACADEMICS: scholarly achievement within a specific subject, field, or academic discipline characterizes this group; they plan to go on to graduate school, a Ph.D. and a career of research and scholarship; middle class, relatively well-educated parents; serious and highly organized in their study routines and habits; slightly left of center in politics; not activists but would be sympathizers, or participants, in some broadly based student movement (marginal ambivalents).

Now, here are some excerpted taped comments about passion, sex, love, and marriage – as seen by the MA *males,* with a brief sketch of each. A sense of the more open, radically changing attitudes of MAs towards sex is illustrated in the following statements.

B.F. (24 years old, teacher in the ghetto, conscientious objector, occupational deferment; WASP; wealthy parents; Ivy League graduate; handsome; two sisters, father a wealthy businessman.)

> Too damn many people are up tight about sex. It's just great! I don't ball every chick I get the hots for; I just ball those I really like. Lately I've only been balling one gal. We're living together and it's real fine. No, I don't want to get married. I'm not ready for that kind of permanent responsibility. But it's sure great to have the apartment looking so clean and the meals and my laundry always clean. I had three or four gals a week – juniors or seniors – when I had an apartment off campus. Most were virgins.

J.R. (22 years old; Ph.D. student, Harvard; two sisters, two brothers; father a college professor; graduate of Yale, good looking, Catholic.)

> There isn't a gal alive who can't be made by the right guy. Fucking is the freest, healthiest activity a human being can indulge in. I did it with twenty or thirty females while an undergraduate at Yale and eventually every one loved it and came (orgasm) almost every time I did. They all wanted it

but most were scared of getting pregnant, or of being talked about, or of not being good, or doing it right. Way over half were virgins – juniors and seniors.

R.T. (21, City University graduate; Catholic, working-class, ignorant parents; awkward, sincere, naïve; psychology graduate student, Queens College; prominent nose and bad complexion; "sweet" guy.)

I don't make it with girls very well or often. I think about it all the time but I'm not very smooth. I've done it three or four times, but I've pulled out too soon – afraid of knocking up the girl. But I'm usually so excited I come too soon. If I can get inside her brassiere, usually I can go all the way. Every time I can brush back and forth over the bare nipples, I break down all resistance. I walk around with an erection half of every day.

S.V.R. (Black; 22; two brothers, sick father, working mother; ghetto resident, senior, CCNY.)

I go to pot and sex orgies every weekend starting Friday evening. About six to eight couples attend and over the course of the two-and-a-half days, most of us ball each of the others at least once. The guy who has the most orgasms (safes are used for proof) wins sixty dollars to eighty dollars. Ten dollars entrance fee per couple. It's a ball. We're all high – some smoke hash and a few take speed. There's usually several white couples. Several of my Black Nationalist brothers have objected, but they still screw the white chicks.

L.D. (21, Yale Law; father, high school principal; only child; Brooklyn middle class; Jewish.)

I want it almost all the time. Every time I see a well-built chick I can feel a deep ache in my dong. I've got a steady who is a teacher in Brooklyn. We knock each other out and can't get enough of each other twice, three times a day, on the rare weekends and vacations when we get together. She loves me, wants to get married. I like her a lot, but the thought of marrying her now, or anyone, scares the hell out of me. Besides, one woman probably would never satisfy me sexually.

J.W. (23; father, lower-middle-class businessman; two brothers; chemistry B.A. from Brooklyn College; Jewish; grad student in sociology at New School.)

I can't stand aggressive or highly emotional females. I couldn't make love to a cheap, manipulative sexpot to save my life. Phoney middle class dames who dress to the hilt turn me off. I'm a one-woman man and even though J. is confused and sick, she's smart as hell, sweet, and great in bed. It's awfully tough to sleep with her now since I know she was knocked up by another guy, and I'm the one she turned to for help, not him, the bastard . . .

A.L. (21; Boston University senior; upper-middle class; Jewish; very handsome; father, cold businessman; one brother.)

Every chick walking around can be made by the right guy—and I'm always the right guy when I decide to lay the gal who turns me on. I get plenty. Sex is a game and I want to win. I don't trust any gal enough to get too serious. My folks taught me to trust no one, or I'd never get badly hurt. And they were right, particularly in regard to themselves. I like a wide variety and can't come unless I get my partner to go first. I like to keep going half the night till I conk out. Pot and a cold back seat and I can turn on any girl who lights my fire.

E.B. (20, black; senior at Harvard; parents—upper-middle class; integrationist and fighter; ascetic looking.)

I have lots of real girl *friends,* white and black. I'm too young to get serious about any of them. Sex is a very private thing. I don't like to talk much about it. I've got a girl back home and our parents try to push us together on holidays, and so on. I hate exhibitionists who try to prove they're big lovers.

G.J. (20, two brothers, one sister; B.U. junior; Protestant; father, upper-middle class businessman; good-looking.)

> I think it's impossible to love in an open, honest relationship with a female unless you first have an intimate, complete sexual relationship with her. I have many chicks I like and go with; if they're tight and resist me sexually, I find them not ready for any mature kind of relationship.

What is typical in the preceding MA male attitudes is open, unadorned, unadulterated, positive sexual behavior with affection with equals – female classmates, not whores or lower-class townies. No apparent guilt or good girl–bad girl dichotomous conflict seems to exist, but a zest for intercourse. No real evidence of the old double standard nor any feeling that their future wives must be virgins comes across in the tapes or interactions with females.

Permissiveness with affection; a sharp move towards honesty and openness; a moral, single standard (unlike left-hippie males indulging in group sex), and full and unrestrained sexual expression seems to be the consensus. Many of the male MAs are frightened of permanent heterosexual relationships with heavy responsibility and emotional commitment. They tend to divide the passion involvement from long-range commitment, which protects them from their own immaturity and ambivalence. Their virility and manhood must be established at all costs. The MA males *talk* like the left-hippie males about sex. But in practice they make love and have singular, affectionate relationships. The left-hippie males "ball" indiscriminately in crash pads and groups, rebelling totally against adult values – not ambivalently and partially like the MAs.

Much more significant, however, is the accelerating evidence (particularly between April 1966 and March 1970) that premarital coitus has become almost as accepted among college females as with college males. Holding off sexual intercourse – curbing passion – until after marriage is becoming rare. *This dramatic change in middle-class college-female behavior is one of the key factors in the open, passion-sexual revolution now sweeping the campuses.*

The internalized value that premarital coitus is wrong, however, along with guilt feelings from its violation, continues to be a conflict for a significant number of American girls. The girl has to decide how far she will go. If she is not permissive, she may lose him! Yet, if she's too permissive, he may define her negatively as too easy or too great an emotional commitment!

The following MA females, though much more open and free than their parents, still remain far different from the SDS and hippie crash-pad followers. Promiscuity and open permissive behavior with many guys is not the female MA style. Their clothing is more modest (skirts above the knee two inches, not to the crotch and they generally wear bras).

To both MAs and left-hippies, passion can often be a cultish effort to replace thought with sensation. In the crisis of values many students obviously use sexual display openly as a shock weapon of protest against the establishment.

C.R. (21; upper-middle class; only child; father, businessman; college, a year and a half at Brandeis; WASP.)

> I was bored at college and had to get out. My parents finally agreed that I ought to try living in Cambridge. I lived there a month, took acid: it was an empty-nothing. I tried everything . . . bored. I came to New York City in June 1966 and started sleeping with a grad student whom I had met in Boston and whom my parents had met and approved of. We've slept together almost every night for two years; all our friends know this and we now live openly together in his apartment. I'm sure his parents and mine, too, know we sleep together, but we've kept the fact of our living together away from them. I don't know how they'd all react. We just don't want to hurt them. I keep an apartment address. Marriage? I really never think of that. I'm taking night courses at City University, working, having a ball with Jim and hoping eventually to do child psychological creative programming at child care centers. On second thought, sure, I'd marry him at the drop of a hat, but he's not ready yet; and I'm nowhere ready to have a kid. Until I'm ready for that, I guess I'm not

ready for marriage either. I've used pills now for three years and I just love to groove and go with him all the time.

L.E. (22, San Diego Junior College; upper-middle class; college graduate; father a businessman; one sister, one brother; Catholic; suburbanite; swinger.)

Though I have trouble coming, I had intercourse with one guy pretty regularly; he made me try *everything,* like oral intercourse (I wasn't too thrilled about that; he really expected me to swallow his semen as a sign of love, but I spit it out – *ugh!*). My first lover, D., had steady intercourse with me and it didn't hurt at all; the big myth of first-time pain or ecstasy didn't come to pass. We did it under the porch of the fraternity house at San Diego. After my first guy wrote he was marrying another girl, I rebounded to Tom, a very old friend, very quickly. The first time I slept with him he mumbled something and I answered yes and it turned out he had asked me if he could "come" in me. I obviously didn't understand the question; three weeks later I had a positive rabbit test. Tom had gotten a previous girl friend pregnant and saw her through an abortion, so we went to New York City to a motel (where I shook for hours in fear), and then I went alone to a street corner in Manhattan where I waited with a red carnation in my lapel, and was picked up by a guy in a black car. Three other girls were in the back seat and he asked for the envelope immediately (containing six hundred dollars in cash). I gave a fake name, and sat with a half dozen others in an apartment who talked openly of the imminent abortions they were having, and then they gave me a D and C. I was six weeks pregnant. I heard the toilet flush as I lay down for an hour on a cot with blankets (ugh). I had no pain or hemorrhaging at all. I started sleeping with Tom regularly again soon after, but I went on pills and shortly thereafter I met a married (separated) lawyer in New York City whom I started having intercourse with. I have a much more satisfactory sexual relationship with him. He's trying to get a divorce but feels guilty about not seeing his two little kids. My folks think he's single and he's visited our home three or four times. They'd die if they knew he's married. I hope it works out.

R.O. (21; lower-middle class; one married brother; senior at Boston University; sleeps home; father, truck driver; Jewish.)

My dad still thinks I'm his little precious doll and treats me that way. My mother is a suspicious, domineering, compulsive cleaner; all she talks about is my having a good marriage to a doctor, lawyer, or successful businessman. I couldn't go away to college – have to sleep home every night . . . I'm a little girl because I'm single, but if I had got married at eighteen, I would have been a mature woman of the world. I can't stand most boys my age; they're so young. There was one boy who used to talk me into visiting his apartment when his mother went shopping weekly. He taught me to soul kiss and it got me all hot and flushed and he pushed and pressed me through the usual high school four stages of petting [outside above the waist; inside above the waist; outside below the waist; inside below the waist] and then, he'd get on top of me and squirm and push. It got me very excited but we fought all the time because I was scared of getting pregnant. Once he took it out and spurted all over my panties. God, I didn't sleep for three weeks till I had my period and nobody touched me again until I finally went all the way two years later with an older grad student. He was adorable and got me worked up petting in bed. He slipped it in without hurting me one night, inside my panties while lying side by side, and later, when he opened me up, he drove me nuts by plunging in and out – hard! He hurt both of us he drove so deep and hard but it drove us crazy. He wouldn't use a safe. He said it was like going in swimming with his shoes on. I wouldn't get a diaphragm or take pills; it sort of turned me off, thinking of getting ready for a mechanical act; I trusted him absolutely; he always pulled it out just before he came, and I think that was why I never had a full orgasm. I didn't like his hands touching and playing with me. I wanted it all or nothing. No, there has never been a real chance of anything permanent happening between us. I have to have a nice home, nice furniture, clothes; all the things I've never had. He just wants to save the world. Yes, I'm crazy about him, but we want different things out of life. It has to break up sooner or later.

P.H. (22; upper-middle class; father, businessman; New Jersey; senior at Brooklyn College; parents, Catholic and Jewish.)

The first guy I ever really fell in love with I never slept with. I wanted to give myself to him unashamedly but was scared and then he just off and dumped me. He started going with a much prettier and vivacious girl and told a mutual friend that I was OK but just a plain Jane, a nice girl, not too much upstairs and only so-so in the chassis. My pride, self-esteem, confidence were all nil. I transferred from Chatham to Brooklyn College to start all over again at nineteen. I met Frank at Brooklyn College with my defenses down. Within six weeks we were living together. We went to concerts, plays, museums, skiing and slept together night and day. My parents found out, violently disapproved, and called me a slut. I told them I loved Frank. No difference. "Nice girls don't sleep around before marriage!!!" said Mama. They put enormous pressure on me. I wanted their approval, needed their financial support, but I also wanted and needed Frank. We moved into separate apartments but still made love with great frequency. Neither of us could get enough but he never would talk of love, or even hint at any kind of long-range future together. Naturally, I'd marry him if he asked. I love him. But he keeps talking about seeing others and not counting on him. Two summers in a row I had brief affairs with other men abroad but back again to Frank. He had several girls while I was away, but neither of us ever sleep with anyone else when we are together. I'm pretty sure he'll run from marriage for years. I don't want anybody else but I'm probably not going to get him. But we see and sleep with each other two or three times a week. My folks suspect, but don't know for sure. I'd like to break with them, but if I do, I won't have anybody if Frank and I don't make it. I'm afraid of every alternative and don't know what to do or who to talk with.

The terrible ambivalence, the guilt, the defiant behavior, the repetitive rationalizations of love, the conflict between parental values and female premarital sexual behavior is strikingly exemplified in the above tapes.

Howard Whitman, author of *The Sex Age,* writes:

> . . . unlike the female, who has an innate tendency to associate sex with love and to reject it without love, the male must overcome a tendency toward the lustful [passionate] use of sex versus an expression of love.

The interrelationship of love and sex is confusing for the MA girls. They are often brought up to believe that strong sexual desire flows solely from being in love. Thus, if they have strong sexual arousal or interest, they rationalize their feelings by declaring themselves "in love." Many so-called nice or good girls have never been fully aroused sexually until they meet a certain boy. At that point, it *has* to be love, otherwise, they are bad girls and easily aroused by any man.[7] And in a love relationship, she thinks or talks of love and marriage, while the young male shies from talk of love and runs from thoughts of marriage. Thus, the MA females (unlike left-hippie females) are ambivalent . . . torn between hopes and realities, between fears of not really being in love, not having a real marriage possibility—and having rationalizations and dreams stripped away, together with the wish that the affection, warmth and stability of a love relationship be maintained.

As we stratify MA *female* college students we find four major typologies which I have classified as a result of analyzing "Passion" data:

1. Virgin, religious: idealistic, scared, unwanted.
2. Virgin, technical: pet to orgasm, genital stimulation.
3. Permissive with affection: selective intercourse with someone whom she believes she loves.
4. "Plumber": permissiveness for curiosity, hedonism, popularity, rebellion; promiscuous with regularity.

Looking at the MAs and reflecting on the votes of over fifteen hundred students I had in classes over three years, it becomes quite clear (as pointed out before) that at least 60 percent of the MA female college students and perhaps 65 percent of all females at college indulge in premarital sexual intercourse.[8]

When asking students to vote in classes, I always prefaced the vote by stating:

> I'm asking you to vote "yes" or "no" in terms of how you perceive the overwhelming majority of your *roommates, friends,* sorority or fraternity sisters or brothers, and *close* (in terms of age) *relatives* behave and act.

So it was their *peers* that received a 65 percent female sexual indulgence vote in class. Utilizing this technique to prevent personal disclosure or embarrassment and to promote accuracy, I prompted many students to think in broader terms and become more analytical about the behavior patterns (in groups) of their peers, rather than to think of only isolated and specific individual cases.[9]

At the end of each semester, after the students had repeatedly voted their estimation of the sex, drug, and political behavior of their peers, I'd make the following statement:

"I'm sure you're all aware that for the most part you were voting on your own personal behavior, not just that of your peers, roommates, friends, and so on." Deadly silence, amused and surprised faces, then nervous laughter usually followed this flat, declarative statement. I'd continue:

"Many social scientists have estimated that there is only a minute discrepancy between students' estimates of their peers' behavior and their own. In other words, how many of you agree that there is virtually no difference between the way you and the entire class voted all semester and your own personal behavior?" Way over half of the class put up their hands in every case each semester. "How many of you agree that there would only be a *one point five* to a *one point* discrepancy between your behavior and your peers' behavior as you voted?" About two thirds accepted this.

Although the above is obviously not a scientifically flawless research technique, most of the votes over three years squared with my own personal observations and discussions with MA students.

There has been a steady but slow upward curve on college campuses starting from the spring of 1966 in regard to drug consumption and premarital sexual intercourse, but the most radical acceleration has been the upsurge of unmarried college girl pregnancies and abortions which climaxed between October 1, 1968, and June 1969.

For unwanted pregnancies to proliferate at a time of growing female freedom; rising intelligence of college students; growing public knowledge through publicity and mass media coverage of birth control information; the breakdown of the Catholic Church's hierarchial control of its members' sexual practices; the advent of the pill; and the sophistication of students about sex — this indicates a complex sociological phenomenon that demands further analysis.

This analysis needs further study and thousands more samples, but based on my own research and talks with other teachers and clergymen at five different campuses in Boston, New York City, and San Francisco, I tentatively propose the following:

First, there is little basic communication between high school students and their parents concerning detailed and specific information about intercourse. There is never any discussion about petting to orgasm as related to the necking and petting problems faced by high school students every weekend. Books and charts are turned over to kids by parents but most of these are boring, formal and scientific and bear little relationship to the weekend petting in back seats.

There are occasional sex lectures held in schools but they are for the most part formal and rigid, and very careful not to go too far or to offend religious, political, and parental fears and objections.[10] The students are wary and careful, too. They must remain cool, sophisticated, and avoid basic bread-and-butter questions for fear their peers will laugh and hoot at their naïveté.

College juniors have told me how they were ridiculed and laughed at in dorm bull sessions when they dared to ask basic questions like: "How close to semen can I come before it can impregnate me?" . . . "Does semen penetrate through cotton panties?" . . . "If my boyfriend has it on his hand, can it be dangerous if he fondles and holds me 'down there' when I come?" . . . "When he gets on top of me with his shorts still on, can it get through his shorts and my pants even if my hymen is still intact?" . . . "I can't get pregnant, can I . . . so long as my boyfriend just spurts against the outside of me? . . . he never puts it inside . . . at least deep enough to feel . . . ?"

Gross, abysmal ignorance is the *number one reason for pregnancies* simply because parents, schools, and society at large still think it immoral and wrong for adolescents to have premarital intercourse and shudder at the thought of their children petting to orgasm. Therefore, they are unable to educate youngsters in this area and have not yet resolved their own hypocrisy about discrepancies between their own youthful sexual behavior and their adult and contradictory verbal values and attitudes. Mothers who had premarital intercourse repeatedly tell researchers that they are unyielding in their opposition to their own daughters doing likewise. They cajole and frighten their children probably because they remember so vividly their own curiosity and experiments with sex and passion.

Secondly, many MA females who have made the decision to make love fully with a lover *don't* know doctors, *don't* trust their family physicians to keep their requests for pills and diaphragms confidential, and just *don't* have the personality, contacts or guts (unlike left-hippie females) to go to a strange doctor and face potential exposure or embarrassment. These girls inevitably count on their male partner to take care of things.

C.R. reasoned: "I trusted him enough to be my lover. How could I *not* trust him to be sure I didn't get pregnant? I was so crazy about him and had idealized him so much. Of course I'd count on him and knew he'd take care of things."

Likewise, R.M.: "My roommate said her boyfriend had always pulled it out and spurted all over the back seat. She trusted him completely. He was mature and strong and knowledgeable and she trusted him. I lent her three hundred dollars to get an abortion."

And R.O.: "When I was in France, this boy was so mature and sophisticated and cool, I was afraid to even raise the question. I assumed he'd take care of everything. He really knew the score and I didn't want him to think me a baby or ninny. He relaxed and calmed me and told me to relax and enjoy it. I did and my friend's father had to give me pills which started me menstruating five weeks late. What a break. My friend's dad is a gynecologist!"

Another tragic and poignant reason for many girls getting pregnant is their fear of having a love relationship drift into a mechanical, back-seat affair.

O.R.: We were getting more intimate all the time. I knew sooner or later we'd go all the way. But I didn't know where to go for pills. Everyone talks about it, but ask them where to go, and they mumble something about "see your doctor . . ." My doctor is at home, and my dad's best friend and golf partner. Could I ask him? I saw a doctor last week, right off campus, and he gave me a long, pompous lecture and made me feel like a bum or tramp. Also he wanted to know my real name and my parents' name and address. No sir! My roomie got a diaphragm at a discount store and had trouble getting it in place properly and safely. Besides, I didn't feel right about mechanically preparing for love. It spoiled it.

G.J.: (male MA) We have a slush fund in my dorm that actually keeps a revolving sum of six hundred dollars in it for any guy's girl who needs an abortion. We raised thirty-six hundred dollars last month and some of the guys last semester (eleven of twenty-nine on my floor) went deeply into hock to get abortions for their girls. A guy who doesn't stand up and pay for and see his girl friend through the abortion is a bastard. I know of at least three other dorms on campus that have slush funds going. One of them is a large female dorm. Well, no guy wants to go in swimming with his shoes on. Did you ever use a safe? It feels like shit, nothing at all, it takes away all the feeling. I think (and most of my friends agree) that the pills are easily available and the girl has the responsibility to get them or buy a diaphragm. She's a college woman and old and smart enough to take care of herself. Besides, there's only a few days a month when she can actually conceive and the rhythm cycle works pretty damned well most of the time.

R.M.: A lot of the girls have got caught when juiced or stoned. It's like liquor. All the inhibitions are lifted and you're floating in another world far away from college and parents and reality. Four girls on my floor, all virgins, got pregnant this month at pot parties. Yes, I asked them why they hadn't used pills or a diaphragm, and they angrily replied with statements to the effect of: "I don't go around waiting to get laid. I wasn't prepared for any Tom or Harry to give it to me. It just happened because we were excited and it was spontaneous and beautiful and full of love. I'm not going around all prepared for any eventuality and plan to be safe like I bring my notebooks and pads to class."

G.J.: A tremendous number of guys and their girl friends get into trouble because they look at sex freely and with no hangups and rigid controls and fears. It's a natural, beautiful experience and talk of practical plans to prevent pregnancy somehow spoils the open and free and spontaneous naturalness of the relationship.

M.P.: My best friend got pregnant because she lost control. She told me that they had been "coming" [petting to orgasm] for six months and everything seemed under control, but suddenly her boyfriend, high on pot or speed, began to handle her differently and insisted while stroking her continuously that he had to have it and actually under great tension and excitement, pushed it in and came all over.

R.O.: I had always been under complete control. I never really came or shuddered like it reads in the hot books but when I start getting wet and my breasts are squeezed hard I sometimes can't say no or stop anything that's going on. I can't stand it if he stops and I didn't really know when he put his penis in and stopped using his hand. It was unbearable and I couldn't hold him back and I didn't really care what happened.

S.W.: Donna and Paula both had long trips and were seduced on the trips. They told me it was erotic and silky and they couldn't stop for the life of them. They knew they had no protection in a vague and distant sort of way but the sensation was overpowering and they wanted more. Only when they came out of it did they begin to get scared.

G.J.: I don't think many girls feel it's bad or dirty anymore. If the guy is cool and sure of himself and gives his word that he'll take it out . . . most of the girls I've helped with abortions believed their boyfriends . . . they cared for the guys and trusted them. It's sort of scary. Besides, they thought it was the right time of the month.

W.B.: Three of my high school roommates had abortions before the end of their sophomore year at college. All three were virgins, technically, until then, but all of them just talked about the pills they were going to take. It was sort of the thing to do, live freely and dangerously and take chances. Besides, wouldn't it really "shake up the old man." That would get some attention. Two of the three were grinning when they told their parents and both of them got pregnant a second time. They later joined me in a sanitorium since we were all flipped on drugs and had been pregnant five times between us. We used to swap stories about how badly we hated our dads and how we pitied our moms. Two of us tried to commit suicide. I guess all our fathers made over seventy-five thousand dollars a year, but never, *never* had time for us as we were growing up. Stern rules and long lectures on Sunday nights but no real talking and genuine concern for us as kids. Sure we went on drugs and got pregnant to punish them. That's what the shrink agreed was our main motive.

J.P.: There used to be a line ten deep every Monday morning at the medical services clinic after weekend orgies. Pot and booze were the reasons for blackouts and fears of being knocked up. My roomie was a doctor at the clinic and he was appalled.

Thus, on a social-psychological level, gross ignorance; fear of reducing love to cheap, mechanical sex; getting high on pot and other drugs; losing control under sexual stimulation, trusting young, immature males to "take it out"; punishing Mom and Dad for over- or underattention seem to be some of the main reasons unmarried MA college females are getting pregnant.

On a cultural-institutional level, media-talk about sexual freedom; supposed easy availability of contraceptives; disgust with the older generation's hypocritical attitudes, approving alcohol while disapproving drugs; the folly and fear of the Vietnam war intruding into the lives of young college couples; and the desperate need for openness, honesty, and integrity in human relationships seem to be some of the major sociological patterns helping to generate far more permissive sexual behavior which inevitably leads to sharply accelerated rates of unwed student pregnancies and abortions.

Any college teacher of Marriage and Family courses who is warm, over thirty-five, and has his own children, is simply overwhelmed with unwed pregnant students who desperately want help in getting an abortion. Perhaps a father-figure image is an essential ingredient.

Many students are terrified of parental discovery, and often mumble words to the effect of, "I'll kill myself if I can't quickly get rid of this baby." Homemade, old-wives-tale threats of lye douches, coat hangers, and over-the-counter drugs via pharmacists permeate this traumatic atmosphere.

Despite rumors galore of medically safe (campus-religious) abortion rings operating in New York City, New Jersey and Baltimore, where scores of students report that a thousand D and C's per week are performed, it is extremely difficult if not impossible for students to find a direct link to a *good doctor* who will perform an abortion.

Medieval, antiquated, religiously imposed state laws are a severe deterrent to intermediaries who could be charged with a felony and sentenced up to ten years in prison for being just an accessory to an abortion. Yet how many friends and teachers can walk away from a young, panicky girl in trouble?

Practically no pregnant students are aware of the laws in most states that allow legal, therapeutic D and C abortions. These legalized abortions, though often narrow in legal applicability and scope, nevertheless allow hospitals, doctors, and psychiatrists to generally recommend and approve abortions on psychiatric grounds under the "life of the mother" provision. Only convincing evidence that the mother will otherwise commit suicide legally justifies medical intervention in most states, except Maryland, New York, Hawaii and Washington, D.C., which have far broader statutes allowing patients, hospital committees and doctors to make a joint, private abortion decision.

It is within this ambiguous area that a teacher or adult can lawfully give advice and help, and send the panicky student to a competent medical doctor, religious advisor or a member of the prestigious and reputable American Psychoanalytical Association, who is also an M.D.

A rising curve of therapeutic abortions has recently emerged because it is almost impossible to distinguish between genuine and artificially staged demonstrations of suicidal intent on the part of the terrorized, unwed pregnant coed. Even acting and exaggerating can be a true definition of reality.

The usual hospital or medical doctor abortion (a procedure known technically as dilation and curettage, hence, D and C) is a relatively simple surgical intervention which, when performed by doctors in the early weeks of pregnancy, preferably before the tenth week, is quite harmless.

How ironic that the open, legal, and medically sound D and C abortion is so harmless and safe while obsolete, unworkable laws, religious taboos, ignorance, fear of discovery, lead thousands of girls to crooks, perverts, midwives, and immature friends. There are other equally dangerous paths: drugs, hangers, uterus lacerations, high douches, and tubes inserted into the uterus by non-doctors.

Thus, lifetime female trouble, unhealthy or crippled children, tumors, disease, sexual incompatibility are the bitter fruits we reap from:

1. Not having honest, open sex education in high schools.
2. Not having widespread contraceptive education programs, availability of medical personnel, or information and material devices vigorously presented at hospitals and health clinics for those who want them.
3. Not removing all present abortion laws through legislative or judiciary processes and allowing a single-standard policy of free choice, a socially approved extension to women in areas of personal freedom that should be their birthright.

Such legalized abortion laws as are now present in Japan, England, Hawaii, Washington, D.C., New York and even Puerto Rico, lead to growing hope that sanity and open, legalized, medical abortions will soon be a fact of life in the entire United States.

The radical increase since 1966 of sexual experience by college females firms up earlier sociological analyses which indicated that more highly educated women believe they are:

1. Equal to men in the area of sexual rights, and
2. Less subject to social control through fear, superstition, or a belief in sin.

Thus, this leads to later marriages and more premarital intercourse. College students as a whole are influenced by their peers and subgroups far more than by the decreasing control of traditional institution. There are very few students who feel free to fully discuss their sexual dilemmas with their parents! Therefore, responsibility for control over pregnancy is increasingly with the girl. Since American society is characterized by confusion, contradiction, and hypocrisy in the general area of sex, the result is a tug and pull on the individual and especially on the girl as to what is right in the area of sexual intimacy.[11]

Most leading sociologists in the field agree that the most important single factor with regard to present premarital sexual values has been the drastic alteration in the traditional double standard (men indulging in intercourse before and during marriage with other women while their women are supposed to be virgins first, then sleep only with their husbands). For the first time in thousands of years we have sexual standards which tend to unify rather than divide men and women. Especially in permissiveness with affection, coitus is no longer forbidden, and the motivation to deceive the opposite sex in order to obtain pleasure is greatly reduced.[12] All the greater is the tragedy that so many young unmarried college women are increasingly and ambivalently becoming pregnant at the same time the birth control pill usage curve is rising so astronomically. This shocking factor is heightened by the general professional projection that premarital coitus within the setting of permissiveness with affection will increasingly be the accepted pattern for larger numbers of young people.

The MAs have led the way to working out some of the contradictions inherent in winning personal freedom and handling it maturely in a stifling, rigidified, bureaucratic setting on campuses.[13]

What is characteristic of the MAs is that though they are in the midst of a sexual revolution, it is primarily *permissiveness with affection* and almost always with just one partner at a time! They have a revulsion to promiscuity, unlike the SDS and hippies. The major typical quote to illustrate this is MA C.O.'s comment: "Anybody who uses the word fuck in regard to an act of love is really describing his or her own animal behaviorism. Likewise, the indiscriminate balling and screwing of chicks by two of my radical pals indicates sharply the general male hippie/New Left attitude toward women; they are objects to be used and exploited, not lovers, partners, enhancing each other's deep needs for love and affection."[14]

On the basis of my observations the revolutionary left, in its defiant rebellion against *all* institutions in American society, in putting down all liberal, egalitarian and reformist values, desperately asserts a new, bold revolutionary life style in which there can be no restraint, no selectivity, no attempt to seek out qualitative common values for permanent relationships (the dominant attitude of MAs). But rather, it's fucking (at the drop of a hat) anyone and everyone who's around. This is amply seen and demonstrated in the wide-open communal pads. Dozens are functioning on Buswell and Bigelow Street just off the Boston University and Harvard campuses. There are regular left-hippie weekend orgies in which circular and continuous sharing of reefers, speed and bodies is well known to the B.U. *News* and the Harvard *Crimson* staffers.

Total sexual and drug rebellion against old norms and Protestant ethic values is sometimes "socio-psychotherapy" to resolve the frustrations and tensions of many radicals and New Leftists as they unsuccessfully try to overcome the bureaucratic institutions – the polity, economy and education – in American life. What the Left cannot accomplish politically they can substitute and try to effectuate through their own revolutionary personal sexual and drug behavior! The MAs aren't as developed politically (nor as frustrated) and they are only marginally in rebellion versus old adult values in hard drugs and sexual behavior. The left-hippies are in total rebellion in all three areas as we shall now delineate.

10

Pot

Pot or grass (marijuana) along with hash, is part of the Cannabis family and is by far the most popular drug used by students on American campuses.

As a chapter title, pot is defined, in this instance only, to mean drugs used in general, on the college scene.

My study of MAs, starting with classroom polls in Marriage and the Family courses (Northeastern University, Brooklyn College and Boston University) numbering over eleven hundred students, indicate an acceleration of their use of drugs since April 1966. At no time, however, have they approached the quantitative or qualitative drug consumption of the hippies or left-radicals (except Progressive Labor Maoists). Though MAs, mostly females, have experimented with the milder forms of speed (dex and bennies), and a small percentage have tried LSD (before knowledge of chromosome changes and psychotic episodes became widely reported), and a handful have tried heroin, cocaine, mescaline and the STP "hard" amphetamines, by and large, the overwhelming majority of MAs don't use the hard drugs (STP, heroin, cocaine, LSD, mescaline and peyote). The

MAs, as a specific, differentiated group almost exclusively use pot (marijuana) and only on a fairly regular weekend basis.

The hippie-left-radical crowd, generally (never numbering more than 10 percent of the student population, according to all surveys) use the hard drugs (especially LSD, STP, mescaline and peyote) on a systematic, almost daily basis in conjunction with their total rejection of the mainstream "system" or culture. It's all part of their overall rebellion: the ultra-long hair, the beards and moustaches; the neuter, beaten clothing; (Indian-black) soul language, rock, hard drug, crash-pad "balling" life style.

The hippie-left-radical drug consumption is mostly in group sessions, just as much of their sexual behavior is an open-group-switch activity. There is no ambivalence, restraint, or confusion about the total commitment to long-range drug experimentation and alteration of basic life styles, as there is among MAs. The need for instant impulse gratification is part of the repetitive pattern of their radical (sexual, drug and political) revolution, their rebellion against the adult, middle class, square, materialistic "system."

It would be a serious mistake to underestimate the full implications of the drug revolution which has swept college campuses, even though only 10 percent of the students are hard drug users. But the drug revolution has enveloped the MAs, numbering from 30 to 40 percent of the student population, who have obviously been influenced by the hippie-radicals. Yet, the MAs, having tried some of the hard drugs at the initiating or peripheral level of experimentation, nevertheless, are also largely influenced by credible, scientific information about the physiological and psychological dangers inherent in hard drug usage!

The ambivalence of the MAs toward drugs is the ambivalence of historic liberalism. The absence of catechism and dogma panaceas and the need for empirically proven data as to the dangers of marijuana or hash, leads to regular weekly consumption of this mild drug though it's against the law and leads to long jail sentences, criminal records, and conflict with parents and adult authorities. Yet, the MAs generally don't use pot anywhere near the level of the all-day, day-in-day-out usage of their countercultural colleagues to the radical left. And the presence of some responsible data about LSD (acid), STP, heroin and cocaine leads them to confusing, uncertain, and contradictory behavior with hard drugs – and diminishing, non-repetitive usage if they start hard drug usage at all.

The following chart[1] conclusively illustrates the differentiated drug behavior of the majority of MAs – in sharp contrast to left-hippies.[2]

Stratified Chart of Drug Usage

Based on questions asked in classes from June 1966 to May 1969, with a definite upward curve, in usage, each year. Sixty percent of these students are estimated to be MAs; 5 percent SDS-hippies; 5 percent jocks; 20 percent "Greeks"; 10 percent miscellaneous. More than 60 percent of students herein are MAs. Their weight dominates this survey.

1. Cannabis Family	
Pot	60 percent have tried it at least once; 35 percent use it weekly.
Hash	No clearly defined pattern.
THC	No information.
2. Psychedelic-Synthetics Family	
LSD	50 percent tried it once before chromosome reports indicated changes; 5 percent use it now (1969).
STP	10 percent tried it once; 5 percent use it now.
DMT	Same as STP.
3. Amphetamine (Speed) Family	
General	35 percent tried it once, 20 percent use it weekly now.
Crystal Methedrine	14 percent use it weekly now.
Dexedrine-Benzedrine	Begins at age 14 to 16; especially females; most common among females 16 and older. 38 percent use it now.

4. Psychedelic-Organic Family	
Mescaline	5 percent tried it; 2 percent use it now.
Peyote	1 percent use it now.
5. Heroin, Cocaine	5 percent tried it; approximately 2 percent use it now.
6. Qualifications of this survey:	1 Lack of natural (physical) science students. 2 Primarily students of education and liberal arts. 3 Mostly white, middle and upper class, from Eastern seaboard.

The most ominous development in drug usage evaluation and control is the deep credibility gap that exists between narcotic and police officials and high school and college students. Adult authorities and parents compound this gap when they lump all drugs together, under one umbrella, and condemn them as *equally* dangerous. The mass media are also guilty of this slovenly and inaccurate practice. As long as the students see establishment authorities speaking, prosecuting and punishing marijuana users in exactly the same way as hard drug users; and if marijuana continues to be falsely labeled as the predecessor or precursor or link to hard drugs — the tendency will be for many students to ignore and disbelieve the legitimate and scientifically knowledgeable information about hard drugs.[3] Heroin, LSD, STP, mescaline, peyote are dangerous and need intelligent, widespread, and repeated dissemination of factual evidence to students, from parents, from narcotic, police and judiciary officials, and from health and psychiatric experts. This information is vital and must be believable. But hypocrisy, lies, and misinformation about marijuana must be stopped first. The dangerously repressive penalties and criminal records handed down by adult authority for marijuana usage — in the name of archaic, immoral and hypocritical laws and institutions — must be drastically altered, repealed, and revoked before the serious attack against hard drugs is to be successful – in my judgement.

Therefore, an analysis and exposure of hypocrisy and double standards practiced by most adults is in order if we're ever going to break down the student mistrust presently generated by the generational credibility gap.

The term "drug" covers a multitude of consumer products that critically affect human physiology, psychology, and physical functioning.

The New York *Times* of June 28, 1968, reported that eighty million persons in the United States have used drugs containing meprobamate (tranquilizers) in the eleven years since they have been marketed. (Truly a "stoned" adult population.)

Sixty to 75 percent of adult Americans use prescribed and unprescribed drugs like aspirin, Bufferin, sleeping pills, wake-up pills, reducing pills, tranquilizers.

These people are not junkies addicted to hard narcotics, nor bearded hippies tripping on LSD; they are ordinary, "stoned" middle-class people who take pills to keep calm, stay awake, or pep up. These pills, most of them legally available by prescription (or OTC), are what are known as psychotropic drugs. Researchers and authorities until recently have been so dazzled by the glamour of narcotic and psychedelic drugs that they know almost nothing about the OTC psychotropics, according to Hugh J. Parry of George Washington University, writing in *Public Health Reports,* October 1968.

Eight billion consumer dollars per year go to the cigarette industry, which sells the addictive drug, nicotine. Also sold indirectly, through cigarettes, are arsenic and coumaraine (a flavoring agent, using tonka leaves, so deadly and dangerous it rips the lining of the alimentary canal as well as degenerates the tissue surrounding the ganglia of the nervous system). The Food and Drug Administration does not allow any use of coumaraine in food, drugs and pastries; cigarettes, ironically, aren't under or subject to the jurisdiction of the Food & Drug Administration. In addition, the concomitant polycyclic hydrocarbons, generated by cigarette smoke, lead to cancer (Surgeon General's Report, 1966, 1968 and 1969) as surely as nicotine constricts the vessels leading to the heart and causes heart disease.

Five billion dollars in yearly sales of liquor and beer also brings that desperately needed adult high or buzz from that ever-popular drug alcohol — which wrecks the liver and other internal organs.

Finally, three billion is spent yearly in the United States for debilitating drugs like caffeine (coffee) and tannic acid (tea) which upset the dendrites and ganglia of the nervous system.

So, practically every adult American is a willing and quasi-addictive consumer of harmful drugs to pep up, calm down, put to sleep, awaken, keep going, or relax.

In the face of this overwhelming adult reliance on different drugs, it is difficult to understand and respect the mass adult revulsion and almost total opposition to youth's experimentation with marijuana.

"Do as I say — not as I do," is hypocritical as you urge Junior not to smoke, while you are inhaling a Salem. ("I'm too old to break the habit, dear, don't *you* get caught.") Even more hypocritical is drinking to relieve pressure, to forget your troubles, or just feel free, good, or high while condemning your children and attacking most young people for presumably trying to achieve the same ends with a different, often less medically dangerous drug, marijuana.

It seems obvious that there will be continuing suspicion of adult authority — especially in relation to the danger of hard drug usage — until the hypocrisy surrounding the so-called health dangers of marijuana are eliminated. Narcotic, educational, and political leaders keep mumbling that there isn't sufficient data, not enough empirical medical information, to take a firm stand on the long-range dangers inherent in smoking marijuana. But that simply is not true.

Boston University and Harvard Medical School researchers, and the University of Toronto Narcotic Control Center, have completed studies of the effects of marijuana. Their findings generally were in complete accord with the 1944 New York Academy of Medicine complete study of the marijuana problem. That report, requested by the mayor of New York City, is an exhaustive study of the medical, sociological, and addiction problems of marijuana by a corps of experts. The academy's main points may be briefly summarized:

1. Smoking marijuana does *not* lead directly to mental or physical deterioration.
2. The habitual smoker knows when to stop, as excessive doses reverse its usually pleasant effects.
3. Marijuana does *not* lead to addiction (in the medical sense), and while it is naturally habit-forming, its withdrawal does not lead to the horrible withdrawal symptoms of the opiates.
4. No deaths have ever been recorded that can be ascribed to marijuana.
5. Marijuana is not a direct causal factor in sexual or criminal misconduct.

Dr. Robert S. deRopp, in his *Drugs and the Mind* quotes the opinion of many "that marijuana never hurt anybody and that the Narcotics Bureau would do better to devote its time and energies to the control of the really dangerous drugs, morphine, heroin, and cocaine, instead of chasing after a relatively innocuous weed."

During the 1937 hearings before a House subcommittee, Representative John Dingell of Michigan asked the head of the Bureau of Narcotics, H. Anslinger: "I am just wondering whether the marijuana addict [sic] graduates into a heroin, an opium, or a cocaine user?" Mr. Anslinger replied: "No, sir; I have not heard of a case of that kind. I think it is an entirely different class. The marijuana addict [sic] does not go in that direction."

Yet the federal legislation that was passed at the end of the 1937 congressional session was virtually a fear reaction (spearheaded hypocritically by Mr. Anslinger). Congress blindly accepted all the harsh recommendations of the Bureau of Narcotics.

Five years imprisonment; a two thousand dollar fine, or both, were the penalties provided for possession of even a minute quantity of the herb, under the Marijuana Tax Act.

Like alcohol, marijuana will never be easy to control – nor can the law be enforced adequately. It's easy to grow; easy to manufacture; easy to peddle, and is a quick source of easy money with a minimal investment. It can be grown anywhere, harvested quickly and secretly, and shaped up with no outlay for equipment or processing. Finally, every cigarette smoker is a prime potential user.

As David Solomon and Dr. Alfred Lindesmith point out in *The Marijuana Papers,* "The penalty provisions applicable to marijuana users under state and federal laws are about the same as those applied to heroin users. These penalties are entirely disproportionate to the seriousness of the offending behavior and lead to gross injustice and undesirable social consequences."[4] Crimes which could be shown to the satisfaction of a court of law to be linked with the use of marijuana, ought to be dealt with in the way that crimes arising from the use of alcohol are handled. Laws such as this, with penalties of a reasonable nature, would probably be more effective than those now in effect, because they would be more enforceable and more in accord with the nature of the problem being dealt with. They would have the effect of reducing the discrepancy that now exists between the laws as written and the laws as they are actually enforced. A more matter-of-fact and realistic handling of the marijuana problem would also probably reduce the aura of sensationalism that now surrounds the subject and diminish the illicit glamor which is now attached to the hemp plant.

But college students, including scores of MAs, are regularly being busted and then have criminal records. And this in the face of constant adult drinking on weekends, leading sometimes to abusive personal behavior, as well as to crimes, leading often to misdemeanor penalties and minor fines. Students are well acquainted with the fact that pot is certainly less harmful to the body than alcohol. And bitterly resent the legality of alcohol consumption and the illegality of pot consumption – a true double standard and one of the key illustrations constantly being mentioned of adult hypocrisy.

Therefore, if pot is less harmful; if their parents are double-standard hypocrites; if the police and courts are heavy-handed and sanctimonious about law and order; the illegal act of smoking pot takes on the magical mystique, the courageous aura of rebellion against unfair, immoral, repressive laws which discriminate against youth and are in favor of adults. It becomes a striking blow for freedom and morality in a highly self-righteous manner and provides this deviant behavior with a Robin Hood-ish rationalization.

What is different and unique about MA student usage of pot as opposed to adult alcohol attitudes is their claim that pot is used for conscious altering of mood and changing one's state of consciousness in an open, overt manner. Pot also "relieves boredom, breaks down inhibitions, elevates one's status as a cool swinger, fights depression, relieves anxieties."

Where adults claim that they only drink to be sociable and to relax, hiding their underlying needs, the MA students generally use pot as part of a general pattern of experimentation and search for relevance within and without the college experience. They make a conscious effort to find meaning in life. They are seekers of an intensifying experience, waiting to expand their awareness, to break out of flatness, deadness, and overwhelming depression. "Immersion in drug use is part of a phase of disengagement from American society."[5] And it's openly expressed and articulated unlike adult convictions and attitudes which are largely suppressed or ignored.[6]

But even if MA students are rationalizing their use of drugs or are tasting forbidden fruit, there is an honesty and integrity clearly evident as they describe their attitudes and values, an honesty which is missing in most adult explanations or rationalizations of adult double standard behavior towards the use of alcohol and OTC drugs and cigarettes.

H.D.: It's easier to make friends when on a high. Smoking pot really relaxes me. I'm inclined then to talk of more personal matters. But after a while I began to lose other "straight" friends, because most of my free time was spent turning on. Most of my pothead friends, also, had no time free for their straight friends.

G.J.: When on a high, my senses are always much more acute. I respond quicker to unusual or different colors, sounds, forms. I'm much more creative on a high, as most of my turned-on friends are. I'm fascinated with words and pictures and lots of us have started to draw and write poetry.

S.W.: Pot appeals to my intelligence with no interference with my intellect (I read that somewhere). I use it sometimes to hide or cover my true feelings, sometimes to expand them, sometimes just to avoid thinking at all.

H.D.: You always know what adults will talk about: weather, college, babies, clothes. But when I turn on with my friends, when we get high, not only is the conversation unexpected, but it's so new you can't control it. It's very adventuresome and appeals to the wanderlust impulses deep inside of me and many of my friends.

P.H. (Senior, Brooklyn College):
Why shouldn't I use grass or pot? Is it more harmful than alcohol? My parents and their friends get juiced every weekend and high with cocktails nightly. This is okay, legal and proper?

G.J. (Junior, Brooklyn College):
The law says pot and all that is illegal. Why? It makes no sense. Pot is medically far less dangerous than booze, so why are my parents and most older people so uptight over our using pot?

O.R. (Graduate student, Tufts):
A search for a sort of mystic unity . . . a feeling of oneness with the entire universe . . . is what I am for when I turn on.

S.V.R. (Senior, City University of New York):
It's cheaper to get high on pot than on booze. Most weekend social grass users can get a nice high on one-half to a full cigarette, costing fifty cents.

G.J. (Brooklyn College):
Pot is sold in bulk – small matchbox-fuls – and you roll your own. Usually with one-dollar "roll your own" hand cigarette

makers, using national brand advertised cigarette papers. You can roll between a dozen and eighteen joints per matchbox, which costs between six and eight dollars for an average quality. Four to five boxes make an economy-size lid [one ounce] which runs eighteen to twenty dollars.

J.R. (Grad student, Harvard, describing a pot party):

It was a clandestine thing. Legally criminal, religiously immoral: it left a feeling of guilt, social and religious guilt, a feeling, and then, inevitable action of compensatory bravado and infantile exhibitionism. We were all still neurotically rebellious! . . . versus our unmastered guilt and fear.

E.O. (Junior, Brooklyn College):

Dexedrine pills (Bennies) kept me awake during last week, cramming for finals — freshman year. They're a steady habit now.

J.R. (Grad student, Duke):

Government hypocrisy in enforcing strict laws against pot, which I see as a nonaddictive, relatively mild intoxicant used as a recreational drug, much in the manner most parents use alcohol, destroys the government's credibility in warning of dangerous drugs such as heroin.

P.L.: Grass tells me who I am, where my life may go, provides an escape from the trials and tribulations of college life.

A.L.: I know I use pot as a social crutch. I want to join in. When I'm floating and lighter-headed, I can make it easier with chicks.

However, even after a comparative analysis which, I believe, indicates the superiority of student drug-consumption values versus adult drug values (including alcohol), one must conclude that understanding is necessary but cannot be an excuse for condoning even the limited MA drug behavior patterns.

Primarily, the steady use of marijuana is a student escape from reality just as alcohol is an escape for adults. Some of these MAs admit honestly, that "pot is an escape from the boredom, ugliness, and complexities of the real world." To the degree they use it, they tend to stabilize and legitimate the status quo in politics, education, and in their own personal interactions and problems.

Whether it's alcohol, pot, or promiscuous sexual behavior, the basic, causative problem still remains. The factors provoking the fears and anxieties remain unchanged after the "escape tranquilizers" have worn off.

The real danger to the MAs (and to most other pot-using students), it must be repeatedly pointed out, is the crutch syndrome pot engenders. You can try to run away, ease the pressure, and even pretend the problem or trouble has gone away. But real problems just don't disappear. They come back repeatedly — as Freud brilliantly observed — in new and differing forms, often disguised, but generally more severe.

It's the substitute pot affords, of avoiding reality, failing to try to meet problems head on, that constitutes the real danger. Anything that reduces MA students' capacity to cope with normal anxieties and frustrations, should be understood as providing only an illusory and temporary escape from reality.

More seriously, as a result of the relaxed, euphoric, pot-induced state, the individual is far more suggestible; therefore, more easily influenced to believe something, accept a new state of affairs, which may be a clear distortion or an unwanted result. Many unwanted pregnancies, quack-butcher abortions, twisted personal and career decisions result from this state. Many students have told me tales of jams and crises they've gotten into as a result of pot parties and false euphoria. And, generally, they can't undo the blunder or mistake.

Quite a few MAs stress their conviction that they increase their sensitivity through the use of pot. Actually, the New York Academy of Medicine reports also indicate that marijuana often tends to distort human perception, carrying users further and further from the truth and clarity they seek through its use.

Freedom, independence, and autonomy are the traditional goals of youth. But these values and goals can only be achieved if they are supported and disciplined by skills, knowledge, judgment, and emotional maturity — which are not always present during the late adolescent years. Quickie-sensation-substitutes are counterfeit. They lead to anarchy, deterioration, and aimlessness, in many cases.

In the last analysis, there are no instant solutions to the youth-drug problem, which grows steadily worse. Certainly the starting point is the drug-ridden, guilt-driven adult population. They simply have to begin to take a new, single-standard, flexible approach. An open mind; understanding the inevitable adolescent-identity crisis; abolishing the unworkable and immoral marijuana laws, are but a few of the necessary and vital actions to be explored. Otherwise, we can only perpetuate the anxiety, resentment and defensiveness of the student generation.

Obviously, smoking, pill-taking, drinking, and drug use (even pot) cannot be anything but harmful to the human physiology. Each contributes medically, in some way, to the inevitable deterioration and dehabilitation of the human body.

MAs, and adults alike, have no rational alternative but to get to the root cause of social-psychological factors leading to alienation, powerlessness and subsequent fears and anxieties; not hide in bouts or scenes of fake euphoria and chemical escapism.

Political action, to reform old, or build new institutions, may show MAs the way towards linking their personal troubles to the solutions of public issues.

11

Politics

Many political myths, some undoubtedly fostered by machine politicians and professionals, permeate our culture. They help to discourage most people from participating actively in politics, the legitimate source of power in American society.

– You can't fight City Hall.
– Politics is a dirty business.
– Politics is a tricky, back-room business.
– Never trust a politician. He promises everything . . . before elections.
– Voting Democratic is an old family tradition.
– I vote Republican; it was good enough for my grandfather . . . why not for me?
– You have to be a lawyer to understand the laws.
– Whatever the "big boys" want, they get.
– My vote doesn't count – it just won't matter.
– You gotta be rich to run for office; poor people can't afford to run for office or be in politics.
– Most elections are rigged, crooked. It's all decided in advance by the bosses.

Like their parents, most students, especially the MAs, are either ignorant or cynical about politics. Their knowledge of American political history is engulfed in a huge smog of names, dates, places, and 1, 2, 3, and 4s (treaty points and platforms), which all become disconnected and mostly forgotten.

Particularly important is the fact that the university or college is the prelude to citizenship; the last adolescent opportunity to acquire a feeling for contesting power, politically, before entering the national political scene.

Most MAs haven't begun to understand that if they can't and don't organize to win, democratically, on campus, they'll indubitably feel – and be – powerless to work toward changes in society at large in the future.

The campus is truly a microcosm of the future, politically. The administration, composed of politically adroit personalities who reflect wealthy and powerful alumni and/or legislative interests, is in many ways just as rigidified, conservative, and committed to order, conformity, and status quo policies as is big government and big business. The faculty, preoccupied with their own research, publishing, and intra- and interdepartmental struggles for power, are generally just as unresponsive to the needs of students as bureaucratic governmental and business leaders are unresponsive to the daily needs of the voters – the public. The rules and regulations of the university are just as rigid, dehumanized, impersonal and backed by threats of legal punishment (injunctions, dismissal, probation) as many archaic institutions in business and governmental hierarchies are backed by a rigid, bureaucratic, "law and order" philosophy.

Thus, political action to reform university and college institutions is a necessary maturation process that MAs must engage in, if they ever hope to be effective at institutional reform of bureaucratic institutions in the larger society.

This is contrasted by the political behavior of the radical Rudd-Hayden-Rubin-Hoffman, hippie-left-type students. They are engaged in total revolution against the older generation, old values, old politics, old parties, the "power structure," the "system," in exactly the same flamboyant fashion that they revolt in their sexual and drug behavior. Riots, explosive bombs, classroom disruptions, booing and hissing at professors, administration building occupations (with chained doors and guns in some cases), constant calls for overthrowing the system via violence in the streets (always in response to system violence in Vietnam and against blacks and Indians, of course), disrupting and clogging the wheels of the structure and system are but some of the extremist patterns of political behavior of the left-extremists and many hippies.

Contempt for the political (two-party) process and system, abusive attacks on liberals for attempting to work for reform within the system, and reverence for socialist-communist, revolutionary slogans and heroes are the strategic and tactical directions of hippie-left political operations on university and college campuses.

They attack the MAs for their attempts at changing the system by working for reform from "within." They abused and vilified the MAs for supporting McCarthy and Kennedy in the 1968 presidential primaries. They ridiculed them for trying to restructure the universities and to win representation in decision-making bodies that run the university. They tell the MAs in revolutionary lectures and leaflets that no piecemeal reforms at university or college institutions can be accomplished. If they are, it will be meaningless in terms of the necessity to join the third world revolutionary struggle. Students must change the *total* economic and political system from top to bottom — not be co-opted or seduced by liberal reformism.

The MAs are far less verbal, more tentative and exploratory, less willing to engage in confrontations with clear-cut slogans and tactics sharply delineating right and wrong absolutes. They are not totally in revolt at all against the society, the government, the establishment. They still have some faith in the democratic process, despite their confused, ignorant groping, and hesitancy when faced with direct participation. They are definitely, however, opposed to monocausal, monolithic, simplistic, Mao-like and Castro-like (unfamiliar) supra-left solutions.

The MAs don't even begin to rebel politically on the same intensive level as they do in sexual and drug behavior (where they are infinitely more creative and innovative, though still much more moderate than the left-hippies!). As pointed out in previous chapters, the MAs are probing for ways to change and redefine the old norms and old values in a more sensitive, rational, and liberal fashion in relation to their sexual and drug behavior – not through the total revolutionary behavior of the left-hippies.

The MAs' ambivalence, therefore, is nakedly evident in the political arena, where they are most ignorant, inconsistent, and contradictory. There is no total correlation or interaction in the three key areas of MA behavior (passion, pot and politics). This is in contrast to the left-hippies who are in total revolt with consistent, repetitive, behavior patterns in all three key areas of behavior which connect and interact as if one, flowing, overall, variable – passion, pot and politics.

The MAs don't have final, definitive answers, particularly in political terms. They can't buy the easy Marxist or revolutionary panaceas. They are seeking change in all three areas and, heretofore, have lost most acutely in the political area because they believe in much of the rhetoric inherent in the historic tradition of the democratic process.

Unlike some of the left activists,[1] the MAs parents are not of the liberal-left spectrum, for the most part, as Keniston, Flacks and Lipset have pointed out. The MAs parents are mostly apolitical, conservative Democrats, or liberal Republicans. They support safe, stolid candidates who reflect a bureaucratic, middle, status-quo viewpoint and can comfortably live under a Nixon, Eisenhower, Humphrey or LBJ administration. Most of the MAs' parents vote once a year, or every other year, and surely every fourth (presidential) year. They think they're good citizens simply because they do vote.

The scars from the Depression drove most middle- and upper-middle-class parents of today's MA students toward obsessive economic security and social status. This comes out constantly in discussions with MAs about their parents, and is a source of MA generational conflict.

The educational system – reflecting the driven culture's values and preparing students to fit smoothly into the postindustrial, affluent (only for middle class) technological society – polishes the students, with the family's help, to fit into the expanding bureaucratic institutions.

The schools teach nothing about how American politics really work. And the students see war, poverty, racism, Madison Avenue values, and IBM technology coldly enveloping them.

Most MA students don't know how laws are passed, how to even organize a primary election, or how frightened elected officials become when written protests of voters flood their offices.

Their parents are afraid of signing petitions, of supporting too liberal a candidate or issue, and are constantly warning their kids not to get too involved in politics on or off campus. Every parent has a story of a dear friend or relative caught up in the madness of Senator Joseph McCarthy, or the House Un-American Activities Committee's "Red hunt" in the 1950s. And most MAs have come to fear and abhor the publicity, acrimony and violence (even if only vocal) of student politics, especially SDS-left confrontations.

Even more significant is the inability of most adults and students to see the direct connection between the polity (Democratic and Republican parties) and issues and problems like war, peace, the Bomb, the draft, marijuana and abortion laws, taxes, education, police, housing, healthcare, pollution, sanitation.

The closeness of the 51 to 49 vote in the United States Senate for pro-Pentagon antiballistic missile forces, and also the closeness of the defeat of the military-industrial juggernaut's baby, the SST supersonic transport program – their first defeat since World War Two – should hammer home this connection and irrevocably establish the importance of the political electoral process. Otherwise, powerful economic interests and right-wingers vitally influencing the growing military-industrial complex will see to it that inordinate political pressure is continually poured onto legislators to vote on behalf of conservative interests.[2] Even on campus, a few students try to negotiate for power, while most are ignorant and just bitch or are apathetic about working toward change.

It is illuminating to see much of the conservative Right obsessively active in politics, nominating Goldwater as the Republican candidate for president in 1964, and helping elect Nixon president in 1968. Meanwhile, the New and Old Left scorn two-party electoral politics and see no difference between New-Dealing Ex-Governor Pat Brown of California and ultra-Right Governor Ronald Reagan. Peoples' Park police violence, spurred on by Governor Reagan, and a crackdown on academic freedom at the state university level by his administration, might begin to shake this unreal view of no differentiation which the Left often helps to self-fulfill as its own prophecy. So, the Right is strongly connected to positive political action within the very system they have now begun to control. And the Left is mostly alienated—and perpetuates that alienation by disengagement, and by abusive attacks on the very establishment in politics that they purportedly state they can't influence.

Most students can't begin to understand what's happening to them at a large university; their personal troubles (loneliness, sexual and identity confusion, alienation, frustration, grade, curriculum and accreditation pressures) are not as isolated from the larger public issues at both national and campus levels as they appear to be.[3] Large-scale bureaucratic institutions on campus and in the private and public sectors of the larger society dominate the lives of most of the people they allegedly serve. These institutions and their corrollary value systems impose conformist, status-quo values on everyone. The university institutions control and socialize the students to fit into an expanding, bureaucratic, postindustrial, technologically computerized society.[4]

It is against this background that we begin to analyze significant examples of student political behavior (Boston University: thirty-two thousand students), as perhaps, illuminating evidence of university political behavior that has generalizing potentiality to other comparable situations.

As we shall see, a prototypical cross section of Boston University MA students seemingly understood that their sense of powerlessness was shared by many others, and not capable of solution by any one individual. They began to articulate the idea that only by restructuring the university where they study and live (for a longer period than students ever have before) could they begin to solve some of the daily conflicts they had as members (nonvoting) of a community — an institution.

We will take a serious, studious look at a sociology professor and at marginal ambivalent students at B.U., as they battle the ironically coupled SDS-Progressive Labor forces and a rigidly bureaucratic B.U. administration.

Boston University is perhaps a typical model of the large big-city, municipal, state or private university; considerably above average in academic and admissions requirements, very similar in size and standing to: City University of New York City (Queens, Hunter, City College of New York and Brooklyn College); Wayne State University in Detroit; Western Reserve in Cleveland; Rutgers University in New Jersey; Washington University of St. Louis; State University of New York at Buffalo, Albany, and Stony Brook (Long Island, New York); George Washington University, Washington, D.C.; San Francisco State; UCLA; Los Angeles; to name some of the better examples. These schools are a notch below Harvard, Yale, Princeton, Cornell, Penn, Columbia, Swarthmore, Stanford, Amherst, Reed, Brandeis — private schools; and not on a par with state universities like Michigan, Wisconsin, and Berkeley.

Boston University is also typical and representative of many other universities and colleges with constant student-faculty-administration conflict.[5] The Charles River campus has been a boiling pot of demonstrations, sit-ins, and takeovers of buildings.

It is very representative of a large cross section of universities and colleges that require their middle and upper-middle class white students to have between 550 and 650 averages on their college entrance SAT scores. They also have a typical militant handful of black students clamoring and winning black studies programs and increasingly separatist demands for housing and food. And lastly, B.U. has many bright high school underachievers in its College of Basic Studies (CBS) who copped out, or lost the grade-test competition, but wanted or were forced into a "good" college to get an education, polishing, or four-year refuge from marriage, career or vocation.

The average social scientist (usually a professor, instructor or teacher) speaks (if he so chooses) to large numbers of students with regularity; he lectures to neighboring pressure and political organizations and addresses written work to larger "publics" (social scientists across the United States via trade journals; and magazine and issue-oriented readers and citizens who are vitally concerned with the breadth and depth of key social issues).

To train a student to read, write, be a mechanic or engineer, practice a vocation, is in large part a training of skill which preoccupies most teachers. To help someone decide what he really wants out of his or her life; or to debate with him Stoic, Judeo-Christian or Humanist values, is part of the rarely practiced scholarly tradition of helping students with a sort of therapy to clarify one's knowledge of self. Only a handful of teachers attempt the latter. In contrast to Professor Lipset's definition of existing roles and norms of college teaching, the involved B.U. professor also falls into the debating, Humanist, therapy (relevant to societal problems) category of teaching.

There are at least two more breakdowns or categories of college teachers. The first kind is an associate or full professor. He has tenure, a lifelong guarantee of a teaching job where he is if he chooses to stay at that university.

The rest of the teachers are lecturers, instructors, or assistant professors, having no tenure. They usually have one, two, or three year appointments and are on trial by their tenured colleagues and at the mercy of the administration. They teach more hours. They haven't yet made it, insofar as research and academic publishing are concerned.

The research and the publishing that they do, plus getting on well personally (socially and politically) with their colleagues, are the chief criteria for tenured advancement. Teaching is a chore, is tolerated, and ungraciously practiced by most tenured faculty. They don't value teaching highly — nor does the administration.

In the social sciences (quoting Max Weber only in part) being objective, value-free, and neutral is the biblical catechism of the vast majority of college professors. And they write and teach solidly in this rigid mold!

Social scientist Fred Machlup disagrees:

> It is neither possible nor desirable in a good teacher to be neutral and to suppress his value judgments. As scholars, professors have only one obligation: to search for truth and speak the truth as they see it.[6]

Now moving directly to the Boston University battleground, mid-January 1969, beginning of the spring semester, some of the key, involved, MA students are tape recording for the campus radio station and for involved-observer sociologists, their descriptions, comments, and analysis of the first MA-led political struggle at Boston University:

> [P.B. (female, junior, Boston University)]: Disenchanted with our sterile and abstract semi-education at B.U., and *completely* turned off by the hysterical, grungy, and disorganized factions of the far Left-SDS-Progressive Labor students, several of my friends and I became interested in rumors we were hearing about some "wild" sociology professor, who, with another more conservative professor, had the entire sociology department turned inside out and, apparently, feeling very embarrassed and exposed. All this, the rumor went, had been due to a "Resolution," submitted to the sociology department by Professors Schaflander and Phillips,

calling for a reorganizing of the department, giving some representation to undergraduate sociology majors and graduate students, as well as to part-time and full-time nontenured instructors.

We started going regularly to Schaflander's classes (as he was the one deemed "crazy" by several sociology teachers, the SDS, and certain deans in the College of Liberal Arts), and began to really probe and question just about everything he said. Needless to say, we were somewhat confused as we began to realize he wasn't really crazy or "flipped out" but rather, he was trying to evoke social change, beginning with the B.U. sociology department. He was not a detached, value-free teacher. He was vitally concerned with confronting bureaucracy, achievement of social change, redistribution of power . . . democratically . . . and he constantly connected theory with practice and action.

He read a restructuring resolution at the end of his classes, and it was received with enthusiasm and approval by the vast majority of students, including many quiet, moderate, dean's list members.

The very next day after the resolution was submitted to the sociology department meeting (and was defeated by a vote of 8 to 2 with 13 abstentions), Professor Schaflander was informed that the fight for his teaching contract to be renewed for 1969–1970 would only be supported by two of his colleagues in the sociology department. The acting chairman of the department, Professor George Psathas, told Schaflander that he'd "better start looking for another position." Psathas also refused consistently to reveal who, if any, were the members of the department who opposed Schaflander's returning.

In short, after two years at Boston University, Schaflander was being fired with no hearing or reasons offered or given for his dismissal.

For three previous months Schaflander had been pressing his colleagues for a decision about his appointment. He had circulated galleys of his first book, *Ghetto Crisis,* which only Professor B. Phillips had read. He had given Professor Psathas two chapters of his second book, *Passion and Politics,* and again, only Phillips had read them. Psathas admitted that no one else in the department had read them (he evidentally didn't circulate them) before a decision on Schaflander had been reached by the department (by informal, individual polling). Yet, that decision was reached only one day after Schaflander led the fight for the restructuring of the sociology department. I know these facts are true because I attended a subsequent meeting of the department, with five other students, and heard Professor Schaflander confront Psathas and the whole faculty with these facts. And not only were they not denied or refuted, Psathas refused to allow any discussion or reconsideration, or open or closed hearing of the "Schaflander Case" from that moment on . . . as acting chairman of the department.

* * *

RESOLUTION: Presented to the Sociology Department Meeting, January 13, 1969.

SUBMITTED BY: Professor Bernard Phillips; Instructor Gerald M. Schaflander.

Resolved that a new decision-making process be instituted within the Sociology Department of the College of Liberal Arts, Boston University, to give broad and full democratic representation to all the groups and elements involved within the Sociology Department.

1. Two representatives apiece, elected by each group, shall comprise eight votes out of sixteen in the newly proposed Department Committee.
2. The four groups (having two representatives apiece) will be:
   a. Elected Undergraduate Majors in Sociology (2)
   b. Graduate Students in Sociology (2)
   c. Part-time Instructors in the Sociology Department (2)
   d. Full-time (non-tenured) Instructors in the Sociology Department (2)
3. The other eight votes will automatically go to the present tenured faculty (Associate Professors and Full Professors) as selected by themselves.
4. We are circulating this within the Department so that all groups will have a full opportunity to read and discuss the pros and cons accordingly. Thus, we plan

to bring this Resolution to a formal vote at the January meeting of the Department Committee.

* * *

Excerpts from Boston University Sociology Faculty Meeting, January 13, 1969, when the restructuring resolution was presented. The following faculty comments were taped by two students and Professor Schaflander.

J.M.: This participant democracy is an eighteenth-century model. Modern complex formal organizations require different procedures.

F.S.: Only a small committee of tenured faculty can be trusted with private papers and records for job applicants. A broad committee of non-tenured faculty, graduate students and undergraduates might lack vital information and ruin the applicant.

J.M.: Non-tenured faculty, graduate students, and undergraduates have to prove they could be trusted before I would want them to see confidential information.[7]

D.S.: I wouldn't want to vote and participate in decisions with anyone except my peers. Who? The people of equal rank, and professional sociologists.

F.S.: We should give students a voice, but not a vote.

J.G.: As a part-time teacher, I'm not really competent to vote and neither are students competent nor do they possess the criteria necessary to vote intelligently.

* * *

[G.B. (B.U. senior, black, co-chairman of the student Voice and Vote Committee)]: The news of Professor Schaflander's dismissal spread rapidly. Literally hundreds of former and present students of his stopped me asking what could be done. Answering the mass of students who stopped him on the street, or called his home, Professor Schaflander and I both continually agreed that a carefully planned and democratic fight should be made. We both stressed that it shouldn't just be for his job, but most importantly, for a public hearing for all dismissed teachers, and, for the restructuring of the university, emphasizing the necessity for a "voice and vote" for undergraduates and graduates in all departments and schools at B.U.

After several long talks between Schaflander and key students who had studied and worked with him in the Community Development Center in Roxbury, we hammered out a strategy and tactics around the formation of the Voice and Vote Committee. Extending the committee to include several student leaders, a number of disturbed liberals, and some of the brightest passive students who had now been spurred to active protest because of the unfair and discriminatory dismissal of this stimulating sociologist and teacher, we began work on a manifesto. It was to be sort of a constitution, credo, bill of rights and procedural rules and regulations (minimal) for the actual functioning of the V and V Committee. It further spelled out how members would be recruited, and who could vote and share power and decision-making in this hoped-to-be active, democratic organization. When we finished the first draft, we circulated it to about forty key students who opposed the administration, were turned off by the SDS and hippies, and yet believed in militant, democratic, non-violent protest and political action. Some of us had worked with Schaflander in the Roxbury ghetto, and in New Hampshire, Connecticut, Wisconsin or California for McCarthy-for-President primary campaigns. We shared a set of common values and goals. Finally, thirty-two people signed the manifesto and we elected Professor Schaflander as our faculty adviser. From that moment on – he never voted on the policy worked out by our six-person executive board. This later accelerated to twelve. Before we issued our first press release, mimeo'd and distributed the manifesto, and went into the George Sherman Union ballroom, we agreed on the following basic ideas, steps, and actions:

1. We agreed that we would not disrupt classes or any communication or administration building or function. This would not deny others their freedom to move, or curb their civil liberties.

2. Nothing we would do would impose our ideas or actions on others – nor impinge on any other person's freedom to ignore or oppose us.

3. The Sherman Union was supported by student fees. It was there for our use. If we didn't deface it, touch university papers or files, or damage or dirty it, attorneys advised us that we had a perfect legal right to create an educational and political center –

smack in the huge ballroom — and eat and sleep there if we didn't endanger health and safety rules and regulations. We planned to attend all classes; to eat lunch and dinner in the ballroom; have seminars, speeches, debates, and entertainment for several hours each night — to inform, educate and mobilize students to join our committee. Students had to sign our manifesto, agree with its moral and political principles, and eat meals and sleep in the ballroom with us for two days and nights — before having a voice and vote in any and all decision-making. The ballroom belonged to us; was financed by us; and offered a central place to organize students to mass, democratic action. Ingress and egress to the ballroom had to be free and open. No one was to be blocked from use of offices. Students participating were urged to attend all classes and allow everyone to pursue all educational and administrative functions, uninterrupted.

4. Lastly, we agreed that we'd stay in that ballroom until the president, and the faculty-administration committees, agreed to students having a voice and vote on each and every committee in every department and school (not parity or control — but a minimum of two elected students to every committee). It was assumed that the new sociology department committee (to be accomplished) would press for an open hearing for Professor Schaflander so students would learn — once and for all — what criteria go into hiring, firing and tenure for faculty.

[B.W., B.U. junior (taped)]: At 4:30 P.M., Thursday, January 16, 1969, after Professor Schaflander's Minorities class, he invited those students to join him at the Union ballroom for an important meeting. Two thirds of that class walked into the ballroom — on the second floor of the Union — unannounced — and joined about one hundred other students who wandered in following a fast distribution of the leaflet.

We insisted it was not a takeover. How could you take over a ballroom which was part of the Union which was yours; which your student fees financed. You couldn't take over yourself. But no one ever called it anything but a takeover — including our executive board.

[S.W., B.U. senior (taped)]: Professor Schaflander made a short speech telling of his dismissal; how he as faculty adviser to the V and V Committee hoped open hearings for all nontenured faculty could be instituted as policy at B.U.; then, he wished us all luck and turned the meeting back to our black co-chairman Griselda Brown. Griselda started to read the manifesto. A hush settled over the ballroom. By now over three hundred students were quietly milling around and listening to Gris. Dean S. S. Curtis, the red-faced, portly, pompous dean of student affairs, was all over the ballroom urging a meeting with proper administration and faculty officials. He was told to read the manifesto; that no negotiating would take place until two hundred students had signed the manifesto; until the entire student body had been thoroughly exposed to the strategy and tactics of the committee. He was super-smooth, disturbed, greasy, sticky, omnipresent, but never agreed to have a faculty-administration committee meeting called to discuss the students' negotiable demands. Gris kept reading the manifesto. Would it receive support? What would the radicals do? Would the administration try to throw us out, illegally? Would TV, radio and press write this up and put public pressure on President Christ-Janer? Would the manifesto help us keep the ballroom orderly and democratic? Gris kept reading the manifesto.

VOICE AND VOTE COMMITTEE MANIFESTO

Until President Christ-Janer and the faculty-administration committee agree to *restructure the university,* we are pledged to live in *our* Union ballroom (Sherman Union – 2nd floor). We are powerless without a VOICE AND VOTE in each school, each department, on each committee – in all university affairs including financial matters (such as investments, salaries, budgets and accepting and giving of grants).

We are incapable of accepting the firing of professors like Siegel (SED '67), Cherniak (CLA '68), Crawford (CLA '68), Riddell (CLA '68), and O'Toole (SPC '67), – and Tuesday, January 14, Professor Gerald Schaflander (CLA '68) was not "invited" back next fall, the day after leading and losing the fight for a restructured sociology department – a fight to give students representation.

For how long must we lose our most stimulating, innovative,

and concerned professors because they threaten the majority of the reactionary tenured faculty and administrators who wield the bureaucratic axe!!!

Classes are packed to the windows; there is an acute shortage of full-time and part-time teachers; students are routinely programmed, closed out and shuttled back and forth like cattle; no one to advise and help us; forced into trying for night classes; degraded into pleading with teachers, lying and forging drop-add slips to get into classes that are closed.

Is it inevitable that we continue to bitch and moan? Is it inevitable that we take to the streets in pseudo-revolutionary boyscout guerrillaism?

NO!!! These polarized alternatives are not the only ones available to us. Students—majors in each department or school—must have the democratic right to elect two undergraduate and two graduate students as representatives with a VOICE AND VOTE on:

1) Hiring and firing, appointments, tenure of teachers.
2) Course content changes.
3) Graduation, M.A. and Ph.D. requirements.
4) In all University affairs including financial matters (such as investments, salaries, budgets and accepting and giving of grants).

We are not disrupting the administration of the university or blocking communications. *The Union belongs to us.* All students and teachers are urged to continue classes.

No one's civil liberties or rights will be impinged upon or abridged if you join us to eat and sleep in *our* Ballroom until we have a real VOICE AND VOTE.

We are nonviolent; we believe in freedom and democracy; we believe in the power of dissent and redress of grievance. We will not tolerate any more rhetoric or administration committee vacillation and promises. This is our university. This is our future.

Protect democracy and be a part of this legitimate democratic struggle for our rights. If we cannot succeed in negotiating in this democratic way, then tragically, the cops and revolutionary guerrillas will take over with billy clubs and violence in the streets, in their way. What a tragedy if students who believe in democracy have to give up and are forced to cop out or go to the streets.

How can genuinely sincere and reasonable administrators and faculty reject such urgent and necessary democratic representation. *The responsibility lies with you* — President Christ-Janer!!!

We, the undersigned students of Boston University, are herein pledging to live in *our* Union ballroom, to eat lunch and dinner and sleep there *until* we have a VOICE AND VOTE on *all* university committees.

Signed:
[23 Boston University undergraduate students]
January 16, 1969

* * *

[Griselda Brown]: The revolutionary guerrillas — taken aback by the ballroom action emanating for the first time from liberals and moderates [marginal ambivalents] — quickly rallied their forces and stormed into the ballroom, thirty-five strong, led by Craig Kaplan and David Lewis of SDS, and Emily Perkins, head of the Maoist Progressive Labor [Communist] Party.

They broke in at 8 P.M. on Jesse, who was speaking to about 275 students, telling them that the first of a nightly series of "open mike" sessions would begin the following evening. Jesse stressed the fact that the Committee needed 24 hours to organize food, sanitation, press committees, and also, wanted to circulate the Voice & Vote manifesto in the ballroom and around campus to build "sleep-in" support.

[Three SDS'ers, bellowing]: Bullshit! Turn over the mike to Dave . . . what kind of a democratic meeting is this . . . we want to expose this liberal and phoney Voice and Vote Committee and we're gonna read a statement.

[Griselda Brown]: The Executive Committee voted to organize committees tonight. Tomorrow night you can have the floor and mike and we'll all debate and discuss strategy and tactics — but not tonight. We're tired; we don't have time now to do anything but organize our committees . . .

[Cries, catcalls broke off what she was saying; then four SDS people grabbed the microphone and the following statement was read and later distributed as a leaflet]:

VOICE OF THE PSEUDO-REVOLUTIONARY BOYSCOUT-GIRLSCOUT GUERILLA CONTINGENT

We too oppose the arbitrary firing of good professors. We too oppose B.U.'s investments in South Africa, and its research for the Defense Department.

But we doubt that giving students "a voice and a vote" on university committees will enable students to change these things. For in the last resort, it is not academic committees that set the goals and policies of the university. Such committees cannot change the fact that the university serves certain clearly defined functions in society: manpower training for corporations, school systems, government; training ROTC for the military; and research for business and government. *These functions are a given* that even the most radical committee member rarely calls into question and certainly has little power to change.

In addition, even within the university structure, academic committees don't have much power. It is the trustees who have the power — which is only logical considering that the trustees' business connections are the major source of funds for the university.

"A Voice and a Vote" then won't change the fact that the trustees have the power, or that the money the trustees raise for the university comes from investments we find reprehensible. (For example, B.U. has investments in South Africa, placed through the State Street Bank, one of whose executives is a B.U. trustee.)

Yet we absolutely agree that students should not continue "to bitch and moan." It is important that students act to defend their professors. But we must understand the limits of that defense: even if we are successful in controlling the hiring and firing of professors, we do not thereby change the nature of the university and the function it serves in our society — which is our most important fight.

It is very difficult for any of us to be democratic in a society based on economic exploitation and control by a ruling elite. But that economic and political oppression is the *real* problem in this country. And we think that if students are going to put their academic lives on the line, it should be around demands that, if won, will really change the nature of this university and its role in society.

Signed,
[4 S.D.S. members and 14 other B.U. undergraduate students]

* * *

[B.W. (taped)]: Professor Schaflander advised us that we were in trouble if we couldn't protect our own meetings through nonviolent ejections of extremists, disrupters, and anarchists, who wouldn't accept the right of the V and V Committee to run its own organization and meetings.

We learned that several thousand of the revolutionary leaflets (just read out at the first meeting) had been circulated all over campus. I felt we had to answer this and engage in a straightforward debate with the radical extremists.

After a long policy meeting of the expanded V and V executive board (now fourteen members) the following statement was issued, both as a leaflet for campus distribution and as a press release. It was posted at all dorms, mess halls, libe, gym, and Union.

We are unalterably opposed to "takeover"; to taking over president's and administration offices; to taking over communications centers and switchboards; to jamming and blocking free in and out access to any classroom or library. This is totalitarianism, not democracy.

We are unalterably opposed to the guerrilla Left policy of taking the law into "Our own hands"; opposed to vulgar and vile name-calling and all nondemocratic forms of protest.

We believe in democratic debate and free speech for all. We believe in nonviolence. We believe in serious negotiations and dignified and sober deliberations with the administration and faculty. As students, we believe we are presently powerless, alienated and . . .

We must have a voice and vote in all university affairs. We don't demand control or even parity. But we do demand that the Bill of Rights and Constitution begin to become operable for us right here – right now – on campus!

We may be naive and idealistic and branded phoney liberals – but we still have faith and hope in the democratic dream that our parents and schools have drummed into us.

If we lose – if we can't become part of the democratic process here at Boston University – then the cops and their billy clubs; then the guerrilla Left and their violent take-to-the-streets nihilism will inevitably take over.

[S.S. (tape-radio interview)]: We advertised (by leaflet and over campus radio) a mass meeting on January 17, with open mikes. Invited as speakers were the three most popular and outspoken professors on campus; Professor Murray Levin, and Professor Howard Zinn of the government department, and Gerald Schaflander of the sociology department. There were over five hundred people in the ballroom by eight o'clock. A number of the leaders of Progressive Labor and SDS swiftly came to the mike and leveled an attack on our committee and what we were doing. Their two major points were:

1. Everyone should have a voice and a vote *anytime* they want without having to commit themselves to any constitutional provisions of the Voice and Vote Committee.
2. What difference does it make if a few professors get their jobs back and students get a voice and a vote . . . in the last analysis, only socialism and total revolutionary change is relevant . . . everything else is irrelevant.

[From tape of S.W.'s speech during meeting]: I don't like to make speeches and to stand up and harangue in wild impassioned exchanges; but something terribly important must be said: there are different methods of operation and organization and obviously different types of democracy. Some of the people here from the SDS-PL seem to believe in "participant democracy." They define this as a group of people in concert making all the decisions together without any formal structure, constitution, or leadership. There need be no requirements for work before voting, or any membership criteria . . . mere interest and being present in effect entitles a participant democracy supporter to a voice and a vote at any time, any place, and in any situation. To those of you who agree with this kind of democracy, all I can say is I sharply differ. But I respect your right to have your own kind of organization and meeting and have never tried to change, break into, disrupt or take over any SDS activities or meeting.

I believe in a different kind of democracy. I believe that people with common values have the right to form their own organization, set up their own rules and procedures, structure and written constitution if they want, which clearly states that anyone who agrees with their strategy and tactics can join and have a voice and a vote in the deliberations of the organization they have joined. Democratic and Republican parties do this, as do Communist and revolutionary parties all around the world. So long as we don't impinge on the rights of other organizations or prevent them from forming their own counterorganizations, this seems to be an inalienable right. But many of those in SDS-PL seem to feel that they have the right to come into our meetings, take them over, disrupt them, and try to give their own radical direction to the course of events. I don't believe they have that right. I think it's totalitarianism and undemocratic to try to prevent in any way the Voice and Vote Committee from staking out its own distinctive, partisan principles and attempting to recruit supporters to its cause.

If you think we're phonies, if you think our attempts to save meaningful teachers' jobs and trying to democratically reform and restructure the university are meaningless, then you're free, of course, to express your opinion by leaflet or even speaking over a microphone, here, *if invited,* or elsewhere. But you don't and never have had the right to try to take over our organization by preventing us from functioning on our *own terms* – to try to build a liberal reform movement on this campus. We intend to run our own organization our own way, just as you have that right.

Thus, the battle was drawn!

The Boston University *News,* issue of January 30, 1969, reported on the balance of that night's crucial meeting:

As a result of widespread publicity and the presence of several controversial members of the faculty on stage, the takeover grew into full ballroom proportions by Wednesday evening. Sixty-two students signed the manifesto.

"I don't think this fight should be made for Schaflander," CLA Sociology Instructor Gerald Schaflander claimed. "It should be made for every single teacher who does not have tenure." [*And gets dismissed without a hearing; four in 1968, three in 1969.*]

Mr. Schaflander's contract was recently terminated for what he believed to be his "controversial nature" and his endeavors to democratize the sociology department. Schaflander made this statement in response to CLA Government Professor Murray Levin's questioning of student competence to evaluate a professor's scholarship as well as his teaching capacity.

Skeptical, at any rate, about the effect four students would have on every university committee, Levin said: "If the university were very smart, it would give you this symbolic power only. Besides, students aren't really equipped for this."

Schaflander disagreed, asking: "What makes one person more competent than another? If students can go to war and be killed, they should have the right to vote in this society, in this university, in every single school, in administrative committees, to be involved with all decisions that affect their lives."

Defending his "naive liberal egalitarianism" in his advocacy of the Manifesto Committee's democratic takeover, Schaflander concluded: "If you disobey civilly, you should be prepared to pay the consequences."

Advocating student involvement in all decisions that effect their lives, CLA Government Professor Howard Zinn spoke next, saying he was in favor of this gathering of students, even though he was not sure what had been said before his arrival. "Somehow we need a kind of parliament gathering — students and faculty together — with whoever is concerned with their problems. This is a step toward the kind of democracy that we can claim as people."

The debate over different types of democracy and what tactics could be used to reconstruct the University was in full swing when suddenly at 11 P.M., Griselda Brown called an abrupt end to the meeting. Professor Zinn took the mike and began to speak. Schaflander took the microphone back and loudly directed the exit from the ballroom, claiming that the manifesto signers of the committee had a prior legal right to remain according to "First Amendment Precedent."

As this article went to press, several student groups were still carrying on discussions in scattered parts of the Union — with university security police maintaining a nervous watch.

There was a great deal of confusion and disagreement in the ranks of the Voice and Vote Committee after the stormy meeting climaxed by the dismissal of Zinn and the radicals.

The campus radio station was taping running commentaries of the ballroom "happening" and taped this short speech of Schaflander's to the executive board and another group of perhaps fifty interested students, during a long debate which culminated in at least a dozen manifesto signers leaving the ballroom – and resigning from the committee – that same night of the Zinn-Schaflander confrontation.

> [The G.S. tape]: There were several basic issues at stake in the confrontation between Professor Howard Zinn and myself.
>
> First, The Voice and Vote Committee elected me to be their faculty adviser. Mistakenly or not, the committee also decided that the first big public meeting would be ended at 11 P.M., so that everyone could get some sleep and get to classes the next day. After Professor Zinn had spoken and I had answered him I told him the meeting was ending at eleven. I urged him to reply before that time, *prior to eleven.* I warned him of the time at 10:30; Griselda at 10:40. Professor Zinn did not acknowledge either of these two warnings. He neither nodded nor acknowledged either of us. He looked right through me, when I repeated the 11 P.M. curfew bit.
>
> Therefore, when Griselda Brown announced the meeting was over at 11 P.M., I was angry when Professor Zinn stood up, took the microphone, and started to talk. I should not have been surprised, however, because he had told students at campus gatherings for over a year that it was justifiable for them to "take the law into their own hands." And now, here he was, doing just that! Despite the clearly stated rule (as democratically voted upon by the Voice and Vote Committee) Zinn tried to take this meeting into his own hands, though it had been legally closed by the co-chairman.
>
> I walked up to Professor Zinn and told him the meeting was over and that it was my obligation as the faculty adviser to support the decision of the Voice and Vote Committee. He spoke directly into the microphone and said, "This reminds me of the Central Committee of the Communist Party."
>
> I replied that I had never had the pleasure of being Red-baited by such a devoted supporter of the extreme Left, but the meeting was still over, and that I was going to carry out the committee's decision.
>
> Griselda Brown and I attempted to take the microphone away from Professor Zinn, who continued talking with loud vocal support from a claque of leaders and supporters of the SDS and

> Progressive Labor (worker-student alliance) organizations in the first several rows. And then I made a decision which, unfortunately shifted the focus of controversy away from the program of the V and V committee. I decided that I absolutely would not — could not — allow the extremists to take over this crucial meeting; and that I would carry out the committee's decision to close the meeting forthwith.
>
> So, I took the mike out of Zinn's hands and loudly and repeatedly ordered the meeting over and the ballroom cleared. In all the years I worked in the South opposing the KKK and the White Citizens Council, or battling Tammany and the Mafia in New York City while working with the Reform Democrats, I have never been attacked on a personal basis so violently. Never had I heard such vile, gutter language as was now directed at me by SDS and PL leaders and supporters. They encircled me at the speakers stand and called me "motherfucker, paranoid, dictator, bastard, fascist, Communist, ego-tripper, insane, psychotic, madman."
>
> I was told to relinquish the mike by loud commands of "your head will be cracked open." I was pushed and shoved (I shoved back — in a vigorous, nonpacifist fashion) and general chaos and pandemonium seemed to take over the ballroom. My wife was seated in the audience and was in her fourth month of pregnancy. As the screaming, yelling, and milling-shoving bodies accelerated, I became scared and very frightened for her safety. I couldn't see her. I raised my voice to a very high level and, by name, charged leaders of the SDS and PL with responsibility for seeing to it that order be restored and that my wife be escorted safely from the ballroom. I repeated this charge loudly, monotonously, and angrily until the ballroom was cleared. It was my firm conviction that the time had come for the revolutionary Left to understand that on this one campus at least, there were teachers and students who would protect their meeting and would do all in their power to nonviolently prevent disruption and *takeover* by the Left.

For too long SDS has been speaking for the moderate-liberal marginal ambivalent students and faculty because a vacuum has existed. A growing number of students across the country have begun to see that the results of New Left actions are often counterproductive; that they don't result in reform but in disengagement or anarchic disorder. There also is a growing conviction that New Left activists are often willing to trample on the civil liberties and academic freedom of others while attempting to gain their own nobly proclaimed ends.

Although large numbers of liberal and moderate marginal ambivalents were shocked by my emotional intensity, and deeply disturbed by my confrontation with Zinn – everyone finally left the meeting. We preserved the right to hold, open, and close our own meeting, on our own terms – free of mob rule. Hopefully this will encourage MAs and other students and faculty across the United States, as this story gets circulated, to become more militant, more openly ready to confront and meet the extremists head on, in a nonviolent but uncompromising manner. Hopefully it will motivate more students and faculty to defend democracy in democratic terms.

Slowly but surely the Voice and Vote Committee started to rebuild eat-in and sleep-in support in the ballroom. Various committees were organized and speakers were circulating in the dorms and campus organizations drumming up support for a voice and vote in all decision-making bodies at the university.

Dean S. S. Curtis looked worse every day that students remained in the ballroom (his offices were directly overhead – one floor up). He repeatedly tried to split up the committee by proposing meetings with nondecision-making deans and faculty. Several were held and nobody had or wanted to wield the power to say yes or no to the voice and vote demand. Of course Curtis wanted the ballroom vacated before anything could be done. When these tactics failed, Dean Curtis, widely recognized as the strong hatchetman for the trustees (Christ-Janer was an innocuous public relations and fund-raising president), moved into another level of counterattack. He told five or six student leaders of the Voice and Vote Committee that he was very concerned about the mental and emotional stability of that "splendid man," Professor Schaflander. This was followed by Dean Lee, head of the College of Liberal Arts, refusing to talk with Schaflander about threats of violence directed against MA student leaders and himself.

On January 30, at 1:45 A.M., Dean Curtis brilliantly struck a blow at the ballroom sleepers and Voice and Vote Committee. He had a staff psychologist file an arrest request for Professor Schaflander, under Boston Municipal Law 79. This law allows a psychologist to sign a commitment form and have the police arrest a citizen who allegedly is disturbed and psychologically unstable (in the psychologist's judgment) and endangering the public. To pull off this creative manuscript out of the Living Theater, the campus police chief awakened Schaflander at 1:30 A.M. in the ballroom. He requested a meeting outside to discuss potential violence in the ballroom. Schaflander reluctantly agreed.

[G.S. (taped)]: We walked downstairs, [Schaflander's affidavit states] and then walked outside to get a breath of air, while the captain outlined some dangers he anticipated because of the continuing ballroom sleep-ins. Suddenly, a police car drew up; two officers climbed out and grabbed me, and dragged me into the police wagon. I verbally protested but didn't resist physically.

They drove me, they said, to the Massachusetts Mental Hospital in Boston – for incarceration and treatment.

When I arrived, held by the two officers, I was greeted by Dr. Kenerson, examining psychiatrist (he was an M.D., and psychoanalyst). He asked me to come into his office and told me that he was required to examine me under Municipal Law 79 – which, he told me, Boston U. had utilized against several students recently.

Thirty-seven minutes later, Dr. Kenerson told me "go on home and get some sleep. You appear quite tired. There's absolutely nothing wrong or disturbed about you or your conduct. And I'll so state or testify in court if I'm asked."

And so I went home, tired, but angry and frustrated. I had three witnesses who were with me all day and that evening in the ballroom. They will confirm that I was never examined by any staff psychologist at any time preceding my arrest. In fact, I had never met the staff psychologist who had signed my arrest form; though I had regularly attacked the B.U. psychological counseling service for revealing confidential information given them by students to graduate schools and potential employers.

While I was under arrest and psychiatric examination, Dean Curtis entered the ballroom and told the students their adviser,

Professor Schaflander, was "arrested and under psychiatric observation and care."

[D.P., MA executive board member, tells the rest of the story]: Curtis came in about 2:00 A.M. and woke us all up. There were about twenty of us sleeping in rented sleeping bags. He turned on the blinding overhead ballroom lights. He told us Schaflander was in jail and had "flipped out." He told us the ballroom sleep-in was all over. He told us to go home now and no disciplinary punishments would be imposed. Most of the students were tired, bewildered, and shocked by what had happened to Professor Schaflander. All but three went back to their dorms or apartments. Three of us decided to stay until we heard from Schaflander, or the co-chairmen, or Rothschild or Fee, who were with Schaflander. They started to threaten us – and they finally dragged me out – by my heels at 4 A.M. As I was slid out on my rear, I heard Dean Curtis say, "Well, that fixes Schaflander's clock."

The next night, bolstered by the administration's arrest and psychiatric charges against Schaflander, and the forced withdrawal of the V and V Committee from the ballroom, SDS and PL leaders packed an emergency meeting (not attended by Schaflander or the two co-chairmen who were out of town after a pseudo-threat on their lives). They elected their own, new, officers of the new Voice and Vote Committee. Most of the old board members were still in a state of shock, reeling from the psychiatric charges against their faculty adviser. Most of them didn't even attend the emergency meeting.

The new Voice and Vote Committee, run by PL and SDS leaders, decided to have a series of symposiums. After two sparsely attended meetings (not held in the ballroom), the new V and V Committee literally disappeared.

The old V and V Committee members were discouraged, bitter and frustrated. But they were hardly up for another mass action. Midsemester exams were at hand, and now, the rumors were hot and heavy that "Prof. Schaflander would be dropped as a teacher, right in the middle of the semester."

For the first time in the history of Boston University, right in the middle of the semester, a series of new, parallel classes – same course, same time; new, different teachers – was opened up. Students were told that Professor Schaflander was "not well," and if they stayed in his classes they might not get credit for those classes. Over five hundred students were registered in Schaflander's three courses in Minorities, Marriage and Family, and Sociological Theory. Approximately two hundred and fifty immediately transferred out — some needing the credit to graduate. What was ironic, was that at the beginning of the semester, the university turned its back on those seniors, and hundreds of other sociology majors. They said, at that time, that they had neither funds nor teachers available to open new classes. So Schaflander and several others overloaded their classes (five hundred students for three courses), so that students could take vitally needed courses. Now, flushed with victory over the ballroom incident, the B.U. administration tried to clean out Schaflander's classes first, then tried to ease him out as a teacher.

[G.S. (taped)]: I, of course, threatened the university with a lawsuit, both for false arrest and now, for wrecking my classes in midsemester. The rumors and veiled threats about closing down my classes ceased.

I taught all three classes — to about two hundred and fifty students (and hundreds of visitors) for the rest of the semester, without incident. I told my students the truth about what happened, as best I knew it. I felt they should know how far their university administration would go to defeat legitimate student protest and dissent. That the attacks and libelous action against me would have to be met in the courts. I told them I was trying to engage counsel to initiate a lawsuit against B.U. I told them that it would cost a fortune (pretrial examinations, cross-examinations) and could take at least a year; would cost thousands of dollars). Also, no prominent attorneys in Boston wanted to sue Boston University. One told me that even if I won, I'd only receive a token amount of dollar damages. Nevertheless, I'm still committed to a lawsuit, when and if funds and competent counsel can be raised and arranged.

[There remain, however, some questions requiring answers. Why did the MAs allow their committee to be taken over — when they clearly had the majority on campus?]:

F.W.: I couldn't take all the yelling and noise in the ballroom and I decided there was no point in continuing to fight against the maniacs in the SDS.

M.F.: One PL female called me a "whore" and two SDS spokesmen spit at me when I stood up and tried to prevent the Left takeover of the Voice and Vote Committee. I was shouted down and when no one defended me, I walked out with four of my friends.

M.P.: I can't yell and fight in public. It's undignified.

S.W.: I was always hoping for a larger, broad coalition against the administration. I naively believed cooperating with the Left could accomplish more. I was badly mistaken.

B.W.: Constant physical threats made it difficult to function.

G.J.: I just lose my cool when the Left moves in; and I just antagonize potential supporters.

M.F.: Who needs all the vilification and noise?

In *Up Against the Ivy Wall: A History of the Columbia Crisis,* by Jerry L. Avorn et al., it is brilliantly stated that "the tactical elegance of confrontation politics lay in the fact that radicals had a good chance of winning whether the administration gave in to their substantive demands or overcame them by repression. The use of coercive force on the part of the adversary – whether it came in the form of university discipline or police violence – could be a powerful force to 'radicalize' liberal or moderate students. For the crucial part of the SDS view is that while escalated tactics are necessary to bring pressure for change on substantive issues, the 'radicalization' of large segments of the population is far more important."

As Mark Rudd, SDS leader said later: "Confrontation politics puts the enemy up against the wall and forces him to define himself. In addition, it puts the individual up against the wall. He has to make a choice. Radicalization of the individual means that he must commit himself to the struggle to change society as well as share the radical view of what is wrong with society."

Rudd later admitted at Emerson Hall, Harvard, in late fall 1968, that the stopping of the gymnasium and ROTC were not really basic issues at Columbia. "We only used them to whip up and radicalize the students to a revolutionary takeover!"

At Boston University, the SDS-PL took over the MAs' "take-over." And instead of achieving large student radicalization, and a mass uprising against the "system," the extremists killed the first, B.U. liberal-moderate, student-initiated, political action with neototalitarian violence and coercion (and with the administration as their ironic partners). And all in the name of peace and love (sic).

The MAs were, for the most part, inexperienced and somewhat ineffective tactically. For most of them, this was the first time they had taken part, directly, in such confrontation political activity. Conversely, the SDS at B.U., and elsewhere, stresses militant confrontation and exciting mass demonstrations. The marginal ambivalents, trying to work within the boundaries of democracy, and infringing on no one's civil liberties, were much more academic, and much less clear-cut and exciting.

With the noted exceptions of three or four faculty members, the B.U. faculty completely ducked this explosive issue, giving the MA students none of the much needed support that was vital to the democratic process at this time. Professor Murray Levin, nationally recognized for his perceptive analysis of Senator Ted Kennedy's election, and of the Massachusetts political process, was very confused and torn between the far left and the MAs. Consequently, he switched back and forth, giving no real aid to the MAs, who certainly could have used his prestigious support.

Also, the "Schaflander personality" became far too much the issue. Either students were too wrapped up in just trying to get his job back, or they were overstimulated or bothered by some aspect of his charisma or style; in neither case giving major attention to the issues (strategy and tactics) themselves, as delineated by the Voice and Vote Committee. The marginal ambivalents should have gone into the ballroom alone, and thus taken and met all problems and confrontations alone, confined to the *issues* and not personalities.

The error made in the ballroom by the marginal ambivalents

and their adviser was the same one that the McCarthy people made – expecting instant national success (after five months of work), instead of planning extensively, organizing, and building a solid constituency for the long haul.

Three months should have been taken to build up the ballroom instead of nine days; starting first with twenty supporters, then to forty, and so on. When there were one hundred people – not thirty-two – of whom fifty were very solid, and of whom twenty could be counted on to speak out strongly in support of policy and issues agreed upon – against breach of the Voice and Vote constitution – the SDS and hippie anarchists might have been successfully isolated.

When the membership had reached one hundred, a public meeting or confrontation could have taken place wherein each of the one hundred could have brought one close friend. There would then be two hundred Voice and Vote supporters! It can be safely estimated that the SDS could never mobilize two hundred people – at B.U., Harvard, Columbia or even Berkeley – particularly when the mobilization wasn't against the administration but against fellow "liberal" students.

Interestingly enough, the B.U. administration, according to "swinging" Assistant Dean Trachtenberg – long sideburned, and boot-shod – never has felt really threatened by Howard Zinn and the far left extremists. Their revolutionary aspirations were amorphous, hysterical, and could safely be dismissed or ignored – since they had no applicability to the B.U. power struggle. The administration, however, was deeply concerned and worried by the reasonable, calm, straightforward, change-in-power proposals of the Voice and Vote restructuring committee. Dean S. S. Curtis, head of student affairs, stayed in his office above the ballroom night after night, constantly trying to negotiate, pacify or split the MAs. He set up meeting after meeting with high administration officials and faculty-administration committees trying to stop the broad and growing pressure emanating from the ballroom. He couldn't call the police (since no laws were being broken) and saw no legitimate way to obtain an injunction. So, he and the administration were sweating heavily with the stark alternatives of recognizing the Voice and Vote Committee – or just hoping the committee would blow away, disappear, lose interest, or be split up by internal dissension.

The left-extremists, through their lawless takeover (of the original Voice and Vote Committee), exposed themselves as wild, irresponsible and solely interested in Che-Mao-or-Fidel-type revolutions – not in positive action to radically reform B.U. as an institution within the democratic process. After they took over the Voice and Vote Committee itself, they talked the new committee to death.

The liberals and/or the marginal ambivalents managed to unhappily refocus the attention of the administration, faculty, and students away from the revolutionary initiative of the left-SDS and towards attainable objectives, toward institutional reform on *issues,* which could draw broad support. But only for ten days.

However, like the SDS at Harvard, Columbia, Berkeley, Wisconsin, Michigan, Brooklyn College and San Francisco State (as reported by Jerry Avorn, James Kunen, Tom Hayden, the *Guardian, New Left Notes,* the *Mole* and *Ramparts*), the SDS at B.U. is showing further and continuing signs of splitting and disintegrating, as the short-haired, Worker-Student Alliance (Progressive Labor) faction, and the Weathermen and nihilists, and anarchist factions, battle each other – and drive the humanist, rational, less radical forces in SDS toward a marginal ambivalent reform position. Only the lack of effective, national leadership prevents the MAs from fully taking advantage of this trend.

Therefore, MAs, both students and teachers, clearly must stand up, speak up, take militant steps to preserve and extend democracy on campus – and fill the old, SDS vacuum.[8]

One of the repetitive questions, continually asked by curious and skeptical observers of the historic B.U. ballroom Voice and Vote Committee was: "How was taking over part of the Student Union different from taking over administrative buildings or classrooms?"

The Student Union, on most campuses (assuredly at B.U.),

belongs to the students, and is financed almost totally by student activity fees. It offers a place for students to read, listen to music, play pool or ping-pong, buy books, magazines or papers, write letters or term papers, generally relax, and have educational and political experiences outside the classroom. In this particular case the most prominent difference in the B.U. student protest was the fact that ingress and egress to the Union building and ballroom, was free and open; no one was blocked from the use of offices or any facilities in the building; nor was anyone prevented from fully pursuing the educational function of the university. All students participating were strongly encouraged to attend all their classes.

Another question constantly raised was: "Why, if the V and V Committee was so clearly intent on changing the administration's structure of power and organization, wasn't the left-extremist group cooperative with the marginal ambivalents?"

If the MAs really fill the vacuum between the far left and the conservatives, providing effective leadership, most of the "uncommitted" students, the chief, potential recruits for the SDS-type radical revolutionaries, will be lost. The liberal-reformist MAs are the chief threat to the far left, the number one enemy, because MA success inevitably leaves the extremists without troops, supporters, and large audiences.

As pointed out, most administrations don't fear the revolutionary leftists. They're too preoccupied with third world and utopian revolutions to threaten existing university power relationships. But militant, civil-libertarian MA types, who want reform and change *now,* are a disturbance to bureaucratic patterns, do upset equilibrium, do threaten to achieve broad support, and thus are dangerous — and must be stifled and decimated. Their threat is to the existing system, and calls for specific, realizable changes within that very system.

The MAs must continue to take initiating, creative, militant action on campuses to become a part of the decision-making process. But by the very nature of the MAs, this action must never be hysterical or outside the boundaries of democracy.

Tactics thus indicated would be: massive petitions signed at large meetings; followed by representative, small, delegations meeting with and pressuring university presidents, deans and other power figures in the administration with waves of visitations (nonviolent and orderly, though persistent); and lastly, student assumption of legitimate control of their own student centers and unions — as a political and educational center of their own.

Only this kind of basic training might prepare most MAs for the macroscopic struggles to halt the tide of war, militarization, pollution, overpopulation, racism and poverty in America.

12

Proposed Solutions to the University Crisis

Before I conclude with my proposed solutions to the university crisis, I think it is necessary to understand the theoretical framework which underlies and is central to my work. I am opposed to Robert Michel's classical theory: "Oligarchy – government by a small group of persons who co-opt their successors . . . [is] a process common to all large organizations."

This negativistic approach to the analysis of social problems is central to the intellectual orientation of many social scientists. These scientists also constantly quote Max Weber to the effect: "[I am] pessimistic about the ultimate effects of growing bureaucratization on democracy and freedom." Then they proceed to place the phenomenon of student protest under the pessimistic umbrella of "inevitable historical repetitiveness."

This theoretical analysis, in my opinion, hardly leaves much hope for combating bureaucracy and achieving social change through new coalitions and new social movements.

These status quo social scientists build their case by selecting existing research that inexorably leads the reader to believe that history is indeed cyclical and inevitably repetitive. They illustrate that student protest and demonstrations come and go in waves provoked mainly by wars, depressions or sporadic and disruptive national and international political events. In short, protest is stimulated by and follows economic and political historical disruptions and is not the result of institutional decay and/or adult value betrayal and hypocrisy.

It follows logically, if not implicitly, that protest and struggle by students (or anyone) against current values in the United States is hopeless. It also follows that one must be realistic and recognize that there is nothing new or significant in current student efforts to challenge the status quo, to bring about social change, and to reform or build new institutions on or off campus.

If the old institutions (". . . and who has better ones?" asks the dominant school of social science) have been attacked unsuccessfully before; if the students will inevitably be co-opted if they take over or build new organizations and institutions (even if they only share power) ; and if students stop protesting once the Southeast Asian war has ended, this "inevitable" thesis or theory can well become the apologia, even though inadvertently, for the maintenance of the status quo.

If there are good reasons for faculty teaching less; if there are understandable reasons for university administrators becoming increasingly impersonal and committed to bureaucratic equilibrium; if there are sound, equalitarian, and practical reasons for grades, stiff exams, and fierce competition for accreditation – after insufferable memorization and regurgitation – then this becomes, albeit unwillingly, an anti-student-change theory, or, a pro–United States institution-perpetuation theory. Behind the rubric of scholarship and objectivity, this "inevitable" school of social scientists actually defines an interpretation of reality that becomes increasingly accepted with repetition. If sufficient legions of intellectuals, scholars, and concerned citizens accept this definition of reality it will, in fact, become a legitimization of the status quo.

To turn away from unprecedented polarization via class, age, race and ethnic variable groupings; to ignore institutional anarchy as control of family and educational institutions disintegrates; to believe that Michel is correct—is to become a functioning cog in the acting out of the self-fulfilling prophecy of "oligarchic inevitability."

One can then safely or sadly retreat to the pursuit of making money; collecting stamps or bugs; becoming a do-it-yourself expert; becoming an experimenter of drugs, aberrational sex practices, astrology, mythical, Eastern or fundamentalist religiosity, occult yoga, energy transformation, rural Indian communes, "touch and tell" group sensitivity exploration . . . or any type of retreatist privatization that will guarantee the perpetuation of the military-industrial-political control of American life.

This brief exploration into probable consequences flowing from acceptance of the "cyclical (cynical) inevitable" theoretical analysis provides a springboard into my own positive "confrontation-conflict," due-process radicalism (nonviolent) theory of institutional formation or reformation. Usually, the traditional scholarly response to my own theoretical approach to social change is: "This is advocacy, exhortation, nonscholarly subjective politicalization." But these attacks against me which became departmental feuds at Brooklyn College and Boston University, twice leading to my dismissal, can best be answered by referring to Professor Joseph Bensman's classic sociological study, *"Dollars and Sense,"*[1] where he points out:

> There are no forms of ethical leprosy that are beneath the faculty participants of a feud. . . . In no other institution is there as much cruelty and barbarism openly practiced as among ethically superior academic men. . . . The contradiction between [expressed] ethical ideals or ideology, and practice in the University, is greater than in most institutions. . . . In terms of personal ethics, the University all too frequently resembles a cesspool.

This revelation is often shocking to students and to critics of education because the university is also the freest and finest place the society has to function as a thinker and social critic. The irony which permeates this book and many other studies of the present university is that the university itself, a lonely bastion of freedom, has also become a huge, bureaucratic institution.

Actually, I see the university as a research instrument. It seethes with value and role conflicts as struggles over status tear the campus apart. It responds to pressures from other institutions (political, economic and military) outside its cloistered walls, while desperately projecting an image of independence as a scholarly, objective research center – seeking only truth.

If social change might result from analyzing institutions, and then trying to alter, reform, or replace them – it seems logical to try to change the very university institution one is a member of – the very institution that is becoming more powerful quantitatively, while deteriorating qualitatively.

I defined my role as an alienated, salaried, nonvoting, nontenured teacher, and as a social scientist. I tried to connect theory with the actual practice of democratic conflict – on and off the campus. I encouraged students to engage in confrontation – first in the ghetto, and then during the McCarthy presidential primary campaign. And finally, against the bureaucratic power at the administrative and faculty level of the university. I tried to stimulate discussion and action among students concerning alternative strategies and tactics to develop new ideologies and new social movements. I tried to help them create and find new, nonviolent solutions to the necessity of participating in decision-making (on and off campus). I tried to get students to perceive the basic differences between conflicting groups of students.

I learned to be skeptical and mistrust much of the survey research questionnaire type of data. I strove to analyze, weigh, measure, and classify repetitive behavior patterns of students, faculty, and administrators by becoming an involved observer in university institutional conflict.

I had to learn how to defend myself against attacks emanating from most of the administrators and departmental faculty. My attack, as a participant, against bureaucratic order and harmony was also part of my attempt to study the possibilities of developing an ideology to change the university into a nonbureaucratic institution.

Implicit in this joint research-participant activity was the overall thesis that if one couldn't radically alter the university, what chance was there ever to alter the power of the military-industrial complex which dominates much of the decision-making in our society??

Underlying all of the thinking, teaching, organizing, and evaluating was the *constant necessity* of developing a specific ideology which might build a successful social movement to change this and other institutions nonviolently. But, as Bensman points out:

"Ideologists, from the standpoint of their bureaucratic bosses, thus become irresponsible, undisciplined, and disloyal. . . . Wherever possible, high level bureaucrats purge the ideologists. They do this not primarily out of ideological concerns, but only to develop a responsive, disciplined, loyal and technically competent staff. . . . To the bureaucratic elite, the only acceptable ideologists among their staff are those that support the organizational purposes at any given time. . . . The bureaucracy as a form, attacks all independent ideologies and replaces them by forms of ideological expediency. . . . The bureaucratic attack on independent ideologies takes the form of *not hiring* ideologists, *firing them,* retraining personnel to accept the bureaucratic ethos, and promoting those who do. It takes the form of doing these same things at the level of *graduate and undergraduate education* so that, if successful, the system operates to *pre-select only those who can conform.*"[2]

And so it was at Brooklyn College and Boston University. And, according to many firsthand reports, at scores of other educational institutions.

Bensman goes on: "In this sense, we can talk of *the end of ideology.* . . . As bureaucracy grows, all other forms of ideology are depressed because the occupational and economic rewards of nonideological commitment are made more attractive. The morally neutral individual becomes the cynosure of a bureaucratic world."[3]

So, the alternatives are starkly drawn. Accept the inevitability or bureaucratic oligarchy, the inevitability of students being co-opted in a Michelian cycle, becoming just as rigid, impersonal, materialistic and conformist (if they win), as the present bureaucratic elite. Or, measure the stratified breakdown of students — as marginal ambivalents increase in numbers and strength; examine the reasons and source of students' growing independence and radical rejection of many old, Protestant-ethic values; and lastly, recognize that there is a *real potential* for building new coalitions with broader and clearer ideologies and nonbureaucratic institutions.

The evidence for supporting the latter orientation (that the bottle is half full rather than half empty), is abundant. It isn't only that students now fail to automatically respect their parents and teachers, contributing to an accelerating deauthorization process — (the antiauthority student movement is deep, pervasive, and extends down to the junior high schools) — but students today, *unlike any previous generation,* are hostile to adult authority figures, suspicious, and unwilling to automatically accept a compliant, subservient role — as in past, cyclical, historical periods! Students are also resisting the cultural-familial-socialization process, based on impulse-restraint, materialistic-consumption patterns, and sexually inhibited, religious-conformist values. As Margaret Mead perceptively indicates, young people have no acceptable adult role models to emulate today, as they have always had in the past.

War, racism, pollution, atomic and hydrogen bombs, ABMs, accelerating alcoholism, divorce, and mental breakdowns, and conspicuous consumption via obsessive driving for materialistic and social security — are all clear and ever-present facts of life that students see and face daily (unlike any previous cycle or historical period).

Students, in many cases, hold their parents (the adult society) responsible for these chaotic, unstable, unprecedented, apparently unsolvable social problems. They just can't divorce the observable results of this postindustrial technological society from the value system that engendered such naked adult responsibility. How can students be expected to respect adults and adult institutions and values, when they see nothing but madness around them?

Certainly this must be one of the key, underlying sources of the breakdown of the family as the prime institutional base for socialization of children. And history, of course, has absolutely no cyclical precedent for the advent of the bomb, TV, technological pollution, and so on.

The Harris poll, July 1970, in a survey of a cross section of college students, "reveals much wider and broader disenchantment than merely over the war in Vietnam. *Large numbers of* today's student population have *little faith* in the establishment leadership of the country – and believe American society should be *drastically reconstituted.*"

No similar (poll) result can be found in the entire history of polling – or in past student protest history.

In his fourth piece on "Surveying The Campuses," in the Boston *Globe,* Harris concludes: "The fact is . . . this generation of students is militant, dedicated to do something about its convictions, and is willing to suffer for them . . . The students do *not* want to become revolutionaries and turn to violence. Rather they want to get into the system and change it, even wrench it drastically by the roots. They want to do this through politics. They say if they are denied this chance, they will turn to more extreme measures."[4]

Between May 20 and May 28, 1970, a cross section of 820 undergraduates in fifty four-year colleges were surveyed in a study commissioned by the American Council on Education. While students rate Nixon's handling of the war 76 to 22 percent negative, it's evident that even if the war ended tomorrow, the seeds of student dissent and of distrust of the system as it is today would not subside until *major changes* have been made in the United States.

By 78 to 20 percent positive, students believe the "real trouble with U.S. society is that it lacks a sense of values – it's conformist and materialistic." This too, is research data that can't be duplicated from studies of past student values and actions – from past student polls.

Thus we have a *new, and truly unique situation* in the student population. Two of our major institutions, the family and education, are in serious trouble. How adults, faculty and administrators, respond to urgent student demands for change, will largely determine the nature of the counterchallenge from the students.

Anarchy, bombing, right-wing repression, drugs, sexual and political hedonism are all serious possibilities as tension and polarization mount. The fight over values within the university between students, trustees, administrators, faculty, and politicians, is a priority arena — which already commands the mass media and the nation's attention.

Anarchy, race war and gang rule, not utopia, lie at the end of the road on which our instant revolutionaries would put us. The power of the snipers and campus guerrillas is that they can start a widening chain reaction. The inescapable countermeasures (Kent State, and FBI legal powers to penetrate campuses) necessitated by a rash of bombings, threaten to precipitate wider clashes in the ghettos and on the campuses, mobilizing whole communities in war with the police and the National Guard. At its inner core (Weathermen), disruption gives small revolutionary groups a sense of importance and power. They possess a sustaining moral indignation which gives these few the strength to live and die as outlaws. They will not be stopped until this inner sense is undermined.[5]

I am proposing a crucial alternative that will undermine nihilistic radical extremists, leaving them impotent. I am proposing that power relationships, starting with students at universities, be drastically altered. Students must be given — or must win — more power and responsibility, and soon. If you're an integral part of an institution, if you help build and run it, you'll never sit still out of apathy, boredom, or nihilism — and watch it being wrecked (not by radical revolutionaries from the left, or by frightened bureaucrats in the polity, or by the conservative elite councils of the university administrative hierarchy).

An incredibly significant study of the attitudes of almost seven thousand students suggests that most of the tensions and conflicts in junior and senior high schools arise from the "Governance Of The Institutions."[6]

The study, sponsored by the Center for Research and Education in American Liberties at Teachers College, Columbia University, reports that its "findings are in serious conflict with widely circulated reports of student unrest *basically* over racial and national political issues."[7]

The critical perception herein, is that student governance alienation and lack of power and responsibility, are the cause, *and specific unrest over stated racial and national politics are the* effect.

More than 50 percent of the students stressed issues of school governance and individual rights as sources of conflict. The students indicated that "68 percent of their conflicts were with persons in authority, and only 20 percent with their peers."[8]

The Center's director, Dr. Alan F. Westin, professor of public law and government at Columbia University, writes in the report:[9]

"The great majority of the students are angry, frustrated, increasingly alienated by school. They do not believe they receive individual justice or enjoy the rights of dissent or share in the critical decision-making affecting their lives within the school . . . When currents of frustration such as these are running through our schools, we should not be surprised that withdrawal through drugs or revolutionary attacks on school and society are the commitments so many of our students are choosing."

Dr. John F. DeCecco, professor of psychology and education at San Francisco State College, and a principal investigator of the aforementioned study, stressed that "there's a rising demand for *participation in decision-making* in all American Institutions as institutional missions and individual goals and needs more and more *diverge* . . . Of all American institutions, it is particularly ironical that the one institution charged with the mission of teaching democracy is usually perceived by the student as one that leaves him *powerless.*"[10]

When we pick up the student two to five years later, at the

university level, the multiplication of this frustration has increased at least tenfold.

Adult attitudes and actions of indifference, repression, oversimplification and hanging on to the present because "change won't make any difference" – are all enemies of democracy.

All that's inevitable is just how we define reality, and who wins.

Now to proceed to specific and concrete analysis and solutions of the university crisis.

The dramatic upsurge of leftist student activism sources and history, as previously analyzed by Seymour Martin Lipset, is in direct contrast to the personal and political ambivalence of the liberal and moderate student MAs.

Heretofore, the militant student leadership of the small but highly vocal radical left has been the center of focus for student public opinion and the media spotlight. However, the outcome of the inevitable struggle between the marginal ambivalent forces of democratic reform and the revolutionaries of the radical left will largely determine the long-range future of universities and America in crisis.

The following proposed solutions are both socratic and polemical and sometimes lack substantial data to support the conclusions. But these solutions, I believe, logically flow from the analysis in the previous sections. In any event, there must be a continuing debate among those who are vitally concerned about the future of liberal arts education and the future for millions of students yet to attend our universities and colleges. This section is my attempt to begin to clarify some of the solutions to the university crisis.

Students

A significant volume of research data discloses a growing proportion of our better students not anticipating careers in professional or business areas. Increasingly, students are looking to *their* university to help them discover the real meaning of life.

When answers aren't forthcoming, disappointment, anger, and frustration mount. Few university administrators and faculty seem concerned with the moral and political consequences of modern man's life.

Concerned MA students are becoming increasingly dissatisfied (as is widely known) with tense competition for grades, monotonous lectures in large, jammed lecture halls, and the narrow and rigid course and curriculum requirements at most American universities. These dissatisfactions prime many students with rationales and motives strong enough to impel them to support radical confrontations against the administration and faculty—the university. They are beginning to act—not just bitch and moan about the university as students have done in the past. If classes and teachers seem inferior and irrelevant, why should the students support the university when it's attacked and confronted by their radical peers?

Admittedly, the complex process of involving students (particularly marginal ambivalents) in the decision-making process of the university will be difficult. But polarized violence (like that at Buffalo, Santa Barbara, and Harvard Square), repression, or capitulation to anarchy are the visible alternatives. Protests and demonstrations which involve the physical takeover of campus buildings—preventing free movement by teachers, students, and administrators—must be condemned. Classroom disruptions which assault the fundamental principles of free speech, academic freedom, universal civil liberties, and open expression in a free marketplace, must be avoided by radicals, liberals and moderate conservatives alike.

However, the fight to preserve these democratic values must never lead to condoning the status quo or bureaucratic rigidity of administrators and the unresponsiveness of most tenured faculty which often triggers undemocratic student action.

Administration

College administrations, struggling to expand or survive, must insure "don't rock the boat" equilibrium if they are to acquire gifts, grants, and legislative benefits. They must keep conflict at a minimum if yearly, conservative alumni gift-giving is to continue.

This is true despite administrators' prostudent, public-relations efforts at communications, and their open-door-grievance rhetoric, initiated by students and fully and endlessly practiced by administrators. Administrators usually are closer to, and talk more directly with students – unlike faculty – as David Riesman has pointed out. But substantively, no significant structural changes result from these stylized communication exchanges. As stated before, administrators respond primarily to conservative, equilibrium and "order" values.

College administrators *must* reduce faculty and student protests and demands for innovation, change, and alteration of the status quo. They *must* present a stable, conservative image – minimizing disagreements and conflict on campus – to accommodate the orientation of affluent donors (and key legislators) who want to insure immortality.

Therefore, the "grand consensus" is the administration's key objective. No other value, in most cases, is really considered more important at the presidential and administrative level.

Students find pious administration pronouncements about "educating the whole person" . . . "preparing students for a creative, well-rounded life" . . . insulting and hypocritical. Grades, diplomas, certification, order, and conformity are what most administrations concentrate the majority of their time and energy towards.

Student anger (MAs particularly) focuses for the most part on the demand for a more active, decision-making role in their own discipline and education!

Most students – even the blacks – don't really believe they should teach or literally have the ultimate power to hire and fire teachers, or individually outline new courses. But they feel they have the experience and insight into good teaching and know what reading and lectures are the most effective. Thus, they feel they would have a positive influence on the final decision-making in these areas only if they have a voice and a vote at every and all departmental and faculty-administration committee levels.

Therefore, the dearth of MA power is the chief factor in the polarized conflict between left-radicals and bureaucratic administrators – the heart of the university crisis.

Administrators are generally unresponsive (except verbally) to students' needs and problems because (among other reasons) of the tremendous size of the educational institutions and the IBM-depersonalized, bureaucratic decision-making that accompanies accelerated growth.[11] Administrative intractability and resistance to change are the major factors in contributing to the breakdown of "law and order" on the campus. The administration's blocking of vital reforms in the decision-making process is particularly frustrating and alienating to reform and liberal students – and plays into the hands of the campus revolutionaries.

The authority status of the administrations of most universities has virtually collapsed. They have collapsed because there is a moral diffusion of responsibility between the administration and the faculty. They are invariably divided on courses, teacher hiring and firing, degree requirements, disciplinary decisions, investments, and rules and regulations. Therefore, many of the needed reforms proposed by students are not resolved. They are lost between bureaucratic committees and intra-institutional power conflicts. This unresponsiveness to student needs and the failure to act decisively except in response to radicals' confrontations and disruptions, is at the heart of this "de-authorization" process.

Faculty

The *rapid faculty growth* in the universities in the last few years, *burgeoning enrollments, faculty* emphasis on research at the expense of teaching, and the emphasis on preserving faculty prerogatives, even at the expense of student needs, have all created a crisis climate.

A vulnerable administration, weakened and divided in its

exercise of authority, faced by alienated, frustrated, energetic masses of students, creates a state of almost spontaneous combustibility.[12]

The administration's general response to this imminent conflagratory situation is to pompously deplore violence and disruption, attack students as "bums" and unpatriotic, piously call for law and order but not to respond to student initiatives for reform.

The SDS and other radicals, of course, move into this vacuum explosively – with creative confrontations – and we see a variety of reactions from the administration. Perkins (Cornell), and Christ-Janer (ex-Boston University), when faced with building takeovers, gave in to the demands of the revolutionaries (which will never appease them); other administrators like Kirk (Columbia) or Pusey (Harvard) violently overreacted, calling in the police or National Guard, whose vicious and predictable counterviolence enrages most students and obscures the original student demands and undemocratic radical actions.

Both giving in and overreacting with hawk counterviolence play into the hands of radicals and the supra-militants – black and white. Behind the scenes, the law-and-order trustees and the affluent alumni and financial gift-givers pour on their pressure to resist change via and through the administrators.[13]

The Boston University administration, under A. Christ-Janer, was the first major university to collapse and capitulate to a building takeover by a group of black militant students – members of UMOJA – in the spring of 1968. Boston University is not a racist school (it is practically bankrupt, with negligible endowments and barely existing on high tuition income). Yet, Christ-Janer agreed in three hours – with a figurative gun to his head – to one hundred additional black student full scholarships for the fall of 1968. The white radicals were deliriously happy at the "revolutionary" victory. Christ-Janer (and the administration) sounded exactly like Chamberlain at Munich as they praised the neatness and good manners of the blacks during the takeover and ignored the chains on the administration building doors and guns in the hands of several militants, led by a seventeen-year-old, nonstudent gang leader from Bedford-Stuyvesant, Chris Stanley. Little wonder that Boston University has been a madhouse of constant classroom invasions and building takeovers.

Enlightened and emboldened by the black student victory at B.U., the front page of the New York *Times* a year later carried a picture of black students holding guns striding out of Willard Straight Hall at Cornell University after capturing and holding the student center, cafeteria, and "Straight Hotel" overnight. President Perkins of Cornell collapsed, too, encouraging a state of neo-anarchy at Cornell while giving in to Harry Edwards, Douglas Dowd and the black student demands, and encouraging violence and totalitarianism by awarding amnesty to the black gun-toters.

What of the one hundred black freshmen (fruits of the UMOJA takeover) who entered Boston University in the fall of 1968? Over 75 percent flunked out by spring. The B.U. administration, UMOJA, and white radicals ignored the necessity of remedial tutoring. They were too flushed with victory! They were indifferent and bored with the necessary hard tutoring work.

But the same reasons for opposing SDS-PL's undemocratic actions – no matter how noble the self-proclaimed goals may be – applies to many of the rash of black, Afro-student takeovers!

For example, demands for twenty-five dollars per week special black spending allowances ("we have different 'soul' needs than white students"); separate "apartheid" dorms; exclusive all-black member organizations;[14] separate kitchens (for soul food); segregated black-studies programs (instead of mulatto studies programs emphasizing Hawaii's integrated, multiracial ethnic society and the evils of ethnocentrism); are but a few of the demands by black separatists that should be rejected; but they are often seriously negotiated by reverse-racist, supine administrations – who remain covert racists.

Myths about Student Radicals

The public at large seriously believes several misconceptions or myths about the SDS, radicals, and other left-hippie students in general. The first major myth is that SDS, radicals and hippies are a majority or represent a substantial body of students. My own research and additional studies indicate that the Left and committed hippies *together,* constitute at most only about 5 to 10 percent of all students (as pointed out previously by Seymour Martin Lipset and myself).

The second major myth is that the New Left really wants to reform or restructure American society or the university. The overwhelming evidence indicates that since 1969 this is untrue. The vast majority of the leaders of the SDS want to *destroy* the soft underbelly of our society—the university; they want "instant socialism" and an antiimperialist revolution. The SDS openly takes the position that there are no victories (by the nature of their analyses of the condition of society, government and the university in this country there can be *no victories*) except in the undefinable, basic revolution.

The aim of all SDS, left-radical campus action is never its immediate, ostensible end. The slogan is only a tactic . . . to aid "further radicalization," to build the cadres or the "movement." What justifies this position, of course, is the supposed irrevocable corruption of society and its institutions, therefore legitimizing any means to bring it all down.[15]

The third and by far the most popular myth is that the New Left is superior intellectually, that the leadership comprises the best, most cultured, and brightest students. Cursory examination will indicate that since the early days (pre-1968) few of the New Left attend operas, symphony concerts, art museums, ballet or the classical theater. Also, most of the leadership of the New Left as I've observed at Brooklyn College, New School (New York City), Boston University, Harvard, and checked out carefully at Wisconsin, Michigan and Berkeley, has contempt for anything that is not relevant now; and they generally (since 1968) do not read or understand Shakespeare, Shaw, Freud, William James, Harold Lasswell, George Simmel, Max Weber, Charles Beard, Stuart Hughes, or Jules Henry.

There is obviously little time left – after organizing revolutions off and on campus, and promiscuous involvement in sexual and drug crash-padding – for much studying, reading or intellectual discourse.

Any teachers or students who get involved in a debate with most leaders of the New Left, will find the majority appallingly ignorant of the most elementary knowledge of American history, the Rennaissance and Reformation, psychology, sociology, or economics.

There is definitely a pro-Che; pro-Fidel; pro-Mao, romantic-revolutionary-Marxist orientation that has become dominant in all sections of SDS and radical-left student leadership. Even the "non-Progressive Labor forces" pursue the unreal, illusionary, fantasy dreams of a working class or student-women-black revolution (backed by Black Panthers and liberated women) and the inevitability of a Marxist working-class revolution.[16] This is as unreal as the pitiful PL-Maoist-WSA "Workers and students unite and fight" chants, along the streets and campus walks, as you strain to find one adult worker! Many workers are busily beating up war resisters and anti-Vietnam demonstrators, and fighting blacks by denying them jobs, integrated schools, busing and equal housing. Note the construction workers (with police indirect aid) beating up student war protestors at New York City Hall on May 8, 1970.

The Kafka-like factionalism at the July 1969 SDS Convention – with PL-WSA-Maoists, Mark Rudd RYM Weathermen, and RYM II National Office antagonists calling each other counterrevolutionists and racists, competing hysterically by chanting Mao's quotes from the Red Book at each other – culminated with the Rudd (Weatherman-RYM) forces undemocratically expelling the WSA-Progressive Labor Party faction.[17] Regional conventions subsequently erupted in scuffles for the microphones and both factions have declared themselves the "only true believers" – the sole leaders of SDS. Each has violently threatened the other with physical beatings and abuse.

The factional split in SDS (July 1969) gives the liberal-moderate MAs on college campuses a new chance to organize the large group of students who have heretofore been attracted to the excitement, sense of community and confrontationist tactics of radical-SDS attacks on the society and university administrations. Only if the marginal ambivalents meet the revolutionaries head-on with a creative, relevant program for institutional reform which will interest and provoke the majority of students, can there be any real hope to defeat bureaucratic repression or polarized anarchy on the campuses.

The MAs are just beginning to mount counterattacks involving liberal and moderate students and initiate pressure on faculty and administrators for democratic social change on university campuses.

Jack Newfield, author of "The Prophetic Minority," in the October 2, 1969, issue of *The Village Voice,* makes this analysis of the importance of marginal ambivalents as the major key to social change when he says:

> SDS has become isolated in a fantasy world of vulgarized Marxist rhetoric, karate classes, and rumbles with white gangs . . . a penchant for tactics so absurdly counterproductive that one might reasonably expect they are really CIA double agents. The January, 1969, *Fortune* estimated there are three million college students sympathetic to [many] of the goals of SDS [but are not members]. Most student activists are resisting the war, organizing, helping the poor. They yearn for less materialistic definitions of success.

Sam Brown, Senator Gene McCarthy's head student organizer in 1968, one of the leaders of the 1969–70 Anti-Vietnam War Moratorium, helped trigger a massive national (nonviolent) demonstration by the MAs in October and November of 1969 which was ignored or viciously attacked by all factions of the SDS and the far left. Yet it made the front page in the press and every television news broadcast across the country as a stunning though temporary peaceful success.

The wildness and unreality of the rival SDS countercharges – "racist, adventurer, and counterrevolutionary," – the epithets and blows thrust back and forth by each rival SDS faction – forces observers to read Franz Kafka or Lewis Carroll to perceive the thin line between fantasy and reality.

The popular theory or analysis of SDS strategy as nonconspiratorial and spontaneous is also rapidly changing since July 1969. Full-time organizers, like Eric Mann (Weathermen, New England)[18] move back and forth between campus chapter meetings and coordinate, counsel and tie together strategy, tactics and timing around settled, nationally determined issues. So do Jeff Gordon of the Progressive Labor-WSA faction in New York City and Jared Israel (PL-WSA) in Boston.

And lastly the SDS has been praised, encouraged, and honored by educators and social scientists like Edgar Z. Friedenberg, Richard Flacks, John Holt, Douglas Dowd and Howard Zinn as being comprised of morally and humanistically ethical students who are dedicated and concerned human beings. Although some followers, supporters and even some of the original '65–'67 leaders of SDS certainly fit this category, the overwhelming majority of present radical leaders (including the RYM-I, the anarchists, the yippie-left group led by Abbie Hoffman and Jerry Rubin and the Weathermen-RYM II) by and large are hedonistic, out-and-out revolutionaries who are often emotionally unstable male chauvinists whose contempt and hatred for liberals, moderates, and the lower-middle-class adult American is usually greater than their hatred for the industrial-military complex and the radical right. Character assassinations and personal disruption of liberal teachers' classrooms (à la Nazi storm troopers) are the kind of tactics generally followed.[19] Observers at Wisconsin, Michigan, Berkeley, Harvard, Boston University, Brooklyn College, CCNY, Queens College, Cornell, SUNY at Stoney Brook, New York, have repeatedly verified these systematic behavior patterns of the current SDS-radicals.

The CBS Yankelovich studies also indicate that it is *not* the radicals but the liberal-moderate reformers (MAs) who are the ultimate key to winning the majority of students to relevant political action and social change.

Although Vietnam, racism, poverty, violence, assassinations and pollution, along with increasing institutional-bureaucratic rigidity are serious evils in the United States needing immediate change, totalitarianism, anarchy, violence, and anti–civil libertarian acts to eradicate those evils cannot be condoned!

What do SDS-type radicals offer liberals, reformers, and moderates as the fruits of victory? The anarchy and riots in China? The political prison and control of all media in Castro Cuba? The undemocratic suppression of freedom in the Soviet Union? The rape of Czechoslovakia? The assassinations and anarchy in Algeria? And Ghana?[20]

When radicals and revolutionaries talk about overthrowing this society, can they show the model for a better one? They have failed miserably on this major point. Thus, how can anyone look to them as any relevant agency for social change in bringing about the necessary radical reforms in American society?

Even though liberalism has declined and the word "liberal" has now become odiously identified with McGeorge Bundy, George Meany, Pat Moynihan, Hubert Humphrey, Walt Rostow, Richard Daley and Lyndon Johnson, no radical movement can hope to gain the support of marginal ambivalent students or Americans at large *unless it is identified with the liberal rule of reason; openness to another man's argument, personal tolerance of someone who disagrees, faith in the power of persuasion, and belief in free speech for opponents as well as allies.*

The tragic consequences of unleashing violence in premature and abortive attempts at revolution can only be destructive. If fascism or right-wing reactionism results from such tantrumlike rebellions, we will all drown in a sea of violence.[21]

Today's SDS and radical revolutionaries show no evidence that they wish to control or moderate the level of violence. Their sloganeering, wild "pig" rhetoric, and "bomb banks" threats indicate that they want to escalate violence as much as possible!

Consistent with accomplishing their limited objectives, the SDS, Black Panthers, and hippie-radical revolutionaries have consistently demonstrated a high degree of irresponsibility in promoting violence over rational debate and nonviolent, democratic social change analysis.

They have dangerously and defiantly antagonized or "turned off" a large percentage of the student and adult population. They have consistently shown that their revolutionary theory is primarily concerned with promoting their own immediate psychological, leadership and power interests, not that of the entire society, its history, or its American revolutionary traditions.[22]

They only know how to identify with each other, trying to perpetuate their own narrow sense of "community" through defiantly wearing and pushing their own conformist clothing, and long, neuter hair styles; through indiscriminate drug and sexual behavior, and single-shot (weekend Woodstock-grass-love-rock) festivals which provide no permanent foundation or hope for real social change. (They are commercially sponsored, pseudorevolutionary events that sell "community" to the alienated, hippies, and New Left.)

You can't make a revolution by talking slogans and jargon to select people like yourself. There must be familiar, positive symbols to latch onto.[23] Masses of people must be able to identify with the history and unique American characteristics of the American Revolution.[24] Otherwise, there will only be a pseudorevolution – pyrrhic rebellions and, inevitably, right-wing reaction.

The endless, boring lessons we all suffered in school couldn't obscure the positive values inherent in the symbols and rhetoric of democracy and freedom. The authoritarian-memorization teachings of the Judeo-Christian ethic in school, church, and synagogue remain a positive and indigenous part of the socialization process that invaded every American's unconscious – often his deep sense of culture. To be successful, it seems imperative to wage the fight to democratize our institutions in the very name, smell, and stamp of the Judeo-Christian values inherent in these old, familiar, traditional, and nostalgic symbols, i.e., fairness, tolerance, respect for differences, leading inevitably to acceptance of the Bill of Rights, the Declaration of Independence and the Constitution (guaranteeing voting, electing, nonviolent pressuring of elected officials, free speech, due process, picketing, and demonstrating). Cuban, Russian, and Chinese theories, jargon, language and symbols are unfamiliar and strange to most Americans. Che, Mao, Ho, and Fidel are jarring to our ears, removed from our cultural heritage. Marx undoubtedly would have rewritten much of his work in the face of the advent of the bomb, TV, and the technological revolution.

Particularly confusing to MAs are the actions of faculty members and administrators who, when pushed hard, often find elaborate justifications for student recourse to nontraditional revolutionary building takeovers and force, in violation of everyone else's rights. This often stems from fear, guilt or political ambivalence. The radical students, when accused of hypocrisy, or of having a double standard, or of using totalitarian methods or tactics in a takeover, respond glibly as in the following exchange at Harvard Yard, April 9, 1969:[25]

> SDS Female: . . . we've talked long enough; we're taking over this building (University Hall). You're responsible for killing people in Vietnam.
>
> Dean Epps: I'm not responsible for killing people in Vietnam. You are using methods here that I thought you objected to – violence and force.
>
> SDS Female: What the fuck do you know about it?

Dean Epps, a black, was then *pushed* out the east door and into the crowd.

Even more penetrating is the SDS radical analogy, "You condone violence in Vietnam . . . and exert violence through the oppression imposed on blacks and on students in the classroom every day."

If you reply that you have been and are opposed to Vietnam since the fall of 1965 and have spoken and written publicly in opposition to it; or, that boredom or oppressive words in a classroom can be ignored, or one can disengage or leave the "pseudo-violence" in the classroom – no intellectual response will be forthcoming. The simplistic SDS-radical analogy remains, nevertheless, oft-used and repetitively self-proclaimed.

The administrators of a university greatly aid the left-radicals when they call in police. The cops, underpaid, low in status, low in education, often ethnocentric (racist or super-ethnic), are primed and ready for force and violence; violence against the blacks, antiwar kids, longhairs; against the youth who reject the superpatriotic, materialistic values and goals which the upwardly mobile cops want so desperately.

So, the cops are often uncontrollable. The SDS, yippies, crazies and Hayden-Hoffman-Rubin-Davis leftists cynically provoked the kind of violent response[26] they wanted and needed from the police at the 1968 Convention in Chicago. Both sides wanted and needed it. They repeat the performance every chance they get (Columbia, Buffalo, Harvard, Berkeley).

If the Left can incite the authorities and cops to overrespond to violence and brutality, the violence will inevitably involve reformers, liberals, moderates and the media, as well as innocent bystanders. It happened in Chicago, Berkeley, Cambridge, Morningside Heights, on many other campuses, and in urban centers.[27]

The Left achieves vast publicity and attention to its propaganda, which radicalizes many others, invokes sympathy for its own ranks who are beaten up and arrested and turns the entire situation into a self-fulfilling prophecy about the corruption, violence, and insensitivity of the police as representative of the entire society.

Yet, where did the violence start at Harvard (for one example)?

When the students went into a building occupied by deans working peacefully at their jobs, they forcefully ejected the deans in a violent fashion.

Completely forgotten then, is the original, the initiating violence or transgression by the student-left. The injustices (war, racism, and poverty), the rigidified bureaucratic administration, the classroom boredom, the faculty indifference to students – all remain as constant, legitimate, burning grievances and unsolved issues.

But do two wrongs make one right? Did Columbia, Berkeley, or Harvard confrontations change or alter one iota of the problems of war, poverty and racism? The rebellions obviously weren't intended to alleviate these "liberal" problems.

Did Attila the Hun, Hitler, Stalin, Franco, Marshal Ky (South Vietnamese Vice-Chairman and Hitler admirer), or any despot or totalitarian ever commit a nondemocratic act . . . or start a rebellion, riot or revolution for an ignoble or undemocratic reason? Never! They always acted with elaborate justifications. The totalitarians have always acted, and always will, in the name of reason, peace, democracy, and freedom.

Yet each violent or campus totalitarian act must be judged for its own intrinsic and indigenous substance. The students involved, their records, their emotional and psychological maturity must be weighed. Their past commitments to tolerance, dissent, open and democratic controversy must be carefully judged.

Justice must always be primary! Trials before peers, counsel, all the substance of what due process and democracy should be, *must* be made available and operable for *all* students charged with violating others' democratic rights, civil liberties, or freedom. (Student-faculty courts must be substituted for arbitrary, bureaucratic-administrator discipline via fiat.) [28]

Sterile bureaucratic compliance with "law and order" (rules) is the central refuge of conservatives, too many liberals, and a majority of administrators.

No elaborate faculty or administration justifications – no amnesty – will ever appease the revolutionaries. They have different aims and values! However, they must be fought, democratically, but only in terms of their totalitarian, undemocratic actions. They should no longer be allowed to act in the name of morality, justice, or peace without marginal ambivalents exposing them, opposing them!

Of course, there are *some* well-meaning, humanistic, intelligent and sensitive radicals. Some of them have attended my classes. But they're in a minority and do *not publically attack* the undemocratic and totalitarian actions of their radical leadership.

Columbia, Harvard, Berkeley, Boston University, Dartmouth, Brooklyn College, CCNY, Rutgers, Stanford, UCLA and Swarthmore are but a few of the campuses where initiating violence, anti–civil libertarian acts and anarchic takeovers have flourished, without *any* open dissent and opposition from the "nice" radicals or SDSers. Either they're afraid to be ostracized, can't handle being attacked, or have been able to successfully rationalize keeping quiet for the sake of internal unity.

The silence of the "nice" rank-and-file SDSers legitimates the totalitarian actions of their SDS leaders and forces the "nice guys" to accept their share of responsibility for the broadsided attacks on the SDS-radical-left from liberals and moderates.

But it is not enough to oppose or expose the radical left. Positive, concrete steps must be undertaken to preserve a free market place for *all* ideas on campus and to extend civil liberties and democratic processes and representation to all divergent groups on campus without abridging anyone's freedom of speech, right to dissent, or right to teach and learn.

A non-armed, democratically elected thirty-person security committee, equally divided between students, faculty, and administration, should take over the policing and protection of a free, open campus. Administrations' calling in police inevitably leads to police violence – as pointed out before.

It is inconceivable that three fourths of campus violence would ever occur if such a committee replaced outside cops. And the polarization, blurring of initiating undemocratic acts, and inevitable radicalization of liberals and moderates in reaction to police violence can mostly be avoided if thirty nonviolent members of the academic community attempt to bring justice into play – preceding attempts at order. If radicals don't accept the decisions and discipline of such a committee, they will lose most of their (MA antiadministration) support on campus. Their revolutionary opposition to fair, open, democratic processes will isolate them.

Referendums, college constitutional conventions, all-day teach-ings will defuse artificially contrived confrontations and violence around conflicts as they did at Amherst and MIT in the spring of 1969. The radicals will then have to calmly, rationally and democratically debate their demands and charges! MA students and faculty will have the opportunity to answer the nihilism, cynicism and negligible support the SDS-radical position eventually commands. Obviously scholarly and intellectual logic, factuality and reason, will prevail more often in such an atmosphere.

Restructuring and reforming the total and basic decision-making apparatus through giving elected students (plus non-tenured faculty) a voice and a vote on all committees on all campuses is one real structural solution to the university crisis. (Governor Sargent of Massachusetts is pushing legislation to achieve such student participation in Massachusetts state education committees.)

The Faculty Ambivalence

A continuing hypocritical thread runs through all the faculty arguments against MA students having a voice and vote in faculty hiring, firing, and tenure.

Implicit – if not downright explicit – is the constant faculty theme implying a lack of trust in the integrity and trustworthiness of students. The expressed fear is over the ultra-private, confidential files each faculty department has compiled on every new faculty member – and, how dangerous it would be for students, to become privy to these secret files.

The older, tenured faculty constantly express grave, almost paranoidal concern about protecting nontenured faculty files from the eyes and indiscretions of mere students.

In half a dozen known cases – including my own – tenured faculty was totally unwilling to discuss or disclose any reasons for not rehiring or granting tenure — with students, or even with the concerned faculty member himself, even when he agreed to open discussion of his own case.

What begins to emerge is a murky kind of bureaucratic hypocrisy on the part of many tenured faculty.

What scares them, it is widely felt, is not the reputation of the rejected faculty member or the students' potential disclosure of confidential information (unfounded and generational as this attack is). It is the apparent fear of disclosure of the substantive or specific reasons why the tenured faculty actually fires — or rejects tenure to — many creative, change-oriented nontenured faculty.

What terrifies most faculty is the possible disclosure or public scrutiny of the shallow and petty reasons offered and often utilized in determining a colleague's career. They cannot allow superficial, catty letters of recommendation and meeting notes to receive public attention and the exposure and contempt they might richly deserve. If these letters and confidential files, full of nonscholarly garbage ("He has a pleasant personality and he and his wife will fit in well . . .") became known, the intrigues and factionalism of many petty faculty bureaucrats and their conformist, conservative academic and administrative policies would be held up to ridicule.[29]

The identical reasons political reformers have traditionally fought backroom, smoke-filled machine political deals is the exact reason fresh air, openness, and broader, more democratic decision-making has become essential in opening up the cloistered nests of academic bureaucracy at the departmental-faculty level.

If students can't be trusted, they can't be taught!

Students are the integral part of the university. They must have at the very least a small minority vote and full-time participation in all decision-making at the various levels of policy-making. If not, how can they be expected to participate later as adults in struggles over issues like war, taxes, racism, and pollution? And why should they defend the university from violence or artificial confrontations by the radical left if they feel no commitment or structural involvement with the faculty and administration – in a community of scholars? Finally, the tenured faculty, in many cases, have become petty bureaucrats and hang onto departmental grading, hiring-firing, tenure and curriculum power without any consideration for broadening the decision-making process to include students (even minor participation is often fought bitterly).

Most of the liberal faculty doesn't even speak out sharply against the far-left students and faculty. They rarely defend the American Civil Liberties Union (ACLU), single-standard, civil-libertarian position, which sometimes badly needs explaining and defending.

Most of the faculty doesn't speak out in strong opposition to the military-industrial complex, the Vietnam war, racism and bureaucratic bungling – off and on campus. All too often they are objective, value-free, scholarly, and removed from the conflict inherent in undemocratic actions on campus which require liberal, civil-libertarian opposition. The faculty must learn to find and live with a middle position between capitulating on high scholastic standards and classroom freedom and bureaucratically controlling all departmental decision-making.

Solutions

The faculty must begin to assume the kind of mature, liberal, understanding role – as adults – that is so often lacking in the students' own homes and, in most of American life.

The separation of research and writing from teaching, as faculty functions, is another essential and necessary step.

A new kind of graduate degree should also be awarded on the basis of superior knowledge in a specific field combined with teaching ability. Teaching must be the major concern on university and college campuses.

Research institutes at every university can be established so that those professors (Ph.D. thesis writers) who are preoccupied with scientific research and publishing more than teaching can concentrate on research without the burdensome additional responsibility of teaching. Where both can be accomplished without teaching's suffering, so much the better.

Universities should give course credit for, and encourage students to volunteer to work on, some of the acute urban problems. The necessity of tutorial work with young blacks, lower-middle-class whites, Mexican-Americans, and Indian and Puerto Rican students, and the urgency of staffing infant care centers for low income and welfare mothers to allow them to work, acquire job training skills, go back to school, or receive psychiatric and medical care, are but two areas where students can do exciting work connecting theory with practical life problems.[30]

Students who are accepted at college should not be failed by teachers whose responsibility should be solely to provoke, teach and counsel students. Fear of poor grades never motivates students to full study and learning potential. Only stimulating teachers and less structured classrooms and more creative and flexible interdisciplinary curriculum and course content can make the university an exciting learning and teaching experience.

Martin Duberman, professor at Princeton, in his article, "An Experiment In Education," in the winter 1968 issue of *Daedalus,* perceptively comments:

". . . I was moved by Neill's candor and exhilarated by his demonstration that children flourish when they are allowed freedom . . .[31] The willingness to suspend judgment of one another in the name of understanding, the tolerance of mistakes, the opportunity to reveal and examine one's inner self without fear of punition – all encourage growth.

"My experience in therapy made me impatient with other group enterprises that were narrowly functional – like a university seminar that merely engaged in the transmission of factual information. I knew that much more than information could be exchanged when a permissive, nonjudgmental atmosphere prevailed. Indeed, little important information can be transmitted if an emotional transaction is not simultaneously in process, for an individual will not expose his deepest assumptions nor be able to perceive those of another if their relationship is purely intellectual. (I continue to use outmoded, dualistic terminology like *intellectual* and *emotional* because more accurate vocabulary is not yet available.)

"The job of self-discovery is never, of course, complete; it is hardly surprising that twenty-one-year-olds do not fully know 'who the hell they are.' But the point is that they have not begun to know. In many cases, four years of college do not initiate or further, but dampen or destroy efforts of self-exploration. This may not be the intent, but it is nonetheless the result of the tactics employed by those who administer and teach in a university. They make certain that the student's energies are directed at fulfilling tasks set by them rather than by himself; they encourage him to define his worth in terms of his success in winning their approval; high grades, good letters of recommendation, departmental honors, prizes. He is taught to regard these tangible signs . . . as the only important evidence or kind of achievement, and as the indispensable precondition, almost the guarantee, of a satisfying life. What he is not taught is that orientation toward gaining the approval of others carries high costs: the acceptance of disguise as a necessity of life; the unconscious determination to manipulate others in the way one has been manipulated; the conviction that productivity is more important than character and 'success' superior to satisfaction; the loss of curiosity, of a willingness to ask questions, of the capacity to take risks.

"The removal of grades is a necessary, but hardly sufficient, means for reversing this disastrous orientation. Grading is but one way in which we turn potentially creative individuals into data processing machines, adapting them to their society but alienating them from themselves. More than grades must go. The entire superstructure of authoritarian control in our schools must give way if we are to enable people to assume responsibility for and to take pleasure in their own lives. We cannot expect aliveness and involvement when we are busy inculcating docility and compliance.

"In this regard, the false distinctions that separate student from teacher must be broken down. What do we think titles like 'professor,' 'sir,' or 'mister' achieve? Perhaps the illusion of respect, but certainly not its reality. Those qualities which are worth admiring in a given person – perception, experience, honesty, empathy, openness, will be admired regardless of title, and no title can create admiration when such qualities are absent. But a title can – and often does – establish a pattern of formality that prevents free exchange and common pursuit by student and teacher of understanding. Titles also provide the professor with a subtle means of discipline and a false sense of self-importance, neither of which is conducive to humanness or communication.

"There is no agreement as to what knowledge is essential . . . Schools, as Holt puts it, should be places where students 'learn what they most want to know, instead of what we think they ought to know.'

"Finally, there is the matter of leadership. A crucial distinction must be made between authority and authoritarianism. The former represents accumulated experience, knowledge, and insight. The latter represents their counterfeits: age masquerading as maturity, information as understanding, technique as originality. Authoritarianism is forced to demand the respect that authority draws naturally to itself. The former, like all demands, is likely to meet with hostility; the latter, like all authenticity, with emulation. Our universities, our schools at every level, are rife with authoritarianism, all but devoid of authority.

"And it is the rare authoritarian who, when given power – when put, say, in charge of adolescents – can resist the satisfaction of reducing them to his level. So it is that one generation, desperate lest its own achievement be exceeded, corrupts the next – all the while protesting benevolence. Fathers are not known to encourage patricide – and few youths grow to manhood.

"No one has a corner on truth, that competence is never across the board, and that therefore leadership (in a classroom discussion, in life) should shift as areas of competence shift. If he can convey that much to Joe Smith, Professor Jones will have given him the one encouragement essential to true education: ultimately each man can, must, become his own authority. This is the one path to adulthood – and democracy.

"We need to recognize that when a seminar is functioning well, the emotions of its members are engaged and, once engaged, will be transmuted.

"Intellectual development does not, cannot, take place *in vacuo.* Indeed, it can be argued that intellectual development is predicated on the simultaneous development of the emotions. By intellectual development, I don't mean the amassing of facts (we all know walking encyclopedias who are emotional infants), but rather, what William Kessen, professor of psychology at Yale, has called the individual's 'delight in the solution of problems, pursuit of the orderly, joy in his own active inquiry, the relief and excitement of setting his own goals.' For that kind of intellectual development one needs emotional growth as well. The two are inextricably linked, and it's because we have tried to separate them – have tried to exclude emotion from the classroom – that we have turned out many more pedants and parrots than human beings."

Peter Clecak goes on to specific solutions: "We should begin to imagine new programs and structures that simultaneously engage the student in the present and teach him more sophisticated modes of understanding, evaluating and valuing his experience . . . We should devise a liberal arts curriculum based on the work-study principle.[32]

"Students should begin their university lives by selecting from a variety of full-time positions – in government, welfare agencies, schools, churches and perhaps in industry.

"To integrate work and study, students might attend seminars on topics related to their work . . . They would begin to examine and reflect upon their immediate activities and upon themselves, exploring the complex inter-relationships between consciousness and social structure (culture versus man). They would move from analysis of local institutions to theoretical speculation about American society and the culture as a whole.[33]

"This synthesization seems to be an essential precondition for creating a desire to learn from the past (and prepare for the future).

"A couple of years of structured (self-analytical) experience in the outside world should generate confusion and the desire for deeper perspective offered by history, philosophy, literature (sociology and psychology).

"Work-study programs have been tried for many years at Antioch, Bennington, and more recently, Old Westbury. Some of these experiments have been moderately successful, although they inherently tend to dissociate work from study . . . But nowhere has the principle been thoroughly tested."

But to solve the university crisis in a fundamental and basic fashion, the illness and malaise of the outside society has to be simultaneously cured. Restructured or new institutions on and off university campuses must be initiated and built if peace, freedom and democracy are to flourish.[34]

Chapter Notes

Introduction

1. Henry Etzkowitz and Gerald M. Schaflander, *Ghetto Crisis* (Boston: Little, Brown, 1969).
2. For a statement on the Berkeley issues during the revolt year see S. M. Lipset and Paul Seabury, "The Lesson of Berkeley," *The Reporter* (January 28, 1965), pp. 36–40; reprinted in revised form in Seymour Martin Lipset and Sheldon S. Wolin, eds., *The Berkeley Student Revolt* (Garden City: Doubleday, Anchor Books, 1965), pp. 340–349.
3. For a statement by Steve Weissman, second to Mario Savio in the leadership of the FSM, boasting of the provocative tactics the FSM radicals had in mind to continue confrontations, see Calvin Trillin, "Letter from Berkeley," in Michael V. Miller and Susan Gilmore, eds., *Revolution at Berkeley* (New York: Dial, 1965), p. 280. See also pp. 277–279.
4. Lipset and Seabury, "The Lesson of Berkeley," p. 40, and in Lipset and Wolin, *The Berkeley Student Revolt,* p. 349.
5. Trillin, "Letter from Berkeley," pp. 277–280.
6. "Stokely Carmichael, Carl Oglesby Talk Strategy and Tactics," *National Guardian* (December 16, 1967), pp. 1, 14.
7. Cited in Eric Ashby and Mary Anderson, *The Rise of the Student Estate in Britain* (London: Macmillan, 1970), p. 125, from *New Left Review* 50 (1968), p. 59.
8. Quoted in Maryl Levine and John Naisbitt, *Right On* (New York: Bantam, 1970), p. 70.
9. Sam Brown, "The Politics of Peace," *The Washington Monthly* 2 (August 1970), pp. 24–46.
10. For a description of the position of the YPSL during the Harvard crisis of 1969 and a sharp attack on the undemocratic tactics of SDS, see Steven Kelman, *Push Comes to Shove* (Boston: Houghton Mifflin, 1970).
11. See articles in S. M. Lipset, ed., *Student Politics* (New York: Basic Books, 1967); Seymour Martin Lipset and Philip G. Altbach, eds., *Students in Revolt* (Boston: Houghton Mifflin, 1969), and Lipset and Wolin, *The Berkeley Student Revolt.*
12. S. M. Lipset, "University Students and Politics in Underdeveloped Countries," *Minerva* 3 (Autumn 1964), pp. 15–56. A much earlier article by Lipset dealing with student opinion during the 1949–50 California loyalty oath crisis is "Opinion Formation in a Crisis Situation," *Public Opinion Quarterly* (Spring 1953), pp. 20–46.
13. Typical of attacks on Lipset as a "conservative" in his treatment of student activism are the writings of Tom Bottomore; see "Conservative Man," *New York Review of Books* 15 (October 8, 1970), pp. 20–24; and James Petras, review of *Confrontation: The Student Rebellion and Universities,* in *New Politics* (Fall 1968), p. 88.
14. "Fué Abucheado el Agitador Lipset," *El Universal* (Mexico City: February 12, 1970), p. 1.
15. Church League of America, "Subversion by the Volume: The Sad State of the Publishing Industry Today," multilithed (New York: August 1970), p. 43.
16. Lipset has discussed the varying reactions to his writings with specific citations to many of them in the preface to the revised paperback edition

of a collection of his essays, *Revolution and Counterrevolution* (Garden City: Doubleday, Anchor Books, 1970).

Chapter 1

1. There is a very extensive literature dealing with student activism comparatively as well as in assorted individual countries. See Philip G. Altbach, *A Select Bibliography on Students, Politics and Higher Education* (Cambridge: Center for International Affairs, Harvard University, 1967); and the bibliography in S. M. Lipset and Philip G. Altbach, eds., *Students in Revolt* (Boston: Houghton Mifflin, 1969), pp. 528–533. Articles dealing with a variety of countries are included in that volume. See also S. M. Lipset, ed., *Student Politics* (New York: Basic Books, 1967); Donald Emerson, ed., *Students and Politics in Developing Countries* (New York: Praeger, 1968); and Julian Nagel, ed., *Student Power* (London: Merlin Press, 1969). The most comprehensive single effort to treat student movements historically and comparatively is Lewis Feuer, *The Conflict of Generations* (New York: Basic Books, 1969).
2. To evaluate the American New Left it is necessary to read various periodicals representing different moderate and extreme leftist groups. These include *New America* (Socialist Party), *The Guardian* (unaffiliated, pro–New Left), *New Left Notes* (two versions put out by different factions), *The Militant* (Socialist Workers Party–Trotskyist), *Challenge* (Maoist), *International Socialist* (Revolutionary Marxist).
3. See, for example, Robert Nisbet, "Who Killed the Student Revolution?" *Encounter* 34 (February 1970), pp. 10–18.
4. Wayne Kind, "Campus Protests Reported on Rise," New York *Times*, March 29, 1970, p. 53. For a report on the previous academic year see Urban Research Corporation, *Student Protests 1969: Summary* (Chicago: 1970). Garth Buchanan and Joan Brackett, *Summary Results of the Survey for the President's Commission on Campus Unrest* (Washington, D.C.: The Urban Institute, September 1970), pp. 9–10.
5. See Urban Research Corporation, *On Strike . . . Shut It Down: A Report on the First National Student Strike in U.S. History* (Chicago: May 1970); and Buchanan and Brackett, *Summary Results,* for statistical data on the extent of the strike.
6. Sam Brown, "The Politics of Peace," *The Washington Monthly* 2 (August 1970), pp. 24–46, especially pp. 24–25.
7. Ernest Gellner, "The Panther and the Dove: Reflections on Rebelliousness and Its Milieux," in David Martin, ed., *Anarchy and Culture: The Problem of the Contemporary University* (London: Routledge and Kegan Paul, 1969), pp. 133–134; Alberto Martinelli and Alessandro Cavalli, "Toward a Conceptual Framework for the Comparative Analysis of Student Movements," (paper presented at the Seventh World Congress of Sociology, Varna, Bulgaria, September 1970), pp. 3–4.
8. Many have written on this phenomenon. See especially Nathan Glazer, *The Social Basis of American Communism* (New York: Harcourt, Brace

and World, 1962), pp. 130–168; Lawrence Fuchs, *The Political Behavior of American Jews* (Glencoe: The Free Press, 1956); Werner Cohn, "The Politics of American Jews," in Marshall Sklare, ed., *The Jews* (Glencoe: The Free Press, 1958), pp. 614–626. See also Charles Liebman, "Toward a Theory of Jewish Liberalism," in Donald R. Cutler, ed., *The Religious Situation: 1969* (Boston: Beacon, 1969), pp. 1034–1061; Nathaniel Weyl, *The Jew in American Politics* (New Rochelle, N.Y.: Arlington House, 1968); Milton Himmelfarb, "Is American Jewry in Crisis?" *Commentary* 47 (March 1969), pp. 33–42; S. M. Lipset, *Revolution and Counter-revolution* (Garden City: Doubleday, Anchor Books, 1970), pp. 375–400. See also for an analysis of the relationship of the Jewish propensity to "intellectuality" to their politics, S. M. Lipset and Everett Ladd, Jr., "Jewish and Gentile Academics: Achievements, Culture, and Politics," *The American Jewish Year Book 1971,* vol. 72 (New York: The American Jewish Committee, Philadelphia: The Jewish Publication Society, 1971).

9. See articles in James McEvoy and Abraham Miller, eds., *Black Power and Student Rebellion* (Belmont, Calif.: Wadsworth, 1969), especially pp. 222–306, 379–418.
10. Brown, "The Politics of Peace," p. 27.
11. Sol Tax, "War and the Draft," in Morton Fried, Marvin Harris, and Robert Murphy, eds., *War* (Garden City: Doubleday, The Natural History Press, 1968), pp. 199–203. Actually Tax concluded that there were seven wars out of twelve fought by the United States which were less popular than the Vietnam one. The twelve, however, include various Indian wars, the Civil War, and the Revolutionary War.
12. Samuel Eliot Morison, "Dissent in the War of 1812," in Samuel Eliot Morison, Frederick Merk and Frank Freidel, *Dissent in Three American Wars* (Cambridge: Harvard University Press, 1970), pp. 3–31.
13. Alice Felt Tyler, *Freedom's Ferment* (New York: Harper, Torchbooks, 1962), p. 407.
14. Frederick Merk, "Dissent in the Mexican War," in Morison et al., *Dissent in Three American Wars,* pp. 33–63; Edward S. Wallace, "Notes and Comment — Deserters in the Mexican War," *The Hispanic American Historical Review* 15 (1935), p. 374.
15. David Donald, "Died of Democracy," in David Donald, ed., *Why the North Won the Civil War* (Baton Rouge: Lousiana State University Press, 1960), pp. 85–89; James McCague, *The Second Rebellion: The New York City Draft Riots of 1863* (New York: Dial, 1968); Basil L. Lee, *Discontent in New York City, 1861–65* (Washington: Catholic University of America Press, 1943).
16. Frank Freidel, "Dissent in the Spanish-American War and the Philippine Insurrection," in Morison et al., *Dissent in Three American Wars,* pp. 65–95, especially p. 77.
17. H. C. Peterson and Gilbert C. Fite, *Opponents of War, 1917–1918* (Seattle: University of Washington Press, 1957), pp. 39, 123–135, 234; Daniel Bell, "The Background and Development of Marxian Socialism in the United States," in Donald Drew Egbert and Stow Persons, eds.,

Socialism and American Life, vol. 1 (Princeton: Princeton University Press, 1952), pp. 314–315.

18. Hazel Erskine, "The Polls: Is War a Mistake?" *Public Opinion Quarterly* 34 (1970), pp. 138–141; Edward Suchman, Rose K. Goldsen and Robin Williams, Jr., "Attitudes Toward the Korean War," *Public Opinion Quarterly* 17 (1953), pp. 173, 182.
19. I have discussed these elements in the relationship of American Protestantism and American political morality elsewhere. See *The First New Nation: The United States in Historical and Comparative Perspective* (Garden City: Doubleday, Anchor Books, 1967), pp. 184–187; *Revolution and Counterrevolution* (New York: Basic Books, 1968), pp. 255–258, 299–303; and, with Earl Raab, *The Politics of Unreason: Right-Wing Extremism in the United States, 1790–1970* (New York: Harper & Row, 1970), pp. 61–67.
20. See especially Feuer, *Conflict of Generations;* Lipset and Altbach, *Students in Revolt;* and Nagel, *Student Power.*
21. Kingsley Davis, "The Sociology of Parent-Youth Conflict," *American Sociological Review* 5 (August 1940), p. 535 and passim; for more recent versions of this approach, see Margaret Mead, *Culture and Commitment: A Study of the Generation Gap* (Garden City: Doubleday, Natural History Press, 1970), especially pp. 51–76; Kenneth Keniston, "The Fire Outside," *The Journal* 9 (September–October 1970), pp. 5–7.
22. Norman Birnbaum, *The Crisis of Industrial Society* (New York: Oxford University Press, 1969), p. 148.
23. Feuer, *Conflict of Generations,* p. 528; Edward Shils, "Comments," in François Duchêne, ed., *The Endless Crisis: America in the Seventies* (New York: Simon and Schuster, 1970), pp. 171–172.
24. [Aristotle,] *Rhetoric,* in *The Basic Works of Aristotle,* edited by Richard McKeon (New York: Random House, 1941), p. 1404.
25. Erik H. Erikson, *Identity, Youth and Crisis* (New York: Norton, 1968), pp. 128–129.
26. Gordon W. Allport, *Pattern and Growth in Personality* (New York: Holt, Rinehart, and Winston, 1961), pp. 283–304; Erikson, *Identity, Youth and Crisis,* pp. 139–140.
27. See especially the recent works of Alain Touraine, *Le mouvement de mai ou le communisme utopique* (Paris: Seuil, 1968), especially pp. 14–15; *La société post-industrielle* (Paris: Denoel, 1969), p. 26 and passim.
28. John and Margaret Rowntree, "The Political Economy of Youth," *Our Generation* 6 (May-June-July 1968), p. 173.
29. Ernest Mandel, "The New Vanguard," in Tariq Ali, ed., *The New Revolutionaries* (New York: Morrow, 1969), p. 47.
30. For a summary, see S. M. Lipset and Philip G. Altbach, "Student Politics and Higher Education in the United States," in Lipset, *Student Politics,* pp. 234–237.
31. "Prudence is really a hateful thing in youth. A prudent youth is prematurely old." Randolph S. Bourne, *Youth and Life* (Boston: Houghton Mifflin, 1913), p. 10.

32. I have developed this point at length in my book *The First New Nation: The United States in Historical and Comparative Perspective.*
33. Max Weber, *From Max Weber: Essays in Sociology,* edited by Hans H. Gerth and C. Wright Mills (New York: Oxford University Press, 1946), pp. 120–128.
34. David K. Cohen, "Public Education: The Coming Decade," mimeographed (Center for Educational Policy Research, Harvard University, April 30, 1970), pp. 7–9.
35. Charles Hampden-Turner, *Radical Man* (Cambridge, Mass.: Schenkman, 1970), p. 364; for a similar analysis to those of Cohen and Hampden-Turner, see Richard Flacks, "Who Protests: The Social Bases of the Student Movement," in Julian Foster and Durward Long, eds., *Protest: Student Activism in America* (New York: Morrow, 1970), pp. 151–152.
36. S. N. Eisenstadt, *From Generation to Generation* (Glencoe: The Free Press, 1956), pp. 163–166.
37. David Easton and Robert D. Hess, "Youth and the Political System," in S. M. Lipset and Leo Lowenthal, eds., *Culture and Social Character* (New York: The Free Press, 1961), pp. 244–247.
38. S. N. Eisenstadt "Archetypal Patterns of Youth," *Daedalus* 91 (Winter 1962), pp. 28–46; and Eisenstadt, "Changing Patterns of Youth Protest in Different Stages of Development of Modern Societies," *Youth and Society* (December 1969), pp. 135–148; Talcott Parsons, *Social Structure and Personality* (New York: The Free Press, 1964), pp. 150–153; 172–180; Talcott Parsons, "Age and Sex in the Social Structure of the United States," *American Sociological Review* 7 (1942), pp. 604–616; Bennett M. Berger, "On the Youthfulness of Youth Cultures," *Social Research* 30 (Autumn 1963), pp. 319–342; Jack D. Douglas, *Youth in Turmoil* (Chevy Chase, Md.: National Institute for Mental Health, 1970), pp. 17–80.
39. César Graña, *Modernity and Its Discontents* (New York: Harper Torchbooks, 1964), pp. 73–74. For excellent as yet unpublished analyses of rebellious youth in Germany and France in the first half of the nineteenth century, see the papers by Anthony Esler of the History Department of William and Mary College: "Rebellious Younger Generations as a Force in Modern History," and "Youth in Revolt: The French Generation of 1830."
40. D.M.W. [Donald Mackenzie Wallace], "Nihilism," *Encyclopaedia Britannica,* 11th ed., vol. 19, pp. 686–688.
41. Ludwig Von Mises, *Bureaucracy* (New Haven: Yale University Press, 1944), pp. 94–95.
42. Donald G. MacRae, "The Culture of a Generation: Students and Others," in Walter Laqueur and George L. Mosse, eds., *Education and Social Structure in the Twentieth Century* (New York: Harper Torchbooks, 1967), pp. 7–8.
43. Eisenstadt, "Changing Patterns of Youth," p. 136.
44. Herbert Moller, "Youth as a Force in the Modern World," *Comparative Studies in Society and History* 10 (April 1968), p. 238.
45. Feuer, *Conflict of Generations,* p. 511.

46. Engels to Marx, April 25, 1870, as quoted in Shlomo Avineri, "Feuer on Marx and the Intellectuals," *Survey,* no. 62 (January 1967), p. 154.
47. D.M.W., "Nihilism," pp. 687–688.
48. Daniel Guerin, *Fascism and Big Business* (New York: Pioneer, 1939), pp. 47–50, 62–63; Karl Bracher, *Die Auflösung der Weimarer Republik* (Villingen, Schwarzwald: Ring Verlag, 1964), pp. 146–149; Hans Peter Bleuel and Ernst Klinnert, *Deutsche Studenten auf dem Weg ins Dritte Reich* (Gütersloh: Sigbert Mohn, 1967).
49. Letter from Max Weber to Herman Baumgarten, July 14, 1885, in Max Weber, *Jugendbriefe* (Tübingen: Mohr, 1930), p. 174, as presented in Reinhard Bendix and Guenther Roth, *Scholarship and Partisanship* (Berkeley: University of California Press, 1971).
50. Walter Laqueur, "Reflections on Youth Movements," *Commentary* 47 (June 1969), pp. 34, 35, 36.
51. See Klara Zetkin, *Reminiscences of Lenin* (London: Modern Books, Ltd., 1929), pp. 55–60.
52. "Report of Commission on Campus Unrest," *The Chronicle of Higher Education* 5 (October 5, 1970), pp. 7, 8–9. Other recent variants of this position may be found in Edgar Friedenberg, "Current Patterns of Generational Conflict," *Journal of Social Issues* 25, no. 2 (1969), pp. 21–38; Friedenberg, "The Generation Gap," *The Annals of the American Academy of Political and Social Science* 382 (March 1969), pp. 32–42; John Seeley, "Youth in Revolt," *Britannica Book of the Year.* (Chicago: University of Chicago Press, 1969), pp. 313–315.
53. Laqueur, "Reflections on Youth Movements," pp. 36–37.
54. For a summary of the many studies dealing with the politics of faculty, see S. M. Lipset, "The Politics of Academia," in David C. Nichols, ed., *Perspectives on Campus Tensions* (Washington, D.C.: American Council on Education, 1970), pp. 85–118. See chap. 6, pp. 197–235 of this book for an elaboration on some of the themes in that article.
55. Kenneth A. Feldman and Theodore M. Newcomb, *The Impact of College on Students,* vol. 1 (San Francisco: Jossey-Bass, 1969), especially pp. 8–10, 19–28, 30–32, 99–100, 101–102; and Feldman and Newcomb, vol. 2, pp. 19–36, 49–56, for summaries of results of the large number of separate studies.
56. For a detailed description of those processes that predicted a student revolt directed against faculty neglect of undergraduates, see Clark Kerr, *The Uses of the University* (Cambridge: Harvard University Press, 1964). A more recent analysis and denunciation of the consequences of these trends which focuses on the University of California as its prototype example is Robert Nisbet, *The Degradation of the Academic Dogma* (New York: Basic Books, 1971), esp. pp. 69–111.
57. See Christopher Jencks and David Riesman, *The Academic Revolution* (New York: Doubleday, 1968), especially pp. 236–250, 531–535.
58. Lawrence Veysey, *The Emergence of the American University* (Chicago: University of Chicago Press, 1965), pp. 295–299.
59. David Matza, "Position and Behavior Patterns of Youth," in Robert

E. L. Faris, ed., *Handbook of Modern Sociology* (Chicago: Rand McNally, 1964), p. 210.

60. Max Weber, *From Max Weber,* pp. 84–85.
61. Daniel and Gabriel Cohn-Bendit, *Obsolete Communism* (New York McGraw-Hill, 1968), p. 47. "The student, at least, in the modern system of higher education, still preserves a considerable degree of personal freedom, if he chooses to exercise it. . . . He can, if he so chooses, take extreme political positions without any personal danger; in general, he is not subjected to formal sanctions or even reprimands."

Chapter 2

1. For a discussion of youth backing for Wallace and racism see S. M. Lipset and Earl Raab, *The Politics of Unreason: Right-Wing Extremism in America 1790–1970* (New York: Harper & Row, 1970), pp. 367–367, 371–372, 394, 418, 513.
2. Hazel Erskine, "The Polls: Is War a Mistake?" *Public Opinion Quarterly* 34 (Spring 1970), p. 134.
3. Philip E. Converse and Howard Schuman, " 'Silent Majorities' and the Vietnam War," *The Scientific American* 222 (June 1970), p. 22. See also Milton J. Rosenberg, Sidney Verba and Philip E. Converse, *Vietnam and the Silent Majority* (New York: Harper & Row, 1970), pp. 65–73.
4. "The Student Revolution – A Special Report," *Gallup Opinion Index,* no. 66 (June 1970), p. 15.
5. "Campus '65," *Newsweek,* March 22, 1965, p. 53.
6. Samuel Lubell, "The People Speak" (news releases reporting on a study of American college students).
7. Gallup Poll release, July 1966.
8. "Results of a New Gallup Survey of College Students," *Gallup Opinion Index,* no. 55 (January 1970), p. 16.
9. "Special Survey of College Students," Gallup Poll release, June 29, 1968.
10. Samuel Lubell, "Where the New Left Dissidents Come From," Boston *Globe,* October 10, 1968.
11. Gallup Poll release, June 29, 1968.
12. "Profile of a Generation," multilithed report of a survey prepared for CBS News (New York: Daniel Yankelovich Associates, April 1969), p. 158.
13. "Aversion to Vietnam War Reaches High Among College Students," Harris Survey, June 30, 1969.
14. "Young Hawks on Decrease," National Gilbert Youth Poll (newspaper release through Newspaper Enterprise Association, December 12, 1969); "A Study of Youth and the Establishment," multilithed report (New York: Daniel Yankelovich Associates, December 1970), p. 76.
15. "Special Report on the Attitudes of College Students," *Gallup Opinion Index,* no. 48 (June 1969), p. 42.
16. "The New Mood on Campus," *Newsweek,* December 29, 1969, p. 42.
17. "Results of a New Gallup Survey of College Students," *Gallup Opinion Index,* no. 55 (January 1970), p. 16.

18. National Gilbert Youth Poll.
19. "*Playboy*'s Student Survey," *Playboy* 17 (September 1970), p. 182; report of the May 1970 Harris Survey, p. 49.
20. *Playboy* Student Poll news release, November 1965.
21. Report of May 1970 Harris Survey, p. 20.
22. Ibid., p. 35.
23. Ibid., p. 51.
24. Anthony Ripley, "Survey Finds Spring Campus Protests Were Greatest in History," New York *Times,* October 3, 1970.
25. Kenneth Gergen and Mary K. Gergen, "Vietnam and the Students: A Brief Summary of Research Results" (mimeographed report, Department of Psychology, Swarthmore College, June 1970), p. 2.
26. Report of May 1970 Harris Survey, p. 140. See table in chap. 3, p. 93.
27. Gergen and Gergen, "Vietnam and the Students," p. 1.
28. Samuel Lubell, "Unresolved Crises Cause Youth Dissension," Boston *Globe,* October 9, 1968.
29. *A Study of the Beliefs and Attitudes of Male College Seniors, Freshmen, and Alumni* (New York: Roper Research Associates, May 1969), p. 5.
30. Yankelovich, "Youth and the Establishment," p. 35.
31. Gilbert Marketing Group, February 1970 Omnibus Youth Survey, Table 22.
32. A report on this study was published as "Youth in College," *Fortune* 13 (June 1936), pp. 99–102, 156–162. The data reported here, however, are from the unpublished report prepared by the Roper Research Associates. I am indebted to Burns Roper for a copy of this report.
33. A preliminary journalistic account of the findings of the Rossi study may be found in Malcolm G. Scully, "Students Found Tolerant on Sex, Marijuana, Even 'the System,'" *The Chronicle of Higher Education* 5 (February 15, 1971), p. 6.
34. Lubell, "The People Speak," no. 6, pp. 1–3.
35. "A Study of the Inward Generation," special report published by *Psychology Today,* October 1969.
36. Yankelovich, "Profile."
37. James A. Foley and Robert K. Foley, *The College Scene* (New York: Cowles, 1969), p. 128.
38. Ibid., p. 132.
39. Ibid., p. 19.
40. Ibid., p. 36.
41. Yankelovich, "Youth and the Establishment," pp. 67–68, 73–74.
42. Gilbert Marketing Group, February 1970 Survey, Tables 31, 24, 25.
43. Scully, "Students Found Tolerant," p. 6.
44. "The Student Revolution," *Gallup Opinion Index,* no. 55, pp. 22, 23.
45. Report of May 1970 Harris Survey, p. 88.
46. Ibid., p. 112.
47. Ibid., p. 110.
48. Ibid., p. 114.
49. Ibid., p. 163. "*Playboy*'s Student Survey," p. 184.
50. Report of May 1970 Harris Survey, pp. 165, 167, 171.

51. For report on this survey see "Students Avoid Party Labels; Also Reject Radical Politics," Gallup Poll release, Sunday, February 14, 1971; "The U.S. Campus Mood, '71: A Newsweek Poll," *Newsweek,* February 22, 1971, p. 61.
52. Louis Harris and Associates, *Youth Attitudes for* Life *Magazine Year End Issue* (New York: November 1970) , passim.
53. The College Poll surveys are published weekly in various Sunday newspapers. Those cited here are from releases of January 10 and 24, April 14, and May 23, 1971. The Campus Poll reports are carried in newspapers across the country on Thursdays. Those reported here are from the releases of November 12, 1970, November 26, 1970, January 14, 1971, and March 11, 1971.
54. See Philippe Bénéton and Jean Touchard, "Les Interprétations de la Crise de Mai-Juin 1968," *Revue Française de Science Politique* 22 (June 1970) , pp. 520, 525, for summary of and references to various French surveys. See also F. Netzler and J. La Brousse, *Diverses Opinions et Attitudes des Etudiants de la Faculté des Lettres de Nanterre* (Paris: Institut Français d'Opinion Publique, June 1970) , p. 20.
55. Enzo Montillo, "Italy: The Youth of the Opinion Surveys," *SIPE* [International Student Press Service], 2 (July 1, 1970) , pp. 13–14.
56. Michiya Shimbori, "The Sociology of a Student Movement — A Japanese Case Study," in Seymour M. Lipset and Philip G. Altbach, eds., *Students in Revolt* (Boston: Houghton Mifflin, 1969) , p. 309, n. 12.
57. See report on nineteenth-century student conflicts in chap. 4; Veysey's analysis is discussed on page 135.
58. Bryan Wilson, *The Youth Culture and the Universities* (London: Faber and Faber, 1970) , p. 227.
59. Robert H. Somers, "The Mainsprings of the Rebellion: A Survey of Berkeley Students in November, 1964," in S. M. Lipset and Sheldon S. Wolin, eds., *The Berkeley Student Revolt* (Garden City: Doubleday, Anchor Books, 1965) , pp. 549–550.
60. Kathleen Gales, "A Campus Revolution," *British Journal of Sociology* 17, (March 1966) , p. 14.
61. Glen Lyonns, "The Police Car Demonstration: A Survey of Participants," in Lipset and Wolin, *The Berkeley Student Revolt,* pp. 525–527.
62. Robert H. Somers, "The Berkeley Campus in the Twilight of the Free Speech Movement: Hope or Futility?" in James McEvoy and Abraham Miller, eds., *Black Power and Student Rebellion* (Belmont, Calif.: Wadsworth, 1969) , p. 427.
63. Gergen and Gergen, "Vietnam and the Students," p. 1.
64. Roper Research Associates, *Beliefs and Attitudes,* p. 52.
65. Daniel Yankelovich, "The Generation Gap — A Misleading Half-Truth" (New York, Spring 1970) , pp. 10–11, and Table 4.
66. Ibid., Table 4.
67. "The New Mood on Campus," *Newsweek,* December 29, 1969, p. 43.
68. For the results of the 1969 Carnegie Survey, see Philip W. Semas, "Students 'Satisfied' with Education, Most of Them and Teachers Agree," *The Chronicle of Higher Education* 5 (January 18, 1971) , p. 1.

69. Harris and Associates, *Youth Attitudes,* p. 53.
70. Gallup Poll release on student survey, May 25, 1969. Yankelovich, "The Generation Gap."
71. Marshall W. Meyer, "Harvard Students in the Midst of Crisis," mimeographed (New York State School of Industrial Relations and Department of Sociology, Cornell University, 1970), p. 43, Table 8.
72. Robert B. Smith, "Campus Protest and the Vietnam War" mimeographed (Department of Sociology, University of California, Santa Barbara, 1970), pp. 1, 46–47; for a summary of evidence from various studies at different institutions which comes to similar conclusions, see Riley Dunlap, "A Comment on 'Multiversity, University Size, University Quality, and Student Protest: An Empirical Study,'" *American Sociological Review* 35 (June 1970), pp. 525–528.
73. Richard Peterson, *The Scope of Organized Student Protest in 1967–68* (Princeton: Educational Testing Service, 1968), pp. 10–11; Alan E. Bayer and Alexander W. Astin, *Campus Disruption During 1968–1969* (Washington, D.C.: Office of Research, American Council on Education, ACE Research Reports, August 1969), pp. 22–23; Urban Research Corporation, *Student Protests 1969: Summary* (Chicago: 1970), pp. 4, 6–8; Wayne King, "Campus Protest Reported on Rise," New York *Times,* March 29, 1970; Garth Buchanan and Joan Brackett, *Summary Results of the Survey for the President's Commission on Campus Unrest* (Washington, D.C.: The Urban Institute, September 1970), pp. 36, 43.
74. See chap. 1, n. 61.
75. Gilbert Marketing Group, Tables 20A and 27A.
76. Kenneth Keniston, "Heads and Seekers," *The American Scholar* 38 (Winter 1968–69), pp. 97–112.
77. Roper Research Associates, *Beliefs and Attitudes,* p. 198.
78. "The New Mood on Campus," *Newsweek,* December 29, 1969, p. 44.
79. Foley and Foley, *The College Scene,* p. 66.
80. Yankelovich, "A Study of Youth," p. 65.
81. *"Playboy's* Student Survey," p. 236.
82. "Twice as Many College Students Today as in 1969 Admit They Have Tried Marijuana," Gallup Poll release, Sunday, January 17, 1971.
83. Harris and Associates, *Youth Attitudes,* p. 58.
84. "Special Report on the Attitudes of College Students," *Gallup Opinion Index,* no. 48, p. 26; Gallup Poll release, February 26, 1971.
85. Yankelovich, *"Profile,"* pp. 74, 77.
86. Ibid., p. 151.
87. "Student Protests Focus on Domestic Injustices," Boston Sunday *Globe,* January 24, 1971.
88. See, for example, Charles A. Krause, "Campaign Help Unexpected. Students Stun Conservatives," Washington *Post,* October 25, 1970, p. 1; Thomas Oliphant, "Students in Politics: Fewer Than Expected," Boston Sunday *Globe,* October 25, 1970, p. 1; Nina Housman, "Adam Smith and John Wayne: Gurus of the New Student Right," *New America,* January 27, 1971, p. 8; Stephen Schlesinger, "The Buckley Kids," *New York,* November 2, 1970, pp. 8, 10.

89. Nicholas Bagnall and Duff Hart-Davis, "What Happened to the Oxbridge Revolution? Student Radicals Run Out of Steam," (London) *Sunday Telegraph,* March 14, 1971, p. 19; Ellen Lentz, "Student Disorder Ebbs in Germany," *New York Times,* April 11, 1971, p. 19; Masuru Ogawa, "Student-Gangsters," *Japan Times Weekly,* April 3, 1971, p. 3; Raymond Boudon, "Sources of Student Protest in France," *The Annals of the American Academy of Political and Social Science* 395 (May 1971), pp. 148–149; Michiya Shimbori, "Student Radicals in Japan," in ibid., pp. 154–156.
90. Milton Mankoff and Richard Flacks, "The Changing Social Base of the American Student Movement," *The Annals of the American Academy of Political and Social Science* 395 (May 1971), p. 62. n. 10.
91. Kenneth Keniston, "The Chilling Shame of Violence," Boston *Globe,* June 7, 1971, p. 10.
92. The Rossi survey taken in the spring of 1970 found that 29 percent of the female freshmen and 36 percent of the juniors "said they had had sexual intercourse." Scully, "Students Found Tolerant," p. 6.

Chapter 3

1. Richard Flacks, "The Liberated Generation: An Explanation of the Roots of Student Protest," *Journal of Social Issues* 23, no. 3 (1967), pp. 66, 68. Kenneth Keniston, "Notes on Young Radicals," *Change* 1 (November–December, 1969), p. 29. For a summary of various studies bearing on this point, see also Richard G. Braungart, "Family Status, Socialization and Student Politics: A Multivariate Analysis" (Ph.D. thesis, Department of Sociology, Pennsylvania State University, 1969), p. 61; Kenneth Keniston, "The Fire Outside," *The Journal* 9 (September–October 1970), pp. 9–10.
2. See Richard Flacks, "Who Protests: The Social Bases of the Student Movement," in Julian Foster and Durwood Long, eds., *Protest: Student Activism in America* (New York: Morrow, 1970), pp. 147–152; and S. M. Lipset, *Political Man* (New York: Doubleday, 1960), pp. 109–110, 285–294. On the Jewish contribution to activism, see Nathan Glazer, "The New Left and the Jews," *The Jewish Journal of Sociology* 11 (December 1969), pp. 122, 127–131; Flacks, "The Liberated Generation," p. 65; Nathan Glazer, "The Jewish Role in Student Activism," *Fortune* 79 (January 1969), pp. 112–113, 126–129; Lipset, *Revolution and Counterrevolution,* rev. ed. (New York: Doubleday, Anchor Books, 1970), pp. 375–400.
3. Michiya Shimbori, "Zengakuren: A Japanese Case Study of a Student Movement," *Sociology of Education* 37 (Spring 1964), pp. 232–233; C. J. Lammers, "Student Unionism in the Netherlands," mimeographed (Leyden: Institute of Sociology, University of Leyden, 1970), pp. 25–26, 31; Walter Korp, "Vansterstudenterna: Barn ar bongare el ler proletaria at," Sociologiska Forskning 4 (1969), pp. 286–287, 292–293; Ted Goertzel, "Political Attitudes of Brazilian Youth" (paper presented at session on politics of students and young workers, Seventh World Congress of Sociology, Varna, Bulgaria, September 1970), p. 3; Klaus R. Allerbeck, "Alternative Explanations of Participation in Student Move-

ments" (paper prepared for the Seventh World Congress of the International Political Science Association, Munich, September 1970), pp. 13–14; Tessa Blackstone, Kathleen Gales, Roger Hadley and Wyn Lewis, *Students in Conflict* (London: Weidenfeld and Nicolson, 1970), p. 200.

4. Allerbeck, "Alternative Explanations," p. 14.
5. Reports on the membership of the YAF may be found in David L. Westby and Richard G. Braungart, "Class and Politics in the Family Backgrounds of Student Political Activists," *American Sociological Review* 31 (October 1966), pp. 690–692; Braungart, "Family Status," p. 142; David L. Westby and Richard G. Braungart, "The Alienation of Generations and Status Politics: Alternative Explanations of Student Political Activism," in Roberta S. Sigel, ed., *Learning About Politics* (New York: Random House, 1970), pp. 476–488; David G. Jansen, Bob B. Winborn and William D. Martinson, "Characteristics Associated with Campus Social-Political Action Leadership," *Journal of Counseling Psychology* 15 (November 1968), pp. 552–562.
6. Bruno Bettelheim, "The Anatomy of Academic Discontent," *Change* 1 (May–June 1969), pp. 23–24.
7. Lipset, *Revolution and Counterrevolution,* pp. 310–342; Lipset, "The Politics of Academia," in David C. Nichols, ed., *Perspectives on Campus Tensions* (Washington, D.C.: American Council on Education, 1970), pp. 85–118; see also chap. 6 of this book.
8. Roger M. Kahn and William J. Bowers, "The Social Context of the Rank-and-File Student Activist: A Test of Four Hypotheses," *Sociology of Education* 43 (Winter 1970), pp. 39, 45–47, 48–49; Braungart, "Family Status," pp. 61–62; Flacks, "The Liberated Generation," pp. 69–70; Paul Heist, "Intellect and Commitment: the Faces of Discontent," in O. W. Knorr and W. J. Minter, eds., *Order and Freedom on Campus* (Boulder, Colo.: Western Interstate Commission for Higher Education, 1965), pp. 61–69.
9. For a summary of the literature see Kenneth A. Feldman and Theodore M. Newcomb, *The Impact of College on Students,* 1 (San Francisco: Jossey-Bass, 1969), p. 161; see also Kahn and Bowers, "Social Context," pp. 39, 46–48.
10. Selvin Hanan and Warren Hagstrom, "Determinants of Support for Civil Liberties," in S. M. Lipset and Sheldon S. Wolin, eds., *The Berkeley Student Revolt* (New York: Doubleday, Anchor Books, 1965), p. 513.
11. Morris Rosenberg, *Occupations and Values* (Glencoe: The Free Press, 1957), pp. 19–22; see also James A. Davis, *Undergraduate Career Patterns* (Chicago: Aldine, 1965), pp. 52–53.
12. Westby and Braungart, "Class and Politics," pp. 690–692.
13. Braungart, "Family Status," p. 142.
14. Milton Mankoff and Richard Flacks, "The Changing Social Base of the American Student Movement: Its Meaning and Implications," *The Annals of the American Academy of Political and Social Science,* May 1971; for an earlier presentation of a similar thesis with more limited data, see A. Riley Dunlap, "Radical and Conservative Student Activists: A Com-

parison of Family Backgrounds," *Pacific Sociological Review* 13 (Summer 1970), pp. 178–179.

15. For more detailed discussion of and evidence for this thesis, see S. M. Lipset, *Agrarian Socialism,* rev. ed. (Garden City: Doubleday, Anchor Books, 1968), pp. 201–207, 214–217, 221–242; and Lipset, *Political Man,* pp. 116–121.
16. For example, see "Profile of a Generation" multilithed report of a survey prepared for CBS News (New York: Daniel Yankelovich Associates, April 1969).
17. Charles V. Hamilton, "Minority Groups," in Robert H. Connery, ed., *The Corporation and the Campus,* Proceedings of the Academy of Political Sciences, vol. 30, no. 1, pp. 20–21.
18. Anthony M. and Amy W. Orum, "The Class and Status Bases of Negro Student Protest," *Social Science Quarterly* 49 (December 1968), p. 528, n. 30, and references to other works there included.
19. Mary K. and Kenneth J. Gergen, "How the War Affects the Campuses," *Change* 3 (January–February 1971), p. 70.
20. Report of Harris Survey, May 20–28, 1970, pp. 155–156.
21. Yankelovich, "Profile," pp. 159–172 and passim.
22. See Report of Harris Survey, and Yankelovich, "Profile."
23. For a summary of the evidence, see Lipset, "The Politics of Academia."
24. Alexander W. Astin, "Personal and Environmental Determinants of Student Activism," *Measurement and Evaluation in Guidance* 1 (Fall 1968), pp. 161–162; Alan E. Bayer and Alexander W. Astin, "Violence and Disruption in the U.S. Campus, 1968–1969," *Educational Record* 50 (Fall 1969), p. 341. Another study of the characteristics of schools which had protests in 1969 indicated that larger ones "with student bodies that had high scholastic aptitudes were more likely to face protests than other schools." Urban Research Corporation, *Student Protests 1969: Summary* (Chicago: 1970), pp. 14, 13.
25. Bayer and Astin, "Violence and Disruption," p. 341; see also Urban Research Corporation *Student Protests 1969,* p. 13; Joseph W. Scott and Mohamed El-Assal, "Multiversity, University Size, University Quality and Student Protest: An Empirical Study," *American Sociological Review* 34 (October 1969), pp. 702–709.
26. Harold Hodgkinson, "Student Protest — An Institutional and National Profile," *The Record* 71 (May 1970), p. 537.
27. Ibid., pp. 540–542, 547–548.
28. Anthony Ripley, "Survey Finds Spring Campus Protests Were Greatest in History," New York *Times,* October 3, 1970, p. 35; Garth Buchanan and Joan Brackett, *Summary Results of the Survey for the President's Commission on Campus Unrest* (Washington, D.C.: The Urban Institute, 1970), pp. 18–21.
29. Hodgkinson, "Student Protest," pp. 549–550.
30. Quotations are from Kenneth Keniston and Michael Lerner, "Campus Characteristics and Campus Unrest," *The Annals of the American Academy of Political and Social Science* 395 (May 1971), pp. 49, 52.

31. See George R. Stewart, *The Year of the Oath* (Garden City: Doubleday, 1950) ; David P. Gardner, *The California Oath Controversy* (Berkeley: University of California Press, 1967) ; S. M. Lipset, "Opinion Formation in a Crisis Situation," *Public Opinion Quarterly* (Spring 1953) , pp. 20–46.
32. Glen Lyonns, "The Police Car Demonstration: A Survey of Participants," in Lipset and Wolin, *The Berkeley Student Revolt,* p. 522.
33. Jürgen Habermas, *Toward a Rational Society: Student Protest, Science, and Politics* (Boston: Beacon, 1970) , p. 20.
34. Alexander W. Astin and Alan E. Bayer, "Antecedents and Consequents of Disruptive Campus Protests," *Measurement and Evaluation in Guidance* 4 (April 1971) , pp. 22–24; and Astin, "New Evidence on Campus Unrest," *Educational Record* 52 (Winter 1971) , pp. 44–46.
35. Peter M. Blau and Ellen L. Slaughter, "Institutional Conditions and Student Demonstrations" (mimeographed paper, Department of Sociology, Columbia University, 1970) .
36. Keniston, "Notes on Young Radicals," pp. 31–32; R. William Cowdry and Kenneth Keniston, "The War and Military Obligation: Attitudes, Actions and Their Consistency" (mimeographed paper, Department of Psychiatry, Yale University, 1969) , pp. 22, 26–27, 30; Jeanne H. Block, Norma Haan and M. Brewster Smith, "Socialization Correlates of Student Activism," *Journal of Social Issues* 25, no. 4 (1969) , pp. 164–165. The latter study differentiates between "activists" and "dissenters."
37. Lyonns, "The Police Car Demonstration," in Lipset and Wolin, *The Berkeley Student Revolt,* p. 521.
38. Flacks, "The Liberated Generation"; Braungart, "Family Status."
39. Lamar E. Thomas, "Family Congruence in Political Orientations of Politically Active Parents and Their College-Age Children (Ph.D. thesis, Committee on Human Development, University of Chicago, 1968) , p. 46. Liberal parents were much more "cause-oriented" than conservatives. Whether the children of the former were activist or not correlated strongly with degree of cause orientation rather than child-rearing practices.
40. Block et al., "Socialization Correlates," pp. 163–164 and Table 7. It is not clear from the report whether the investigators inquired as to respondents' religion or that of their parents. Left-oriented people tend to say "none" for their own religion. Hence, unless family religious background is probed, many of the "none" turn out to in fact come from Jewish backgrounds.
41. Keniston, "Notes on Young Radicals," p. 31.
42. David Matza, "Subterranean Traditions of Youth," *Annals of the American Academy of Political and Social Science* 338 (November 1961) , p. 106; David Matza, "Position and Behavior Patterns of Youth," in Robert E. L. Faris, ed., *Handbook of Modern Sociology* (Chicago: Rand McNally, 1964) , pp. 209–214.
43. Kenneth Keniston, "The Sources of Student Dissent," *Journal of Social Issues* 23, no. 3 (1967) , pp. 110–115; Kenneth Keniston, "The Fire Outside," *The Journal* 9 (September–October 1970) , pp. 9–10.

44. Alvin W. Gouldner, *The Coming Crisis of Western Sociology* (New York: Basic Books, 1970), p. 78.
45. Keniston, "Notes on Young Radicals," p. 32.
46. Block et al., pp. 146–147, 163–165.
47. Richard Blum, "Epilogue: Students and Drugs," in Richard Blum and Associates, *Students and Drugs: Drugs II* (San Francisco: Jossey-Bass, 1969), p. 366.
48. Blum, "Prologue: Students and Drugs," ibid., p. 8.
49. James W. Trent and Judith L. Craise, "Commitment and Conformity in the American College," *Journal of Social Issues* 23 (1967), p. 39; a more recent work of this sort is Robert Liebert, *Radical and Militant Youth* (New York: Praeger, 1971).
50. S. M. Lipset and Philip G. Altbach, "Student Politics and Higher Education in the United States," *Comparative Education Review* 10 (June 1966), pp. 320–349. The review of the literature is on pages 331–334. This article was reprinted and updated in S. M. Lipset, *Student Politics* (New York: Basic Books, 1967); see pp. 222–224. See also Braungart, "Family Status," pp. 331–332; and Larry C. Kerpelman, "Student Political Activism and Ideology: Comparative Characteristics of Activists and Non-activists," *Journal of Counseling Psychology* 16 (1969), pp. 8–13.
51. Larry C. Kerpelman, *Student Activism and Ideology in Higher Education Institutions* (Washington, D.C.: Bureau of Research, Office of Research, U.S. Department of Health, Education, and Welfare, March 1970), pp. xv, 79, 85.
52. Cowdry and Keniston, "The War and Military Obligation," pp. 21–23.
53. Roy E. Miller and David H. Everson, "Personality and Ideology: The Case of Student Power" (paper presented at the Midwest Political Science Association, April 30–May 2, 1970, Public Affairs Research Bureau and Department of Government, Southern Illinois University), p. 36.
54. Kerpelman, *Student Activism and Ideology*, pp. 5–6, 42, 80; for a similar point, see Lipset and Altbach, "Student Politics and Higher Education," pp. 223–224; for recent data on this, see Block et al., "Socialization Correlates," p. 31.
55. Kerpelman, *Student Activism and Ideology*, p. 80; see also Lipset and Altbach, "Student Politics and Higher Education," p. 250, n. 61.
56. Enunciated as a possibility in S. M. Lipset, "The Activists: A Profile," in Daniel Bell and Irving Kristol, eds., *Confrontation: The Student Rebellion and the Universities* (New York: Basic Books, 1969), p. 56.
57. Miller and Everson, "Personality and Ideology," pp. 35, 38–39.
58. Blum, "Epilogue: Students and Drugs," p. 377.
59. Dennis H. Wrong, "The Case of the *New York Review*," *Commentary* 50 (November 1970), pp. 62–63. The Keniston review of the book by Kelman was published in the *New York Review of Books*, September 24, 1970.
60. Glaucio A. D. Soares, "The Active Few: Student Ideology and Participation in Developing Countries," in S. M. Lipset, ed., *Student Politics* (New York: Basic Books, 1967), pp. 124–147.

61. Paul Goodman, "The New Reformation," *New York Times Magazine,* September 14, 1969, pp. 33, 143, 144. Similar criticisms have been advanced by Norman Birnbaum, the Amherst sociologist, who was founding editor of the *New Left Review* in London, and who is both an identified Marxist scholar and a disciple of C. Wright Mills.

    "The ahistoricism and pragmatism of American thought has found a parody in the disdain for political thinking exhibited by most of the militants of the American student left. An unreflected doctrine of immediacy, an explicit fear of academicism (and an implicit incapacity, engendered by a defective university system, for sustained thought), a considerable ignorance of nearly everything and especially of the history of socialism, combine in the jargon, the slogans, and the bewilderment of the *avant-garde* of the new American left." Norman Birnbaum and Marjorie Childers, "The American Student Movement," Julian Nagel, ed., *Student Power* (London: Merlin, 1969), p. 139.
62. "Rightists Launch Offensive," *The Guardian* 21 (February 8, 1969), p. 8.
63. *The Campaigner* 1 (September 1968), p. 9.
64. C. LaRouche and L. Marcus, "The New Left, Local Control and Fascism," *The Campaigner* 1 (September 1968), pp. 10–33, passim.
65. Irving Louis Horowitz, *The Struggle Is the Message* (Berkeley: The Glendessary Press, 1970), pp. 84–85, 97, 101. (Emphasis mine. S.M.L.)
66. Peter L. Berger, "Between System and Horde," in Peter L. Berger and Richard J. Neuhaus, *Movement and Revolution* (New York: Doubleday, Anchor Books, 1970), pp. 44–45.
67. Daniel Guerin, *Fascism and Big Business* (New York: Pioneer, 1939), pp. 47–50, 62–63; Guido Martinotti, "The Positive Marginality: Notes on Italian Students in Periods of Political Mobilization," in Lipset and Altbach, *Students in Revolt,* pp. 173–175; Karl Bracher, *Die Auflösung der Weimarer Republik* (Villingen, Schwarzwald: Ring Verlag, 1964), pp. 146–149; Peter Gay, *Weimar Culture* (New York: Harper & Row, 1968), pp. 139–140; Fritz K. Ringer, *The Decline of the German Mandarin* (Cambridge: Harvard University Press, 1969), pp. 250–251; John Orr, "The Radical Right," in Julian Nagel, *Student Power,* pp. 73–90; Lewis Feuer, *The Conflict of Generations* (New York: Basic Books, 1969), pp. 284–291.
68. Randolph S. Bourne, *Youth and Life* (Boston: Houghton Mifflin, 1913), pp. 23, 266, 304, 305.
69. [Aristotle,] *Rhetoric,* in *The Basic Works of Aristotle,* edited by Richard McKeon (New York: Random House, 1941), p. 1404. Aristotle goes on, of course, to say equally unflattering things about the character of the "Elderly," who err on the side of caution, small-mindedness, cynicism, concern for the useful rather than the noble, and so forth. Typically, the best are those in the middle, "Men in their Prime," who tend to have the "right amount" of each relevant trait. The Prime age for "the mind [is] about forty-nine," pp. 1405–1406.
70. See S. M. Lipset and Earl Raab, *The Politics of Unreason: Right-*

Wing Extremism in the United States 1790–1970 (New York: Harper & Row, 1970), chaps. 1, 11, and 12, for this discussion.

71. "Poll Finds Voters Aged 18 to 21 Favor Democrats and Kennedy," New York *Times,* April 18, 1971, p. 37.
72. This discussion of the youth support for Wallace and the ideology of the National Youth Alliance is taken from Lipset and Raab, *The Politics of Unreason,* pp. 418–419, 513–514.
73. "Rightists Launch Offensive," p. 8.
74. Dennis C. McMahon, "The National Youth Alliance," *The American Mercury* 105 (Spring 1969), p. 63.
75. National Youth Alliance leaflet headed "Lost and Alone."
76. Ralph Blumenthal, "Infusion of Youth Strengthens Radical Rightist Party in West Germany," New York *Times,* March 2, 1969.
77. Boris Kidel, "German Rightists Shift to Disruption," Boston Sunday *Globe,* December 27, 1970.
78. Noël-Jean Bergeroux, "Shot in the Right Arm," *Le Monde — Weekly Selection,* March 25, 1970, p. 2.
79. Cosimo Di Fazio, "Italy: The Menace of the Extremist Groups of the Right," *SIPE* 3 (March 10, 1971), pp. 3–6.

Chapter 4

1. S. M. Lipset, "University Students and Politics in Underdeveloped Countries," in S. M. Lipset, ed., *Student Politics* (New York: Basic Books, 1967), pp. 3–53; "Introduction: Students and Politics in Comparative Perspective," and "The Possible Effects of Student Activism on International Politics," in S. M. Lipset and Philip G. Altbach, eds., *Students in Revolt* (Boston: Houghton Mifflin, 1969), pp. xv–xxiv, 495–521.
2. Richard Holfstadter, *Academic Freedom in the Age of the College* (New York: Columbia University Press, 1961), p. 206. See also Samuel Eliot Morison, *Three Centuries of Harvard* (Cambridge: Harvard University Press, 1936), pp. 132–148. A recent historian of American education suggests that from the early nineteenth century on, students through their protest activities and extracurricular institutional innovations have been the "most creative and imaginative force in the shaping of the American college and university" (Frederick Rudolph, "Neglect of Students As a Historical Tradition," in Lawrence E. Dennis and Joseph F. Kaufman, eds., *The College and the Student* [Washington: American Council on Education, 1966], p. 47; see also pp. 47–58).
3. Morison, *Three Centuries of Harvard,* p. 138.
4. W. H. Cowley, unpublished "Notes on Universities," chap. 11, "Student Participation," pp. 11–25.
5. Granville Stanley Hall, *Adolescence: Its Psychology* (New York: D. Appleton, 1904), p. 138.
6. Ibid.
7. Morison, *Three Centuries of Harvard,* p. 185; Frederick Rudolph, *The American College and University: A History* (New York: Knopf, 1962), p. 38.

8. Harry P. Bowes, "University and College Student Rebellion in Retrospect and Some Sociological Implications" (Ed.D. thesis, School of Education, University of Colorado, 1964), p. 96; see also Charles A. Wagner, *Harvard: Four Centuries of Freedom* (New York: Dutton, 1950), p. 87.
9. Morison, *Three Centuries of Harvard,* pp. 252–253.
10. Bowes, "Rebellion in Retrospect."
11. Cowley, "Notes on Universities," chap. 11, p. 15.
12. Bowes, "Rebellion in Retrospect," pp. 75–76.
13. Thomas Jefferson, *Writings* (Washington: Thomas Jefferson Memorial Association, 1890), vol. 11, p. 455.
14. Morison, *Three Centuries of Harvard,* pp. 179–180.
15. Bowes, "Rebellion in Retrospect," p. 84; see also Rudolph, *The American College,* pp. 96–97; and Oscar and Mary Handlin, *The American College and American Culture* (New York: McGraw-Hill, 1970), pp. 37–38.
16. Bowes, "Rebellion in Retrospect," p. 76; T. J. Wertenbaker, *Princeton, 1846–1896* (Princeton: Princeton University Press, 1946), p. 136.
17. E. Earnest, *Academic Procession: An Informal History of the American College 1636 to 1953* (Indianapolis: Bobbs-Merrill, 1953), p. 31; Hofstadter, *Academic Freedom,* pp. 241–242.
18. Sister M. Kennedy, "The Changing Academic Characteristics of the Nineteenth Century American College Teacher" (Ph.D. thesis, Department of Education, St. Louis University, 1961), p. 52.
19. Ibid., p. 72; see also John Brubacher and Willis Rudy, *Higher Education in Transition* (New York: Harper, 1958), p. 53.
20. Morison, *Three Centuries of Harvard,* pp. 211–212.
21. John R. Bodo, *The Protestant Clergy and Public Issues: 1812–1848* (Princeton: Princeton University Press, 1954), pp. 39–43; Anson P. Stokes, *Church and State in the United States* (New York: Harper, 1950) vol. 2, pp. 12–20.
22. Richard M. Johnson, "Sunday Observance and the Mail," reprinted in George E. Probst, ed., *The Happy Republic* (New York: Harper Torchbooks, 1962); pp. 250–254.
23. S. M. Lipset and Earl Raab, *The Politics of Unreason: Right-Wing Extremism in America, 1790–1970* (New York: Harper & Row, 1970), chap. 2.
24. Bowes, "Rebellion in Retrospect," pp. 104–105, 108.
25. Wagner, *Harvard,* p. 87.
26. Bowes, "Rebellion in Retrospect," pp. 115–116.
27. A Graduate of '69 [Lyman H. Bagg], *Four Years at Yale* (New Haven: Charles C. Chatfield, 1871), p. 516.
28. Handlin and Handlin, *American College,* pp. 40–41.
29. C. A. Bristed, *Five Years in an English University* (New York: G. P. R. Putnam, 1874), p. 61.
30. Howard H. Peckham, *The Making of the University of Michigan: 1817–1967* (Ann Arbor: University of Michigan Press, 1967), p. 46.
31. Russel Nye, *Fettered Freedom: Civil Liberties and the Slavery Controversy* (East Lansing: Michigan State University Press, 1949), p. 93; Hofstadter,

Academic Freedom, pp. 259–261; Earnest, *Academic Procession,* pp. 66–68, 85, 90.

32. Cowley, "Notes on Universities," chap. 11, p. 26.
33. Bowes, "Rebellion in Retrospect," p. 126.
34. Laurence R. Veysey, *The Emergence of the American University* (Chicago: University of Chicago Press, 1965) , pp. 295, 299.
35. Laurence R. Veysey, "The Emergence of the University" (Ph.D. thesis, Department of History, University of California, Berkeley, 1962) , p. 101.
36. Erik H. Erikson, *Identity: Youth and Crisis* (New York: Norton, 1968) , pp. 237–240, 258.
37. Veysey, "Emergence of the University," pp. 101–103.
38. Walter Laqueur, *Young Germany* (New York: Basic Books, 1962) .
39. George E. Peterson, *The New England College in the Age of the University* (Amherst: Amherst College Press, 1964) , p. 146.
40. *The Autobiography of Lincoln Steffens* (New York: Harcourt, Brace, 1931) , pp. 117–118. See also Lewis S. Feuer, *The Conflict of Generations* (New York: Basic Books, 1969) , pp. 327, 332; and Peterson, *The New England College,* pp. 113–148.
41. Feuer, *Conflict of Generations,* p. 332.
42. Veysey, "Emergence of the University," p. 279. Although third-party groups were to attain more support in 1912 and subsequent years than they did earlier, the majority of students seemingly continued to vote Republican, following family patterns, until 1932. For Harvard student preferences in 1912, see "University Notes," *Harvard Graduates' Magazine* 21 (December 1912) , p. 364; for 1908, see "Student Life," ibid. 16 (June 1908) , p. 705: and in earlier years, Francis G. Caffey, "Harvard's Political Preferences Since 1860," ibid. 1 (April 1893) , pp. 407–415.
43. Merle Curti and Vernon Carstensen, *The University of Wisconsin: 1848–1925* (Madison: University of Wisconsin Press, 1949) , pp. 412–418.
44. Winton U. Solberg, *The University of Illinois 1867–1894* (Urbana: University of Illinois Press, 1968) , pp. 207–213, 319–326.
45. Ibid., p. 211.
46. Ibid., p. 318.
47. Ibid., p. 275.
48. Feuer, *The Conflict of Generations,* p. 341.
49. Peterson, *The New England College,* pp. 139–140.
50. Walter P. Metzger, *Academic Freedom in the Age of the University* (New York: Columbia University Press, 1961) , p. 36.
51. Peckham, *The Making of the University of Michigan,* p. 62.
52. "College Discipline," *The Critic* 1 (July 30, 1881) , p. 204. Yet thirty years later, an analyst of the American university scene who contended as of 1909 that "almost every educator, [who] if asked what was the main fault of our large colleges, would . . . [reply] that it was the loss of personal relationship between instructor and student," also argued that the "less personal attention they [students] get from professors the better some of them like it." (Edwin E. Slosson, *Great American Universities* [New York: Macmillan, 1910], pp. 76, 386) .

53. Hugo Münsterberg, "Productive Scholarship in America," *The Atlantic Monthly* 87 (May 1901), p. 624.
54. G. S. Hall, "Research: The Vital Spirit of Teaching," *The Forum* 27 (July 1894), p. 570.
55. Münsterberg, "Scholarship in America," p. 624.
56. Hall, "Research," p. 569.
57. Peterson, *The New England College*, pp. 145–146.
58. N. S. Shaler, "The Problem of Discipline in Higher Education," *The Atlantic Monthly* 54 (July 1889), p. 35.
59. Francis Wayland and H. L. Wayland, *A Memoir of the Life and Labors of Francis Wayland* (New York: Sheldon and Co., 1867), vol. 1, p. 264. A Graduate of '69 assumes in his book on life at Yale "that no peeler can lawfully enter . . . the college yard," *Four Years at Yale*, p. 516.
60. S. C. Bartlett, "College Disturbances," *The Forum* 4 (December 1887), p. 427.
61. "Professor Wilson's Address," *Johns Hopkins University Celebration of the Twenty-Fifth Anniversary* (Baltimore: The Johns Hopkins Press, 1902), pp. 39, 41; see also comments to the same effect by President Dabney of the University of Tennessee, and William Rainey Harper of the University of Chicago, ibid., pp. 54, 59–60.
62. See summary and excerpts of an article by Charles Ramsey in *The Educational Review* for January 1895, in "Needed Reforms in College Teaching," *The Review of Reviews* 11 (February 1895), p. 21.
63. "The Decline of Teaching," *The Nation* 70 (March 8, 1900), p. 18; "For Better Teaching and Better Research," *The World's Work* 2 (July 1901), p. 913.
64. B. P., "College Professors and the Public," *The Atlantic Monthly* 89 (March 1902), p. 284.
65. Abraham Flexner, "The Problems of College Pedagogy," *The Atlantic Monthly* 103 (June 1909), p. 844.
66. E. E. Slosson, *Great American Universities* (New York: Macmillan, 1910), pp. 17–18.
67. B. P., "College Professors," pp. 284–285.
68. Ibid., p. 286.
69. Metzger, *Academic Freedom*, pp. 43–44; for a detailed analytic account of the shift see Veysey, *Emergence of the University*, pp. 121–179.
70. Alexander Francis, *Americans: An Impression* (London: Andrew Melrose, 1909), pp. 228–229.
71. Randolph S. Bourne, *Youth and Life* (Boston: Houghton Mifflin, 1913), pp. 48, 295, 325–326.
72. David A. Shannon, *The Socialist Party of America* (Chicago: Quadrangle, 1967), pp. 55–56; Ira Kipnis, *The American Socialist Movement 1897–1912* (New York: Columbia University Press, 1952), pp. 259–260.
73. Upton Sinclair, *The Goose-Step* (Pasadena: "The Author," 1923), p. 460.
74. John Reed, "The Harvard Renaissance," *The Harvard Progressive* (March 1939), pp. 8, 10, 22. The 1917 essay was somewhat similar in tone: "Students themselves criticized the faculty for not educating them. . . . Some

men, notably Walter Lippmann, had been reading and thinking and talking about politics and economics, not as dry theoretical studies, but as live forces acting on the world, on the university even. . . . [The members of the Socialist Club] . . . wrote articles in the college papers challenging undergraduate ideals, and muckraked the university. . . . The result of this movement upon the undergraduate world was potent. All over the place radicals sprang up, in music, painting, poetry, the theater, etc. The more serious college papers took a socialistic, or at least, progressive tinge. . . ." John Reed, "Almost Thirty," *New Republic* 86 (April 29, 1936), pp. 332–333. For other contemporary accounts of the activities of the Harvard Socialists, see Francis B. Thwing, "Radicalism at Harvard," *Harvard Graduates' Magazine* 20 (December 1911), pp. 260–263; Gerard C. Henderson, "The College and the Radicals," ibid. 20 (March 1912), pp. 463–465.

75. Randolph S. Bourne, "The Price of Radicalism," *The New Republic* 6 (March 11, 1916), p. 161.
76. E. Earnest, *Academic Procession* (Indianapolis: Bobbs-Merrill, 1953), p. 249.
77. S. William Rudy, *The College of the City of New York: A History 1847–1947* (New York: City College Press, 1949), p. 346.
78. Peterson, *The New England College,* pp. 179–184.
79. A. G. Bowden-Smith, *An English Student's Wander-Year in America* (London: Edward Arnold, 1910), p. 267.
80. Allen F. Davis, *Spearheads for Reform: The Social Settlements and the Progressive Movement 1890–1914* (New York: Oxford University Press, 1967), pp. 35–36.
81. Henry F. May, *The End of American Innocence: A Study of the First Years of Our Own Time, 1912–1917* (Chicago: Quadrangle, 1964), p. 281.
82. Ibid., p. 304.
83. Ibid., p. 282.
84. Ibid., pp. 304–308.
85. Davis, *Spearheads for Reform,* p. 183.
86. James H. Leuba, *The Belief in God and Immortality* (Boston: Sherman, French, 1916), pp. 221–288.
87. Paul F. Lazarsfeld and Wagner Thielens, Jr., *The Academic Mind* (Glencoe: The Free Press, 1958), pp. 144–146, 150–151, 161–163.
88. Leuba, *God and Immortality,* pp. 202–203.
89. Cornelia A. P. Comer, "A Letter to the Rising Generation," *The Atlantic Monthly* 107 (February 1911), pp. 147–148, 149.
90. Randolph S. Bourne, "The Two Generations," *The Atlantic Monthly* 107 (May 1911), pp. 592, 596.

Chapter 5

1. Henry May, "Shifting Perspectives on the 1920s," *The Mississippi Valley Historical Review* 43 (1956–57), p. 425.
2. Cited in William Leuchtenberg, *The Perils of Prosperity* (Chicago: University of Chicago Press, 1958), p. 176.

3. Martin J. Sklar, "On the Proletarian Revolution and the End of Political-Economic Society," *Radical America* 3 (May–June, 1969), p. 33; for a general analysis and description of the radical young intellectuals see pp. 23–36.
4. Frederick J. Hoffman, "Philistine and Puritan in the 1920s," *American Quarterly* 1 (Fall 1949), pp. 249–250, 251–252. *See also* Henry May, *The Discontent of the Intellectuals: A Problem of the Twenties* (Chicago: Rand McNally, 1963).
5. Cited in Arthur M. Schlesinger, Jr., *The Crisis of the Old Order, 1919–1933* (Boston: Houghton Mifflin, 1957), p. 49, from Arthur Pound and S. T. Moore, eds., *They Told Barron* (New York, 1930), pp. 13–14.
6. Calvin Coolidge, "Are the Reds Stalking Our College Women?" *The Delineator* (1921), as cited in "Mr. Coolidge on Direct Action," *The Freeman* (June 1, 1921), p. 268, and citations from the Coolidge article in Robert W. Iversen, *The Communists and the Schools* (New York: Harcourt, Brace, 1959), p. 14.
7. Ibid., p. 13.
8. Upton Sinclair, *The Goose-Step* (Pasadena: "The Author," 1923), p. 130; see also pp. 412–424.
9. Harold Lewack, *Campus Rebels* (New York: Student League for Industrial Democracy, 1953), p. 8.
10. E. Earnest, *Academic Procession* (Indianapolis: Bobbs-Merrill, 1953), p. 265; Oscar Handlin and Mary F. Handlin, *Facing Life* (Boston: Little, Brown, 1971).
11. George Santayana, "America's Young Radicals," *The Forum* 67 (May 1922), pp. 373–374. A comprehensive attack on the spreading collegiate socialist movement by a conservative group which advocated suppression of its rights may be found in Henry Campbell Black, "Socialism in American Colleges," *Bulletin of the National Association for Constitutional Government,* no. 4 (December 1920), pp. 3–46.
12. Herbert Adolphus Miller, "Youth and Age," *The New Student* 2 (November 4, 1922), p. 1.
13. C. Hartley Grattan, "The College Student and Contemporary Writers," *The New Student* 4 (February 28, 1925), pp. 8–12.
14. D.P.H., "This Paper," *The New Student* 3 (October 20, 1923), pp. 1–2.
15. W. H. Cowley, unpublished "Notes on Universities," chap. 11, pp. 32, 36.
16. See "Coolidge Carries Colleges," *The New Student* 4 (November 1, 1924), pp. 1–4.
17. "The Students Buck the Drill-Master," the New York *World* (November 18, 1925), as reprinted in *The New Student* 5 (December 9, 1925), p. 15.
18. *Students in Revolt* (New York: League for Industrial Democracy, 1933), p. 7.
19. Earnest, *Academic Procession,* p. 279.
20. Ibid., pp. 281–282. For contemporary accounts of campus activities on behalf of Sacco and Vanzetti, see articles in *The New Student* 6 (1927), e.g., "Proper Case for Clemency" (April 27, 1927), p. 1; "Students for Sacco, Vanzetti" (May 4, 1927), p. 1; "Sacco-Vanzetti Pleas" (June 1, 1927), p. 2.

21. S. P. Fullinwider, *The Mind and Mood of Black America* (Homewood, Ill.: Dorsey, 1969) , p. 128.
22. Edmund D. Cronon, *Black Moses: The Story of Marcus Garvey and the Universal Negro Improvement Association* (Madison: University of Wisconsin Press, 1955) .
23. John Davis, "Unrest in Negro Colleges," *The New Student* 8 (January 1929) , pp. 13–14.
24. Edward K. Graham, "The Hampton Institute Strike of 1927: A Case Study in Student Protest," *The American Scholar* 38 (Autumn 1969) , pp. 673, 677.
25. Alfred C. Kinsey et al., *Sexual Behavior in the Human Female* (Philadelphia: Saunders, 1953) , pp. 298–302; R. R. Bell, *Premarital Sex in a Changing Society* (Englewood Cliffs, N.J.: Prentice-Hall, 1966) , pp. 33–40; I. R. Reiss, "America's Sex Standards – How and Why They are Changing," *Trans-action* 5 (March 1968) , pp. 26–32.
26. Earnest, *Academic Procession,* pp. 264–265.
27. Robert Gorham Davis, "Rimbaud and Stavrogin in the Harvard Yard," *New York Times Book Review* (June 28, 1970) , p. 2.
28. Oscar Handlin and Mary Handlin, *The American College and American Culture* (New York: McGraw-Hill, 1970) , p. 69.
29. Earnest, *Academic Procession,* p. 249.
30. John Palmer Gavit, *College* (New York: Harcourt, Brace, 1925) , pp. 237, 241, 244, 262.
31. Christian Gauss, *Life in College* (New York: Scribner's, 1930) , pp. 111, 113.
32. Alvin Toffler, *Future Shock* (New York: Random House, 1970) .
33. Gauss, *Life in College,* pp. 101, 108.
34. "The Faculty and Teaching – the Heart of the Dartmouth Report," *The New Student* 5 (November 11, 1925) , pp. 4–5. Other parts of the report are reprinted in *The New Student* (October 3, 1925) , pp. 3–6, and (February 3, 1926) , pp. 11–13. See also "What the Undergraduate Wants," *The New Republic* 39 (July 30, 1924) , pp. 258–260.
35. " 'Too Big' Our Higher Education Is Overgrown – and End of Student Influx Is Not in Sight," *The New Student* 5 (November 11, 1925) , p. 1.
36. The Editors of *The Vagabond,* "Gigantism and the University," *The New Student* 4 (January 24, 1925) , p. 7.
37. Grant Showerman, "Intellect and the Undergraduate," *School and Society* 13 (February 26, 1921) , pp. 241–242.
38. Frank E. Spaulding, "The Passing of Great College Teachers," *The Forum* 75 (March 1926) , p. 447.
39. See the report of his speech in the *Bulletin of the A.A.U.P.* 11 (March–April 1925) , p. 156.
40. Addison Hibbard, "Our Truant Professors," *Outlook* 150 (December 5, 1928) , pp. 1267, 1269.
41. As cited by W. H. Cowley in his unpublished "Notes on Universities," chap. 12, p. 22. I am very grateful to Professor Cowley for this reference.
42. Robert M. Hutchins, "Training Professors and Paying Them," *The Review of Reviews* 81 (February 1930) , p. 99.

43. Somnia Vana, "College Education: An Inquest, II," *The Freeman* 4 (March 1, 1922), pp. 584–585. There is no relationship between *The Freeman* of the 1920s, and the ultraconservative magazine of the same name, which began publication in 1950.
44. Milton Mankoff and Richard Flacks, "The Changing Social Base of the American Student Movement: Its Meaning and Implications," *The Annals of the American Academy of Political and Social Science* 395 (May 1971), p. 62.
45. C. Michael Stanton, "Student Protest: Youth Response to Depression and Affluence," unpublished ms., Boston College, chap. 2, p. 7. William R. McIntyre, "Student Movements," *Editorial Research Reports* 2 (December 1957), p. 925; Murray Kempton, *Part of Our Time* (New York: Simon and Schuster, 1955), pp. 302–303.
46. George P. Rawick, "The New Deal and Youth" (Ph.D. thesis, Department of History, University of Wisconsin, 1957), pp. 281–282, and "*Digest* Helps Poll Articulate College Generation," *The Literary Digest* 119 (January 12, 1935), p. 38; "League Loses by Slim Margin in College Vote," *The Literary Digest* 119 (February 16, 1935), p. 7. For results of the *Literary Digest* poll on Roosevelt, see Harold Seidman, "How Radical Are College Students?" *The American Scholar* 4 (Summer 1935), p. 327.
47. Norman Birnbaum and Majorie Childers, "The American Movement," in Julian Nagel, ed., *Student Power* (London: Merlin, 1969), p. 132.
48. Martin McLaughlin, "Political Processes in American National Student Organizations" (Ph.D. thesis, Department of Political Science, Notre Dame University, 1948), pp. 17–20; Rawick, "The New Deal and Youth," pp. 308–311, 317–322, 335–337; Hal Draper, "The Student Movement of the Thirties: A Political History," in Rita James Simon, ed., *As We Saw the Thirties* (Urbana: University of Illinois Press, 1967), pp. 172–182; Birnbaum and Childers, "The American Movement," pp. 132–133.
49. Kempton, *Part of Our Time,* 320–321.
50. Irving Howe and Lewis Coser, *The American Communist Party* (Boston: Beacon, 1957), p. 529; Morris L. Ernst and David Loth, *Report on the American Communist* (New York: Holt, 1952), p. 14.
51. Ibid., p. 2.
52. Ibid., pp. 3–4.
53. Nathan Glazer, *The Social Basis of American Communism* (New York: Harcourt, Brace and World, 1961), pp. 114–118.
54. Ernst and Loth, *Report on the American Communist,* p. 3.
55. Glazer, *The Social Basis of American Communism,* p. 130.
56. Gardner Murphy and Rensis Likert, *Public Opinion and the Individual* (New York: Harper, 1938), pp. 71–87.
57. Ibid., pp. 110–111.
58. Ibid., pp. 107–108, (emphasis mine. S.M.L.)
59. "The A.S.U. . . . established radical traditions at certain universities . . . which were to be revived a generation later — often by the very children of A.S.U. members." Birnbaum and Childers, "The American Movement," p. 133.

60. "Youth in College," *Fortune* 13 (June 1936), pp. 99–102, 155–162.
61. Unpublished report of 1936 national college student study prepared by Cherington, Roper and Wood. I would like to thank Burns Roper for making this report available to me.
62. "Youth in College," pp. 100, 158.
63. Edward Suchman, Rose K. Goldsen and Robin Williams, Jr., "Attitudes Toward the Korean War," *Public Opinion Quarterly* 17 (1953), pp. 173, 182.
64. Norman Miller, "Social Class and Value Differences Among American College Students" (Ph.D. thesis, Department of Sociology, Columbia University, 1958). This study is based on a comprehensive analysis of a sample of thirteen schools gathered by a Cornell group of sociologists. Similar conclusions in analyzing these materials are reported in Arthur Liebman, "The Active and Silent Generation: Student Politics in the 1950s and 1960s" (draft memo: Center for International Affairs, Harvard University, 1970), p. 9. A study of Berkeley students' reactions to the effort to impose a loyalty oath in 1950 found similar relationships between academic class and liberalism. S. M. Lipset, "Opinion Formation in a Crisis Situation," *Public Opinion Quarterly* 17 (1953), pp. 20–46.
65. Lawrence C. Howard, "The Academic and the Ballot," *School and Society* 86 (November 22, 1958), p. 416. For a summary of the variety of research results bearing on the political orientations and voting behavior of American professors, see S. M. Lipset, "The Politics of Academia," in David C. Nichols, ed., *Perspectives on Campus Tensions* (Washington, D.C.: American Council on Education, 1970), pp. 85–118.
66. Paul F. Lazarsfeld and Wagner Thielens, Jr., *The Academic Mind* (Glencoe: The Free Press, 1958), p. 402.
67. M. Stanton Evans, *Revolt on Campus* (Chicago: Regnery, 1961), p. 217.
68. Liebman, "The Active and Silent Generation," pp. 8–9.
69. See Margaret Mead, *Culture and Commitment: A Study of the Generation Gap* (Garden City: Doubleday, Natural History Press, 1970); Kenneth Keniston, "The Fire Outside," *The Journal* 9 (September–October 1970), pp. 5–6; for a general critique of this approach, see S. M. Lipset, "The Banality of Revolt," *Saturday Review* (July 18, 1970), pp. 23–26, 34.
70. Claude Bowman, *The College Professor in America* (Philadelphia: privately printed, 1938). See especially p. 185. The comparison of literature dealing with the role of the professor between 1900 and 1910, and after World War II, found almost total similarity in content and tone, much to the surprise of the author.

    "Although the nation underwent rapid and extensive change between the turn of the century and the post–World War II period, the arguments and incantations echoing through the university sounded surprisingly similiar in both eras. The force and scope of the major problems affecting the professor may have increased by the late 1940s, but the rhetoric describing them was identical to that employed prior to World War I.

"Appearing again as a prominent issue was the avowed decline in the quality of teaching, especially in undergraduate courses, and the apparent supremacy of research men in the eyes of university administrators. The loss of prestige accorded teachers was blamed on elective courses and the departmental system. Only the researcher was felt to gain recognition and advancement, and many charged that this resulted in the neglect of teaching in favor of the laboratory, library, or field. Research and publication were the invidious bases of promotion. . . .

"The second major issue reappearing in the second period involved the *content* of university courses. Some observers of the academic scene felt that a major responsibility had been abrogated by the universities in their refusal to instruct youth in the moral and spiritual values of American culture. Countervailing opinions suggested that professors could not be expected to survey contemporary life, reduce its complexity to classroom proportions, and derive a single set of values acceptable to all. Such efforts approached indoctrination rather than education and fell beyond the province of the university. Some felt that the values attending liberal arts courses did not, in fact, liberalize but instead inflicted upon students prejudice and disdain for many aspects of American life.

"A third major source of tension remained in relationships between university faculties and administrations. The pyramiding of administrative personnel and power had deprived the teacher of prestige and authority. The administrative chores forced upon the professor detracted from his major responsibility, that of teaching." (Donald F. Allen, "Changes in the Role of the American University Professor" [Ph.D. thesis, Department of Sociology, University of Texas, 1962], pp. 168–169, 171.)

71. Laurence R. Veysey, *The Emergence of the American University* (Chicago: University of Chicago Press, 1965) , pp. 294–302.
72. See Max Ways, "The Faculty Is the Heart of the Trouble," *Fortune* 79 (January 1969) , pp. 94–97, 161–164; William F. Baxter, "Faculty and Government Roles in Campus Unrest," *The Educational Record* 50 (Fall 1969) , pp. 411–419; John P. Roche, "Retreat of the Faculty," *The New Leader* 52 (November 10, 1969) , pp. 15–61. Such claims are, of course, not new. Randolph Bourne discussed the efforts to explain pre–World War I student radicalism as a consequence of the activities of "these agnostic professors who unsettle the faith of our youth, these 'intellectuals who stick a finger in everybody's pie in the name of social justice,' . . . these remorseless scientists who would reveal so many of our reticences." (Randolph Bourne, *History of a Literary Radical* [New York: Huebsch, 1920], pp. 109–110.)

Chapter 6

1. Robert F. Boruch, "The Faculty Role in Campus Unrest," *ACE Research Reports* 4, no. 5 (1969) , pp. 50, 21.
2. S. M. Lipset, "The Politics of Academia," in David C. Nichols, ed., *Perspectives on Campus Tensions* (Washington, D.C.: American Council on Education, 1970) , pp. 85–118. Much of this chapter is taken from the

original, much longer draft of that paper, which was prepared for the ACE's Special Committee on Campus Tensions.

3. "Text of a Pre-Inauguration Memo from Moynihan on Problems Nixon Would Face," New York *Times,* March 11, 1970.
4. "The Scholar in Politics" (a commencement address delivered at Dartmouth and Amherst colleges, and before the alumni of Miami University), *Scribner's Monthly* 6 (1873), pp. 613–614. (Emphasis in original). Twenty-eight years later, speaking at Stanford in 1901, an older Reid saw the same behavior by American academics as bad. "It is a misfortune for the colleges, and no less for the country, when the trusted instructors are out of sympathy with its history, with its development, and with the men who made the one and are guiding the other." Whitelaw Reid, *American and English Studies* (New York: Scribner's, 1913), vol. 1, pp. 241–242.
5. George Stigler, unpublished memorandum, as quoted in Milton Friedman, "The Ivory Tower," *Newsweek* (November 10, 1969), p. 92. For a similar comment from the Left, see Noam Chomsky, "Philosophers and Public Policy," *Ethics* 79 (October 1968), pp. 5–61. "Perhaps the most important role of the intellectual since the enlightenment has been that of unmasking ideology, exposing the injustice and repression that exists in every society that we know, and seeking the way to a new and higher form of social life that will extend the possibilities for a free and creative life." Chomsky goes on to argue that the intellectual will cease this role when he becomes an "administrator" in the postindustrial society.
6. See Lipset, "The Politics of Academia," for documentation based on the large number of studies from 1912 to 1969. For reports on the analysis of the recent massive (60,000 sample) Carnegie Commission on Higher Education survey of the professoriate, see S. M. Lipset and Everett Ladd, Jr., ". . . And What Professors Think," *Psychology Today* 4 (November 1970), pp. 49–51, 61, and "The Divided Professoriate," *Change* 3 (May–June 1971), pp. 54–60.
7. Everett C. Ladd, Jr., "Social Scientists and Opposition to the Vietnam War: The Petition Campaign Revisited" (mimeographed), pp. 28–30.
8. Christopher Lasch, *The Agony of the American Left* (New York: Knopf, 1969), p. 21.
9. Max Weber, *The Methodology of the Social Sciences* (Glencoe: The *Free Press,* 1949), p. 6.
10. Ibid., p. 81.
11. Ibid., p. 76.
12. Ibid., p. 55.
13. Ibid., p. 84.
14. From the *Critique of the Gotha Programme (1875)*, as quoted in Noam Chomsky, "The Function of the University in a Time of Crisis," in Robert M. Hutchins and Mortimer J. Adler, eds., *The Great Ideas Today: 1969* (Chicago: Encyclopaedia Britannica, 1969), p. 58.
15. Robert Paul Wolff, *The Ideal of the University* (Boston: Beacon, 1969), p. 75.

16. Barrington Moore, Jr., "Barrington Moore Asks for Student Restraint," *Harvard Crimson* 146 (November 8, 1967).
17. H. Stuart Hughes, "The Need Now Is to De-politicize the University," *Harvard Alumni Bulletin* 71 (September 15, 1969), p. 37.
18. Eugene D. Genovese, "Black Studies: Trouble Ahead," *The Atlantic* 223 (June 1969), pp. 38–39, 41. Another leftist historian, William Appleton Williams, whose graduate students at Wisconsin had started the earliest New Left journal, *Studies on the Left,* also has commented in extremely critical terms about the recent crop of campus New Leftists. "They are the most selfish people I know. They just terrify me. They are acting out a society I'd like to live in as an orangutan.

 . . . "They say: 'I'm right and you're wrong and you can't talk because you're wrong.' They think the university president should be leading the revolution – it's ludicrous." Quoted in Nan Robertson, "The Student Scene: Angry Militants," New York *Times,* November 20, 1967.
19. Chomsky, "Function of a University," pp. 58–59. At the December 1969 meeting of the A.A.A.S., Chomsky "surprised the radical students and faculty members in the audience at a discussion about academic research and the military. . . . Chomsky, an outspoken critic of the Vietnam war and of military research, argued that chemical and biological warfare research should be conducted on university campuses so that the students and faculty members could keep track of what is going on. . . . Chomsky argued that students should be 'effective revolutionaries' and that 'breaking locks has brought practically no new information.' As an example of why he thinks military research should be conducted on university campuses, Chomsky said the recent revelations about the physical deformations in animals caused by 2, 4, 5-T had gone over 'like a lead balloon' on university campuses because there were no CBW departments to alert people to the importance of these issues. The herbicide 2, 4, 5-T has been widely used in Vietnam as a defoliant." (Los Angeles *Times,* December 19, 1969.)
20. Chomsky, "Function of a University," p. 59.
21. Ibid., p. 60.
22. Moore, "Student Restraint," p. 5.
23. Ernest Gellner, "The Panther and the Dove: Reflections on Rebelliousness and Its Milieux," in David Martin, ed., *Anarchy and Culture: The Problem of the Contemporary University* (London: Routledge and Kegan Paul, 1969), pp. 143–144 (emphases in the original).
24. Christopher Jencks and David Riesman, *The Academic Revolution* (Garden City: Doubleday, 1968), p. 531.
25. For an analysis and description of faculty activities along these lines, see Clark Kerr, *The Uses of the University* (Cambridge: Harvard University Press, 1963). One of the key documents of the Berkeley revolt, one that outlined student grievances, drew heavily on Kerr's analyses of faculty behavior. See Bradford Cleveland, "A Letter to Undergraduates," in S. M. Lipset and Sheldon S. Wolin, eds., *The Berkeley Student Revolt* (New York: Doubleday, Anchor Books, 1965), pp. 66–81.
26. A. H. Raskin, "Where It All Began – Berkeley, 5 Years Later, Is

Radicalized, Reaganized, Mesmerized," *New York Times Magazine,* January 11, 1970, p. 85.

27. Ibid.
28. Paul F. Lazarsfeld and Wagner Thielens, Jr., *The Academic Mind* (Glencoe: The Free Press, 1958), pp. 151–152, 443.
29. C. Edward Noll and Peter H. Rossi, *"General Social and Economic Attitudes of College and University Faculty Members"* (private report; Chicago: National Opinion Research Center, University of Chicago, November 1966), p. 58.
30. Lazarsfeld and Thielens, *The Academic Mind,* p. 443.
31. In the following discussion, I am highly indebted to the brilliant analysis of Michio Nagai, "The Problem of Indoctrination: As Viewed from Sociological and Philosophical Bases" (Ph.D. thesis, Department of Sociology, Ohio State University, 1952).
32. Florian Znaniecki, *The Social Role of the Man of Knowledge* (New York: Columbia University Press, 1940), p. 155.
33. Nagai, "The Problem of Indoctrination," p. 46.
34. Ibid., p. 52.
35. Michael Novak, "Battles of Old Westbury," New York *Times,* July 17, 1971, p. 23.
36. Robert S. Powell, Jr., "Participation Is Learning," *Saturday Review* 53 (January 10, 1970), p. 58.
37. *Felix Frankfurter Reminisces* (Garden City: Doubleday, Anchor Books, 1962), p. 43.
38. Randolph S. Bourne, *Youth and Life* (Boston: Houghton Mifflin, 1913), p. 318.
39. Robert K. Merton, *Social Theory and Social Structures* (Glencoe: The Free Press, 1949), pp. 308–314; Talcott Parsons, *The Social System* (Glencoe: The Free Press, 1951), pp. 342–344, 434.
40. Jencks and Riesman, *The Academic Revolution.*
41. David Riesman and Joseph Gusfield, "Style of Teaching in Two New Public Colleges," in Robert Morrison, ed., *The Contemporary University: USA* (Boston: Houghton Mifflin, 1966), pp. 257–258.
42. Robert Dubin and Frederic Beisse, "The Assistant: Academic Subaltern," *Administrative Science Quarterly* 11 (March 1967), pp. 521–527.
43. William M. Roth, "The Dilemmas of Leadership," *Saturday Review* 53 (January 10, 1970), p. 68.

Chapter 7

1. David J. Finlay, Roberta E. Koplin, and Charles A. Ballard, Jr., "Ghana," in Donald K. Emmerson, ed., *Students and Politics in Developing Countries* (New York: Praeger, 1968), 64–102; Harsja W. Bachtiar, "Indonesia," ibid., pp. 180–214.
2. David Burg, "Observations on Soviet University Students," *Daedalus* 89 (Summer 1960), pp. 520–540; Lewis S. Feuer, *The Conflict of Generations* (New York: Basic Books, 1969), pp. 298–312; Richard Cornell, "Students and Politics in the Communist Countries of Eastern Europe," *Daedalus* 97 (Winter 1968), pp. 166–183; Miluse Kubickova, "Students in Czechoslo-

vakia," in Philip G. Altbach, ed., *The Student Revolution* (Bombay: Lalvani, 1970), pp. 267–285.

3. Dennis J. Doolin, *Communist China: The Politics of Student Opposition* (Stanford: Hoover Institution on War, Revolution, and Peace, 1964); John Israel, "Reflections on the Modern Chinese Student Movement," in Seymour M. Lipset and Philip G. Altbach, eds., *Students in Revolt* (Boston: Houghton Mifflin, 1969), pp. 324–331.
4. A. Beldon Fields, *Student Politics in France* (New York: Basic Books, 1970), pp. 32–40.
5. Ibid., pp. 166–169.
6. A. H. Halsey and Stephen Marks, "British Student Politics," in Lipset and Altbach, eds., *Students in Revolt,* pp. 43–55; Stephen Hatch, "From C.N.D. to Newest Left," in David Martin, ed., *Anarchy and Culture* (London: Routledge and Kegan Paul, 1969), pp. 122–128.
7. John P. Robinson, "Public Reaction to Political Protest: Chicago 1968," *Public Opinion Quarterly* 34 (Spring 1970), pp. 1–3.
8. "Student Unrest Seen as Nation's Top Problem," *The Gallup Political Index,* no. 61 (July 1970), p. 3.
9. Sam Brown, "The Politics of Peace," *The Washington Monthly* 2 (August 1970), pp. 24–46.
10. Kiyoaki Murata, "The JCP-JSP Dispute," *The Japan Times Weekly,* August 29, 1970, p. 4.
11. Pekka Puska and Seppo Naumanen, "Finland: The Struggle for a Democratic University," SIPE [International Student Press Service] 2 (May 5, 1970), pp. 7–12.
12. S. M. Lipset, *Revolution and Counterrevolution,* rev. ed. (New York: Doubleday, Anchor Books, 1970), chap. 9.
13. Robinson, "Public Reaction to Political Protest," p. 7.
14. Enzo Montillo, "The Youth of the Opinion Surveys," SIPE [International Student Press Service] 2 (July 1, 1970), pp. 13–14.
15. Max Kaase, "Determinants of Political Mobilization for Students and Non-Academic Youth" (paper prepared for session on the politics of students and young workers, Seventh World Congress of Sociology, Varna, Bulgaria, September 14–19, 1970), pp. 5–7; Max Kaase, "Democratic Attitudes in the Federal Republic of Germany: Students, Non-Academic Youth and Total Population" (paper prepared for session on youth and politics, (Eighth World Congress of Political Science, Munich, Germany, August 31–September 5, 1970), pp. 4–6.
16. "New Values for Young Workers," *The Japan Times Weekly,* September 19, 1970, p. 12; Neville Meaney, "The Crises in Japanese Universities, 1969," *Vestes: The Australian Universities' Review* 13 (November 1969), pp. 225–231.
17. Ted Goertzel, "Political Attitudes of Brazilian Youth" (paper prepared for session on the politics of students and young workers, Seventh World Congress of Sociology, Varna, Bulgaria, September 14–19, 1970), p. 14.
18. Bernard Pares, *Russia Between Reform and Revolution* (New York: Schocken, 1962; first published in 1910), pp. 161–282.

19. Irving Louis Horowitz, ed., *Power, Politics and People: The Collected Essays of C. Wright Mills* (New York: Ballantine, 1963), pp. 257–258.
20. Much of this discussion is taken from S. M. Lipset and Everett C. Ladd, Jr., "What Happens to College Generations Politically?" *The Public Interest* no. 25 (Fall 1971), in press. This article also presents the results of a variety of opinion surveys.

Chapter 8

1. Jules Henry, *Culture Against Man* (New York: Random House, 1963), p. 13.
2. "Most students today are convinced that their parents and teachers deceive themselves, and profess a traditional set of principles without even being aware that they do not live by them. In the eyes of the children, the generation gap is now a 'hypocrisy gap.'" J. Bronowski, "Protest—Past and Present," *The American Scholar* (Autumn 1969), p. 540.
3. C. Wright Mills, *The Sociological Imagination* (New York: Grove, 1959), pp. 3–5.
4. "Any well-knit way of life molds human behavior into its own design. The individualism of bourgeois society, like the communism of a socialized state, must be inculcated from the nursery to the grave. In the United States, as one among the bourgeois nations, the life of personal achievement and personal responsibility is extolled in song and story from the very beginning of consciousness." Harold Lasswell, *Politics: Who Gets What, When, How* (Cleveland: World, 1958), p. 32.
5. C. Wright Mills and Hans Gerth, *Character & Social Structure: The Psychology of Social Institution* (New York: Harcourt, Brace and World, 1953–1964), p. 26.
6. Henry Etzkowitz and Gerald M. Schaflander, *Ghetto Crisis* (Boston: Little, Brown, 1969), pp. 8–18.
7. Etzkowitz and Schaflander, *Ghetto Crisis,* p. 65.
8. McCarthy held a 65% to 35% presidential primary poll edge over LBJ in Wisconsin one week before Johnson resigned. The entire administration cabinet, en masse, were fiercely campaigning for LBJ in Wisconsin sixteen hours a day until certain defeat drove them back to Washington—prematurely—five days before LBJ's resignation—and the election.
9. "Karl Mannheim has located the concerns of 'adolescents and early adults, particularly students,' for major political or social concerns beyond their personal interests, in the 'uncertainty and doubt' which results when 'one's questions outrun the scope of one's inherited answers.'

   "This occurs when the youth learns that there are other values and ways of life different from those urged on him by his family . . . self-assertion and defiance accompany this new experience . . . rather than remain in a state of doubt, many youths seek a new certainty in beliefs, which are opposed to those taught at home. Intellectual fanaticism is not the product of a tacitly accepted heritage, but the expression of an anxiety to *end the wear and tear of a state of suspense by the adoption of a categorial creed."* (Emphasis mine. G.S.) Seymour Martin Lipset,

"University Students and Politics in Underdeveloped Countries," in S. M. Lipset, ed., *Student Politics* (New York: Basic Books, 1967).

10. Bipartisan bill sponsored by Senator Gaylord A. Nelson (Dem.) of Wisconsin.
11. Most data on left-hippies is of a participant-observer nature.
12. "Mannheim believed that the understanding of history could arise only from acting in it . . . thought was not a detached and static affair; it was intimately involved in the process of living . . . In this view, the intellectual was no mere observer. He represented the conscience of his society — Mannheim saw the greater peril in detachment and apathy." H. Stuart Hughes, *Consciousness and Society* (New York: Vintage, 1958), p. 424.
13. Community Development Center, Roxbury; CDC Store, Boston University; McCarthy campaign, New Hampshire, Connecticut, California; Poor People's March, (lobbying,) 1968, Wash., D.C.; lobbying trips to see Robert Kennedy, and the State and Justice Depts., 1966.
14. See Kenneth Clark, introduction to *Dark Ghetto,* for a definition of the "involved observer," and Etzkowitz and Schaflander, *Ghetto Crisis,* "Institution-Formation," Appendix B.

Chapter 9

1. "Sex refers to the drive originating at puberty toward genital union between men and women . . . an elemental force or drive that promotes life . . . has biological purpose of procreation . . . [as] physiological and psychological manifestation — at every age level — can be a force for pleasure, tenderness and human relatedness." Committee on the College Student: Group for the Advancement of Psychiatry, *Sex and The College Student* (New York: Atheneum, 1966), p. 12.
2. Ira L. Reiss, *Premarital Sexual Standards in America* (New York: The Free Press of Glencoe, 1960); "The Treatment of Premarital Coitus in Marriage and Family Texts," *Social Problems* (April 1957), pp. 334–338.
3. Robert R. Bell, *Premarital Sex in a Changing Society* (Englewood Cliffs, N.J.: Prentice-Hall, 1966).
4. "Princeton, N.J., June 21: The nation's teenagers and college students are on the verge of a revolution in their attitudes toward sex, according to a Gallup Poll, conducted recently throughout the country.

   "But a majority of their parents still cling to the Puritan Ethic in sex, even though today's best-selling novels, the best-attended movies and many of the new magazines would suggest otherwise.

   "Two of three college students interviewed (66 percent) thought it was not wrong for men and women to have premarital sex relations, 55 percent of the young women and 72 percent of the college males holding this view. (A total of 1,502 persons 21 years of age and older were interviewed in more than 300 localities . . .) On the other hand, a majority of all adults interviewed (73 percent) said they would find pictures of nudes in magazines objectionable. Seventy-six percent said they would be offended by topless waitresses and an even higher proportion (81 percent) said they would object to actors and actresses appearing nude on the stage." (New York *Times,* June 21, 1969.)

5. Note the oversimplified abstractions that cover the tremendous variability on many dimensions that indubitably exist within this single typology of marginal ambivalents.
6. Richard E. Peterson, "The Student Left in American Higher Education," *Daedalus* 97 (Winter 1968), p. 293.
7. Bell, *Premarital Sex in a Changing Society.*
8. On a lecture tour of college campuses (16 in Vermont, Maine, New Jersey, New York, Virginia, Minnesota and Massachusetts) in small (50 to 100 students) after-lecture sessions in the fall of 1969, the same percentages held up. More significant were the figures on their younger brothers and sisters in grades 9 to 12. Over 50 percent engaged in coitus; over 50 percent smoked pot regularly; over 25 percent used amphetamines (speed); over 75 percent were rebelling against parents and principals.
9. Certain critics of this methodology point out that many people think others are freer than they are; they do not know facts, and if anything may exaggerate.
10. The John Birch Society sometimes forces cold, impersonal, older teachers to bore or embarrass high school students . . . if not pressuring the banning of sex lectures entirely, by witch-hunting the local school boards.
11. Reiss, *Premarital Sexual Standards in America.*
12. Richard Lewinsohn, *A History of Sexual Customs* (New York: Harper & Row, 1966).
13. As Erik Erikson notes: ". . . whatever the partial abstinences that characterize premarital sex life in various cultures — whether the pleasure and pride of forceful genital activity without commitment, or of erotic states without genital consummation, or of disciplined and divided delay — ego development uses the psycho-sexual powers of adolescence for enhancing a sense of style and identity." (*Daedalus* 91 [Winter 1962], p. 12.)
14. There is ambivalence and contradiction in differing MA male sexual data as enumerated before. Not true of left-hippies.

Chapter 10

1. These statistics differ sharply from almost all research-survey questionnaires. I believe students won't tell the truth about drugs to surveyors for fear of prosecution. This naturalistic, involved-observer research may be the only means to measure accurately the scope and depth of drug usage.
2. "The majority of student drug users who are not disturbed do not volunteer themselves as subjects in research studies of drug users. The reason: the possession of marijuana is a felony under federal law. Thus, while we know something about why some students get into psychological trouble using drugs, we know almost nothing about why most students

apparently do not get into trouble." Helen H. Nowlis, *Drugs on the College Campus* (Garden City: Doubleday, Anchor Books, 1969), p. xiii, introduction by Kenneth Keniston.

3. "We cannot rely on a corresponding increase in the number of enforcement personnel as the solution to social control . . . Experience does suggest that an education approach to social problems may be worth a try, and where better than in an institution in which faith in education should be the highest? . . . Many sex, drug, driving, alcohol and cigarette education programs have been tried in the high schools . . . As we move deeper into such areas as drug education, sex education, cigarette and alcohol education in the colleges — as well — research is desperately needed on the general problem of evaluating results of such programs . . . Many people feel that education in this area should consist simply of saying, "It's against the law — don't do it," and that, since use of drugs is currently illegal, it is not open to further question. When any kind of education program is attempted, the issue of the legal status of the drugs and drug users has to be faced . . . There are many important and continuing questions: Should there be a program? What should such a program try to do? Who should decide on the objectives? For whom should such a program or programs be developed? By whom should the program be developed and carried out? What should be in the program?" (Ibid., pp. 54–58)
4. "The widely shared view that savagely punitive laws will effectively 'stamp out' drug use among college students has no evidence to support it. In fact, the rapid spread of drug use among college students in the face of highly punitive (though erratically enforced) legislation suggests that illegality and stiff punishment have little deterrent effect." (Ibid., p. xi.)
5. Kenneth Keniston, *The American Scholar* (Winter 1969–70).
6. "Adults with their alcohol and tranquilizers and students with their marihuana and LSD are both reacting to conditions which negate human values and human worth. The main difference is that the adults' drugs of choice are depressants, taken to blunt the pain. The students' drugs of choice are perceived by at least some of the more serious, rightly or wrongly, as an attempt to strike back at, to seek insight into, to protest what they feel to be the causes of the pain. It is a reasonable prediction that if all drugs were eliminated from the campus tomorrow the search would go on in some other form, perhaps more tolerable to society, perhaps less." (Nowlis, *Drugs on the College Campus,* p. 76.)

Chapter 11

1. W. Ayers, M. Rudd, C. Wilkerson and dozens of Weathermen, PL, and radical student leaders at Brooklyn College, Boston University and Harvard are children of rich and/or conservative parents. This contradicts Keniston, Flacks and Lipset surveys and reports.
2. Focus of President Eisenhower's Farewell Address.
3. "Many personal troubles can't be solved merely as troubles, but must be understood in terms of overriding public issues — and in terms of the

problems of history making." (C. Wright Mills, *The Sociological Imagination* [New York: Grove, 1959], p. 226.)

4. S. M. Lipset, *Political Man* (Garden City: Doubleday, Anchor Books, 1963), as quoted in J. P. Mayer, *Max Weber and German Politics* (London: Faber and Faber, 1943), p. 11, 128 n. 15. "Weber and Michels were among the first . . . to postulate . . . the problem of modern politics is not capitalism or socialism but the relationship between bureaucracy and democracy . . . Both men tried to demonstrate that socialist organizations and societies were or would necessarily be as bureaucratic and oligarchic as capitalist ones."
5. New York *Times,* March 5, 1970.
6. L. Joughlin, ed., *Academic Freedom and Tenure: A Handbook of the American Association of University Professors* (Madison: University of Wisconsin Press, 1969), pp. 199–201.
7. "There will be many difficulties . . . but they do not justify prejudices which keep half of mankind from participating in planning and decision-making, especially at a time when the other half, by its competitive escalation and acceleration of technical progress, has brought us and our children to the gigantic abyss." Erik H. Erikson, *Identity, Youth and Crisis* (New York: Norton, 1968), pp. 292–293.
8. "To come to the aid of colleagues whose academic freedom is in jeopardy . . . we need and want teachers and scholars to come unhesitatingly to the defense of the 'odd ball,' heretic, dissenter, whose freedom to speak and write is under some threat. . . . [The] task of true freedom-and-progress-loving scholars is to aid the troublemaker under attack, even if they disagree with what he professes and dislike him for his personal traits, manners or practices." (Fred Macklup, in L. Joughlin, *Academic Freedom and Tenure,* pp. 328–329.)

Chapter 12

1. J. Bensman, "Dollars and Sense" (New York: Macmillan, 1967), p. 142.
2. Ibid., pp. 196–197. (Emphasis mine. G.S.)
3. Ibid. (Emphasis mine. G.S.)
4. Louis Harris, "Surveying the Campus," Boston *Globe,* July 7, 1970. (Emphasis mine. G.S.)
5. *I. F. Stone's Weekly,* September 21, 1970.
6. New York *Times,* September 22, 1970.
7. Ibid.
8. Ibid.
9. Ibid.
10. Ibid. (Emphasis mine. G.S.)
11. "Since no institutional mechanisms for student participation in the determination of educational policy have been devised, student comment, in these circumstances, has been a parody of American consumer behavior: the consumer is free to select among goods, but not to alter the structure of the market." (Norman Birnbaum and Marjorie Childers, "The American Movement," in Julian Nagel, ed., *Student Power* [London: Merlin, 1969].)

12. "Profile of a Generation," Daniel Yankelovich Associates, multilithed report of a survey for CBS News issued April 1969.
13. Powerful industrialists endow universities on the implicit condition that they prove "useful" in the education of future elites and their technical subordinates, or in the support of "applied" research.
14. Henry Etzkowitz and Gerald M. Schaflander, *Ghetto Crisis* (Boston: Little, Brown, 1969), pp. 2–8.
15. Nathan Glazer, "Student Politics and the University," *Harper's Magazine*, (July 1969).
16. PLR's wear short hair, dress modestly and abstain from drugs and "free" sexual behavior. They want to avoid turning off the working class.
17. See August and September 1969 articles in *National Guardian, The Old Mole, New Left Notes* and *Militant*.
18. Arrested, convicted and jailed in January 1970 for beating up two female secretaries and a Quaker at the Harvard University Center for International Affairs.
19. Professor A. Inkeles of Harvard was forced to call police to protect his classroom in the spring of 1969 (New York *Times*); Professor J. Bunzel of San Francisco State: "House, office, and classroom wrecked, bombed and mutilated." Readers of the New York *Times* are familiar with many other such examples.
20. Not to overlook the assassinations of Malcolm X, George Lincoln Rockwell, John and Robert Kennedy, Medgar Evers and Martin Luther King in the "good old U.S.A."
21. "Behind this assumption of a 'right' to interfere forcibly with the exercise of the rights of others, even of the large majority, stands the more general postulate that freedom of expression for all members of the community is a 'bourgeois' notion and that freedom belongs properly only to those whose views are 'right' and 'progressive.' And, curiously enough, the elitism of some contemporary radical students also echoes the claim that only the elite have a right to freedom.

    "This view that freedom rightly belongs only to the enlightened minority is clearly manifested when some of the leaders of SDS, for example, talk about the stupidity and political backwardness of their 'unradicalized' fellow students and when they admit that they would not be influenced by a student referendum in which their views were decisively rejected." (Jerry L. Avorn and others, *Up Against the Ivy Wall: A History of the Columbia Crisis* [New York: Atheneum, 1969].)
22. D. Sisson, *Center Magazine*, March 1970 (Santa Barbara, Calif.: Center for the Study of Democratic Institutions).
23. One of the most popular symbols is the color and clothing connections to American Indian culture. Indians stand as an emblem of the simple; a primitive survival on the continent of affluence and technological sophistication. They represent the way white outsiders exploited the native peoples of the American continent. Young people identify powerfully with the deprived and exploited Indian.
24. Thomas Paine and Thomas Jefferson symbolize the roots to potential American revolutionary leadership — not Ho, Fidel or Mao.

25. *Harvard Today* (Spring 1969).
26. But not a conspiratorial effort at initiating violence — as the government and Judge Hoffman "patriotically" tried so hard to prove in the infamous Chicago Seven trial, January 1970.
27. "A minimum of disturbance has been relied upon with unnerving insight, to produce a maximum of repression." (Norman Birnbaum, "Staggering Colossus," in Julian Nagel, ed., *Student Power* [London: Merlin, 1969], p. 161.)
28. The Committee on Rights and Responsibilities at Harvard University is now functioning, apparently with broad student-faculty support.
29. *The American Sociologist* (November 1969).
30. "We must join university scholarly thinking (research and writing) to political and social action — by focusing educational course content on specific environmental and community problems (assigning term projects to teams of students who go into the ghetto — volunteer — and engage in participant-observation research). This provides students with practical 'relevant' experience in the real world and forces the university to use part-time, non-formal, non-academic experts (adults, professionals) as full-status faculty." (William M. Birenbaum, *Overlive* [New York: Dell, 1969], p. 134.)

    This obviously enhances scholarship, and is part of educational reformation that is blocked by those "objective" academicians who rigidly and narrowly claim to fight left extremists who want to politicalize the university — but they also block the MA's — tragically — in a monolithic, syncretic analysis of students.
31. A. S. Neill, founder of Summerhill School and author of *Freedom, Not License!* (New York: Hart, 1966).
32. Peter Clecak, "The Snare of Preparation," *The American Scholar* (Autumn 1969), pp. 65–66; Peter Clecak is professor of English and American culture at the University of California at Irvine.
33. Northeastern University in Boston calls their work-study alternative-semester "Co-op." But it fails totally on a content basis. In reality, Northeastern is a giant employment agency for New England business and industry.
34. And so Schaflander, Dr. Redge Ranyard, and a score of students (black and white and brown) have organized and financed a new, equal, decision-making institution — Citizens College — at Spring Lake, New Jersey — to open September 11, 1972. Theory will be integrated with practice at this "due process radical" college, located in rented garden apartments. There will be no full-time administrators, no departments, no tenure, no grades, no bureaucratic madness, no building ("edifice") complex. Intellectual activism will be the key philosophical thrust as students will help build and run a nonanarchic, nonpermissive, non-crash pad, non-freaked-out, self-generating institution (stove, Laundromats, cafeteria, clinic, newspaper, and FM radio station — plus a school with students from six weeks of age through the twelfth grade of high school). Temporary address: Citizens College, 90 South Main Street, Orange, New Jersey.

Indexes

Subject Index

Name Index